Databases:
A Beginner's Guide

About the Author

Andrew J. (Andy) Oppel is a proud graduate of The Boys' Latin School of Maryland and of Transylvania University (Lexington, Kentucky) where he earned a BA in computer science in 1974. Since then, he has been continuously employed in a wide variety of information technology positions, including programmer, programmer/analyst, systems architect, project manager, senior database administrator, database group manager, consultant, database designer, data modeler, and data architect. In addition, he has served as a part-time instructor with the University of California, Berkeley, Extension for more than 20 years and received the Honored Instructor Award for the year 2000. His teaching work included developing three courses for UC Extension, "Concepts of Database Management Systems," "Introduction to Relational Database Management Systems," and "Data Modeling and Database Design." He also earned his Oracle 9*i* Database Associate certification in 2003. He is currently employed as a senior data modeler for Blue Shield of California. In addition to computer systems, Andy enjoys music (guitar and vocals), amateur radio (Pacific Division Vice Director, American Radio Relay League), and soccer (Referee Instructor, U.S. Soccer).

Andy has designed and implemented hundreds of databases for a wide range of applications, including medical research, banking, insurance, apparel manufacturing, telecommunications, wireless communications, and human resources. He is the author of *Databases Demystified* (McGraw-Hill Professional, 2004) and *SQL Demystified* (McGraw-Hill Professional, 2005), and is co-author of *SQL: A Beginner's Guide* (McGraw-Hill Professional, 2009). His database product experience includes IMS, DB2, Sybase ASE, Microsoft SQL Server, Microsoft Access, MySQL, and Oracle (versions 7, 8, 8*i*, 9*i*, and 10*g*).

If you have any comments, please contact Andy at andy@andyoppel.com.

About the Technical Editor

Todd Meister has been developing using Microsoft technologies for more than ten years. He's been a Technical Editor on more than 50 books with topics ranging from SQL Server to the .NET Framework. In addition to technical editing, he serves as an Assistant Director for Computing Services at Ball State University in Muncie, Indiana. He lives in central Indiana with his wife, Kimberly, and their four incredible children. Contact Todd at tmeister@sycamoresolutions.com.

Databases:
A Beginner's Guide

Andrew J. Oppel

New York   Chicago   San Francisco
Lisbon   London   Madrid   Mexico City
Milan   New Delhi   San Juan
Seoul   Singapore   Sydney   Toronto

The McGraw·Hill Companies

Library of Congress Cataloging-in-Publication Data

Oppel, Andrew J.
  Databases : a beginner's guide / Andrew J. Oppel.
      p. cm.
  Includes index.
  ISBN 978-0-07-160846-6 (alk. paper)
  1. Database design. 2. Database management. 3. Databases. I. Title.
  QA76.9.D26O65 2009
  005.74—dc22

                                                                                    2009004963

McGraw-Hill books are available at special quantity discounts to use as premiums and sales promotions, or for use in corporate training programs. To contact a special sales representative, please visit the Contact Us page at www.mhprofessional.com.

Databases: A Beginner's Guide

1234567890   DOC DOC   019

ISBN 978-0-07-160846-6 05-18-09
MHID   0-07-160846-X

Sponsoring Editor   Wendy Rinaldi

Editorial Supervisor   Jody McKenzie

Project Manager   Aparna Mathur, International Typesetting and Composition

Acquisitions Coordinator   Joya Anthony

Technical Editor   Todd Meister

Copy Editor   Lisa Theobald

Proofreader   Constance Blazewicz

Indexer   Karin Arrigoni

Production Supervisor   Jean Bodeaux

Composition   International Typesetting and Composition

Illustration   International Typesetting and Composition

Cover Designer   Jeff Weeks

Contents

Acknowledgments

Many people were involved in the development of *Databases: A Beginner's Guide*—many of whom I do not know by name. First, the editors and staff at McGraw-Hill provided untold hours of support for this project. I wish to especially thank Editorial Director Wendy Rinaldi as the individual who has provided the most advice and inspiration throughout the development of all my books. In fact, it was Wendy who got me started as a McGraw-Hill author. I also wish to thank Lisa Theobald for her excellent copy editing and all the other editors, proofreaders, indexers, designers, illustrators, and other participants. My special thanks go to Todd Meister, the technical editor, for his attention to detail and his helpful inputs throughout the editing process. Finally, my thanks to my family for their support and understanding as I fit the writing schedule into an already overly busy life.

Introduction

Thirty-five years ago, databases were found only in special research laboratories, where computer scientists struggled with ways to make them efficient and useful, publishing their findings in countless research papers. Today databases are a ubiquitous part of the information technology (IT) industry and business in general. We directly and indirectly use databases every day—banking transactions, travel reservations, employment relationships, website searches, online and offline purchases, and most other transactions are recorded in and served by databases.

As is the case with many fast-growing technologies, industry standards have lagged behind in the development of database technology, resulting in myriad commercial products, each following a particular software vendor's vision. Moreover, a number of different database models have emerged, with the relational model being the most prevalent. *Databases: A Beginner's Guide* examines all of the major database models, including hierarchical, network, relational, object-oriented, and object-relational. This book concentrates heavily on the relational and object-relational models, however, because these are the mainstream of the IT industry and will likely remain so in the foreseeable future.

The most significant challenge in implementing a database is correctly designing the structure of the database. Without a thorough understanding of the problem the database is intended to solve, and without knowledge of the best practices for organizing the required data, the implemented database becomes an unwieldy beast that requires constant attention.

Databases: A Beginner's Guide focuses on the transformation of requirements into a working data model with special emphasis on a process called *normalization*, which has proven to be an effective technique for designing relational databases. In fact, normalization can be applied successfully to other database models. And, in keeping with the notion that you cannot design an automobile if you have never driven one, the Structured Query Language (SQL) is introduced so that the reader may "drive" a database before delving into the details of designing one.

I've drawn on my extensive experience as a database designer, administrator, and instructor to provide you with this self-help guide to the fascinating and complex world of database technology. Examples are included using both Microsoft Access and Oracle. Publicly available sample databases supplied by these vendors (the Microsoft Access Northwind database and the Oracle Human Resources database schema) are used in example figures whenever possible so that you can try the examples directly on your own computer system. A self test is provided at the end of each chapter to help reinforce your learning.

Who Should Read This Book

Databases: A Beginner's Guide is recommended for anyone trying to build a foundation in database design and management, whether for personal or professional use. The book is designed specifically for those who are new or relatively new to database technology; however, those of you who need a refresher in normalization and database design and management will also find this book beneficial. Whether you're an experienced developer, you've had some development experience, you're a database administrator, or you're new to programming and databases, *Databases: A Beginner's Guide* provides a strong foundation that will be useful to any of you wanting to learn more about database technology. In fact, any of the following individuals will find this book helpful when trying to understand and use databases:

- The novice new to database design and SQL programming

- The analyst or manager who wants a better understanding of how to design, implement, and access databases

- The database administrator who wants to learn more about database design

- The technical support professional or testing/QA engineer who must perform ad hoc queries against SQL databases

- The web developer writing applications that require databases for data persistence

- The third-generation language (3GL) programmer embedding SQL within an application's source code

- Any other individual who wants to learn how to design databases and write SQL code to create and access databases within an RDBMS

No matter which category you fit into, you must remember that the book is geared toward anyone wanting to learn standard database design techniques that work on any database, not one specific vendor's product. This lets you apply the skills you learn in this book to real-world situations, without being limited to product standards. You will, of course, still need to be aware of how the product you work on implements databases, particularly dialects of SQL, but with the foundation provided in these pages, you'll be able to move from one RDBMS to the next and still have a solid understanding of database design theory. As a result, you'll find that this book is a useful tool to anyone new to databases, particularly relational databases, regardless of the product used. You will easily be able to adapt your knowledge to the specific RDBMS.

What the Book Covers

Databases: A Beginner's Guide is divided into three parts. Part I introduces you to basic database concepts and explains how to create and access objects within your database using SQL. Part II provides you with a foundation in database development, including the database life cycle, logical design using the normalization process, transforming the logical design into a physical database, and data and process modeling. Part III focuses on database implementation with emphasis on database security, as well as the advanced topics of databases for online analytical processing (OLAP) and integrating objects and XML documents into the database, allowing you to expand on what you learned in Parts I and II. In addition to the three parts, *Databases: A Beginner's Guide* contains appendices that include answers to the self-test questions and solutions to the Try This exercises that appear throughout the book.

Content Description

The following outline describes the contents of the book and shows how the book is broken down into task-focused chapters:

Part I: Database Concepts

Part I introduces you to basic database concepts and explains how to create and access objects within your database using SQL.

Chapter 1: Database Fundamentals   This chapter introduces fundamental concepts and definitions regarding databases, including properties common to databases, prevalent database models, a brief history of databases, and the rationale for focusing on the relational model.

Chapter 2: Exploring Relational Database Components This chapter explores the conceptual, logical, and physical components that make up the relational model. *Conceptual database design* involves studying and modeling the data in a technology-independent manner. *Logical database design* is the process of translating, or *mapping,* the conceptual design into a logical design that fits the chosen database model (relational, object-oriented, object-relational, and so on). The final design step is *physical database design,* which involves mapping the logical design to one or more physical designs—each tailored to the particular DBMS that will manage the database and the particular computer system on which the database will run.

Chapter 3: Forms-based Database Queries This chapter provides an overview of forming and running database queries using the forms-based query tool in Microsoft Access, providing a foundation in database query concepts for the database design theory that follows in later chapters.

Chapter 4: Introduction to SQL This chapter introduces SQL, which has become the universal language for relational databases that nearly every DBMS in modern use supports. The reason for its wide acceptance is clearly the time and effort that went into the development of language features and standards, making SQL highly portable across different RDBMS products.

Part II: Database Development

Part II provides you with a foundation in database development, including the database life cycle, logical design using the normalization process, transforming the logical design into a physical database, and data and process modeling.

Chapter 5: The Database Life Cycle This chapter introduces the framework in which database design takes place, a useful precursor to the particulars of database design. The *life cycle* of a database (or computer system) is the term we use for all the events that take place between the time we first recognize the need for a database, continuing through its development and deployment, and finally ending with the day it is retired from service.

Chapter 6: Database Design Using Normalization In this chapter, you will learn how to perform logical database design using a process called *normalization*. In terms of understanding relational database technology, this is the most important topic in this book, because normalization teaches you how best to organize your data into tables.

Chapter 7: Data and Process Modeling In this chapter, we will look at entity-relationship diagrams (ERDs) and data modeling in more detail. The second part of the chapter includes a high-level survey of process design concepts and diagramming techniques.

Chapter 8: Physical Database Design   This chapter focuses on the database designer's physical design work, which is transforming the logical database design into one or more physical database designs.

Part III: Database Implementation

Part III focuses on database implementation with emphasis on database security as well as the advanced topics of databases for online analytical processing (OLAP) and integrating objects and Extensible Markup Language (XML) documents into the database; this allows you to expand on what you learned in Parts I and II.

Chapter 9: Connecting Databases to the Outside World   This chapter begins with a look at the evolution of database deployment models, meaning the ways that databases have been connected with the database users and the other computer systems within the enterprise computing *infrastructure* (the internal structure that organizes all the computing resources of an enterprise, including databases, applications, computer hardware, and the network). The chapter then explores the methods used to connect databases to applications that use a web browser as the primary user interface, which is the way many modern application systems are constructed. It concludes with a look at current methods for connecting databases to applications, namely using ODBC connections (for most programming languages) and various methods for connecting databases to applications written in Java (a commonly used object-oriented language).

Chapter 10: Database Security   This chapter presents the need for security, the security considerations for deploying database servers and clients that access those servers, and methods for implementing database access security, concluding with a discussion of security monitoring and auditing.

Chapter 11: Deploying Databases   This chapter covers some considerations regarding the development of applications that use the database system. These include cursor processing, transaction management, performance tuning, and change control.

Chapter 12: Databases for Online Analytical Processing   This chapter presents the concepts of databases for analytical processing, including data warehouses and data marts, an overview of data mining and other data analysis techniques, along with the design variations required for these types of databases.

Chapter 13: Integrating XML Documents and Objects into Databases   This chapter explores a number of ways to integrate XML and object content into databases.

Part IV: Appendices

The appendices include answers to the Self Test questions and solutions to the Try This exercises that appear throughout the book.

Appendix A: Answers to Self Tests   This appendix provides the answers to the Self Test questions listed at the end of each chapter.

Appendix B: Solutions to the Try This Exercises   This appendix contains solutions, including diagrams and applicable SQL code, for the Try This exercises that appear in nearly every chapter of the book.

Chapter Content

As you can see from the outline, *Databases: A Beginner's Guide* is organized into chapters. Each chapter focuses on a set of key skills and concepts and contains the background information you need to understand the concepts, plus the skills required to apply these concepts. Each chapter contains additional elements to help you better understand the information covered in that chapter:

Ask the Expert

Each chapter contains one or two Ask the Expert sections that provide information on questions that might arise regarding the information presented in the chapter.

Self Test

Each chapter ends with a Self Test, a set of questions that test you on the information and skills you learned in that chapter. The answers to the Self Tests are included in Appendix A.

Try This Exercises

Most chapters contain one or two Try This exercises that allow you to apply the information that you learned in the chapter. Each exercise is broken down into steps that walk you through the process of completing a particular task. Where applicable, the exercises include related files that you can download from our website at www.mhprofessional.com. Click Computing and then click the Downloads Section link on the left side of the page. On the downloads page, scroll down to the listing for this book and select the files you wish to download. The files usually include the SQL statements or diagrams used within the Try This exercise.

To complete many of the Try This exercises in this book, you'll need to have access to an RDBMS that allows you to enter and execute SQL statements interactively. If you're accessing an RDBMS over a network, check with the database administrator to make sure that you're logging in with the credentials necessary to create a database and schema. You might need special permissions to create these objects. Also verify whether you should include any particular parameters when creating the database (for example, log file size), and whether restrictions on the names you can use or other restrictions apply. Be sure to check the appropriate documentation before working with any database product.

Part I

Database Concepts

Chapter 1
Database
Fundamentals

Key Skills & Concepts

- Properties of a Database
- Prevalent Database Models
- A Brief History of Databases
- Why Focus on Relational?

This chapter introduces fundamental concepts and definitions regarding databases, including properties common to databases, prevalent database models, a brief history of databases, and the rationale for focusing on the relational model.

Properties of a Database

A *database* is a collection of interrelated data items that are managed as a single unit. This definition is deliberately broad because so much variety exists across the various software vendors that provide database systems. For example, Microsoft Access places the entire database in a single data file, so an Access database can be defined as the file that contains the data items. Oracle Corporation defines its database as a collection of physical files that are managed by an instance of its database software product. An *instance* is a copy of the database software running in memory. Microsoft SQL Server and Sybase Adaptive Server Enterprise (ASE) define a database as a collection of data items that have a common owner, and multiple databases are typically managed by a single instance of the database management software. This can all be quite confusing if you work with multiple products, because, for example, a database as defined by Microsoft SQL Server or Sybase ASE is exactly what Oracle Corporation calls a *schema*.

A *database object* is a named data structure that is stored in a database. The specific types of database objects supported in a database vary from vendor to vendor and from one database model to another. *Database model* refers to the way in which a database organizes its data to pattern the real world. The most common database models are presented in the "Prevalent Database Models" section later in this chapter.

A *file* is a collection of related records that are stored as a single unit by an operating system. Given the unfortunately similar definitions of *files* and *databases*, how can we make a distinction? A number of Unix operating system vendors call their password files "databases," yet database experts will quickly point out that, in fact, these are not actually databases. Clearly, we need a bit more rigor in our definitions. The answer lies in an understanding of certain characteristics or properties that databases possess which are not found in ordinary files, including the following:

- Management by a database management system (DBMS)
- Layers of data abstraction
- Physical data independence
- Logical data independence

These properties are discussed in the following subsections.

The Database Management System

The *database management system (DBMS)* is software provided by the database vendor. Software products such as Microsoft Access, Oracle, Microsoft SQL Server, Sybase ASE, DB2, Ingres, and MySQL are all DBMSs. If it seems odd to you that the DBMS acronym is used instead of merely DMS, remember that the term *database* was originally written as two words, and by convention has since become a single compound word.

The DBMS provides all the basic services required to organize and maintain the database, including the following:

- Moves data to and from the physical data files as needed.
- Manages concurrent data access by multiple users, including provisions to prevent simultaneous updates from conflicting with one another.
- Manages transactions so that each transaction's database changes are an all-or-nothing unit of work. In other words, if the transaction succeeds, all database changes made by it are recorded in the database; if the transaction fails, none of the changes it made are recorded in the database.
- Supports a *query language,* which is a system of commands that a database user employs to retrieve data from the database.
- Provides provisions for backing up the database and recovering from failures.
- Provides security mechanisms to prevent unauthorized data access and modification.

Ask the Expert

Q: I've heard the term "data bank" used. What is the difference between a data bank and a database?

A: A data bank and a database are the same thing. *Data bank* is merely an older term that was used by the scientists who developed early database systems. In fact, the term *data bank* is still used in a few human languages, such as *banco de dados* in Portuguese.

Layers of Data Abstraction

Databases are unique in their ability to present multiple users with their own distinct views of the data while storing the underlying data only once. These are collectively called *user views*. A *user* in this context is any person or application that signs on to the database for the purpose of storing and/or retrieving data. An *application* is a set of computer programs designed to solve a particular business problem, such as an order-entry system, a payroll-processing system, or an accounting system.

When an electronic spreadsheet application such as Microsoft Excel is used, all users must share a common view of the data, and that view must match the way the data is physically stored in the underlying data file. If a user hides some columns in a spreadsheet, reorders the rows, and saves the spreadsheet, the next user who opens the spreadsheet will view the data in the manner in which the first user saved it. An alternative, of course, is for each user to save his or her own copy in separate physical files, but then as one user applies updates, the other users' data becomes out of date. Database systems present each user a view of the same data, but the views can be *tailored* to the needs of the individual users, even though they all come from one commonly stored copy of the data. Because views store no actual data, they automatically reflect any data changes made to the underlying database objects. This is all possible through *layers of abstraction*, which is shown in Figure 1-1.

The architecture shown in Figure 1-1 was first developed by ANSI/SPARC (American National Standards Institute/Standards Planning and Requirements Committee) in the 1970s and quickly became a foundation for much of the database research and development efforts that followed. Most modern DBMSs follow this architecture, which is composed of three primary layers: the physical layer, the logical layer, and the external layer. The original architecture included a conceptual layer, which has been omitted here because none of the modern database vendors implement it.

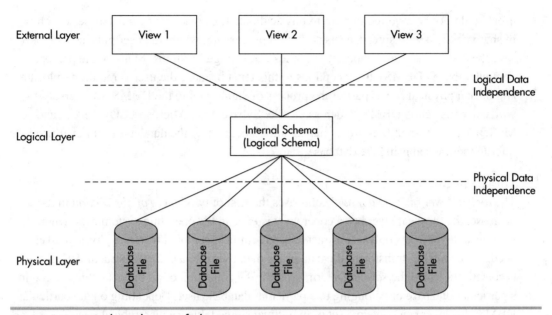

Figure 1-1   Database layers of abstraction

The Physical Layer

The *physical layer* contains the data files that hold all the data for the database. Nearly all modern DBMSs allow the database to be stored in multiple data files, which are usually spread out over multiple physical disk drives. With this arrangement, the disk drives can work in parallel for maximum performance. A notable exception among the DBMSs used as examples in this book is Microsoft Access, which stores the entire database in a single physical file. While simplifying database use on a single-user personal computer system, this arrangement limits the ability of the DBMS to scale to accommodate many concurrent users of the database, making it inappropriate as a solution for large enterprise systems. In all fairness, Microsoft Access was not designed to be a robust enterprise class DBMS. I have included it in discussions in this book not because it competes with products such as Oracle and SQL Server, but because it's a great example of a personal DBMS with a user interface that makes learning database concepts easy and fun.

The database user does not need to understand how the data is actually stored within the data files or even which file contains the data item(s) of interest. In most organizations, a technician known as a *database administrator* (DBA) handles the details of installing and configuring the database software and data files and making the database available to users. The DBMS works with the computer's operating system to manage the data files automatically, including all file opening, closing, reading, and writing operations. The database user should not be required to refer to physical data files when using a database, which is in sharp contrast with spreadsheets and word processing, where the user must consciously save the document(s) and choose file names and storage locations. Many of the personal computer–based DBMSs are exceptions to this tenet because the user is required to locate and open a physical file as part of the process of signing on to the DBMS. Conversely, with enterprise class DBMSs (such as Oracle, Sybase ASE, Microsoft SQL Server, and MySQL), the physical files are managed automatically and the database user never needs to refer to them when using the database.

The Logical Layer

The *logical layer* or *logical model* comprises the first of two *layers of abstraction* in the database: the physical layer has a concrete existence in the operating system files, whereas the logical layer exists only as abstract data structures assembled from the physical layer as needed. The DBMS transforms the data in the data files into a common structure. This layer is sometimes called the *schema*, a term used for the collection of all the data items stored in a particular database or belonging to a particular database user. Depending on the particular DBMS, this layer can contain a set of two-dimensional tables, a hierarchical structure similar to a company's organization chart, or some other structure. The "Prevalent Database Models" section later in this chapter describes the possible structures in more detail.

The External Layer

The *external layer* or *external model* is the second layer of abstraction in the database. This layer is composed of the user views discussed earlier, which are collectively called the *subschema*. In this layer, the database users (application programs as well as individuals) that access the database connect and issue queries against the database. Ideally, only the DBA deals with the physical and logical layers. The DBMS handles the transformation of selected items from one or more data structures in the logical layer to form each user view. The user views in this layer can be predefined and stored in the database for reuse, or they can be temporary items that are built by the DBMS to hold the results of a single ad hoc database query until they are no longer needed by the database user. An *ad hoc* query is a query that is not preconceived and that is not likely to be reused. Views are discussed in more detail in Chapter 2.

Physical Data Independence

The ability to alter the physical file structure of a database without disrupting existing users and processes is known as *physical data independence*. As shown in Figure 1-1, the separation of the physical layer from the logical layer provides physical data independence in a DBMS. It is essential that you understand that physical data independence is not a "have or have not" property, but rather one in which a particular DBMS might have more or less data independence than another. The measure, sometimes called the *degree* of physical data independence, is how much change can be made in the file system without impacting the logical layer. Prior to systems that offered data independence, even the slightest change to the way data was stored required the programming staff to make changes to every computer program that used the data, an expensive and time-consuming process.

All modern computer systems have some degree of physical data independence. For example, a spreadsheet on a personal computer will continue to work properly if copied from a hard disk to a floppy disk or a USB thumb drive. The fact that the performance (speed) of these devices varies markedly is not the point, but rather that the devices have entirely different physical construction and yet the operating system on the personal computer will automatically handle the differences and present the data in the file to the application (that is, the spreadsheet program, such as Microsoft Excel), and therefore to the user, in exactly the same way. However, on most personal systems, the user must still remember where he or she placed the file so that it can be located when needed.

DBMSs expand greatly on the physical data independence provided by the computer system in that they allow database users to access database *objects* (for example, tables in a relational DBMS) without having to reference the physical data files in any way. The DBMS *catalog* stores the object definitions and keeps track of where the objects are physically stored. Here are some examples of physical changes that can be made in a data-independent manner:

- Moving a database data file from one device to another or one directory to another
- Splitting or combining database data files
- Renaming database data files
- Moving a database object from one data file to another
- Adding new database objects or data files

Note that I have made no mention of deleting things. It should be obvious, then, that deleting a database object will cause anything that uses that object to fail. However, everything else should be unaffected, except perhaps availability—some DBMSs will require that the database or DBMS service be shut down while making certain physical layer changes.

Logical Data Independence

The ability to make changes to the logical layer without disrupting existing users and processes is called *logical data independence*. Figure 1-1 shows that it is the transformation between the logical layer and the external layer that provides logical data independence. As with physical data independence, there are degrees of logical data independence. It is important that you understand that most *logical* changes also involve a *physical* change. For example, you cannot add a new database object (such as a table in a relational DBMS) without physically storing the data somewhere; hence, a corresponding change is made in the physical layer. Moreover, deletion of objects in the logical layer will cause anything that uses those objects to fail but should not affect anything else.

Here are some examples of changes in the logical layer that can be safely made thanks to logical data independence:

● Adding a new database object

● Adding data items to an existing object

● Making any change in which a view can be placed in the external model that replaces (and processes the same as) the original object in the logical layer, such as combining or splitting existing objects

Prevalent Database Models

A *database model* is essentially the architecture that the DBMS uses to store objects within the database and relate them to one another. The most prevalent of these models are presented here in the order of their evolution. A brief history of relational databases appears in the next section to help put things in a chronological perspective.

Flat Files

Flat files are "ordinary" operating system files, in that records in a file contain no information to communicate the file structure or any relationship among the records to the application that uses the file. Any information about the structure or meaning of the data in the file must be included in each application that uses the file or must be known to each human who reads the file. In essence, flat files are not databases at all because they do not meet any of the criteria previously discussed. However, it is important that you understand them for two reasons: First, flat files are often used to store database information. In this case, the operating system is still unaware of the contents and structure of the files, but the DBMS has *metadata* that allows it to translate between the flat files in the physical layer and the database structures in the logical layer. *Metadata*, which literally means "data about data," is the term used for the information that the database stores in its catalog to describe the data stored in the database and the relationships among the data. The metadata for a customer, for example, might include all the data items collected about the customer (such as name, address, and account status), along with the length, minimum and maximum data values, and a brief description of each data item. Second, flat files existed before databases, and the earliest database systems *evolved* from the flat file systems that preceded them.

Figure 1-2 shows a sample flat file system, a subset of the data for fictional company Northwind Traders, a supplier of international food items (and a Microsoft sample database). Keep in mind that the column titles (Customer ID, Company Name, and so on) are included for illustration purposes only—only the data records would be stored in the actual files. Customer data is stored in a Customer file, with each record representing a Northwind customer. Each employee of Northwind has a record in the Employee file, and each product sold by Northwind has a record in the Product file. Order data (orders placed with Northwind by its customers) is stored in two other flat files. The Order file contains one record for each customer order with data about the orders, such as the customer ID of the customer who placed the order and the name of the employee who accepted the order from the customer. The Order Detail file contains one record for each line item on an order (an order can contain multiple line items, one for each product ordered), including data such as the unit price and quantity.

An *application program* is a unit of computer program logic that performs a particular function within an application system. Northwind Traders has an application program that prints out a listing of all the orders. This application must correlate the data between the five files by reading an order and performing the following steps:

1. Use the customer ID to find the name of the customer in the Customer file.

2. Use the employee ID to find the name of the related employee in the Employee file.

3. Use the order ID to find the corresponding line items in the Order Detail file.

4. For each line item, use the product ID to find the corresponding product name in the Product file.

This is rather complicated given that we are just trying to print a simple listing of all the orders, yet this is the best possible data design for a flat file system.

One alternative design would be to combine all the information into a single data file with all the data about the customer, employee, and order combined into a single record for each order. Although this would greatly simplify data retrieval, consider the

Customer File

Customer ID	Company Name	Contact First Name	Contact Last Name	Job Title	City	State
6	Company F	Francisco	Pérez-Olaeta	Purchasing Manager	Milwaukee	WI
26	Company Z	Run	Liu	Accounting Assistant	Miami	FL

Employee File

Employee ID	First Name	Last Name	Title
2	Andrew	Cencini	Vice President, Sales
5	Steven	Thrope	Sales Manager
9	Anne	Hellung-Larsen	Sales Representative

Product File

Product ID	Product Code	Product Name	Category	Quantity Per Unit	List Price
5	NWTO-5	Northwind Traders Olive Oil	Oil	36 boxes	$21.35
7	NWTDFN-7	Northwind Traders Dried Pears	Dried Fruit & Nuts	12 - 1 lb pkgs	$30.00
40	NWTCM-40	Northwind Traders Crab Meat	Canned Meat	24 - 4 oz tins	$18.40
41	NWTSO-41	Northwind Traders Clam Chowder	Soups	12 - 12 oz cans	$9.65
48	NWTCA-48	Northwind Traders Chocolate	Candy	10 pkgs	$12.75
51	NWTDFN-51	Northwind Traders Dried Apples	Dried Fruit & Nuts	50 - 300 g pkgs	$53.00

Order File

Order ID	Customer ID	Employee ID	Order Date	Shipped Date	Shipping Fee
51	26	9	4/5/2006	4/5/2006	$60.00
56	6	2	4/3/2006	4/3/2006	$0.00
79	6	2	6/23/2006	6/23/2006	$0.00

Order Detail File

Order ID	Product ID	Unit Price	Quantity
51	5	$21.35	15
51	41	$9.65	21
51	40	$18.40	2
56	48	$12.75	20
79	7	$30.00	14
79	51	$53.00	8

Figure 1-2 Flat file order system

ramifications of repeating all the customer data on every single order line item. You might not be able to add a new customer until the customer has an order ready to place. Also, if someone deletes the last order for a customer, you would lose all the information about the customer. But the worst is when customer information changes because you have to find and update every record in which the customer data is repeated. You will explore these issues in more detail when I present logical database design in Chapter 7.

Another alternative approach often used in flat file–based systems is to combine closely related files, such as the Order file and Order Detail file, into a single file, with the line items for each order following each order header record and a Record Type data item added to help the application distinguish between the two types of records. In this approach, the Order ID would be omitted from the Order Detail record because the application would know to which order the Order Detail record belongs by its position in the file (following the Order record). Although this approach makes correlating the order data easier, it does so by adding the complexity of mixing different kinds of records into the same file, so it provides no net gain in either simplicity or faster application development.

Overall, the worst problem with the flat file approach is that the definition of the contents of each file and the logic required to correlate the data from multiple flat files must be included in every application program that requires those files, thus adding to the expense and complexity of the application programs. This same problem provided computer scientists with the incentive to find a better way to organize data.

The Hierarchical Model

The earliest databases followed the hierarchical model, which evolved from the file systems that the databases replaced, with records arranged in a hierarchy much like an organization chart. Each file from the flat file system became a *record type*, or *node* in hierarchical terminology—but the term *record* is used here for simplicity. Records were connected using *pointers* that contained the address of the related record. Pointers told the computer system where the related record was physically located, much as a street address directs you to a particular building in a city, a URL directs you to a particular web page on the Internet, or GPS coordinates point to a particular location on the planet. Each pointer establishes a parent-child relationship, also called a *one-to-many relationship*, in which one parent can have many children, but each child can have only one parent. This is similar to the situation in a traditional business organization, where each manager can have many employees as direct reports, but each employee can have only one manager. The obvious problem with the hierarchical model is that some data does not exactly fit this strict hierarchical structure, such as an order that must have the customer who placed the order as one parent and the employee who accepted the order as another. (Data relationships are presented in more detail in Chapter 2.) The most popular hierarchical database was Information Management System (IMS) from IBM.

Figure 1-3 shows the hierarchical structure of the hierarchical model for the Northwind Traders database. You will recognize the Customer, Employee, Product, Order, and Order Detail record types as they were introduced previously. Comparing the hierarchical

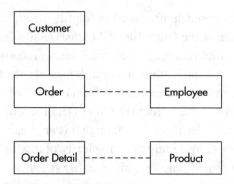

Figure 1-3   Hierarchical model structure for Northwind

structure with the flat file system shown in Figure 1-2, note that the Employee and Product records are shown in the hierarchical structure with dotted lines because they cannot be connected to the other records via pointers. These illustrate the most severe limitation of the hierarchical model that was the main reason for its early demise: No record can have more than one parent. Therefore, we *cannot* connect the Employee records with the Order records because the Order records already have the Customer record as their parent. Similarly, the Product records cannot be related to the Order Detail records because the Order Detail records already have the Order record as their parent. Database technicians would have to work around this shortcoming either by relating the "extra" parent records in application programs, much as was done with flat file systems, or by repeating all the records under each parent, which of course was very wasteful of then-precious disk space— not to mention the challenges of keeping redundant data synchronized. Neither of these was really an acceptable solution, so IBM modified IMS to allow for multiple parents per record. The resultant database model was dubbed the *extended hierarchical* model, which closely resembled the network database model in function, as discussed in the next section.

Figure 1-4 shows the contents of selected records within the hierarchical model design for Northwind. Some data items were eliminated for simplicity, but a look back at Figure 1-2 should make the entire contents of each record clear, if necessary. The record for customer 6 has a pointer to its first order (ID 56), and that order has a pointer to the next order (ID 79). You know that Order 79 is the last order for the customer because it does not have a pointer to a subsequent order. Looking at the next layer in the hierarchy, Order 79 has a pointer to its first Order Detail record (for Product 7), and that record has a pointer to the next detail record (for Product 51). As you can see, at each layer of the hierarchy, a chain of pointers connects the records in the proper sequence. One additional important distinction exists between the flat file system and the hierarchical model: The key (identifier) of the parent

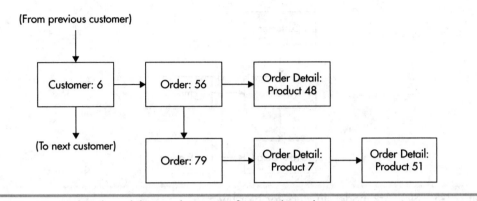

Figure 1-4 Hierarchical model record contents for Northwind

record is removed from the child records in the hierarchical model because the pointers handle the relationships among the records. Therefore, the customer ID and employee ID are removed from the Order record, and the product ID is removed from the Order Detail record. Leaving these in is not a good idea, because this could allow contradictory information to appear in the database, such as an order that is pointed to by one customer and yet contains the ID of a different customer.

The Network Model

The network database model evolved at around the same time as the hierarchical database model. A committee of industry representatives was formed essentially to build a better mousetrap. A cynic would say that a camel is a horse that was designed by a committee, and that might be accurate in this case. The most popular database based on the network model was the Integrated Database Management System (IDMS), originally developed by Cullinane (later renamed Cullinet). The product was enhanced with relational extensions, named IDMS/R and eventually sold to Computer Associates.

As with the hierarchical model, *record types* (or simply *records*) depict what would be separate files in a flat file system, and those records are related using one-to-many relationships, called *owner-member* relationships or *sets* in network model terminology. We'll stick with the terms *parent* and *child*, again for simplicity. As with the hierarchical model, physical address pointers are used to connect related records, and any identification of the parent record(s) is removed from each child record to avoid possible inconsistencies. In contrast with the hierarchical model, the relationships are named so the programmer can direct the DBMS to use a particular relationship to navigate from one record to another in the database, thus allowing a record type to participate as the child in multiple relationships.

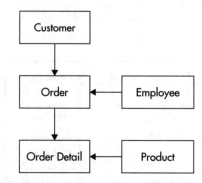

Figure 1-5 Network model structure for Northwind

The network model provided greater flexibility, but—as is often the case with computer systems—with a loss of simplicity.

The network model structure for Northwind, as shown in Figure 1-5, has all the same records as the equivalent hierarchical model structure shown in Figure 1-3. By convention, the arrowhead on the lines points from the parent to the child. Note that the Customer and Employee records now have solid lines in the structure diagram because they can be directly implemented in the database.

In the network model contents example shown in Figure 1-6, each parent-child relationship is depicted with a different type of line, illustrating that each relationship has a different name. This difference is important because it points out the largest downside of the network model—complexity. Instead of a single path that can be used for processing the records, now many paths are used. For example, start with the record for Employee 2 (Sales Vice President Andrew Cencini) and use it to find the first order (ID 56), and you land within the chain of orders that belong to Customer 6 (Company F). Although you actually land on that customer's first order, you have no way of knowing that. To find all the other orders for this customer, you must find a way to work forward from where you are to the end of the chain and then wrap around to the beginning and forward from there until you return to the order from which you started. It is to satisfy this processing need that all pointer chains in network model databases are circular. Thus, you are able to follow pointers from order 56 to the next order (ID 79), and then to the customer record (ID 6) and finally back to order 56. As you might imagine, these circular pointer chains can easily result in an *infinite loop* (a process that never ends) should a database user not keep careful track of where he is in the database and how he got there. The structure of the World Wide Web loosely parallels a network database in that each web page has links to other related web pages, and circular references are not uncommon.

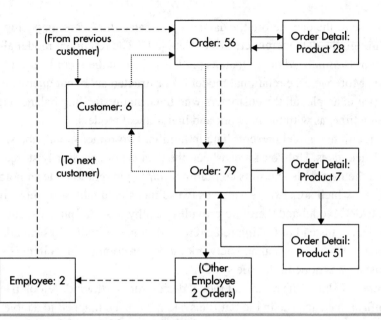

Figure 1-6   Network model record for Northwind

The process of navigating through a network database was called "walking the set," because it involved choosing paths through the database structure much like choosing walking paths through a forest when multiple paths to the same destination are available. Without an up-to-date map, it is easy to get lost, or, worse yet, to find a dead end where you cannot get to the desired destination record without backtracking. The complexity of this model and the expense of the small army of technicians required to maintain it were key factors in its eventual demise.

The Relational Model

In addition to complexity, the network and hierarchical database models share another common problem—they are inflexible. You must follow the preconceived paths through the data to process the data efficiently. Ad hoc queries, such as finding all the orders shipped in a particular month, require scanning the entire database to locate them all. Computer scientists were still looking for a better way. Only a few events in the history of computer development were truly revolutionary, but the research work of E.F. (Ted) Codd that led to the relational model was clearly that.

The *relational model* is based on the notion that any preconceived path through a data structure is too restrictive a solution, especially in light of ever-increasing demands to support ad hoc requests for information. Database users simply cannot think of every possible use of the data before the database is created; therefore, imposing predefined paths through the data merely creates a "data jail." The relational model allows users to relate records *as needed* rather than as predefined when the records are first stored in the database. Moreover, the relational model is constructed such that queries work with *sets* of data (for example, all the customers who have an outstanding balance) rather than one record at a time, as with the network and hierarchical models.

The relational model presents data in familiar two-dimensional tables, much like a spreadsheet does. Unlike a spreadsheet, the data is not necessarily stored in tabular form and the model also permits combining (*joining* in relational terminology) tables to form *views*, which are also presented as two-dimensional tables. In short, it follows the ANSI/SPARC model and therefore provides healthy doses of physical and logical data independence. Instead of linking related records together with physical address pointers, as is done in the hierarchical and network models, a common data item is stored in each table, just as was done in flat file systems.

Figure 1-7 shows the relational model design for Northwind. A look back at Figure 1-2 will confirm that each file in the flat file system has been mapped to a table in the relational model. As you will learn in Chapter 6, this one-to-one correspondence between flat files and relational tables will not always hold true, but it is quite common. In Figure 1-7, lines are drawn between the tables to show the one-to-many relationships, with the single line end denoting the "one" side and the line end that splits into three parts (called a "crow's foot") denoting the "many" side. For example, you can see that "one" customer is related to "many" orders and that "one" order is related to "many" order details merely by inspecting the lines that connect these tables. The diagramming technique shown here, called the *entity-relationship diagram (ERD)*, is covered in more detail in Chapter 7.

In Figure 1-8, three of the five tables have been represented with sample data in selected columns. In particular, note that the Customer ID column is stored in both the

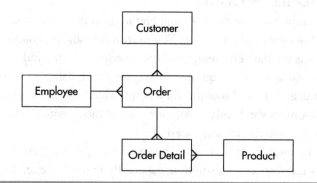

Figure 1-7   Relational model structure for Northwind

Customer Table

Customer ID	Company Name	Contact First Name	Contact Last Name	Job Title	City	State
6	Company F	Francisco	Pérez-Olaeta	Purchasing Manager	Milwaukee	WI
26	Company Z	Run	Liu	Accounting Assistant	Miami	FL

Order Table

Order ID	Customer ID	Employee ID	Order Date	Shipped Date	Shipping Fee
51	26	9	4/5/2006	4/5/2006	$60.00
56	6	2	4/3/2006	4/3/2006	$ 0.00
79	6	2	6/23/2006	6/23/2006	$ 0.00

Employee Table

Employee ID	First Name	Last Name	Title
2	Andrew	Cencini	Vice President, Sales
5	Steven	Thrope	Sales Manager
9	Anne	Hellung-Larsen	Sales Representative

Figure 1-8 Relational table contents for Northwind

Customer table and the Order table. When the customer ID of a row in the Order table matches the customer ID of a row in the Customer table, you know that the order belongs to that particular customer. Similarly, the Employee ID column is stored in both the Employee and Order tables to indicate the employee who accepted each order.

The elegant simplicity of the relational model and the ease with which people can learn and understand it has been the main factor in its universal acceptance. The relational model is the main focus of this book because it is ubiquitous in today's information technology systems and will likely remain so for many years to come.

The Object-Oriented Model

The object-oriented (OO) model actually had its beginnings in the 1970s, but it did not see significant commercial use until the 1990s. This sudden emergence came from the inability of then-existing relational database management systems (RDBMSs) to deal with complex data types such as images, complex drawings, and audio-video files. The sudden explosion of the Internet and the World Wide Web created a sharp demand for mainstream delivery of complex data.

An *object* is a logical grouping of related data and program logic that represents a real-world thing, such as a customer, employee, order, or product. Individual data items, such as customer ID and customer name, are called *variables* in the OO model and are stored within each object. You might also see variables referred to as *instance variables* or *properties*, but I will stick with the term *variables* for consistency. In OO terminology, a *method* is a piece of application program logic that operates on a particular object and provides a finite function, such as checking a customer's credit limit or updating a customer's address. Among the many differences between the OO model and the models already presented, the most significant is that variables can be accessed *only* through methods. This property is called *encapsulation*.

The strict definition of *object* used here applies only to the OO model. The general term *database object,* as used earlier in this chapter, refers to any named item that might be stored in a non-OO database (such as a table, index, or view). As OO concepts have found their way into relational databases, so has the terminology, although often with less precise definitions.

Figure 1-9 shows the Customer object as an example of OO implementation. The circle of methods around the central core of variables reminds us of encapsulation. In fact, you can think of an object much like an atom with an electron field of methods and a nucleus of variables. Each customer for Northwind would have its own copy of the object structure, called an *object instance*, much as each individual customer has a copy of the customer record structure in the flat file system.

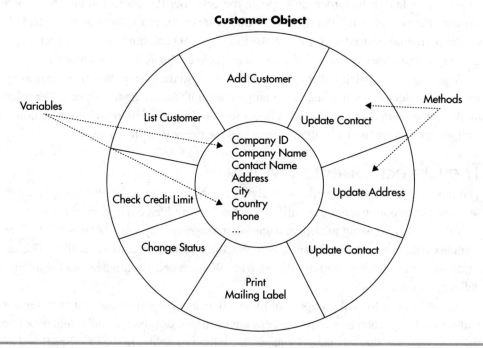

Figure 1-9 The anatomy of an object

At a glance, the OO model looks horribly inefficient because it seems that each instance requires that the methods and the definition of the variables be redundantly stored. However, this is not at all the case. Objects are organized into a *class hierarchy* so that the common methods and variable definitions need only be defined once and then *inherited* by other members of the same class. Variables also belong to classes, and thus new data types can be easily incorporated by simply defining a new class for them.

The OO model also supports *complex objects*, which are objects composed of one or more other objects. Usually, this is implemented using an object *reference*, where one object contains the identifier of one or more other objects. For example, a Customer object might contain a list of Order objects that the customer has placed, and each Order object might contain the identifier of the customer who placed the order. The unique identifier for an object is called the *object identifier (OID)*, the value of which is automatically assigned to each object as it is created and is then invariant (that is, the value never changes). The combination of complex objects and the class hierarchy makes OO databases well suited for managing nonscalar data such as drawings and diagrams.

OO concepts have such benefit that they have found their way into nearly every aspect of modern computer systems. For example, the Microsoft Windows Registry (the directory that stores settings and options for some Windows operating systems) has a class hierarchy, and most computer-aided design (CAD) applications use an OO database to store their data.

The Object-Relational Model

Although the OO model provides some significant benefits in encapsulating data to minimize the effects of system modifications, the lack of ad hoc query capability has relegated it to a niche market in which complex data is required, but ad hoc query ability is not. However, some vendors of relational databases noted the significant benefits of the OO model, particularly its ability to easily map complex data types, and added object-like capability to their relational DBMS products with the hopes of capitalizing on the best of both models. Although object purists have never embraced this approach, the tactic appears to have worked to a large degree, with pure OO databases gaining ground only in niche markets. The original name given to this type of database was *universal database*, and although the marketing folks loved the term, it never caught on in technical circles, so the preferred name for the model became *object-relational (OR)*. Through evolution, the Oracle, DB2, and Informix databases can all be said to be OR DBMSs to varying degrees.

To understand the OR model fully, you need a more detailed knowledge of the relational and OO models. However, keep in mind that the OR DBMS provides a blend of desirable features from the object world, such as the storage of complex data types, with the relative simplicity and ease-of-use of the relational model. Most industry experts believe that object-relational technology will continue to gain market share.

A Brief History of Databases

Space exploration projects led to many significant developments in the science and technology industries, including information technology. As part of the NASA Apollo moon project, North American Aviation (NAA) built a hierarchical file system named Generalized Update Access Method (GUAM) in 1964. IBM joined NAA to develop GUAM into the first commercially available hierarchical model database, called Information Management System (IMS), released in 1966.

Also in the mid 1960s, General Electric internally developed the first database based on the network model, under the direction of prominent computer scientist Charles W. Bachman, and named it Integrated Data Store (IDS). In 1967, the Conference on Data Systems Languages (CODASYL), an industry group, formed the Database Task Group (DBTG) and began work on a set of standards for the network model. In response to criticism of the "single-parent" restriction in the hierarchical model, IBM introduced a version of IMS that circumvented the problem by allowing records to have one "physical" parent and multiple "logical" parents.

In June 1970, E. F. (Ted) Codd, an IBM researcher (later an IBM fellow), published a research paper titled "A Relational Model of Data for Large Shared Data Banks" in *Communications of the ACM*, the Journal of the Association for Computing Machinery, Inc. (The publication can be easily found on the Internet.) In 1971, the CODASYL DBTG published its standards, which were more than three years in the making. This began five years of heated debate over which model was the best.

The CODASYL DBTG advocates argued the following:

- The relational model was too mathematical.
- An efficient implementation of the relational model could not be built.
- Application systems need to process data one record at a time.

The relational model advocates argued the following:

- Nothing as complicated as the DBTG proposal could possibly be the correct way to manage data.
- Set-oriented queries were too difficult in the DBTG language.
- The network model had no formal underpinnings in mathematical theory.

The debate came to a head at the 1975 ACM SIGMOD (Special Interest Group on Management of Data) conference. Codd and two others debated against Bachman and two others over the merits of the two models. At the end, the audience was more confused than ever. In retrospect, this happened because every argument proffered by the two sides was completely correct! However, interest in the network model waned markedly in the late 1970s. It was the evolution of database and computer technology that followed that proved the relational model was the better choice, offering these significant developments:

- Query languages such as the Structured Query Language (SQL) emerged and were not so mathematical.

- Experimental implementations of the relational model proved that reasonable efficiency could be achieved, although it was never as efficient as an equivalent network model database. Also, computer systems continued to drop in price, and flexibility was considered more important than efficiency.

- Provisions were added to SQL to permit processing of a set of data using a record-at-a-time approach.

- Advanced tools made the relational model even easier to use.

- Codd's research led to the development of a new discipline in mathematics known as *relational calculus*.

In the mid-1970s, database research and development was at full steam. A team of 15 IBM researchers in San Jose, California, under the direction of Frank King, worked from 1974 to 1978 to develop a prototype relational database called System R. System R was built commercially and became the basis for HP ALLBASE and IDMS/SQL. Larry Ellison and a company that later became known as Oracle independently implemented the external specifications of System R. It is now common knowledge that Oracle's first customer was the Central Intelligence Agency (CIA). With some rewriting, IBM developed System R into SQL/DS and then into DB2, which remains its flagship database to this day.

A pickup team of University of California, Berkeley, students under the direction of Michael Stonebraker and Eugene Wong worked from 1973 to 1977 to develop the Ingres DBMS. Ingres also became a commercial product and was quite successful. Ingres was later sold to Computer Associates, but it emerged again as an independent company in 2005.

In 1976, Peter Chen presented the entity-relationship (ER) model. His work bolstered the modeling weaknesses in the relational model and became the foundation of many modeling techniques that followed. If Codd is considered the "father" of the relational model, then Chen should be considered the "father" of the ERD. ERDs are explored in Chapter 7.

Sybase, which had a successful RDBMS deployed on Unix servers, entered into a joint agreement with Microsoft to develop the next generation of Sybase (to be called System 10) with a version available on Windows servers. For reasons not publicly known, the relationship soured before the products were completed, but each party walked away with all the work developed up to that point. Microsoft finished the Windows version and marketed the product as Microsoft SQL Server, whereas Sybase rushed to market with Sybase System 10. The products were so similar that SQL Server instructors were known to use the Sybase manuals in class rather than first-generation Microsoft documentation. The product lines have diverged considerably over the years, but Microsoft SQL Server's Sybase roots are still evident in the product.

Relational technology took the market by storm in the 1980s. Object-oriented databases, which first appeared in the 1970s, were also commercially successful during the 1980s. In the 1990s, object-relational systems emerged, with Informix being the first to market, followed relatively quickly by Oracle and DB2.

Not only did the relational technology of the day move around, but so did the people involved. Michael Stonebraker left UC Berkeley to found Illustra, an object-relational database vendor, and he became chief science officer of Informix when it merged with Illustra. He later went on to found Cohera, StreamBase Systems, and Vertica, and he is currently a faculty member at MIT. Bob Epstein, who worked on the Ingres project with Stonebraker, moved to the commercial company along with the Ingres product. From there he went to Britton-Lee (later absorbed by NCR) to work on early *database machines* (computer systems specialized to run only databases) and then to start up Sybase, where he was the chief science officer for a number of years, and he is currently involved in environmental issues and wearable computers. Database machines, incidentally, died on the vine because they were so expensive compared to the combination of an RDBMS running on a general-purpose computer system. The San Francisco Bay Area was an exciting place for database technologists in that era because all the great relational products started there, more or less in parallel with the explosive growth of Silicon Valley. Others have moved on, but DB2, Oracle, and Sybase are still largely based in the Bay Area.

Why Focus on Relational?

The remainder of this book focuses on the relational model, with some coverage of the OO and object-relational models. Aside from the relational model being the most prevalent of all the database models in modern business systems, other important reasons warrant this focus, especially for those of you who are learning about databases for the first time:

- Definition, maintenance, and manipulation of data storage structures is easy.
- Data is retrieved through simple ad hoc queries.
- Data is well protected.
- Well-established ANSI (American National Standards Institute) and ISO (International Organization for Standardization) standards exist.
- Many vendors offer a plethora of products.
- Conversion between vendor implementations is relatively easy.
- RDBMSs are mature and stable products.

Chapter 1 Self Test

Choose the correct responses to each of the multiple-choice and fill-in-the-blank questions. Note that there may be more than one correct response to each question.

1. The logical layer of the ANSI/SPARC model provides which of the following?

   A Physical data independence

   B Parent-child relationships

   C Logical data independence

   D Encapsulation

2. The external layer of the ANSI/SPARC model provides which of the following?

   A Physical data independence

   B Parent-child relationships

   C Logical data independence

   D Encapsulation

3. Which of the following is *not* true regarding user views?

   A Application programs reference them.

   B People querying the database reference them.

    C They can be tailored to the needs of the database user.

    D Data updates are shown in a delayed fashion.

4. The database schema is contained in the _____ layer of the ANSI/SPARC model.

5. User views are contained in the _____ layer of the ANSI/SPARC model.

6. When application programs use flat file systems, where do the file definitions reside?

7. Which of the following is true regarding the hierarchical database model?

    A It was first developed by Peter Chen.

    B Data and methods are stored together in the database.

    C Each node may have many parents.

    D Records are connected using physical address pointers.

8. Which of the following is true regarding the network database model?

    A It was first developed by E.F. Codd.

    B Data and methods are stored together in the database.

    C Each node may have many parents.

    D Records are connected using common physical address pointers.

9. Which of the following is true of the relational database model?

    A It was first developed by Charles Bachman.

    B Data and methods are stored together in the database.

    C Records are connected using physical address pointers.

    D Records are connected using common data items in each record.

10. Which of the following is true regarding the object-oriented model?

    A It was first developed by Charles Bachman.

    B Data and methods are stored together in the database.

    C Data is presented as two-dimensional tables.

    D Records are connected using common data items in each record.

11. Which of the following is true regarding the object-relational model?

   A It serves only a niche market and most experts believe it will stay that way.

   B Records are connected using physical address pointers.

   C It was developed by adding object-like properties to the relational model.

   D It was developed by adding relational-like properties to the object-oriented model.

12. According to advocates of the relational model, which of the following describe the problems with the CODASYL model?

   A It is too mathematical.

   B It is too complicated.

   C Set-oriented queries are too difficult.

   D It has no formal underpinnings in mathematical theory.

13. According to advocates of the CODASYL model, which of the following describe the problems with the relational model?

   A It is too mathematical.

   B Set-oriented queries are too difficult.

   C Application systems need record-at-a-time processing.

   D It is less efficient than CODASYL model databases.

14. The ability to add a new object to a database without disrupting existing processes is an example of _____.

15. The property that most distinguishes a relational database table from a spreadsheet is the ability to present multiple users with their own _____.

Chapter 2

Exploring Relational Database Components

Key Skills & Concepts

- Conceptual Database Design Components
- Logical/Physical Database Design Components

This chapter explores the conceptual, logical, and physical components that make up the relational model. *Conceptual database design* involves studying and modeling the data in a technology-independent manner. The conceptual data model that results can be theoretically implemented on any database or even on a flat file system. The person who performs conceptual database design is often called a *data modeler*. *Logical database design* is the process of translating, or *mapping,* the conceptual design into a logical design that fits the chosen database model (relational, object-oriented, object-relational, and so on). A specialist who performs logical database design is called a *database designer*, but often the database administrator (DBA) performs all or part of this design step. The final design step is *physical database design,* which involves mapping the logical design to one or more physical designs, each tailored to the particular DBMS that will manage the database and the particular computer system on which the database will run. The person who performs physical database design is usually the DBA. The processes involved in database design are covered in Chapter 5.

The sections that follow explore the components of a conceptual database design, and then the components of logical and physical designs.

Conceptual Database Design Components

Figure 2-1 shows the conceptual database design for Northwind. This diagram is similar to Figure 1-7 in Chapter 1, but a few items have been added to illustrate key points. The labeled items (Entity, Attribute, Relationship, Business Rule, and Intersection Data) are the basic components that make up a conceptual database design. Each is presented in sections that follow, except for intersection data, which is presented in "Many-to-Many Relationships."

Entities

An *entity* (or *entity class*) is a person, place, thing, event, or concept about which data is collected. In other words, entities are the real-world things in which we have sufficient interest to capture and store data about in a database. An entity is represented as a rectangle

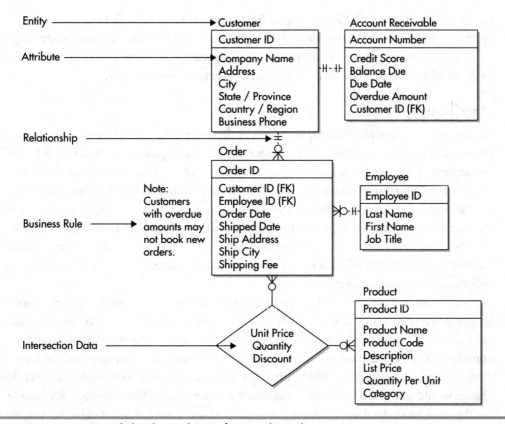

Figure 2-1   Conceptual database design for Northwind

on the diagram. Just about anything that can be named with a noun can be an entity. However, to avoid designing everything on the planet into our database, we restrict ourselves to entities of interest to the people who will use our database. Each entity shown in the conceptual model (Figure 2-1) represents the entire class for that entity. For example, the Customer entity represents the collection of all Northwind customers. The individual customers are called *instances* of the entity.

An *external entity* is an entity with which our database exchanges data (sending data to, receiving data from, or both) but about which we collect no data. For example, most businesses that set up credit accounts for customers purchase credit reports from one or more credit bureaus. They send a customer's identifying information to the credit bureau and receive a credit report, but all this data is about the *customer* rather than the credit bureau itself. Assuming there is no compelling reason for the database to store data about the credit bureau, such as the mailing address of its office, the credit bureau will not appear in the conceptual database design as an entity. In fact, external entities are seldom shown in database designs, but they commonly appear in data flow diagrams as a source or destination of data. Data flow diagrams are discussed in Chapter 7.

Attributes

An *attribute* is a unit fact that characterizes or describes an entity in some way. These are represented on the conceptual design diagram shown in Figure 2-1 as names inside the rectangle that represents the entity to which they belong. The attribute or attributes that appear at the top of the rectangle (above the horizontal line) form the *unique identifier* for the entity. A unique identifier, as the name suggests, provides a unique value for each instance of the entity. For example, the Customer ID attribute is the unique identifier for the Customer entity, so each customer must have a unique value for that attribute. Keep in mind that a unique identifier can comprise multiple attributes, but when this happens, it is still considered just *one* unique identifier.

We say attributes are a *unit* fact because they should be *atomic*, meaning they cannot be broken down into smaller units in any meaningful way. An attribute is therefore the smallest named unit of data that appears in a database system. In this sense, Address should be considered a suspect attribute because it could easily be broken down into Address Line 1, Address Line 2, and perhaps Address Line 3, as is commonly done in business systems. This change would add meaning because it makes it easier to print address labels, for example. On the other hand, database design is not an exact science and judgment calls must be made. Although it is possible to break the Business Phone attribute into component attributes, such as Country Code, Area Code, Prefix, Suffix, and Extension, we must ask ourselves whether such a change adds meaning or value. There is no right or wrong answer here, so we must rely on the people who will be using the database, or perhaps those who are funding the database project, to help us with such decisions. Always remember that an attribute *must* describe or characterize the entity in some way (for example, size, shape, color, quantity, location).

Relationships

Relationships are the associations among the entities. Because databases are all about storing related data, the relationships become the glue that holds the database together. Relationships are shown on the conceptual design diagram (Figure 2-1) as lines connecting one or more entities. Each end of a relationship line shows the *maximum cardinality* of the relationship, which is the maximum number of instances of one entity that can be associated with the entity on the opposite end of the line. The maximum cardinality may be *one* (the line has no special symbol on its end) or *many* (the line has a crow's foot on the end). Just short of the end of the line is another symbol that shows the *minimum cardinality,* which is the minimum number of instances of one entity that can be associated with the entity on the opposite end of the line. The minimum cardinality may be *zero,* denoted with a circle drawn on the line, or *one,* denoted with a short perpendicular line or tick mark drawn across the relationship line. Many data modelers use two perpendicular lines to mean "one and *only one*," as I have done in Figure 2-1.

Learning to read relationships takes practice, and learning to define and draw them correctly takes a *lot* of practice. The trick is to think about the association between the entities in one direction, and then reverse your perspective to think about it in the opposite direction. For the relationship between Customer and Order, for example, we must ask two questions: Each customer can have how many orders? followed by Each order can have how many customers? Relationships may thus be classified into three types: *one-to-one*, *one-to-many*, and *many-to-many*, as discussed in the following sections. Some people will say many-to-one is also a relationship type, but in reality, it is only a one-to-many relationship looked at with a reverse perspective. Relationship types are best learned by example. Getting the relationships right is *essential* to a successful design.

Ask the Expert

Q: You stated that relationships in the conceptual design are between one or more entities. However, I've always been told that relationships in an RDBMS are between only two tables. How can this be?

A: A conceptual database design is usually created at a higher level of abstraction than the physical database. As you will learn later in this chapter, the referential constraints placed in the relational database can support only relationships between two tables, except for a special case called *recursive relationships* that involve only one table. However, nothing stops a designer from being more general in a conceptual design and showing a relationship between more than two entities. For example, the relationship between Order and Product shown in Figure 2-1 might be represented in a conceptual design as one between Order, Product, and Shipping Warehouse (the location that stocks the product on the order line item). Such a relationship would have to be resolved during logical design, just as the intersection data shown in Figure 2-1 must be (it must eventually be stored in a table). Have no fear if this seems confusing; it will all become more clear as you learn about database design in upcoming chapters. In reality, relationships involving more than two entities are reasonably rare, and an advanced topic, so they are not used in this book.

One-to-One Relationships

A *one-to-one relationship* is an association in which an instance of one entity can be associated with *at most* one instance of the other entity, and vice versa. In Figure 2-1, the relationship between the Customer and Account Receivable entities is one-to-one. This means that a customer can have *at most* one associated account receivable, and an account can have *at most* one associated customer. The relationship is also *mandatory* in both directions, meaning that a customer must have *at least* one account receivable associated with it, and an account receivable must have *at least* one customer associated with it. Putting this all together, we can read the relationship between the Customer and Account Receivable entities as "one customer has one and only one associated account receivable, and one account receivable has one and only one associated customer."

Another important concept is *transferability*. A relationship is said to be *transferable* if the parent can be changed over time—or, said another way, if the child can be reassigned to a different parent. In this case, the relationship between Customer and Account Receivable is obviously not transferable because we would never take one customer's account and transfer it to another customer (it would be horribly bad accounting practice to do so). Unfortunately, no widely accepted symbol is available for showing transferability on data models, but it is an important consideration in some cases, particularly with one-to-one relationships that are mandatory in both directions.

One-to-one relationships are surprisingly rare among entities. In practice, one-to-one relationships that are mandatory in both directions *and* not transferable represent a design flaw that should be corrected by combining the two entities. After all, isn't an account receivable merely more information about the customer? We're not going to collect data *about* an account receivable; instead, the information in the Account Receivable entity is simply more data we collect *about* the customer. On the other hand, if we buy our financial software from an independent software vendor (a common practice), the software would almost certainly come with a predefined database that it supports, so we may have no choice but to live with this situation. We won't be able to modify the vendor's database design to add customer data of interest to us, and at the same time, we won't be able to get the vendor's software to recognize anything that we store in our own database.

Figure 2-2 shows a different "flavor" of one-to-one relationship that is *optional* (some say *conditional*) in both directions. Suppose we are designing the database for an automobile dealership. The dealership issues automobiles to some employees, typically sales staff, for them to drive for a finite period of time. They obviously don't issue *all* the automobiles to employees (if they did, they would have none to sell). We can read the relationship between the Employee and Automobile entities as follows: "At any point in time, each employee can have zero or one automobiles issued to him or her,

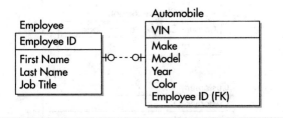

Figure 2-2   Employee-automobile relationship

and each automobile can be assigned to zero or one employee." Note the clause *At any point in time*. If an automobile is taken back from one employee and then reassigned to another, this would still be a one-to-one relationship. This is because when we consider relationships, we are always thinking in terms of a snapshot taken at an arbitrary point in time. Also, from the preceding description, it is obvious that the relationship is transferable.

One-to-Many Relationships

A *one-to-many relationship* is an association between two entities in which any instance of the first entity may be associated with one or more instances of the second, and any instance of the second entity may be associated with at most one instance of the first. Figure 2-1 shows two such relationships: between the Customer and Order entities, and between the Employee and Order entities. The relationship between Customer and Order, which is mandatory in only one direction, is read as follows: "At any point in time, each customer can have zero to many orders, and each order must have one and only one owning customer."

One-to-many relationships are quite common. In fact, they are the fundamental building block of the relational database model in that all relationships in a relational database are implemented as if they are one-to-many. It is rare for them to be optional on the "one" side and even more rare for them to be mandatory on the "many" side, but these situations do happen. Consider the examples shown in Figure 2-3. When a customer account closes, we record the reason it was closed using an account closure reason code. Because some accounts are open at any point in time, this is an optional code. We read the relationship this way: "At any given point in time, each account closure reason code value can have zero, one, or many customers assigned to it, and each customer can have either zero or one account closure reason code assigned to them." Let us next suppose that as a matter of company policy, no customer account can be opened without first obtaining a credit report, and that all credit reports are kept in the database, meaning

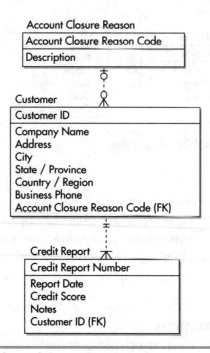

Figure 2-3 One-to-many relationships

that any customer may have more than one credit report in the database. This makes the relationship between the Customer and Credit Report entities one-to-many, and mandatory in both directions. We read the relationship thus: "At any given point in time, each customer can have one or many credit reports, and each credit report belongs to one and only one customer."

Many-to-Many Relationships

A *many-to-many relationship* is an association between two entities in which any instance of the first entity may be associated with zero, one, or more instances of the second, and vice versa. Back in Figure 2-1, the relationship between Order and Product is many-to-many. We read the relationship thus: "At any given point in time, each order contains zero to many products, and each product appears on zero to many orders."

This particular relationship has data associated with it, as shown in the diamond in Figure 2-1. Data that belongs to a many-to-many relationship is called *intersection data*. The data doesn't make sense unless you associate it with both entities at the same time. For example, Quantity doesn't make sense unless you know *who* (which customer) ordered *what* (which product). If you look back in Chapter 1 at Figure 1-7, you will recognize this data as the Order Detail table from Northwind's relational model. So why isn't Order Detail just shown as an entity? The answer is simple: It doesn't fit the definition of an entity. We are not collecting data about the line items on the order; instead, the line items on the order are merely more data about the order.

Many-to-many relationships are quite common, and most of them will have intersection data. The bad news is that the relational model does not directly support many-to-many relationships. There is no problem with having many-to-many relationships in a conceptual design, because such a design is independent of any particular technology. However, if the database is going to be relational, some changes have to be made as you map the conceptual model to the corresponding logical model. The solution is to map the intersection data to a separate table (an *intersection table*) and the many-to-many relationship to two, one-to-many relationships, with the intersection table in the middle and on the "many" side of both relationships. Figure 1-7 shows this outcome, with the Order Detail table holding the intersection data and participating in two one-to-many relationships that replace the original many-to-many relationship. The process for recognizing and dealing with the many-to-many problem is covered in detail in Chapter 6.

Recursive Relationships

So far, you've learned about relationships between instances of different entities. However, relationships can exist between entity instances of the same type. These are called *recursive relationships*. Any one of the relationship types already presented (one-to-one, one-to-many, or many-to-many) can be a recursive relationship. Figure 2-4 and the following list show examples of each:

- **One-to-one**   If we were to track which employees were married to other employees, we would expect each to be married to either zero or one other employee at any one point in time.

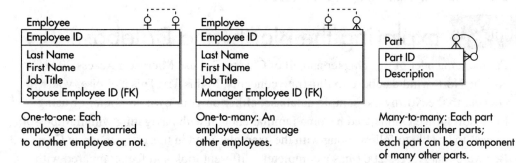

Figure 2-4   Recursive relationship examples

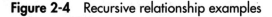

- **One-to-many**   It is common to track the employment "food chain" of who reports to whom. In most organizations, people have only one supervisor or manager. Therefore, we normally expect to see each employee reporting to zero or one other employee, and employees who are managers or supervisors to have one or more direct reports.

- **Many-to-many**   In manufacturing, a common relationship has to do with parts that make up a finished product. If you think about the CD-ROM drive in a personal computer, for example, you can imagine that it comprises multiple parts, and yet, the entire assembly shows as only one item on the parts list for your computer. So any part can be made of many other parts, and at the same time any part can be a component of many other parts.

Business Rules

A *business rule* is a policy, procedure, or standard that an organization has adopted. Business rules are *very* important in database design because they dictate controls that must be placed upon the data. In Figure 2-1, you can see a business rule that states that orders will be accepted only from customers who do not have an overdue balance. Most business rules can be enforced through manual procedures that employees are directed to follow or logic placed in the application programs. However, each of these can be circumvented—employees can forget or can choose not to follow a manual procedure, and databases can be updated directly by authorized people, bypassing the controls included in the application programs. The database can serve nicely as the last line of defense. Business rules can be implemented in the database as *constraints,* which are formally defined rules that restrict the data values in the database in some way. More information on constraints can be found in the "Constraints" section later in this chapter. Note that business rules are not normally shown on a conceptual data model diagram; the one shown in Figure 2-1 is merely for illustration. It is far more common to include them in a text document that accompanies the diagram.

Try This 2-1   Exploring the Northwind Database

For the remainder of this chapter and all of Chapter 3, I use Microsoft Access 2007 and the Northwind database to illustrate concepts. In this Try This exercise, you will connect to the Northwind sample database, either on your own computer or using Microsoft Office Online, and become familiar enough with navigating within Microsoft Access to be able to follow along with the examples used in this chapter and in Chapter 3. Be aware that Access 2007 has a completely different look and feel compared with prior versions, so you may find it difficult to follow along using an earlier version. However, the solution is simple because all you need for Microsoft Office Online is a web browser and a reasonably fast Internet connection.

The selection of Microsoft Access for these conceptual illustrations is merely a matter of convenience and not an endorsement of this product over any other. In fact, as I cover SQL in Chapter 4, I will use other RDMS products for demonstration, including Oracle.

Step by Step

1. If you have Microsoft Access 2007 available, download and install the Northwind sample database by following these steps:

   a. Start Access 2007 from your Start menu with no databases open.

   b. On the left side of the Getting Started panel, click Sample under the heading From Microsoft Office Online.

   c. Click the Northwind 2007 icon.

   d. In the lower-right corner of the panel, click the Download button and respond to any additional prompts.

   e. Once connected to the database, a screen like the one shown in Figure 2-5 will be displayed.

2. If you do not have Microsoft Access 2007 available, you can access it via Microsoft Office Online using only your web browser by following these steps:

   a. Type the URL **http://office.microsoft.com/en-us/products/** into your browser and then press ENTER.

   b. In the center part of the screen, find and click the link that reads Try Office 2007 Online.

   c. On the next page, click Launch Test Drive and respond to any additional prompts. The process of loading the software and establishing your database connection may take several minutes.

   d. On the Tutorial Menu page, click Office Access 2007.

(continued)

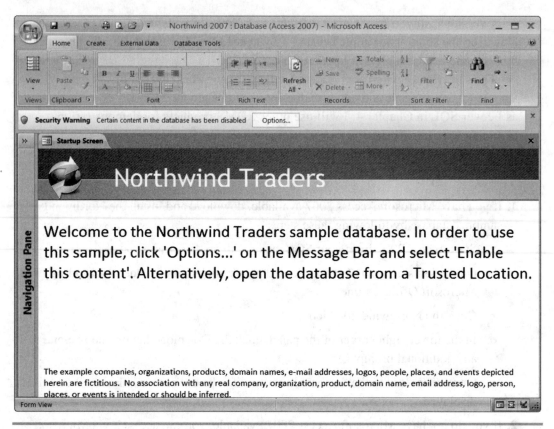

Figure 2-5   Northwind database startup screen

e.   On the left margin of the Getting Started panel, click Sample under the heading From Microsoft Online.

f.   In the lower-right corner of the panel (you may have to expand your browser to full screen to see it), click the Download button and respond to any additional prompts. In particular, note the following:

●   You may get one or more messages about running add-ons from the website. These will appear near the top of the screen, just below the line with the gold star, usually with a light yellow background color (similar to the Security Warning message shown in Figure 2-5).

- You will have to respond to the Security Warning shown on Figure 2-5. Just click the Options button on the message line and choose the option that enables the content.

- When you first open the database, you may be prompted to log in. If this occurs, just click the Cancel option.

   g. Once connected to the database, a screen like the one shown in Figure 2-5 will be displayed.

3. On the ribbon (the area along the top of the panel that contains options), click Database Tools, and then choose the Relationships option. The Relationships panel is displayed, showing 18 tables and the relationships between them. You will see a very busy diagram, but if you follow the lines, you can easily see each relationship.

4. Close the Relationships panel by clicking the X immediately to the right of the Relationships tab.

5. Expand the Navigation Pane (along the left margin of the panel) by clicking the >> icon near the top of the pane. The database contains a number of screens, reports, and other objects used to demonstrate the programming facilities within Microsoft Access 2007. However, we are interested only in the database objects (application programming is beyond the scope of this book). Expand the Supporting Objects to see a list of all the tables included in the Northwind database. For each table, you can right-click its name and select either Open to see the table contents (rows of data) or Design View to see the definition of the table. Don't be concerned if you don't understand everything you are looking at—these panels are described in more detail in upcoming sections.

6. Close Microsoft Access 2007 (or Office 2007 Online and your browser window).

Try This Summary

You have successfully accessed the Northwind sample database that will be used to demonstrate concepts for the remainder of this chapter as well as in the next chapter. You navigated to the Relationships panel and to the Supporting Objects list in the Navigation Pane.

Logical/Physical Database Design Components

The logical database design is implemented in the logical layer of the ANSI/SPARC model discussed in Chapter 1. The physical design is implanted in the ANSI/SPARC physical layer. However, we work through the DBMS to implement the physical layer, making it difficult to separate the two layers. For example, when we create a table, we include a clause in the *create table* command that tells the DBMS where we want to place it. The DBMS then automatically allocates space for the table in the requested operating system file(s). Because so much of the physical implementation is buried in the DBMS definitions of the logical structures, I have elected not to try to separate them here. During logical database design, physical storage properties (file or tablespace name, storage location, and sizing information) can be assigned to each database object as we map them from the conceptual model, or they can be omitted at first and added later in a physical design step that follows logical design. For time efficiency, most DBAs perform the two design steps (logical and physical) in parallel.

Tables

The primary unit of storage in the relational model is the *table*, which is a two-dimensional structure composed of rows and columns. Each row corresponds to one occurrence of the entity that the table represents, and each column corresponds to one attribute for that entity. The process of mapping the entities in the conceptual design to tables in the logical design is called *normalization* and is covered in detail in Chapter 6. Often, an entity in the conceptual model maps to exactly one table in the logical model, but this is not always the case. For reasons you will learn with the normalization process, entities are commonly split into multiple tables, and in rare cases, multiple entities can be combined into one table. Figure 2-6 shows a listing of part of the Northwind Orders table.

You must remember that a relational table is a *logical* storage structure and usually does not exist in tabular form in the physical layer. When the DBA assigns a table to operating system files in the physical layer (called *tablespaces* in most RDBMSs), it is common for multiple tables to be placed in a single tablespace. However, large tables can be placed in their own tablespace or split across multiple tablespaces, and this is called *partitioning*. This flexibility typically does not exist in personal computer-based RDBMSs such as Microsoft Access.

Each table must be given a unique name by the DBA who creates it. The maximum length for these names varies a lot among RDBMS products, from as little as 18 characters to as many as 255. Table names should be descriptive and should reflect the name of the real-world entity they represent. By convention, some DBAs always name entities in the

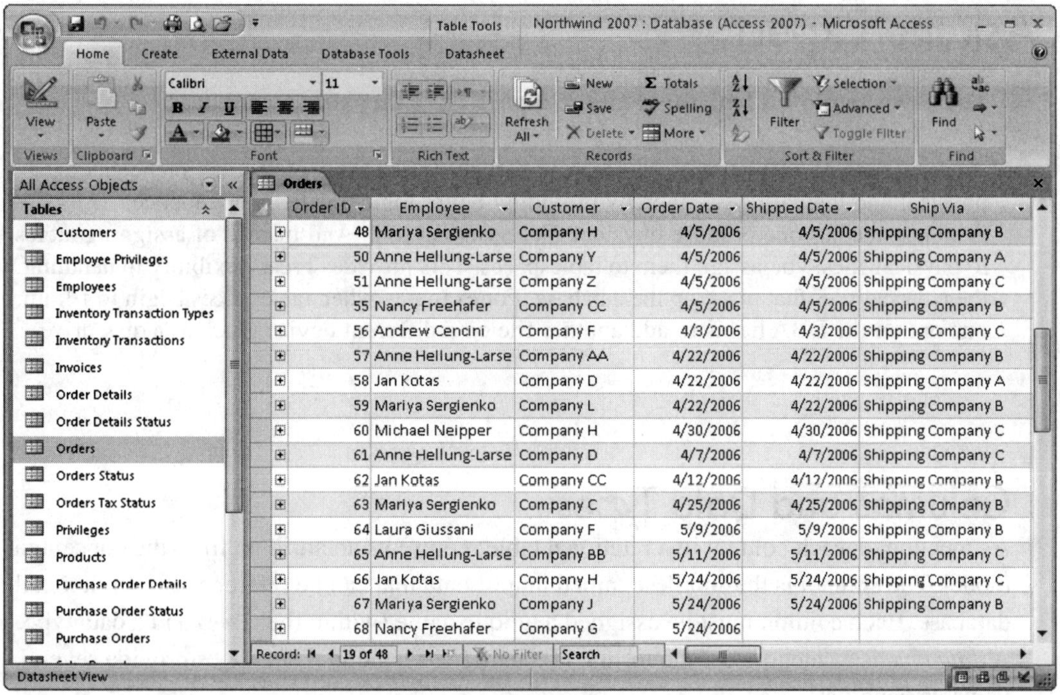

Figure 2-6 Northwind Orders table (partial listing)

singular and tables in the plural, and you will see this convention used in the Northwind database. (I prefer that both be named in the singular, but obviously other learned professionals have counter opinions.) The point here is that you should establish naming standards at the outset so that names are not assigned in a haphazard manner, as this leads to confusion later. As a case in point, Microsoft Access permits embedded spaces in table and column names, which is counter to industry standards. Moreover, Microsoft Access, Sybase ASE, and Microsoft SQL Server allow mixed-case names, such as OrderDetails, whereas Oracle, DB2, MySQL on Windows, and others force all names to be uppercase letters unless they are enclosed in double quotes. Because table names such as ORDERDETAILS are not very readable, the use of an underscore to separate words, per industry standards, is a much better choice. You may want to set standards that forbid the use of names with embedded spaces and names in mixed case because such names are nonstandard and make any conversion between database vendors that much more difficult.

Ask the Expert

Q: You have mentioned both files and tablespaces. Are they the same thing?

A: You can think of a tablespace as a logical file that forms a layer of abstraction between the physical and logical layers, thereby providing better logical data independence. A tablespace has one or more physical files assigned to it. And instead of assigning tables to physical files, you assign them to tablespaces. This provides great flexibility in handling the physical files that make up the database. For example, when tablespaces begin to fill up, one option the DBA has is to add another file on a different device (such as a disk drive).

Columns and Data Types

As mentioned, each column in a relational table represents an attribute from the conceptual model. The *column* is the smallest named unit of data that can be referenced in a relational database. Each column must be assigned a unique name (within the table) and a data type. A *data type* is a category for the format of a particular column. Data types provide several valuable benefits:

- Restricting the data in the column to characters that make sense for the data type (for example, all numeric digits or only valid calendar dates).

- Providing a set of behaviors useful to the database user. For example, if you subtract a number from another number, you get a number as a result; but if you subtract a date from another date, you get a number representing the elapsed days between the two dates as a result.

- Assisting the RDBMS in efficiently storing the column data. For example, numbers can often be stored in an internal numeric format that saves space, compared with merely storing the numeric digits as a string of characters.

Figure 2-7 shows the table definition of the Northwind Orders table from Microsoft Access 2007 (the same table listed in Figure 2-6). The data type for each column appears in the second column. The data type names are usually self-evident, but if you find any of them confusing, you can view definitions of each in the Microsoft Access help pages.

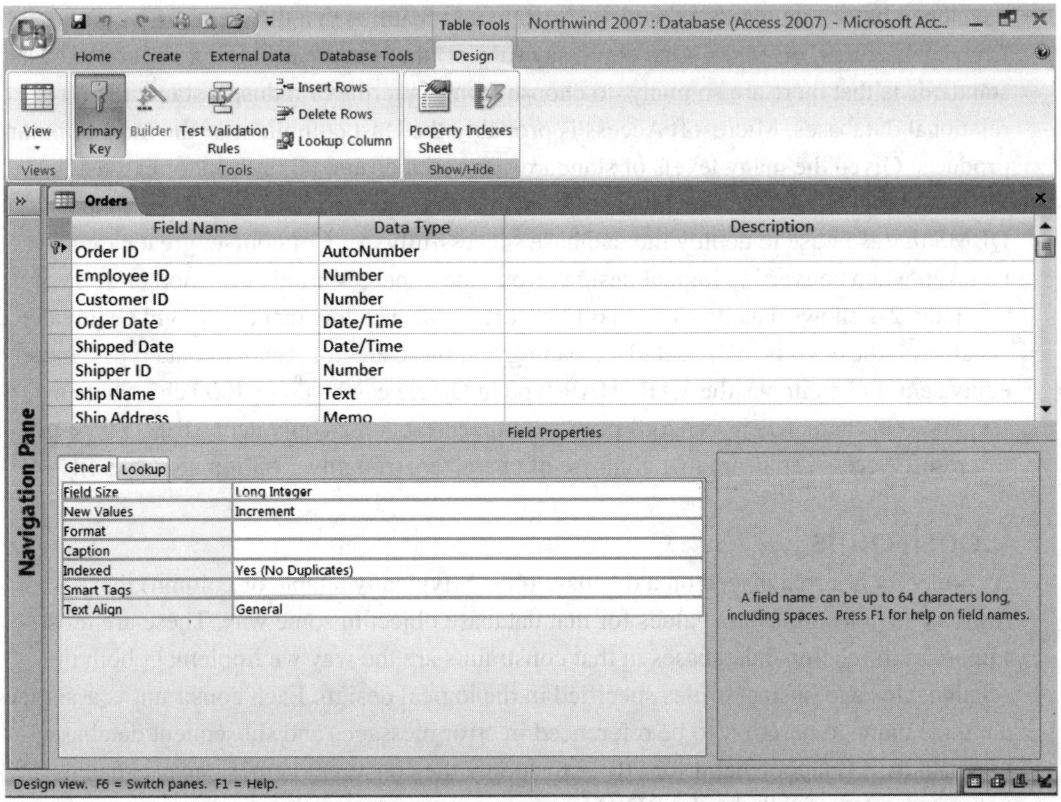

Figure 2-7   Table definition of the Northwind Orders table (Microsoft Access 2007)

NOTE

If you compare Figure 2-6 with Figure 2-7, you will notice that the Employee Name and Customer Name are shown in Figure 2-6 instead of Employee ID and Customer ID as specified in definition in Figure 2-7. This is not an error, but rather a feature of Microsoft Access that is explained in the "Referential Constraints" section later in this chapter.

It is most unfortunate that industry standards lagged behind RDBMS development. Most vendors did their own thing for many years before sitting down with other vendors to develop standards, and this is clearly evident in the wide variation of data type options across the major RDBMS products. Today ANSI/ISO SQL standards cover relational data types, and the major vendors support all or most of the standard types. However, each vendor has its own "extensions" to the standards, largely in support of data types it developed before standards existed, but also to add features that differentiate its product from competitors' offerings. One could say (in jest) that the greatest thing about database standards is that there are so many to choose from. In terms of industry standards for relational databases, Microsoft Access is probably the least compliant of the most popular products. Given the many levels of standards compliance and all the vendor extensions, the DBA must have a detailed knowledge of the data types available on the particular DBMS that is in use to deploy the database successfully. And, of course, great care must be taken when converting logical designs from one vendor's product to another's.

Table 2-1 shows data types from different RDBMS vendors that are roughly equivalent. As always, the devil is in the details, meaning that these are not *identical* data types, merely equivalent. For example, the VARCHAR type in Oracle can be up to 4000 characters in length (2000 characters in versions prior to Oracle8*i*), but the equivalent MEMO type in Microsoft Access can be up to a gigabyte of characters (roughly 1 billion characters)!

Constraints

A *constraint* is a rule placed on a database object (typically a table or column) that restricts the allowable data values for that database object in some way. These are most important in relational databases in that constraints are the way we implement both the relationships and business rules specified in the logical design. Each constraint is assigned a unique name to permit it to be referenced in error messages and subsequent database commands. It is a good habit for DBAs to supply the constraint names because names generated automatically by the RDBMS are never very descriptive.

Data Type	Microsoft Access	Microsoft SQL Server	Oracle
Fixed-length character	TEXT	CHAR	CHAR
Variable-length character	MEMO	VARCHAR	VARCHAR
Long text	MEMO	TEXT	CLOB or LONG (deprecated)
Integer	INTEGER or LONG INTEGER	INTEGER or SMALLINT or TINYINT	NUMBER
Decimal	NUMBER	DECIMAL or NUMERIC	NUMBER
Currency	CURRENCY	MONEY or SMALLMONEY	None, use NUMBER
Date/time	DATE/TIME	DATETIME or SMALLDATETIME	DATE or TIMESTAMP

Table 2-1 Equivalent Data Types in Major RDBMS Products

Primary Key Constraints

A *primary key* is a column or a set of columns that uniquely identifies each row in a table. A unique identifier in the conceptual design is thus implemented as a primary key in the logical design. The small icon that looks like a door key to the left of the Order ID field name in Figure 2-7 indicates that this column has been defined as the primary key of the Orders table. When you define a primary key, the RDBMS implements it as a *primary key constraint* to guarantee that no two rows in the table will ever have duplicate values in the primary key column(s). Note that for primary keys composed of multiple columns, each column by itself *may* have duplicate values in the table, but the *combination* of the values for all the primary key columns must be unique among all rows in the table.

Primary key constraints are nearly always implemented by the RDBMS using an *index*, which is a special type of database object that permits fast searches of column values. As new rows are inserted into the table, the RDBMS *automatically* searches the index to make sure the value for the primary key of the new row is not already in use in the table, rejecting the insert request if it is. Indexes can be searched much faster than tables; therefore, the index on the primary key is essential in tables of any size so that the search for duplicate keys on every insert doesn't create a performance bottleneck.

Referential Constraints

To understand how the RDBMS enforces relationships using referential constraints, you must first understand the concept of foreign keys. When one-to-many relationships are implemented in tables, the column or set of columns that is stored in the child table (the table on the "many" side of the relationship), to associate it with the parent table (the table on the "one" side), is called a *foreign key*. It gets its name from the column(s) copied from another (foreign) table. In the Orders table shown in Figure 2-6, the Employee ID column is a foreign key to the Employees table, and the Customer ID column is a foreign key to the Customers table.

In most relational databases, the foreign key must either be the primary key of the parent table or a column or set of columns for which a unique index is defined. This again is for efficiency. Most people prefer that the foreign key column(s) have names identical to the corresponding primary key column(s), but again there are counter opinions, especially because like-named columns are a little more difficult to use in query languages. It is best to set some standards up front and stick with them throughout your database project.

Each relationship between entities in the conceptual design becomes a referential constraint in the logical design. A *referential constraint* (sometimes called a *referential integrity constraint*) is a constraint that enforces a relationship among tables in a relational database. *Enforces* means that the RDBMS automatically checks to ensure that each foreign key value in a child table always has a corresponding primary key value in the parent table.

Microsoft Access provides a nice feature for foreign key columns, but it takes a bit of getting used to. When you define a referential constraint, you can define an automatic lookup of the parent table rows, as was done throughout the Northwind database. In Figure 2-7, the third column in the table is listed as Customer ID. However, in Figure 2-6, you will notice that the third column of the Orders table displays the customer name and is listed as Customer. If you click in the Customer column for one of the rows, a pull-down menu appears to allow the selection of a valid customer (from the Customers table) to be the parent (owner) of the selected Orders table row. Similarly, the Employee ID column of the table displays the employee name. This is a convenient and easy feature for the database user, and it prevents a nonexistent customer or employee from being associated with an order. However, it hides the foreign key in such a way that Figure 2-6 isn't very useful for illustrating how referential constraints work under the covers. Figure 2-8 lists the Orders table with the lookups removed so you can see the actual foreign key values in the Employee ID and Customer ID columns.

When we update the Orders table, as shown in Figure 2-8, the RDBMS must enforce the referential constraints we have defined on the table. The beauty of database constraints

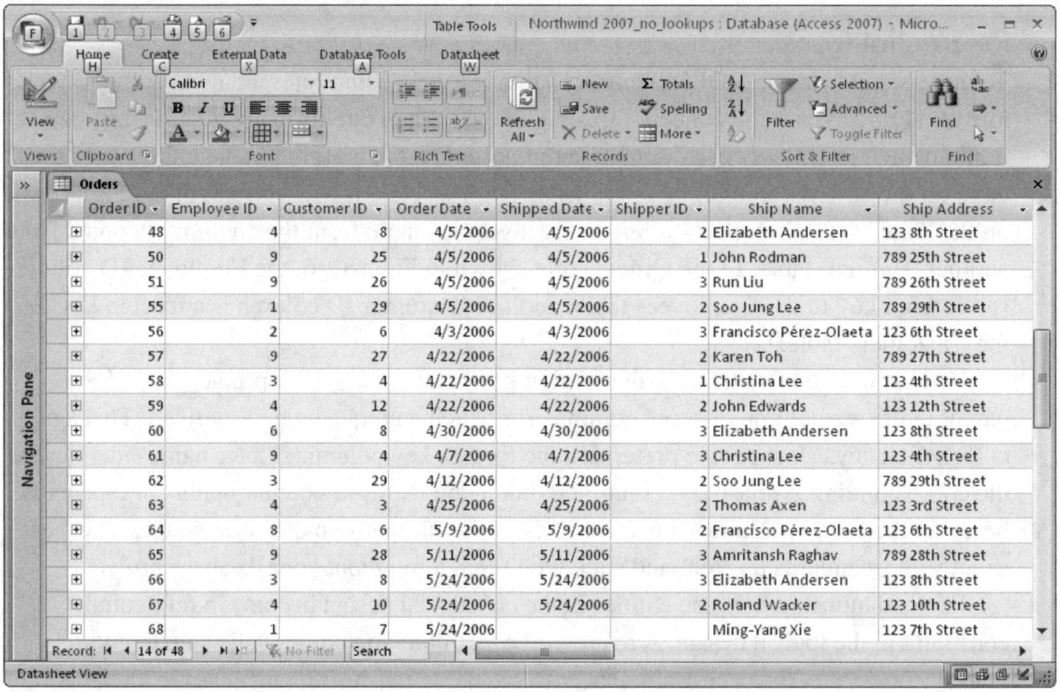

Order ID	Employee ID	Customer ID	Order Date	Shipped Date	Shipper ID	Ship Name	Ship Address
48	4	8	4/5/2006	4/5/2006	2	Elizabeth Andersen	123 8th Street
50	9	25	4/5/2006	4/5/2006	1	John Rodman	789 25th Street
51	9	26	4/5/2006	4/5/2006	3	Run Liu	789 26th Street
55	1	29	4/5/2006	4/5/2006	2	Soo Jung Lee	789 29th Street
56	2	6	4/3/2006	4/3/2006	3	Francisco Pérez-Olaeta	123 6th Street
57	9	27	4/22/2006	4/22/2006	2	Karen Toh	789 27th Street
58	3	4	4/22/2006	4/22/2006	1	Christina Lee	123 4th Street
59	4	12	4/22/2006	4/22/2006	2	John Edwards	123 12th Street
60	6	8	4/30/2006	4/30/2006	3	Elizabeth Andersen	123 8th Street
61	9	4	4/7/2006	4/7/2006	3	Christina Lee	123 4th Street
62	3	29	4/12/2006	4/12/2006	2	Soo Jung Lee	789 29th Street
63	4	3	4/25/2006	4/25/2006	2	Thomas Axen	123 3rd Street
64	8	6	5/9/2006	5/9/2006	2	Francisco Pérez-Olaeta	123 6th Street
65	9	28	5/11/2006	5/11/2006	3	Amritansh Raghav	789 28th Street
66	3	8	5/24/2006	5/24/2006	3	Elizabeth Andersen	123 8th Street
67	4	10	5/24/2006	5/24/2006	2	Roland Wacker	123 10th Street
68	1	7	5/24/2006			Ming-Yang Xie	123 7th Street

Figure 2-8 Northwind Orders table (with foreign key values displayed)

is that they are *automatic* and therefore cannot be circumvented unless the DBA removes or disables them.

Here are the particular events that the RDBMS must handle when enforcing referential constraints:

- When you try to insert a new row into the child table, the insert request is rejected if the corresponding parent table row does not exist. For example, if you insert a row into the Orders table with an Employee ID value of 12345, the RDBMS must check the Employees table to see if a row for Employee ID 12345 already exists. If it doesn't exist, the insert request is rejected.

- When you try to update a foreign key value in the child table, the update request is rejected if the new value for the foreign key does not already exist in the parent table. For example, if you attempt to change the Employee ID for Order 48 from 4 to 12345, the RDBMS must again check the Employees table to see if a row for Employee ID 12345 already exists. If it doesn't exist, the update request is rejected.

- When you try to delete a row from a parent table, and that parent row has related rows in one or more child tables, either the child table rows must be deleted along with the parent row or the delete request must be rejected. Most RDBMSs provide the option of automatically deleting the child rows, called a *cascading delete*. At first, you probably wondered why anyone would ever want automatic deletion of child rows. Consider the Orders and Order Details tables. If an order is to be deleted, why not delete the order and the line items that belong to it in one easy step? However, with the Employee table, you clearly would not want that option. If you attempt to delete Employee 4 from the Employee table (perhaps because the person is no longer an employee), the RDBMS must check for rows assigned to Employee ID 4 in the Orders table and reject the delete request if any are found. It would make no business sense to have orders automatically deleted when an employee left the company.

In most relational databases, an SQL statement is used to define a referential constraint. SQL is introduced in Chapter 4. SQL is the language used in RDBMSs to communicate with the database. Many vendors also provide graphical user interface (GUI) panels for defining database objects such as referential constraints. In SQL Server, for example, these GUI panels are located within the SQL Server Management Studio tool, and in Oracle, a tool named SQL Developer has these capabilities. For Microsoft Access, Figure 2-9 shows the Relationships panel that is used for defining referential constraints.

For simplicity, only the Orders table and its two parent tables, Employees and Customers, are shown in Figure 2-9. The referential constraints are shown as bold lines with the numeric

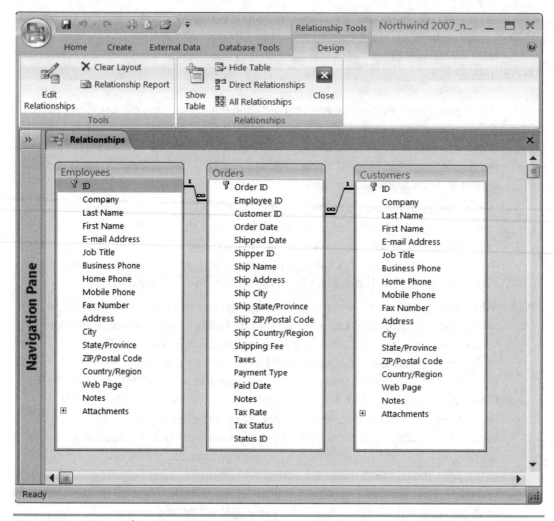

Figure 2-9 Microsoft Access 2007 Relationships panel

symbol *1* near the parent table (the "one" side) and the mathematical symbol for infinity
(a sideways figure 8) near the child table (the "many" side). These constraints are defined
simply by dragging the name of the primary key in the parent table to the name of the foreign
key in the child table. A pop-up window is then automatically displayed to allow
the definition of options for the referential constraint, as shown in Figure 2-10.

At the top of the Edit Relationships panel, the two table names appear with the parent
table on the left and the child table on the right. If you forget which is which, the
Relationship Type field at the bottom of the panel should remind you. Under each table

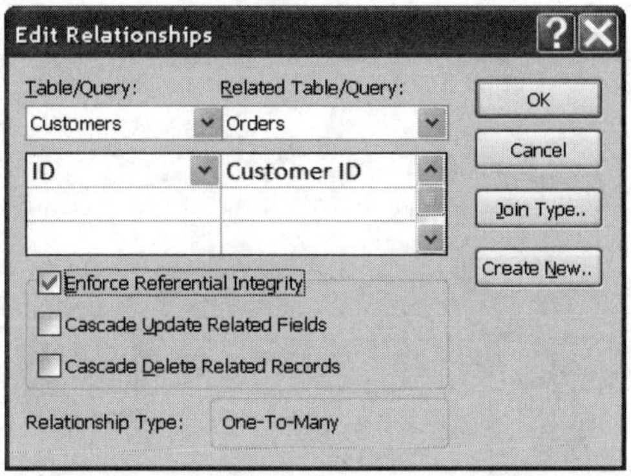

Figure 2-10   Microsoft Access 2007 Edit Relationships panel

name are rows for selection of the column names that make up the primary key and foreign key. Figure 2-10 shows the primary key column ID in the Customers table and foreign key column Customer ID in the Orders table. The check boxes provide some options:

- **Enforce Referential Integrity**   If this box is checked, the constraint is enforced; unchecking the box turns off constraint enforcement.

- **Cascade Update Related Fields**   If this box is checked, any update to the primary key value in the parent table will cause automatic corresponding updates to the related foreign key values. An update of primary key values is a rare situation.

- **Cascade Delete Related Records**   If the box is checked, a delete of a parent table row will cause the automatic cascading deletion of the related child table rows. Think carefully here. There are times when you should use this, such as the constraint between Orders and Order Details, and times when the option can lead to the disastrous unwanted loss of data, such as deleting an employee (perhaps accidentally) and having all the orders that employee handled automatically deleted from the database.

Intersection Tables

The discussion of many-to-many relationships earlier in this chapter pointed out that relational databases cannot implement these relationships directly and that an intersection table is formed to establish them. Figure 2-11 shows the implementation of the Order Details intersection table in Microsoft Access.

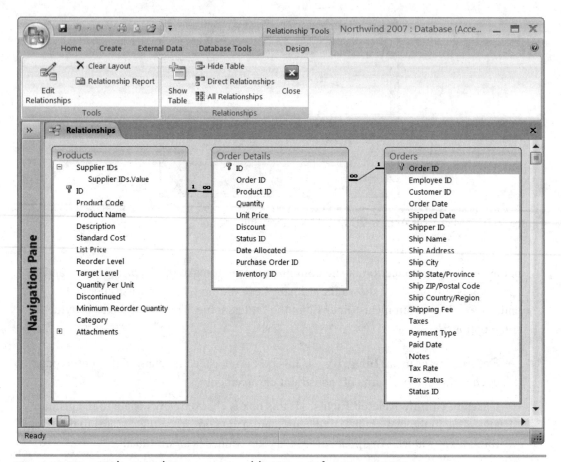

Figure 2-11   Order Details intersection table (Microsoft Access 2007)

The many-to-many relationship between orders and products in the conceptual design becomes an intersection table (Order Details) in the logical design. The relationship is then implemented as two, one-to-many relationships with the intersection table on the "many" side of each. The primary key of the Order Details table could be formed using the combination of Order ID and Product ID, with Order ID being a foreign key to the Orders table and Product ID being a foreign key to the Products table. In this case, however, the designer chose to add a single unique key value, ID, as the primary key of the Order Details table. This arrangement is known as a *surrogate key,* because the so-called *natural key* has been replaced with another one. Take a moment to examine the contents of the intersection table and the two referential constraints. Understanding this arrangement is fundamental to understanding how relational databases work. Here are some points to consider:

- Each row in the Order Details intersection table belongs to the intersection of one product and one order. It would not make sense to include Product Name in this table because that name is the same every time the product appears on an order. Also, it would not make sense to include Customer ID in Order Details because all line items on the same order belong to the same customer.

- Each Products table row may have many related Order Details rows (one for each order line item on which the product was ordered), but each Order Details row belongs to one and only one Products table row.

- Each Orders table row may have many related Order Details rows (one for each line item for that particular order), but each Order Details row belongs to one and only one Orders table row.

Integrity Constraints

As mentioned, business rules from the conceptual design become constraints in the logical design. An *integrity constraint* is a constraint that promotes the accuracy of the data in the database. The key benefit is that these constraints are invoked automatically by the RDBMS and cannot be circumvented (unless you are a DBA) no matter how you connect to the database. The major types of integrity constraints are NOT NULL constraints, CHECK constraints, and constraints enforced with triggers.

NOT NULL Constraints

As you define columns in database tables, you have the option of specifying whether null values are permitted for the column. A *null value* in a relational database is a special code that can be placed in a column that indicates that the value for that column in that row is unknown. A null value is not the same as a blank, an empty string, or a zero—it is indeed a special code that has no other meaning in the database.

A uniform way to treat null values is specified in the ANSI/ISO SQL Standard. However, there has been much debate over the usefulness of the option because the database cannot tell you *why* the value is unknown. If you leave the value for Job Title null in the Northwind Employees table, for example, you don't know whether it is null because it is truly unknown (you know employees must have a title, but you do not know what it is), it doesn't apply (perhaps some employees do not get titles), or it is unassigned (they will get a title eventually, but their manager hasn't figured out which title to use just yet). The other dilemma is that null values are not equal to anything, including other null values, which introduces three-valued logic into database searches. With nulls in use, a search can return the condition *true* (the column value matches), *false* (the column value does not match), or *unknown* (the column value is null). The developers who write the application programs have to handle null values as a special case. You'll see more about nulls when SQL is introduced in Chapter 4.

In Microsoft Access, the NOT NULL constraint is controlled by the Required option on the table design panel. Figure 2-12 shows the definition of the Discount column of the Order Details table. Note that the column is required (that is, it cannot be null) because the Required option is set to Yes. In SQL definitions of tables, you simply include the keyword NULL or NOT NULL in the column definition. Watch out for defaults! In Oracle, if you skip the specification, the default is NULL, which means the column may contain null values.

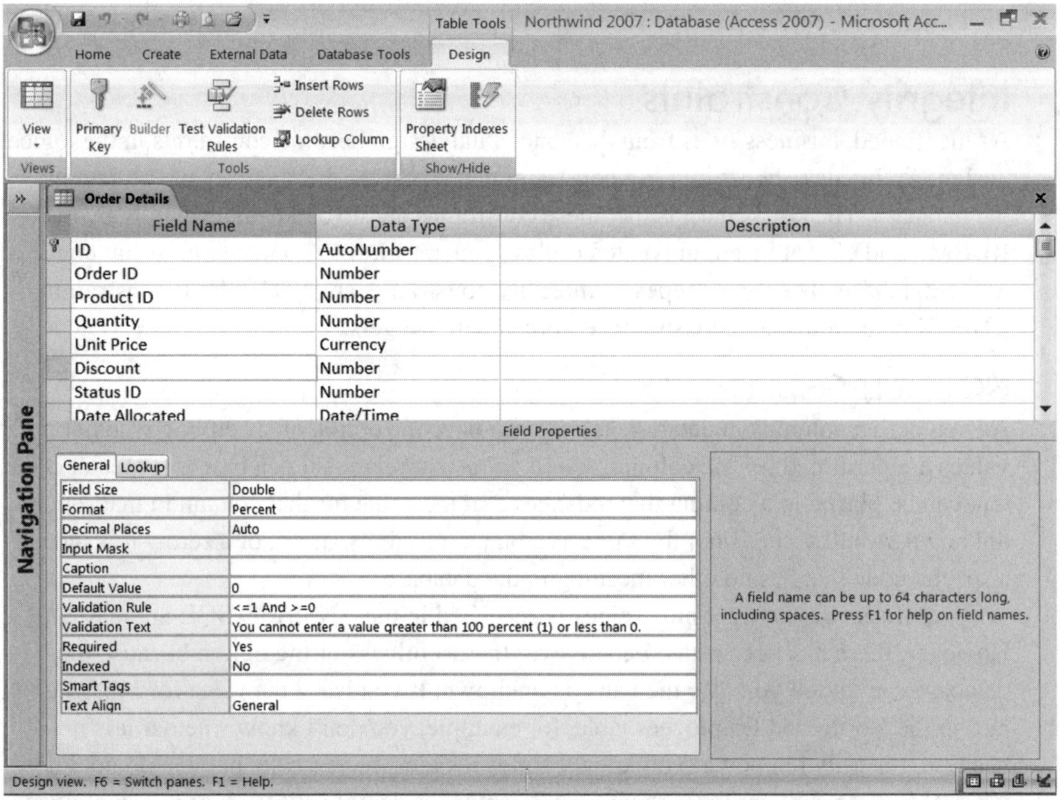

Figure 2-12 Order Details table definition panel, Discount column

But in some implementations of DB2, Microsoft SQL Server, and Sybase ASE, it is just the opposite: if you skip the specification, the default is NOT NULL, meaning the column *may not* contain null values.

CHECK Constraints

A CHECK constraint uses a simple logic statement to validate a column value. The outcome of the statement must be a logical *true* or *false*, with an outcome of *true* allowing the column value to be placed in the table, and a value of *false* causing the column value to be rejected with an appropriate error message. In Figure 2-12, notice that *<=1 And >=0* appears in the Validation Rule option for the Discount column. This rule prevents discounts from being greater than 100 percent (input as 1.00) or less than 0 percent. Although the syntax of the option will vary for other databases, the concept remains the same. In Oracle SQL, it would be written this way:

```
CHECK (DISCOUNT <=1 AND DISCOUNT >=0)
```

Constraint Enforcement Using Triggers

Some constraints are too complicated to be enforced using the declarations. For example, the business rule contained in Figure 2-1 (Customers with overdue amounts may not book new orders) falls into this category because it involves more than one table. We need to prevent new rows from being added to the Orders table if the Account Receivable row for the customer has an overdue amount that is greater than zero. As mentioned, it may be best to implement business rules such as this one in the application logic. However, if we want to add a constraint that will be enforced no matter how the database is updated, a trigger will do the job. A *trigger* is a module of programming logic that "fires" (executes) when a particular event in the database takes place. In this example, we want the trigger to fire whenever a new row is inserted into the Orders table. The trigger obtains the overdue amount for the customer from the Account Receivable table (or wherever the column is physically stored). If this amount is greater than zero, the trigger will raise a database error that stops the insert request and causes an appropriate error message to be displayed.

In Microsoft Access, triggers can be written as macros using the Microsoft Visual Basic for Applications (VBA) language. Some RDBMSs provide a special language for writing program modules such as triggers: PL/SQL in Oracle and Transact SQL in Microsoft SQL Server and Sybase ASE. In other RDBMSs, such as DB2, a generic programming language such as C may be used.

Views

A *view* is a stored database query that provides a database user with a customized subset of the data from one or more tables in the database. Said another way, a view is a *virtual table,* because it looks like a table and for the most part behaves like a table, yet it stores no data (only the defining query is stored). The user views form the external layer in the ANSI/SPARC model. During logical design, each view is created using an appropriate method for the particular database. In many RDBMSs, a view is defined using SQL. In Microsoft Access, views are not directly supported. However, Access supports an equivalent type of object called a *query* that is created using the Query panel. Figure 2-13 shows the Microsoft Access definition of a simple view that lists orders placed by customers who live in Washington state.

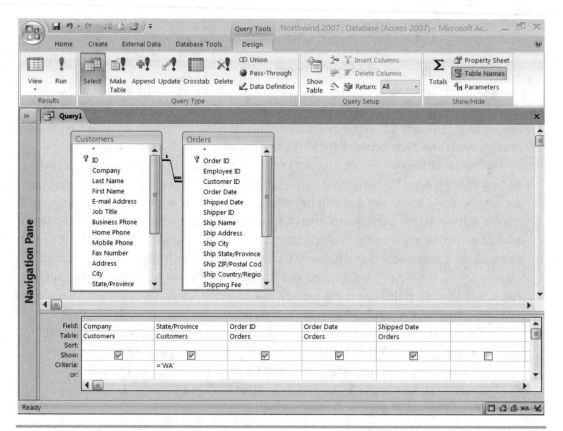

Figure 2-13   Microsoft Access 2007 view definition: list all orders for customers in Washington state

The view in Figure 2-13 displays only two columns from the Customers table along with only three columns from the Orders table. Furthermore, the view specifies the matching (joining) of the Customers and Orders tables and *filters* the rows so that only orders for Washington state customers are included by virtue of the value in the Criteria property for the State/Province column (= '*WA*'). We explore the Microsoft Access Query panel in detail in Chapter 3. Figure 2-14 shows the results of the query when it is run against the database. Although two customers are located in Washington, only one of them has placed orders, and only two such orders appear currently in the table.

Views serve a number of useful functions:

- Hiding columns that the user does not need to see (or should not be allowed to see)

- Hiding rows from tables that a user does not need to see (or should not be allowed to see)

- Hiding complex database operations such as table joins

- Improving query performance (in some RDBMSs, such as Microsoft SQL Server)

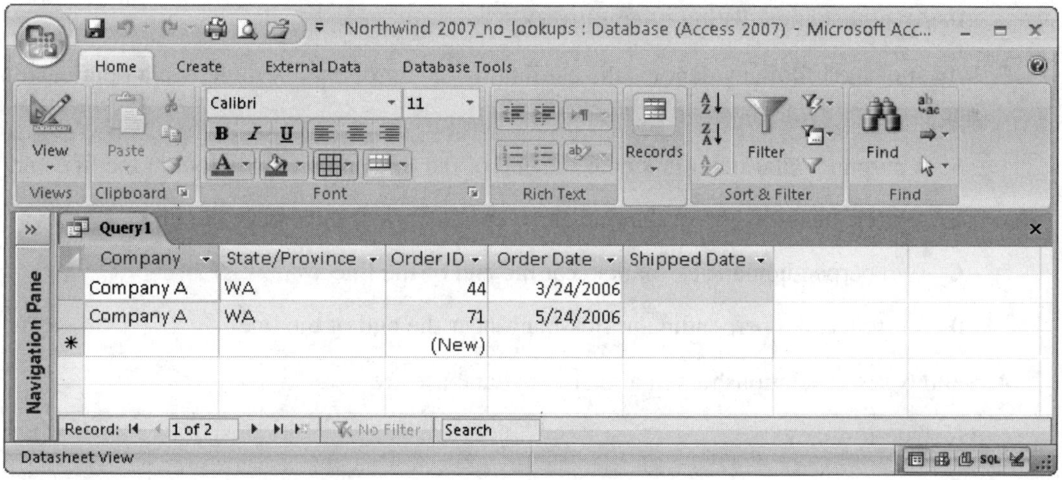

Figure 2-14   Results from running the query shown in Figure 2-13

✔ # Chapter 2 Self Test

Choose the correct responses to each of the multiple-choice and fill-in-the-blank questions. Note that there may be more than one correct response to each question.

1. Examples of an entity are

   A A customer

   B A customer order

   C An employee's paycheck

   D A customer's name

2. Examples of an attribute are

   A An employee

   B An employee's name

   C An employee's paycheck

   D An alphabetical listing of employees

3. Which of the following denotes the cardinality of "zero, one, or more" on a relationship line?

   A A perpendicular tick mark near the end of the line and a crow's foot at the line end

   B A circle near the end of the line and a crow's foot at the end of the line

   C Two perpendicular tick marks near the end of the line

   D A circle and a perpendicular tick mark near the end of the line

4. Valid types of relationships in a relational database are

   A One-to-many

   B None-to-many

   C Many-to-many

   D One-to-one

5. If a product can be manufactured in many plants, and a plant can manufacture many products, this is an example of which type of relationship?

A One-to-one

B One-to-many

C Many-to-many

D Recursive

6. Which of the following are examples of recursive relationships?

A An organizational unit made up of departments

B An employee who manages other employees

C An employee who manages a department

D An employee who has many dependents

7. Examples of a business rule are

A A referential constraint must refer to the primary key of the parent table.

B An employee must be at least 18 years old.

C A database query eliminates columns an employee should not see.

D Employees below pay grade 6 are not permitted to modify orders.

8. A relational table

A Is composed of rows and columns

B Must be assigned a data type

C Must be assigned a unique name

D Is the primary unit of storage in the relational model

9. A column in a relational table

A Must be assigned a data type

B Must be assigned a unique name within the table

C Is derived from an entity in the conceptual design

D Is the smallest named unit of storage in a relational database

10. A data type

    A Assists the DBMS in storing data efficiently

    B Provides a set of behaviors for a column that assists the database user

    C May be selected based on business rules for an attribute

    D Restricts characters allowed in a database column

11. A primary key constraint

    A Must reference one or more columns in a single table

    B Must be defined for every database table

    C Is usually implemented using an index

    D Guarantees that no two rows in a table have duplicate primary key values

12. A referential constraint

    A Must have primary key and foreign key columns that have identical names

    B Ensures that a primary key does not have duplicate values in a table

    C Defines a many-to-many relationship between two tables

    D Ensures that a foreign key value always refers to an existing primary key value in the parent table

13. A referential constraint is defined

    A Using the Relationships panel in Microsoft Access

    B Using SQL in most relational databases

    C Using the referential data type for the foreign key column(s)

    D Using a database trigger

14. Major types of integrity constraints are

    A CHECK constraints

    B One-to-one relationships

    C NOT NULL constraints

    D Constraints enforced with triggers

15. _____ tables are used to resolve many-to-many relationships.

16. An entity in the conceptual design becomes a(n) _____ in the logical design.

17. An attribute in the conceptual design becomes a(n) _____ in the logical design.

18. Items in the external level of the ANSI/SPARC model become _____ in the logical model.

19. A relationship in the conceptual design becomes a(n) _____ in the logical design.

20. A primary key constraint is implemented using a(n) _____ in the logical design.

Chapter 3
Forms-based
Database Queries

Key Skills & Concepts

- QBE: The Roots of Forms-based Queries

- Getting Started in Microsoft Access

- The Microsoft Access Relationships Panel

- Creating Queries in Microsoft Access

With a nod toward the theory that says you cannot design a car if you have never driven one, this chapter offers a brief tour of database queries before delving into the details of database design. This chapter provides an overview of forming and running database queries using the forms-based query tool in Microsoft Access. It is not at all my intent to provide a comprehensive guide to Microsoft Access; I am merely using Microsoft Access as a vehicle to present database query concepts that will provide a foundation for the database design theory that follows later in this book. However, I will attempt to provide enough basic information about using Microsoft Access to allow you to follow along on your own computer as you explore forms-based queries.

QBE: The Roots of Forms-based Queries

A *forms-based* query language uses a GUI panel for the creation of a query. The database user defines queries by entering sample data values directly into a query template to represent the result that the database is to achieve. An alternative query method uses a *command-based* query language, in which queries are written as text commands. SQL is the ubiquitous command-based query language for relational databases and is discussed in Chapter 4. The emphasis with both forms-based and command-based query languages is on *what* the result should be rather than *how* the results are achieved. The difference between the two is in the way the user describes the desired result—similar to the difference between using Microsoft Windows Explorer to copy a file versus using the MS-DOS **copy** command (in the DOS command window) to do the same thing.

The first well-known forms-based query tool was Query By Example (QBE), which was developed by IBM in the 1970s. Personal computers, Microsoft Windows, the mouse, and many other modern computing amenities were unheard of at this time, but the interface was still graphical in nature. A form was displayed, and database users typed

Ask the Expert

Q: You have mentioned both command-based and forms-based queries. It is not clear to me which one I should focus on learning.

A: Which one you learn first depends a lot on what you want to do with the database, and you may eventually want to know both. Command-based queries are essential if you want to embed them in another programming language (you cannot embed a forms-based query in another language). However, when forming ad hoc queries, humans generally prefer an interactive point-and-click GUI over text commands that require more typing. In the 1970s, IBM conducted a controlled study to determine whether QBE or SQL was preferred by database users of the day. IBM learned that most users preferred to use the method they learned first—human nature, it seems.

sample data and simple commands in boxes, where today they would click an onscreen button using a mouse. SQL, also initially developed by IBM, was new in the 1970s.

Experience has shown us that both methods are useful to know. Forms-based queries lend themselves well to individuals who are more accustomed to GUI environments than to touch-typing commands. However, database users familiar with command syntax and possessing reasonable typing skills can enter command-based queries more quickly than their GUI equivalents, and command-based queries can be directly used within a programming language such as Java or C.

Getting Started in Microsoft Access

The queries used in this chapter all feature the Northwind sample database available from Microsoft for use with Access or SQL Server. You will have the best learning experience if you try the queries presented in this chapter as you read. Obviously, the sample database is required, and you should use Microsoft Access 2007 because substantial differences exist between it and its previous versions, including the sample database. Fortunately, you'll find it relatively simple either to download and install the Northwind database (if you already have Access 2007 installed) or to connect to Microsoft Access 2007 remotely using Microsoft Office Online. Just follow the steps in the Try This exercise in Chapter 2 (if you have not already done so). Keep in mind that it is easy to update the database accidentally when using Microsoft Access, and no simple "undo" function is available.

However, if this happens, you can just download the database again and then pick up where you left off.

When you launch Microsoft Access 2007 (whether locally or using Microsoft Office Online), a startup panel similar to the one shown in Figure 3-1 is displayed.

If you have already downloaded and used the Northwind database, it should be listed under the Open Recent Database heading on the right side of the panel. Simply click the listed file name to open the database. If the database is not listed, you can download it by clicking Sample under the From Microsoft Office Online heading on the left side of the panel. A panel similar to the one shown in Figure 3-2 will be displayed. Click the Northwind 2007 icon to select it, and then click the Download button in the lower-right corner of the panel.

You will know that you have successfully connected to the Northwind database when you see the main Microsoft Access 2007 panel with the Startup Screen tab for Northwind Traders displayed, as shown in Figure 3-3. Before we explore the options available on this panel, let's tidy things up a bit. The sample database comes with application code

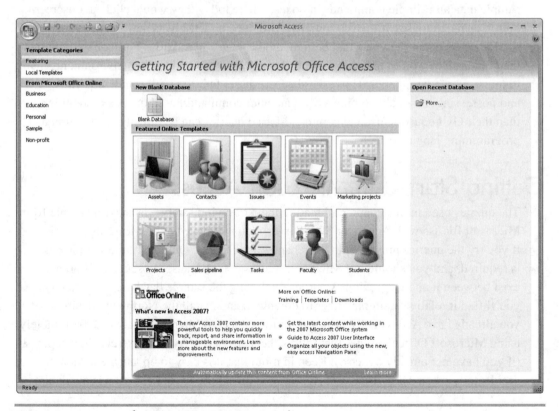

Figure 3-1 Microsoft Access 2007 startup panel

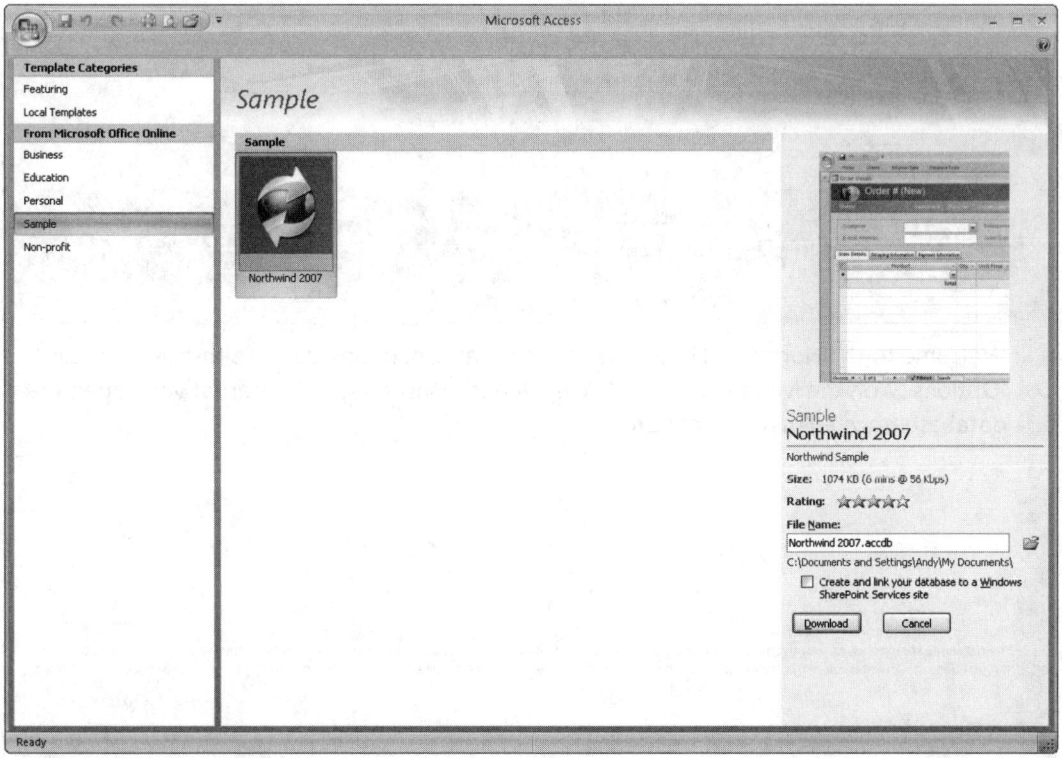

Figure 3-2 Microsoft Access 2007 sample database panel

(Visual Basic macros) that cannot be run until you respond to the security warning that is displayed on the panel. You can follow the instructions on the screen to enable the content if you wish, but we won't be using any of the application content in this chapter, so you can also simply close the message by clicking the Close button (the X) to the far right of the Security Warning message. (Do *not* click the X at the upper-right corner of your screen; that will close Microsoft Access and you will have to start all over.) You can also close the Northwind Traders Startup Screen. To do so, click the Close button to the right of the Startup Screen tab, or right-click the tab and choose Close. Tidying up the panel should make the options available on it that much more apparent.

NOTE

Like most PC-based database tools, Access provides not only a database, but a complete programming environment that supports the creation of screens, reports, and application logic in the form of macros. The development of applications using Access is well beyond the scope of this book. This chapter focuses on those components that are directly related to defining data structures and managing the data stored in them.

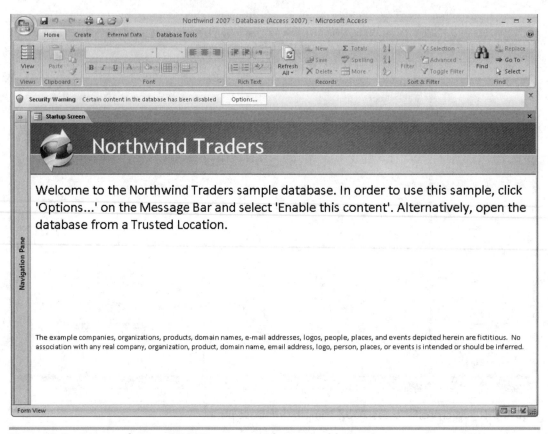

Figure 3-3   Microsoft Access 2007 main panel, Home ribbon

The area along the top of the panel that contains all the options you can use in Access is called the *ribbon*. This user interface is new with Office 2007 (and Access is part of the Office suite of applications) and is a radical departure from previous versions that used a series of drop-down menus. If you are accustomed to using the old interface, it takes a while to adapt to this new one. The Office button in the upper-left corner provides options common to all Microsoft Office applications, such as opening and saving files. You can click it to get to a drop-down menu of options. On the top line of the ribbon (to the right of the Office button) is the Quick Access Toolbar, which has options for Save, Undo, Repeat Typing, Print, Print Preview, and Open a Folder. A final option allows you to customize the toolbar. The icons are reasonably intuitive, but you can allow your cursor pointer to hover over each one for a second or two and see the names of the options. These options are also common to all Microsoft Office 2007 applications and, as the name suggests, provide a quick way to get to options accessible via the Office button.

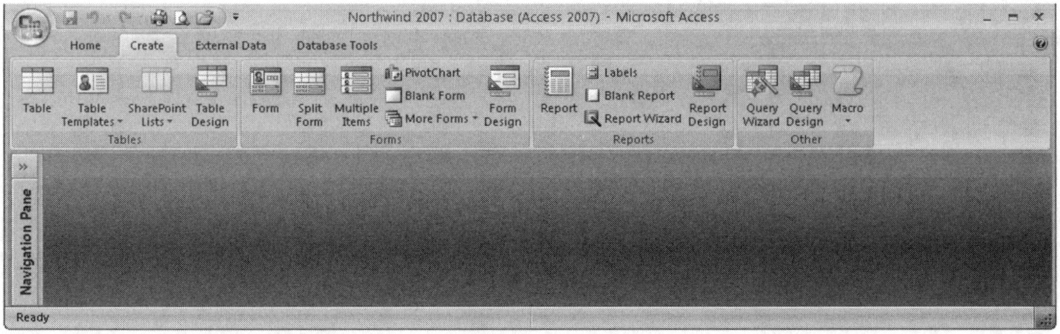

Figure 3-4   Access main panel, Create ribbon

Directly below the Quick Access Toolbar are tabs for the major groupings of ribbon options available within Access. In previous versions, these were used to open drop-down menus; in Office 2007, they are tabs that change the ribbon of options that appears immediately below. Figure 3-3 shows the Home ribbon, for example. Many of the Home ribbon options are related to building application components within Access (forms, reports, and so forth), which are beyond the scope of database work. However, you will use the View option often, because it allows you to switch between the Design View, which shows the metadata that defines a database object, and the Datasheet View, which shows the data that is stored in the database object in rows and columns.

The Create ribbon, shown in Figure 3-4, provides options for creating tables, forms, reports, and other types of objects. We won't be using forms or reports, because these are application programming functions rather than database functions. As you can see, the Tables group of options allows you to create relational tables using various tools. The Other group at the right side of the ribbon contains options for queries. These options let you create, run, and store database queries, which closely resemble what most other DBMSs and the ISO/ANSI SQL standard call *views*.

Figure 3-5 shows the External Data ribbon, which contains options for importing and exporting to and from external sources, including most of the other Office applications. While you will find these options very useful in practice, we won't need them for this tour of features because we are using a sample database that is already populated for us.

The Database Tools ribbon, shown in Figure 3-6, contains various tools that assist in managing the database. The most important of these in terms of database design is the Relationships option, which you will study in the next section. First, though, we need to cover another important navigation feature in Access.

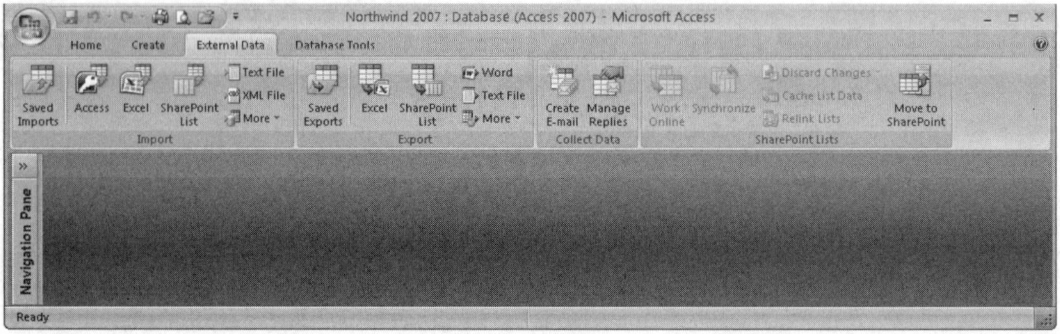

Figure 3-5 Access main panel, External Data ribbon

You might have noticed the Navigation Pane along the left side of the panels we have examined thus far. This is an essential feature of Access because it provides a common method of organizing, listing, and opening (accessing) the objects stored in the database. When you expand it by clicking the double arrowhead (that points to the right), you'll see a panel similar to what is shown in Figure 3-7.

The default organization of the Navigation Pane categorizes the objects by areas within the Northwind Traders application, which isn't all that useful for database work. If you right-click the top of the pane (where the name Northwind Traders appears), and click Category and then Object Type, the Navigation Pane will be organized by database object type, as shown in Figure 3-8. You can expand any category as needed to view the list of objects in that category, and of course minimize the categories that are not of current interest.

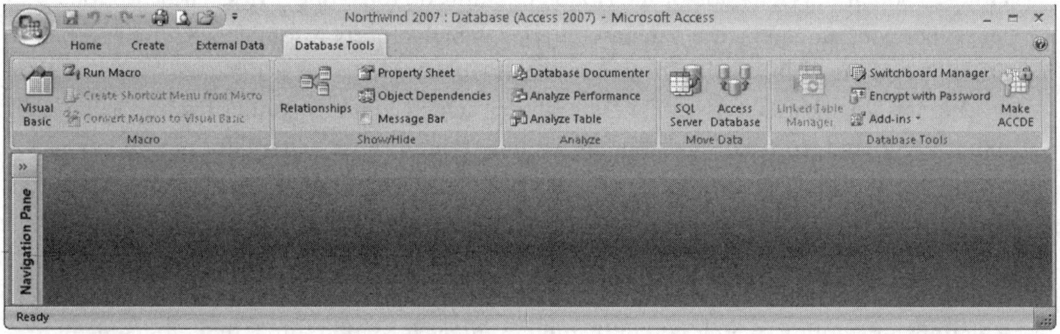

Figure 3-6 Access main panel, Database Tools ribbon

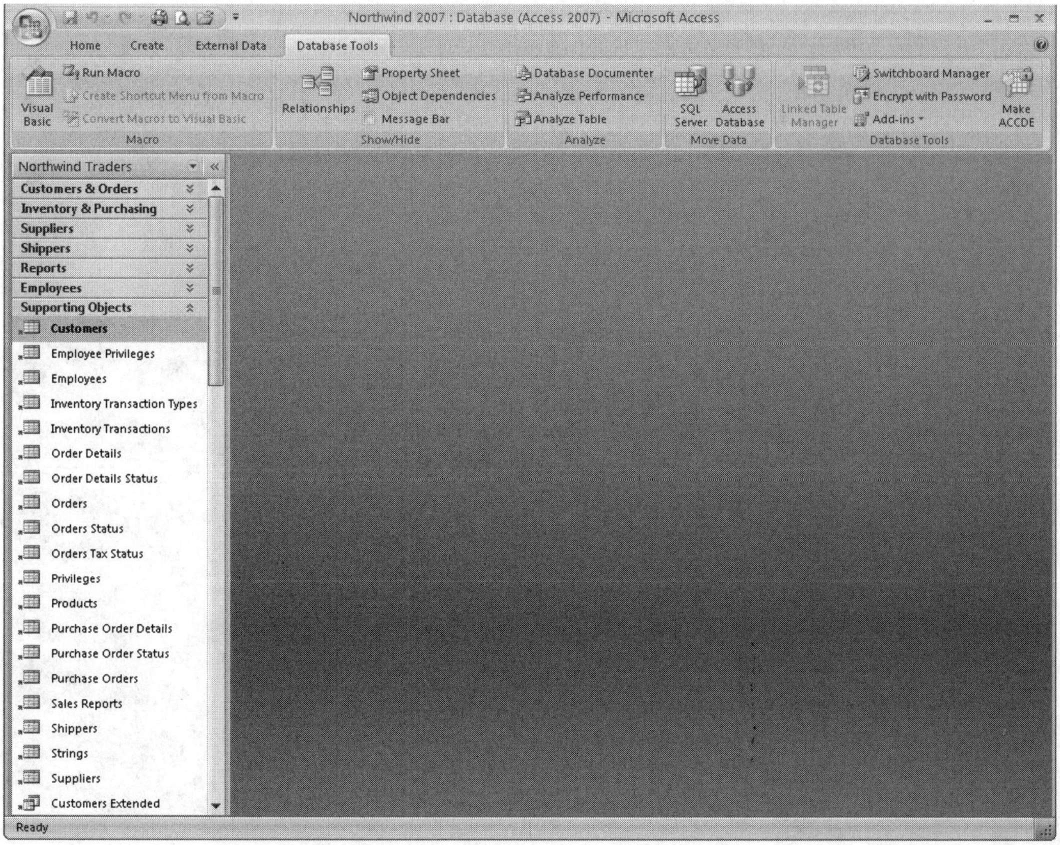

Figure 3-7   Access main panel with expanded Navigation Pane

If you have used older versions of Access, the list of object types shown in Figure 3-8 should look familiar, because it appeared on the main panel of those older versions. Briefly, the types shown can be defined as follows:

- **Tables**   Relational tables. These hold the actual database data in rows and columns.

- **Queries**   Stored database queries. These are called *views* in nearly all other relational databases.

- **Forms**   GUI forms for data entry and/or display within Microsoft Access.

- **Reports**   Reports based on database queries.

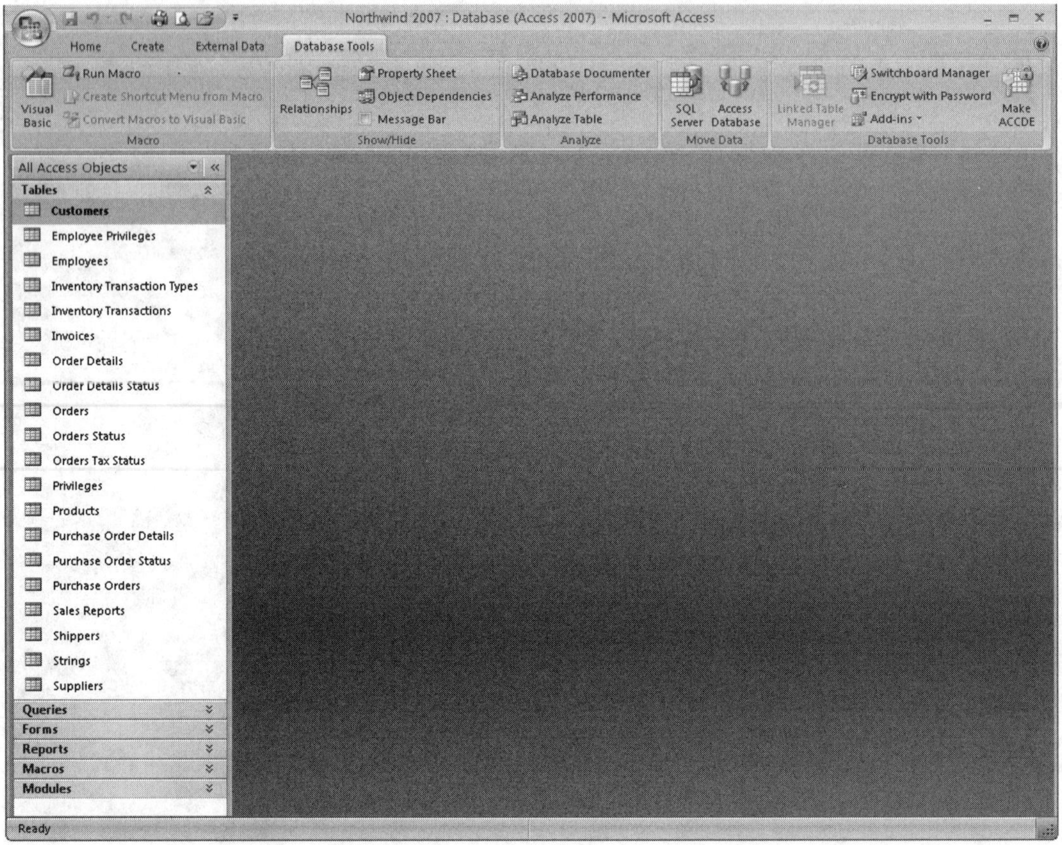

Figure 3-8 Navigation Pane organized by object type

- **Macros** Sets of actions that each perform a particular operation, such as opening a form or printing a report.
- **Modules** Collections of Visual Basic programming language components that are stored as a unit.

As noted earlier, Microsoft Access is not only a database, but also a complete development environment for building and running applications. The enterprise-class database products that usually run on larger, shared computer systems called *servers* typically do *not* come with application-development environments. Learning to build application programs is well outside the scope of this book, so we will not deal with the Forms, Reports, Macros, and Modules types at all. We will focus only on the Tables and Queries types in Microsoft Access.

Maintenance of the objects in the database can be performed from this panel, including the following tasks:

- To add a new object, use the Create ribbon and click the appropriate icon. For example, you can create a new table by clicking the Table or Table Design icon on the Create ribbon.

- To delete an existing object, right-click its name in the Navigation Pane and choose the Delete option.

- To open an object, double-click its name in the Navigation Pane.

- To display the definition (design) of an object, right-click its name in the Navigation Pane and choose the Design View option.

The Microsoft Access Relationships Panel

Microsoft Access provides the Relationships panel, shown in Figure 3-9, for the definition and maintenance of referential constraints between the relational tables. To display this panel, click the Edit Relationships option on the Database Tools ribbon.

NOTE
If you are following along with your own copy of the Northwind database, the panel will show a lot more tables and relationships. I simplified and reorganized my copy to make Figure 3-9 more understandable for the reader. You may also notice the Manager ID column in the Employees table in the figure, which I added to illustrate a recursive relationship, which is covered later in this chapter.

The Relationships panel graphically displays tables, shown as rectangles, and one-to-many relationships, shown as lines between the rectangles. Technically, these are referential constraints (*relationships* being only a conceptual term), but because Microsoft calls them relationships on this panel, I will also use this term for consistency. The symbol *1* shows the "one" side of each relationship, whereas the infinity symbol (similar to the number 8 laying on its side) shows the "many" side of each relationship. You may also notice an arrowhead on the end of some of the lines, which denote relationships that have a lookup (as discussed in Chapter 2) defined.

The relationships can be maintained as follows:

- To add tables that are not displayed, click the Show Table icon (the table and a bold yellow plus sign) on the ribbon, and select the tables from the pop-up window.

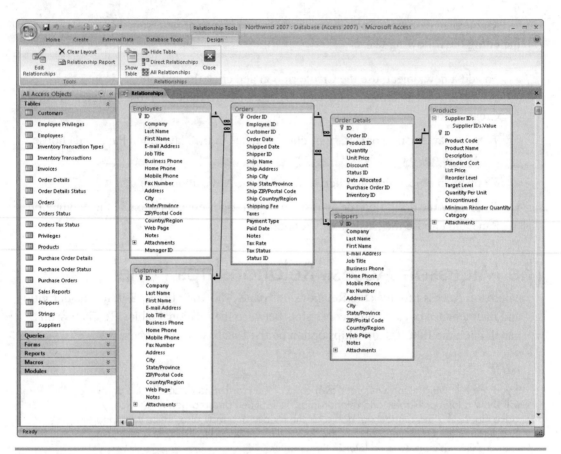

Figure 3-9 The Microsoft Access Relationships panel

- To remove a table from the display, click it so that it is selected and then press DELETE. Note that this does *not* delete the table or any relationships in which the table participates; it merely removes the table from the panel.

- To add a relationship, drag the primary key in one table to the matching foreign key in another. For recursive relationships, the table must be added to the display a second time, and the relationship must be created between one displayed copy of the table and the other. This looks odd at first, but it serves to facilitate the drag-and-drop method of creating the relationship. A table shown multiple times on the panel still exists only one time in the database.

- To delete a relationship, click the narrow part (the middle section) of its line and press DELETE. Selecting relationships can be tricky in Microsoft Access because clicking only the *narrow* part of the line will work, and you might have to stretch short lines by moving a table on the panel to expose the narrow part of the line.

- To edit a relationship, double-click the narrow part of its line. A pop-up window can be used to change various options about the relationship, including toggling enforcement of the relationship as a referential constraint on and off (that is, enabling and disabling the constraint). When a constraint is disabled, the DBMS will not prevent inserts, updates, and deletes from creating "orphan" foreign key values (foreign key values that have no matching primary key values in the parent table). The DBMS will not, however, permit a constraint to be enabled if orphan foreign key values exist in the child table.

To close the Relationships panel, you can either click the Close button (X) at the upper-right corner of the panel or right-click the Relationships tab and choose Close.

The Microsoft Access Table Design View

A table can be selected by double-clicking its name on the Navigation Pane. The default display, called the Datasheet View, is shown in Figure 3-10. The data in the table is displayed in the familiar tabular form, and the data can be updated if desired, including the insertion and deletion of rows. Be careful, because there is no undo feature—once you move the cursor from one row to another, any changes you have made cannot be easily reversed.

You can get to the Design View, which shows the definition of the table, in two ways. You can right-click the tab with the name of the table and choose Design View. Or you can select the Home ribbon (if not already selected), click the View icon, and choose the Design View option. Figure 3-11 shows the Design View for the Employees table.

The Design View for a table displays information such as the following:

- **Field Name**   The name of the column.
- **Data Type**   The data type for the column.
- **Description**   A description of the column, typically provided by a DBA.
- **Field Size**   A subtype within the data type. For example, Long Integer and Short Integer apply to the more general Number data type.

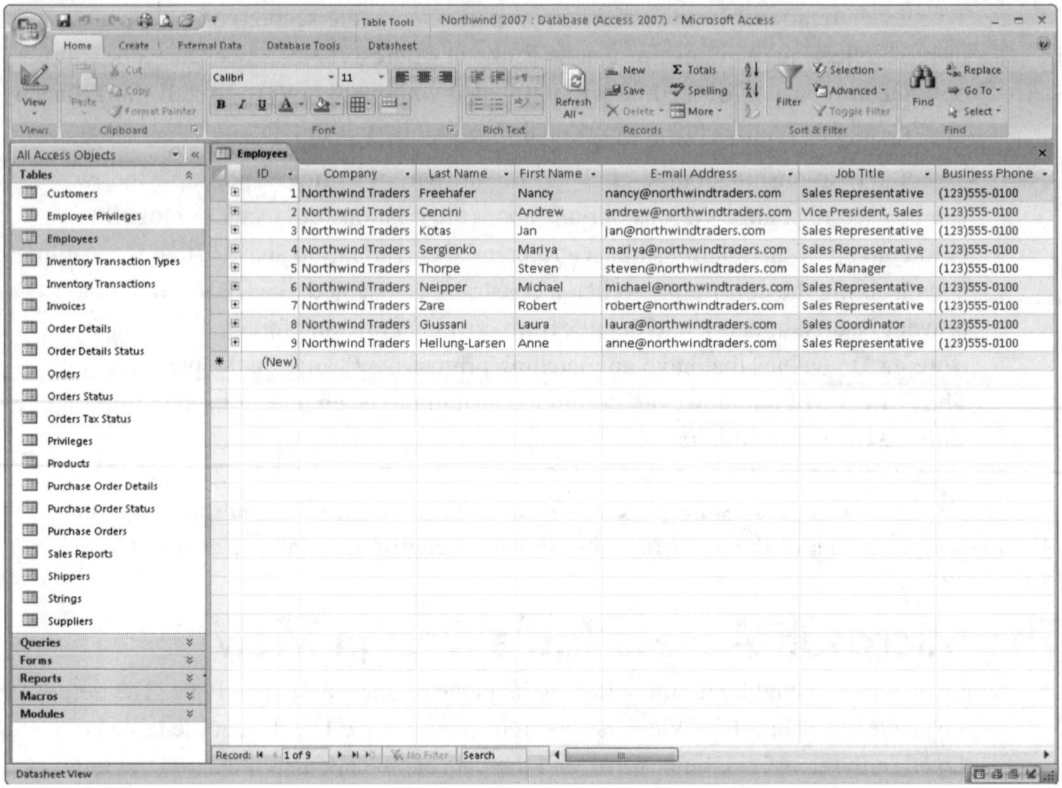

Figure 3-10 Datasheet View (Employees table)

- **Required** Indicates whether the column is optional (that is, whether it may have null values).
- **Indexed** Indicates whether the column has an index.
- **Primary Key** Denoted with a small key icon next to the field name (or names) that make up the primary key.

Hopefully, you recognized that everything on this panel is *metadata*. Many more options are available but not noted here, and Microsoft Access is very clever about hiding and exposing options so that only the applicable ones are displayed. Notice that help text automatically displays in the blue area in the lower-right corner of the panel as you move the cursor from one option to another.

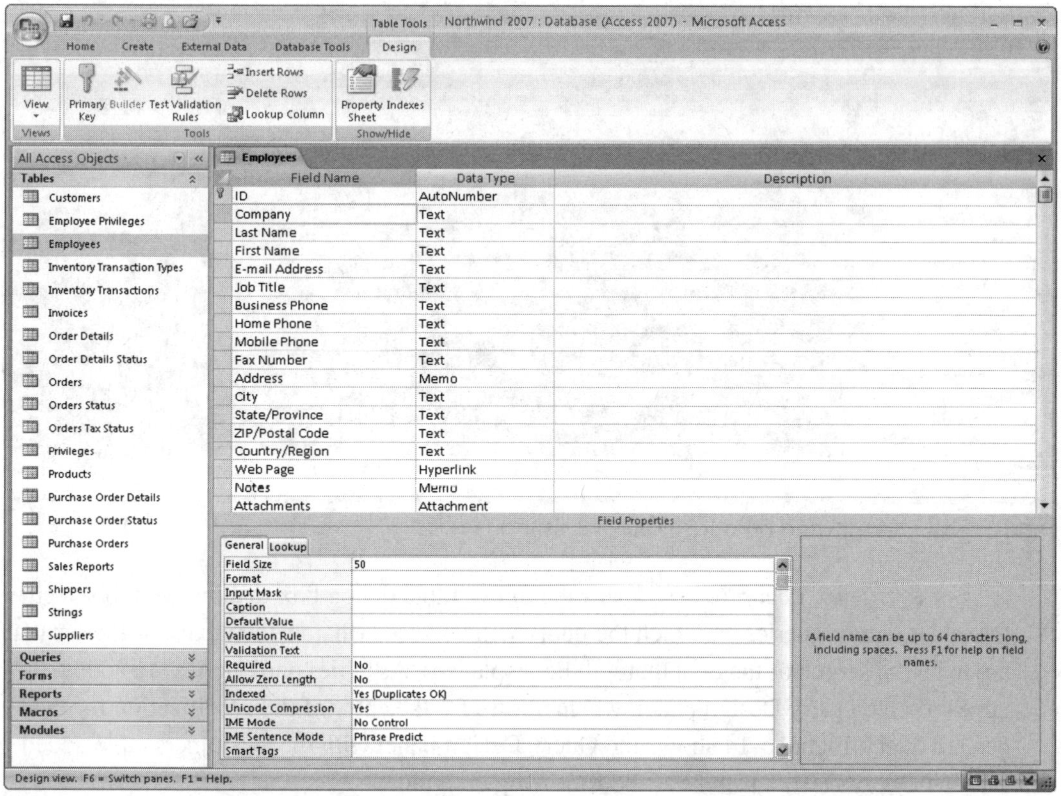

Figure 3-11 Design View (Employees table)

Creating Queries in Microsoft Access

As mentioned, Microsoft Access queries closely resemble what most DBMSs call *views*, because a view is defined in the SQL standard as a stored database query. A key similarity is that Access queries, like views, do not store any data; instead, the data is stored in the tables. However, Access queries have some capabilities not found in views, such as the ability to tailor a query to perform inserts to or updates of data rows in the database. On the Navigation Pane, expanding the Queries category lists all the queries stored in this database, as shown in Figure 3-12.

Although Microsoft Access offers several ways to create a new query, the Query Design option is the easiest for beginners to understand. When you click the Query Design icon (in the Other area of the Create ribbon), Access displays the Show Table dialog box, as shown in Figure 3-13.

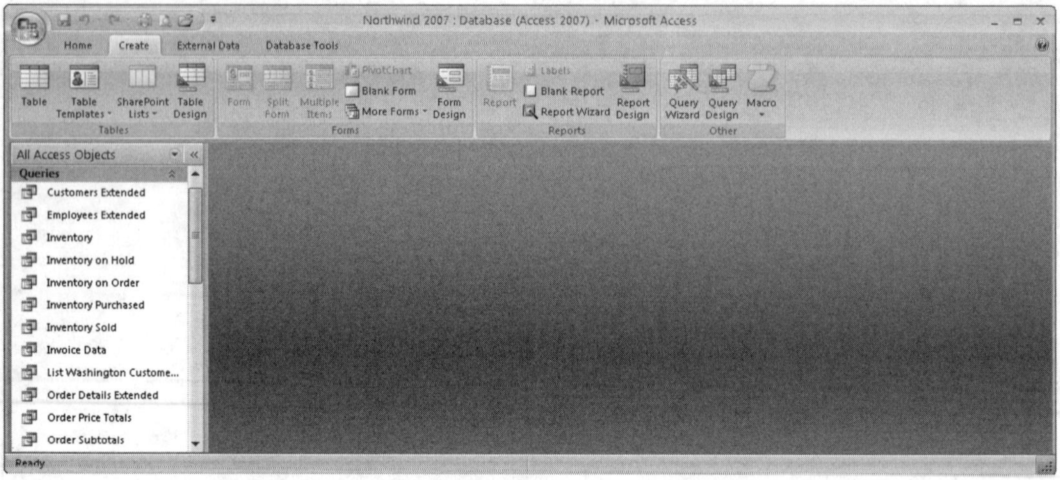

Figure 3-12 Northwind database Queries listing

For every new query, Access opens the Show Table dialog box to allow you to select the tables and/or queries on which the query will be based (that is, the tables or queries that are to be the source of the data that will be displayed). As tables and queries are added, they appear on the Query Design panel, which allows for the entry of the specification for the desired query. Figure 3-14 shows the Query Design panel with the Customers table added.

The Query Design panel has the following components:

● In the open area at the top of the panel (light blue background), a graphical representation of the query's source tables, queries, and their relationships for the query are shown. Any relationships defined for the tables are automatically inherited here.

Figure 3-13 Show Table dialog box

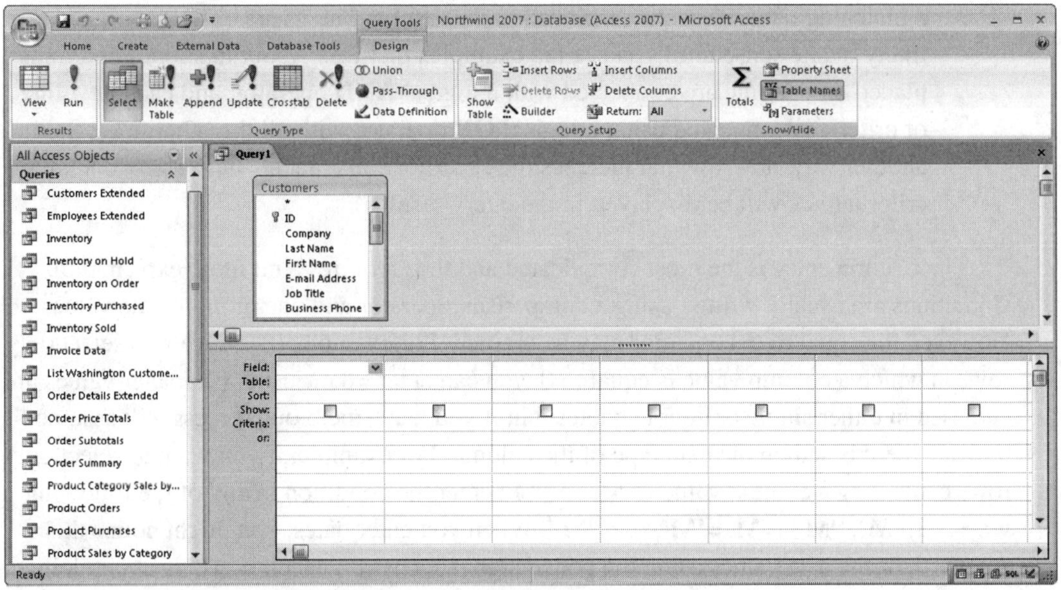

Figure 3-14   Query Design panel (with Customers table added)

- In the grid area in the lower part of the panel, each column represents a column of data that is to be returned in the result set when the query is executed. Rows in the grid area define various options to be applied to the corresponding columns. Usage examples are provided in the sections that follow:

  - **Field**   The specification for the source of the column. This is normally a table or query column name, but it can also be a constant or an expression similar to calculations used in spreadsheets.

  - **Table**   The source table or query name for the column.

  - **Sort**   The specification for any sort sequencing for the column (Ascending, Descending, or None).

  - **Show**   A check box that controls display of the column. If the box is not checked, the column can be used in forming the query but does not appear in the query results.

  - **Criteria**   The specification that determines which rows of data are to appear in the query results. All conditions placed on the same line must be met for a row of data to be displayed in the query results. Conditions placed on subsequent lines (labeled "or" on the panel) are alternative sets of conditions that will also cause a matching data row to be displayed in the results. The usage of these will not likely make sense until you see the examples that follow, but in short, conditions placed on one line are connected with a logical **AND** operator, and each new line of criteria is connected using a logical **OR** operator with all the other lines. Said another way, any row that matches the specifications that appear on any one of the criteria lines will be displayed in the query results.

The Criteria entry is the most complicated and thus requires a bit more explanation. Conditions are usually written using a comparison operator and one or more data values. However, the equal to (=) operator may be omitted. For example, if you want to select only rows in which a column value is equal to 0, you can enter =0 or just **0**. Character values are enclosed in either single or double quotes, but if you leave them out, Access will assume they are there based on the data type of the column. For example, if you want to select only rows containing a column value of M, you can enter the condition in any of the following ways: **M**, '**M**', "**M**", =**M**, ='**M**', or ="**M**". When you enter dates, you might notice that Access delimits date values using the pound sign (#), but you need not worry about doing so yourself. As you might guess, you can use other comparison operations in addition to equal to (=). The following table shows all the supported comparison operators:

Operator	Description
=	Equal to
<	Less than
<=	Less than or equal to
>	Greater than
>=	Greater than or equal to
<>	Not equal to

Once the specification is complete, clicking the Run icon (the exclamation point) runs the query and displays the results using the Datasheet View like the one shown in Figure 3-10. To go back to the Query Design panel, simply click the Design View icon (the ruler, pencil, and triangle icon in the Views group of the Home ribbon). For most queries, data updates can be entered directly in the Datasheet View table, and they are applied directly to the source tables for the query. If a column in the query results cannot be mapped to a single table column—perhaps because it was calculated in some way—then it cannot be updated in the query results.

If all this seems confusing, that's because the best way to learn how to create queries in Microsoft Access is by trying them for yourself. Therefore, the remainder of this chapter will use a series of Try This exercises to demonstrate the powerful features of the Microsoft Access Queries tool. To reduce the amount of work required to complete each one, these exercises build on one another. Each exercise offers a description of the result desired and the steps required to create the specification for the query on the Query Design panel. This is followed by a figure containing two screen shots, the first showing the completed Query Design panel and the other showing the results when the query is executed.

Try This 3-1 **List All Customers**

In this Try This exercise, you will simply list the entire Customers table (all rows and all columns).

Step by Step

1. On the Create ribbon, click Query Design.

2. Perform the following actions in the Show Table dialog box:
   a. Click Customers to select the Customers table.
   b. Click the Add button.
   c. Click the Close button.

3. On the Query Design panel, double-click the asterisk in the Customers table template (near the top of the panel).

4. Click the Run icon on the ribbon (the exclamation point) to run your query. The completed panel is shown at the top of Figure 3-15 with the query results shown below.

5. To get ready for the next exercise, do the following on the query results panel (bottom of Figure 3-15):
   a. Return to the Query Design panel by clicking the View icon (the triangle, ruler, and pencil) just below the Office button.
   b. On the Query Design panel (top of Figure 3-15), clear the existing query specification by clicking the slim gray strip just above the field name Customers* (which changes the entire column to a black background). Then press DELETE to remove the column.

(continued)

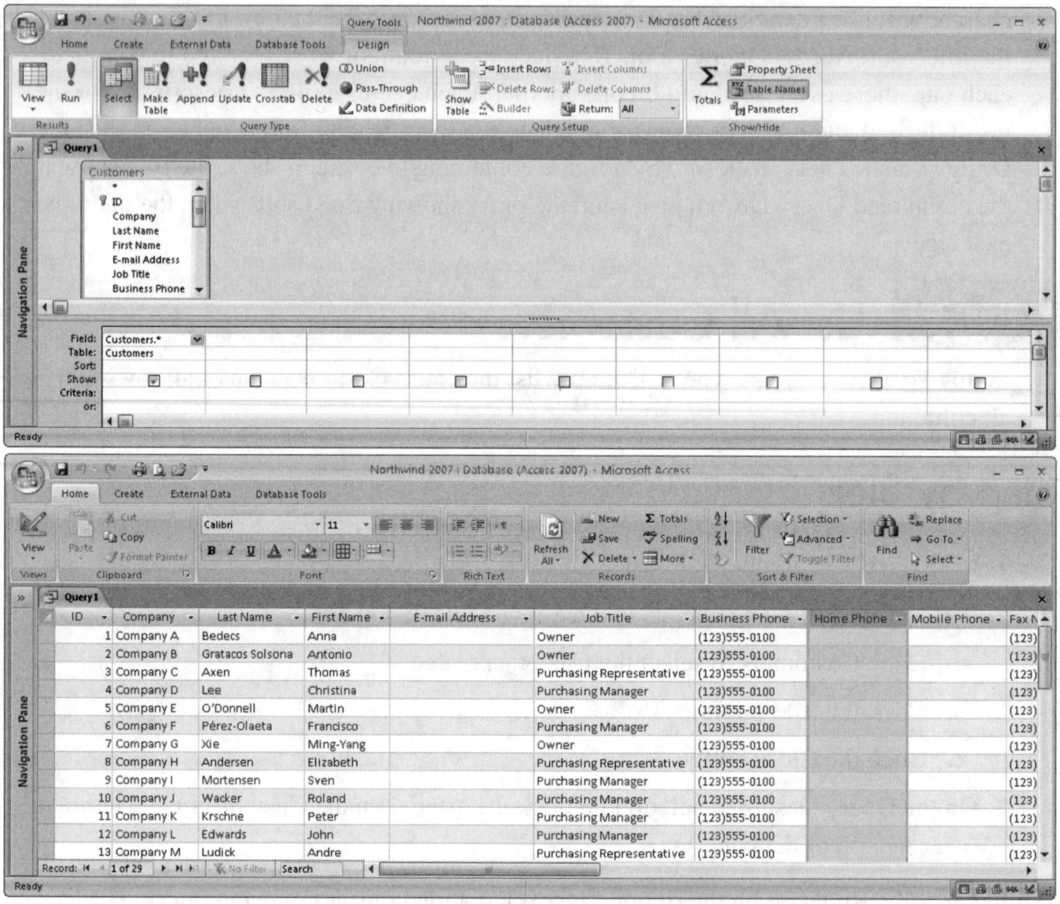

Figure 3-15 Try This 3-1 (List All Customers), query design (top) and query results (bottom)

Try This 3-2 Choose Columns to Display

Instead of displaying all columns, here you'll specify only the ones that you want to see. You will list the ID, Company (company name), City, State/Province, and Country/Region columns for all customers (all rows in the Customers table).

Step by Step

1. You should already have the Query Design panel open with the Customers table added to the query.

2. For each desired column (ID, Company, City, State/Province, and Country/Region), double-click the column name in the table shown at the top of the form. An alternative method is to drag-and-drop the column name from the table shown at the top of the form to the grid in the lower part of the form.

3. Click the Run icon on the ribbon to run your query. The completed panel is shown at the top of Figure 3-16 with the query results shown below.

4. To get ready for the next exercise, return to the Query Design panel by clicking the View icon (the triangle, ruler, and pencil) just below the Office button.

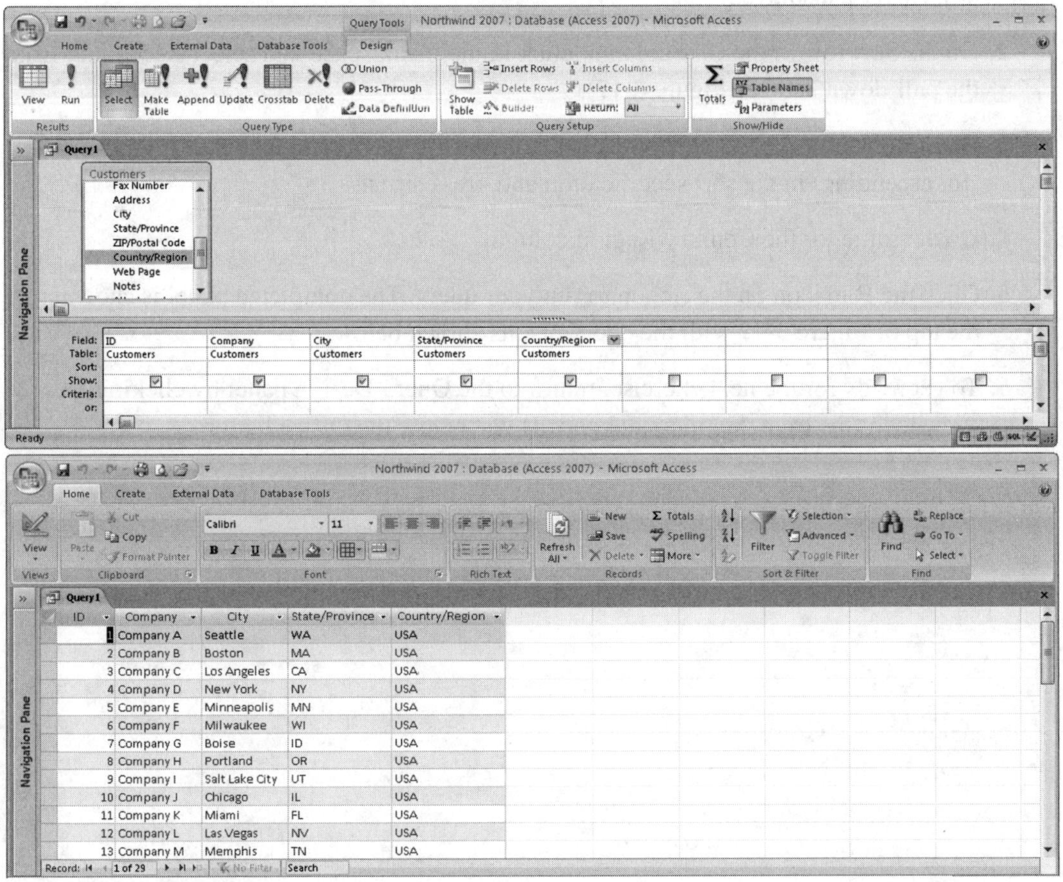

Figure 3-16 Try This 3-2 (Choose Columns to Display), query design (top) and query results (bottom)

Try This 3-3 Sorting Results

In any RDBMS, rows are returned in no particular order unless you request otherwise. Microsoft Access uses the Sort specification to determine the order in which rows are returned in query results. You will modify Try This 3-2 so that rows are sorted in ascending order by City, State/Province, and Country/Region.

Step by Step

1. You should already have the Query Design panel open with the query you created in Try This 3-2 displayed.

2. On the Sort row in the City column, click in the blank space and select Ascending from the pull-down list (see Figure 3-17).

3. Do the same for the State/Province column. A simple alternative method is to type **A** (for ascending) in the sort specification and press ENTER.

4. Do the same for the Country/Region column.

5. Click the Run icon on the ribbon to run your query. The completed panel is shown at the top of Figure 3-17 with the query results shown below.

6. To get ready for the next exercise, return to the Query Design panel by clicking the View icon (the triangle, ruler, and pencil) just below the Office button.

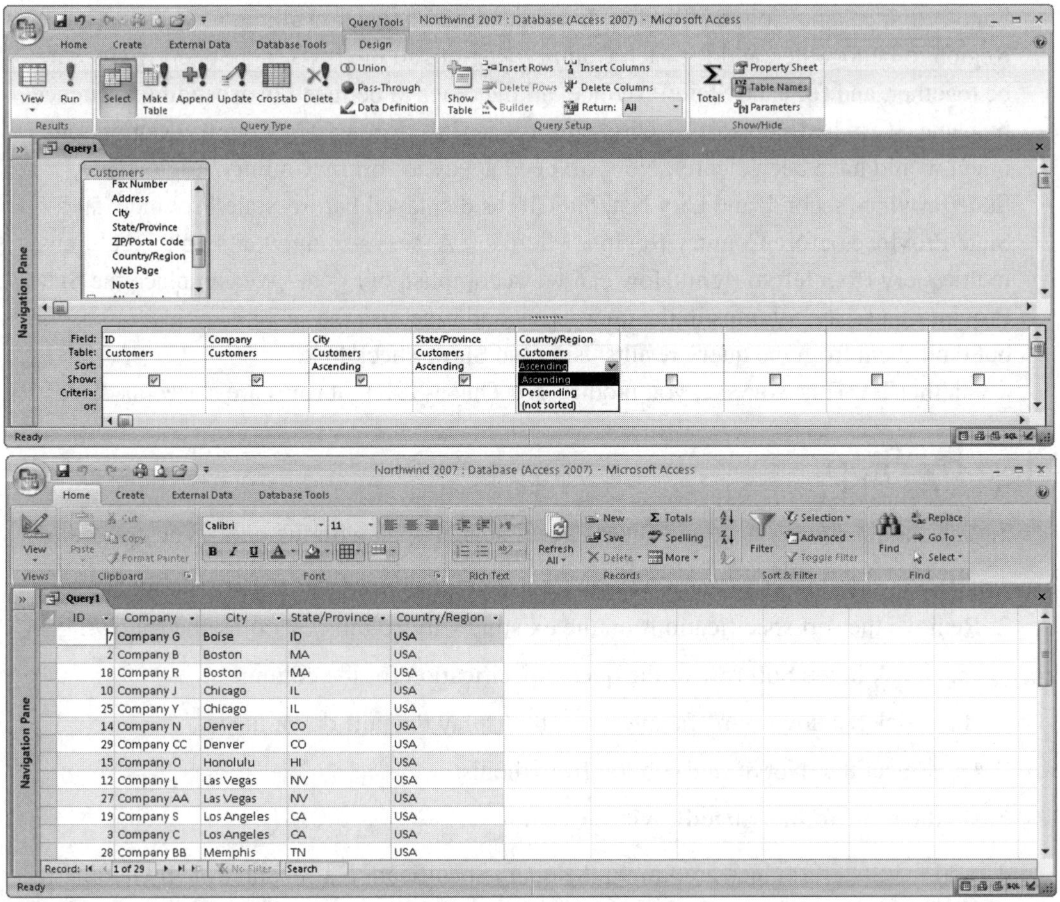

Figure 3-17 Try This 3-3 (Sorting Results), query design (top) and query results (bottom)

Try This 3-4 # Advanced Sorting

Looking at the results of Try This 3-3, you can see that all the cities are listed in ascending sequence and that sorting by State/Province and then by Country/Region had little effect and would matter only if two cities with the same name existed in different states/provinces and countries/regions. Spoken language not always being logically precise, this is unlikely to be what we intended when we said we wanted the data sorted by City,

(continued)

State/Province, and Country/Region. Instead, we likely wanted all the rows for a Country/ Region to be together, and for each Country/Region, all the rows in a State/Province to be together, and for each State/Province, all the cities to be listed in ascending sequence by name. If we had said sort by City *within* State/Province *within* Country/Region, our intent would have been clearer. Now we need a way to sort by Country/Region first, State/Province second, and City last, but City is displayed before State/Province, and State/Province before Country/Region. Microsoft Access sorting works on the columns in the query from left to right. How can we accomplish our goal? We can place the State/ Province and City columns in the query a second time, use the second copies for sorting, but omit them from the query results using the Show check box.

In this Try This exercise, you modify Try This 3-3 so that rows are sorted as discussed.

Step by Step

1. You should already have the Query Design panel open with the query you created in Try This 3-3 displayed.

2. Remove the sort specifications on the existing City column by doing the following:

   a. Click in the Sort row of the query specification for the column.

   b. Click the downward-facing arrow to display the pull-down menu.

   c. Select the (Not Sorted) option from the list.

3. Do the same for the State/Province column.

4. Add the State/Province column to the query specification a second time by double-clicking its name in the Customers table.

5. Do the same for the City column.

6. Add the ascending sort specification to the State/Province and City columns that you just added (the ones to the *right* of the Country/Region column).

7. Remove the check mark in the Show row for the State/Province and City columns that you just added. This will prevent the data in them from displaying a second time in your query results.

8. Since this exercise is a bit complicated, I suggest you compare your Query Design panel with the one shown in Figure 3-18 to make sure you did everything correctly.

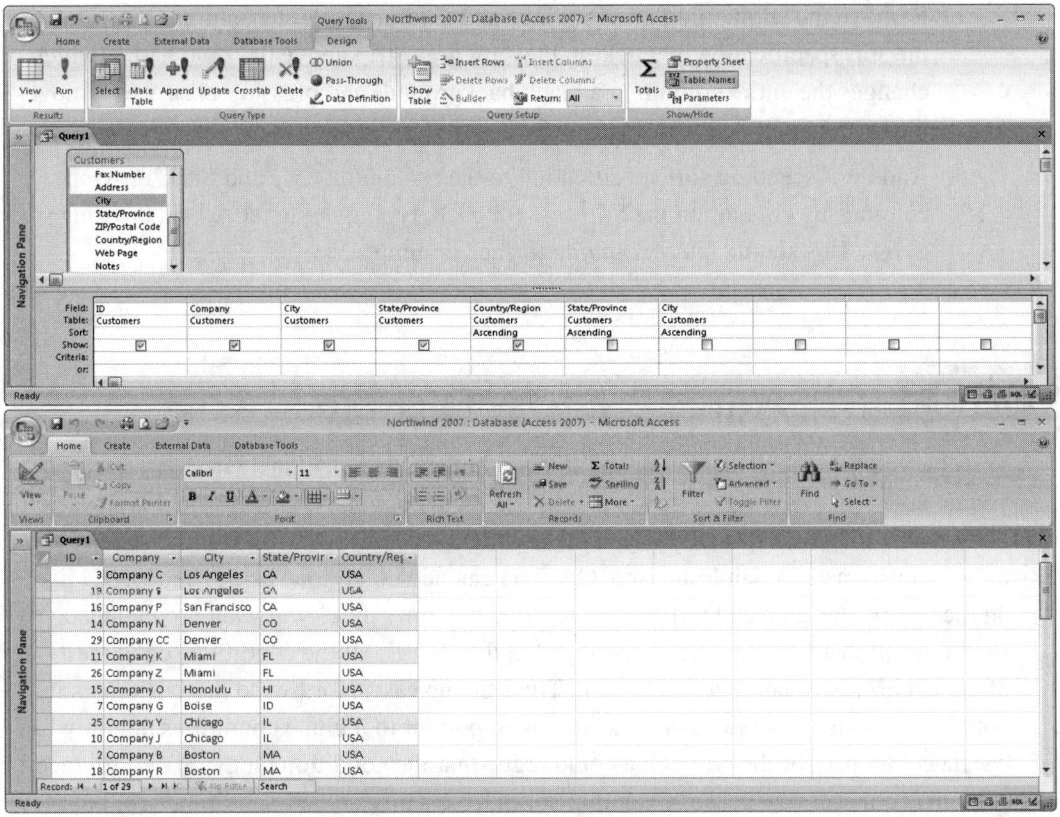

Figure 3-18   Try This 3-4 (Advanced Sorting), query design (top) and query results (bottom)

9. Click the Run icon on the ribbon to run your query. The completed panel is shown at the top of Figure 3-18 with the query results shown below. Note that most languages are read from left to right, so we naturally expect tabular listings to be sorted moving from left to right, starting with the leftmost column. It is unusual, and perhaps poor human engineering, to sort columns another way. But should you ever need to do so, you now know how.

10. To get ready for the next exercise, do the following:

   a. Return to the Query Design panel by clicking the View icon (the triangle, ruler, and pencil) just below the Office button.

   b. To simplify the upcoming Try This exercises, put the query specification back to the way it was at the end of Try This 3-3.

(continued)

c. Remove the additional State/Province and Country/Regions columns you added to the sort specification by clicking the slim gray strip above the field name (which changes the entire column to a black background) and pressing DELETE to remove the column.

d. Add the Ascending sort specification to the remaining City and State/Province columns by clicking in the Sort row for each, typing the letter **A**, and pressing ENTER. This should add *Ascending* to each column.

Try This 3-5 Choosing Rows to Display

Thus far you have been displaying all 26 rows in the Customers table in every query. If you do not want to see all the rows, displaying them could be confusing, and it is wasteful of system resources, especially if you are sorting them. Suppose you want to see rows only for customers in San Francisco, CA. You can add conditions using the Criteria line on the Query Design panel to filter the rows so that only those you want are included. You should recall that for a row to be displayed in the results, all the conditions on at least one of the Criteria lines needs to evaluate to True. In this case, Northwind has customers in both San Francisco and Los Angeles, so it is important to include conditions not only for the state, but also for the city. (One could argue that the condition on the State/Province column is unnecessary because no other states have a city named San Francisco, but it is far better when writing database queries to include additional conditions because they often help the DBMS process the query more efficiently; plus they avoid unnecessary surprises, should the query be reused later for another purpose, such as selecting a city that does not have a unique name.)

In this exercise, you modify the query specification from Try This 3-3 to filter the results to include only customers from San Francisco.

Step by Step

1. You should be starting with a query specification matching the one shown in Figure 3-17.

2. On the Criteria row in the City column, type **San Francisco**. Note that Microsoft Access pays no attention to the case when selecting data in queries, so you can also enter **SAN FRANCISCO** or **san francisco** and achieve the same result. Note that character constants used in an RDBMS are normally enclosed in quotation marks. However, Microsoft Access knows that the City column has a character data type, so it will add the quotes automatically, should you leave them out.

3. On the same row, type **CA** in the State/Province column. It is important to enter the City and State/Province criteria on the same line because you want rows returned only where the City is San Francisco *and* the State/Province is CA.

4. Click the Run icon on the ribbon to run your query. The completed panel is shown at the top of Figure 3-19 with the query results shown below.

5. To get ready for the next exercise, simply return to the Query Design panel by clicking the View icon just below the Office button.

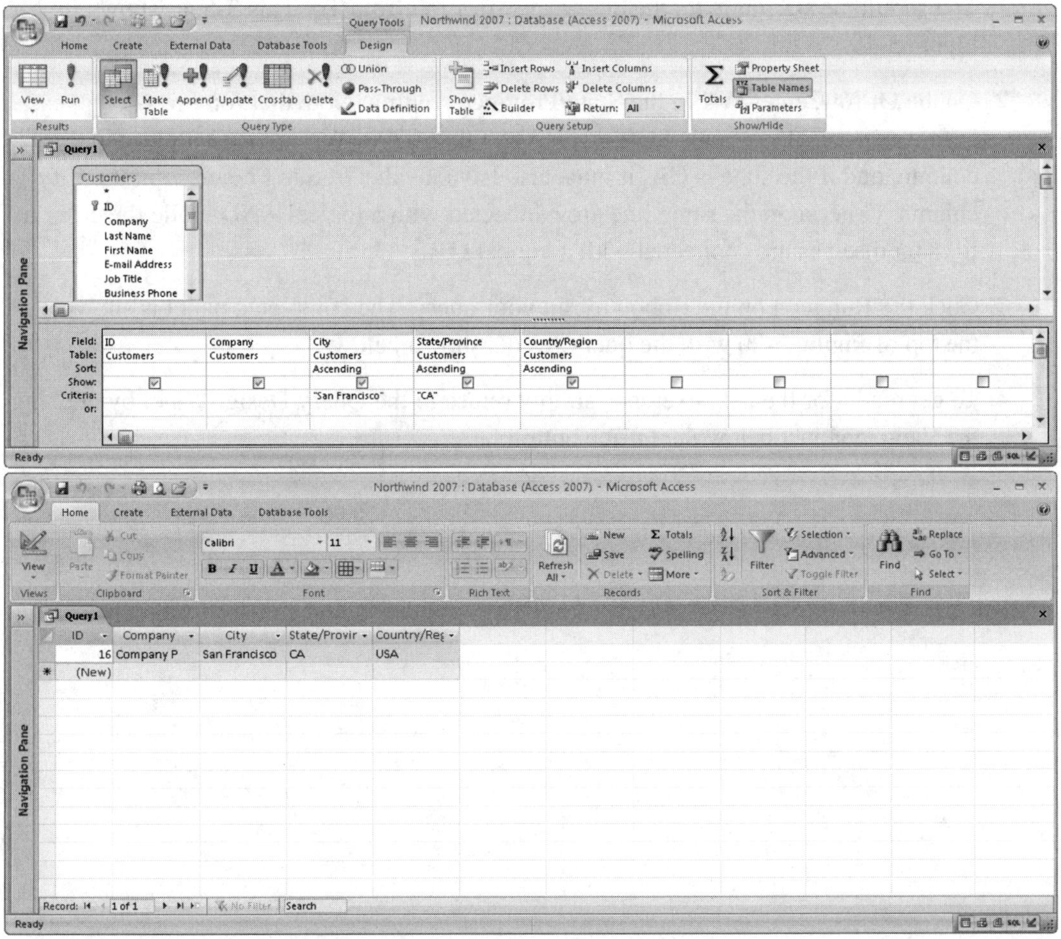

Figure 3-19   Try This 3-5 (Choosing Rows to Display), query design (top) and query results (bottom)

Try This 3-6 Compound Row Selection

Suppose you now want to select all customers in the state of Washington in addition to those in San Francisco. You must add the new criteria on a *different* line of the Query Design panel.

In this Try This exercise, you modify Try This 3-5 to include the additional customers.

Step by Step

1. You should be starting with the query specification from Try This 3-5, as shown in Figure 3-19.

2. On the Or row, enter **WA** in the State/Province column. Note that for a row to appear in the query results, it must have a value of either CA or WA in the State/Province column, and if the state is CA, it must also have a value of San Francisco in the City column. Criteria on the same line are connected with a logical **AND** while the criteria lines themselves are connected with a logical **OR**.

3. Click the Run icon on the ribbon to run your query. The completed panel is shown at the top of Figure 3-20 with the query results shown below.

4. To get ready for the next exercise, simply return to the Query Design panel by clicking the View icon just below the Office button.

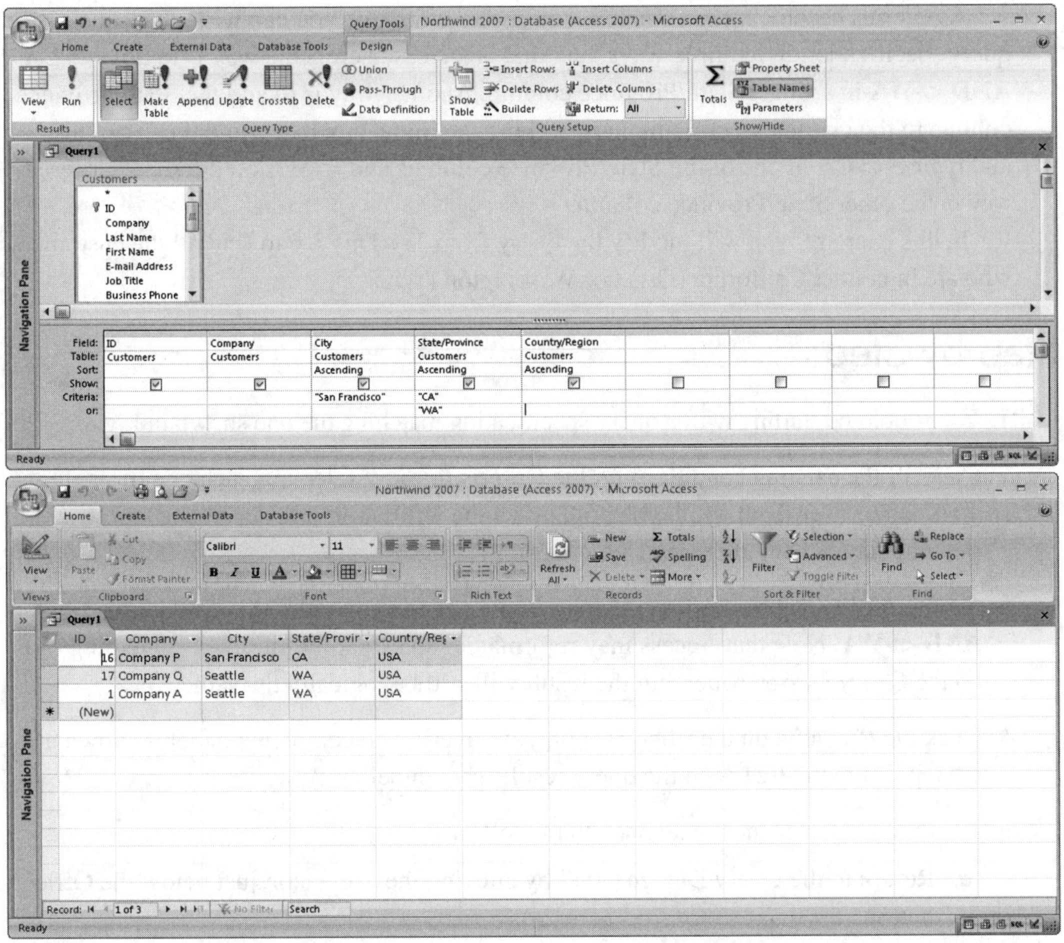

Figure 3-20 Try This 3-6 (Compound Row Selection), query design (top) and query results (bottom)

Try This 3-7 Using Not Equal

Thus far we have looked at search criteria that assumes the equal to (=) comparison operator. However, several other comparison operators can be used, as shown earlier in this chapter. Suppose, for example, you want to list all the customers who are in neither California (CA) nor Washington (WA). The easiest way to do this is to use the not equal to (<>) operator.

(continued)

As queries become more complex, you'll often find that you can write the same query specification in multiple ways, and that is the case here. One way is to type **<>CA AND <>WA** in a single State/Province column. Another way is to add the State/Province column to the query a second time, unchecking the Show box like you did in Try This 3-4, and typing **<>CA** in one of the State/Province columns and **<>WA** on the *same* Criteria row in the other State/Province column.

In this exercise, you will modify the query from Try This 3-6 to find all the customers who are in neither California (CA) nor Washington (WA).

Step by Step

1. You should be starting with a query specification matching the one shown in Figure 3-20.

2. Clear all the existing conditions on the Criteria lines by selecting each one (dragging your cursor over them while you hold down the left button on your mouse or other pointing device) and then pressing DELETE.

3. On one of the Criteria rows in the State/Province column, enter this condition: **<>CA AND <>WA**. Note that Access may reformat it somewhat if you select something else on the Query Design panel, but the result will still be logically the same.

4. Click the Run icon on the ribbon to run your query. The completed panel is shown at the top of Figure 3-21 with the query results shown below.

5. To get ready for the next exercise, do the following:

   a. Return to the Query Design panel by clicking the View icon just below the Office button.

   b. Click the Customers table at the top of the Query Design panel (the rectangle that shows the table name along with a listing of some of the column names) and then press DELETE. This will clear out the form so it contains no tables, columns, or criteria.

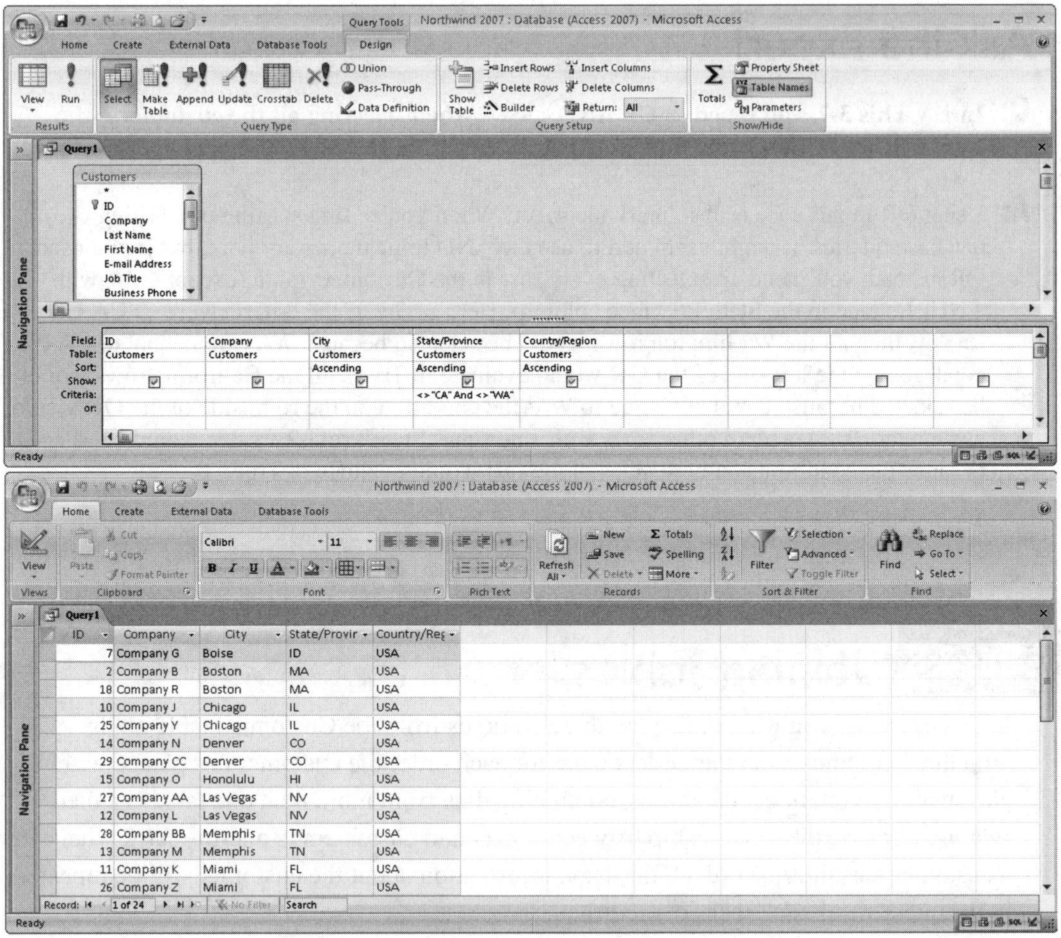

Figure 3-21   Try This 3-7 (Using Not Equal), query design (top) and query results (bottom)

Ask the Expert

Q: In Try This 3-7, you typed <>CA AND <>WA when selecting all the customers who were neither in California nor Washington. Isn't OR the correct logical operator here?

A: Using OR in this case is absolutely incorrect! When you're first starting out writing database queries, it might seem odd to use the AND logical operator here, but if you used OR instead, you'd end up selecting every row in the Customers table (except those with a NULL value in the State/Province column). Here's why. If the criteria were <>CA OR <>WA, then all the Washington rows would be selected because WA is not equal to CA (the condition on the left side of the OR would evaluate to True), all the California rows would be selected because CA is not equal to WA (the condition on the right side of the OR would evaluate to True), and all other rows with a non-null State/Province value would be selected because the conditions on both sides of the OR would evaluate to True.

Try This 3-8   Joining Tables

In this exercise, you want to display three columns from the Customers table along with three columns from the Orders table for each order the customer has placed with Northwind. In relational databases, combining data from more than one table is called *joining*. Because the relationship between orders and customers is one-to-many, whenever a customer has multiple orders, the same information about the customer will be repeated in the query results for each row returned.

Understanding joins is essential to understanding relational databases. Just as one-to-many relationships (implemented in the database as referential constraints) are the fundamental building blocks for relational databases, joins are the fundamental building blocks for relational database queries.

Step by Step

1. You should be starting with an empty Query Design panel (no tables, columns, criteria, and so on, are displayed). If this is not the case, select (click) each table shown and press DELETE to remove it from the query.

2. Click the Show Table icon (with the yellow plus sign) to display the Show Table dialog box, like the one shown in Figure 3-13.

3. Select the name of the Customers table, and then click Add to add it to the query.

4. Do the same for the Orders table, and then close the Add Table dialog box. Notice the line connecting the two tables on the Query Design panel. This tells you that Access already knows how to match up rows in these two tables (foreign key Customer ID in the Orders table matched to primary key ID in the Customers table) based on the metadata supplied by the database designer on the Relationships panel. In other words, this query *inherited* the relationship between the two tables from the one specified at a much earlier time on the Relationships panel. If the join condition were not included, you would get a *Cartesian product* as a result (every row in one table combined with every row in the other—the *product* of multiplying the two tables together) unless you added the condition by dragging your pointer from the foreign key column to the primary key column (the method in Access for manually adding a join condition). You clearly do not want your query results to look like every customer placed every single order, so Microsoft Access has helped you do the right thing by automatically inheriting the join condition.

5. In the Customers table, double-click the ID, Company, City, and State/Province columns to add them to the query specification.

6. In the Orders table, double-click Order Date, Shipped Date, and Shipping Fee to add these columns to the query specification. Notice that you don't have to select the Customer ID column even though the join criteria will use it to find the matching row in the Customers table.

7. Click the Run icon on the ribbon to run your query. The completed panel is shown at the top of Figure 3-22 with the query results shown below. Note the record count at the bottom of the query results. Even though only 29 customers exist, the results contain 48 rows. This is because 48 orders have been placed. When a customer places multiple orders, the company ID, name, city, and state/province is repeated on each order. And customers who have no orders are not included at all because, by default, this query uses an *inner join*—where only matched rows are displayed. You'll try an *outer join*, where unmatched rows are included, in Try This 3-10.

8. To get ready for the next exercise, simply return to the Query Design panel by clicking the View icon just below the Office button.

(continued)

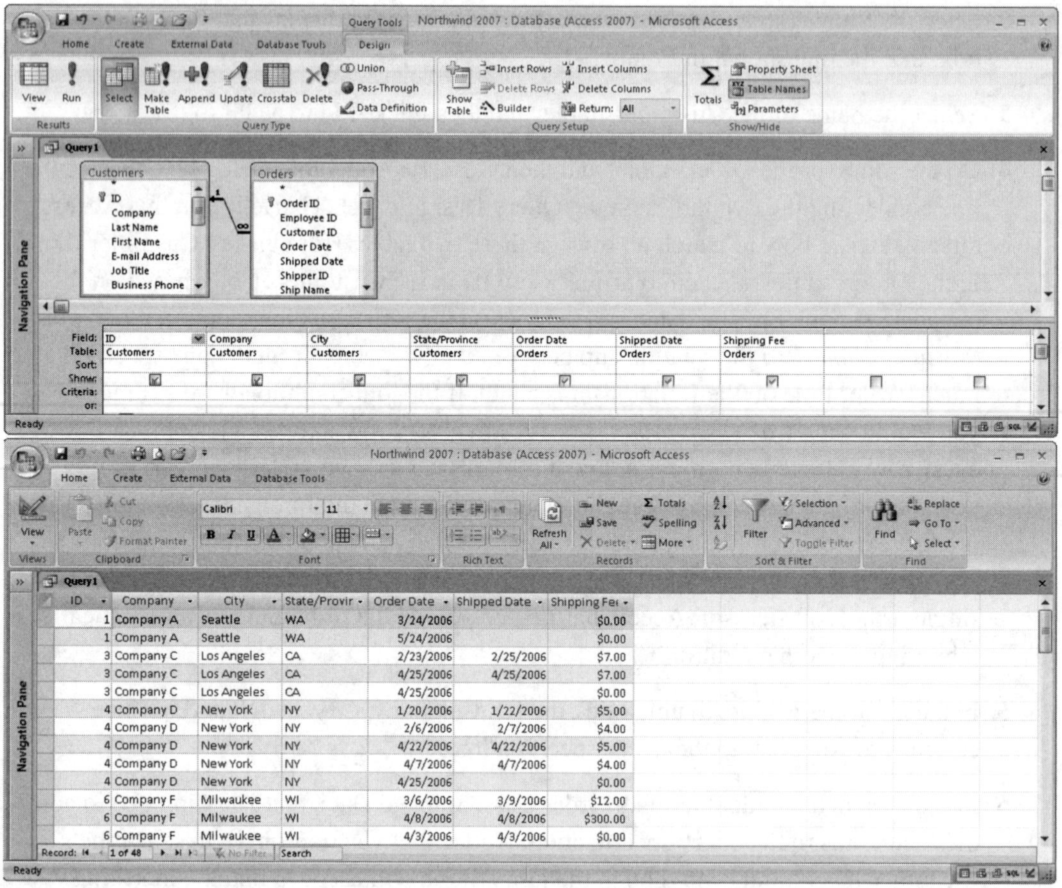

Figure 3-22 Try This 3-8 (Joining Tables), query design (top) and query results (bottom)

Try This 3-9 Limiting Join Results

In Try This 3-8, you joined the Customers and Orders tables, but the results contain all orders and all customers who have orders. However, if you don't want to see all the orders, you can use conditions to limit the rows in the query results, just as you did in earlier exercises. In this Try This exercise, you will limit the rows to include only customers in California (CA) and only orders with an order date of April 1, 2006, (4/1/2006) or later. As in Try This 3-8, you will use an inner join, meaning that California customers who have no orders on or after April 1, 2006, will not appear in the results.

Step by Step

1. You should be starting with the query specification from Try This 3-8, as shown in Figure 3-22.

2. On the Criteria row, enter **CA** in the State/Province column.

3. On the same Criteria row, enter **>=4/1/2006** in the Order Date column. You might notice that Access changes the condition by enclosing the date value in pound signs (**>=#4/1/2006#**). This is merely the way Access *delimits* a date value—most RDBMSs use single quotes around both character strings and date values, so this is atypical behavior.

4. Click the Run icon on the ribbon to run your query. The completed panel is shown at the top of Figure 3-23 with the query results shown below.

5. To get ready for the next exercise, return to the Query Design panel by clicking the View icon just below the Office button.

(continued)

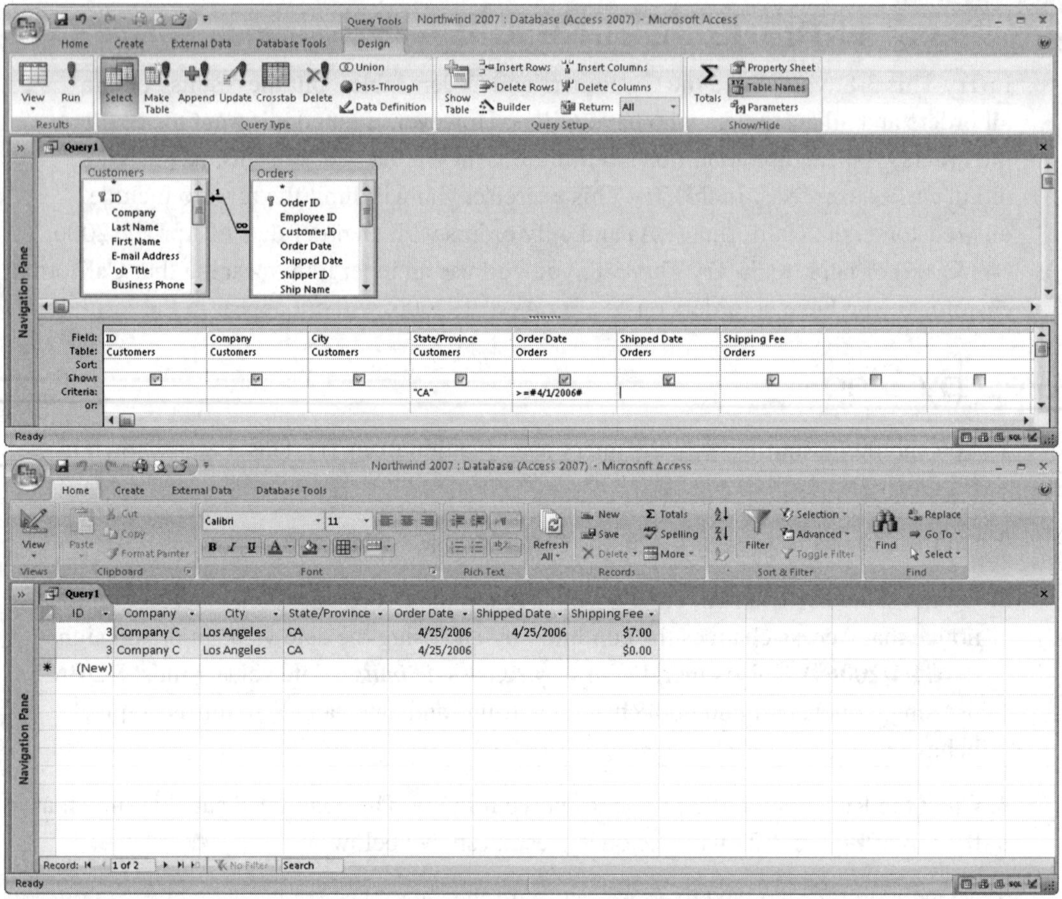

Figure 3-23 Try This 3-9 (Limiting Join Results), query design (top) and query results (bottom)

Try This 3-10 Outer Joins

As described in Try This 3-9, the join technique you have used thus far is the *inner join*. Note that some customers in California have placed no orders, so data for those customers did not appear in the Try This 3-9 results. If you want to include all customers in California in the results, regardless of whether they have placed orders or not, you must use an *outer join* (also called an *inclusive join*). An outer join returns all rows from one (or both) of the tables, regardless of whether matching rows are found in the joined tables. Any data to be displayed from the table where no matching row is found is set to NULL in the query results. (For Microsoft Access, NULL columns appear blank.) For example, for the customer who has no orders, all the columns from the Orders table would be NULL in the results. Keep in mind that the returned data rows are still filtered by other search criteria (for example, only customers from California; only orders with order dates greater than or equal to 4/1/2006), but whether the filtering occurs before, during, or after the join operation is immaterial, so long as the unwanted rows are eliminated from the query results. Remember, you only describe the result you want, not how it is achieved.

Three types of outer joins can be used, and, unfortunately, the industry has settled on potentially confusing names for them:

- **Left Outer Join**   An outer join for which all rows are returned from the left-hand table in the join, and data from any matching rows found in the right-hand table is also returned.

- **Right Outer Join**   An outer join for which all the rows are returned from the right-hand table in the join, and data from any matching rows found in the left-hand table is also returned.

- **Full Outer Join**   An outer join for which all rows are returned from both tables, regardless of whether matching data is found between them. Microsoft Access does not currently support this type of join.

The confusion mentioned comes from the use of *left* and *right* in the names of the join types. All you have to do is reverse the order of the tables in any existing query, and you are essentially switching it from a left outer join to a right outer join, or vice versa. However, Microsoft Access does not make this distinction, so all its joins are simply called *outer joins*. Instead, Access uses a dialog box named Join Properties, shown in Figure 3-24, to specify the type of join you want to use, with an inner join as the default.

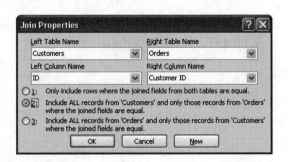

Figure 3-24   Join Properties dialog box

(continued)

In this Try This exercise, you will change the query from Try This 3-9 into an outer join so that all California customers are displayed, regardless of whether they have ordered since 4/1/2006.

Step by Step

1. You should be starting with the query specification from Try this 3-9, as shown in Figure 3-23.

2. To access the Join Properties dialog box (shown in Figure 3-24), double-click somewhere in the middle of the line between the two tables displayed on the Query Design panel, or as an alternative, right-click the line. As with the Relationships panel, it can be tricky to get the cursor pointer in exactly the right place on the line, but practice and a bit of patience always prevails.

3. In the Join Properties dialog box, select the options Include ALL Records From 'Customers' And Only Those Records From 'Orders' Where The Joined Fields Are Equal. It is most likely option 2, but if you added the tables to the query in the reverse order, it could have ended up as option 3. Click OK to close the dialog box.

4. Since you have a condition on Order Date from the Orders table, you need to change it to allow for null values. For customers who have no orders, the value in the Order Date column will be NULL. Add the condition **OR IS NULL** (which can also be written as Or Is Null) to the condition on the Order Date column.

5. Click the Run icon on the ribbon to run your query. The completed panel is shown at the top of Figure 3-25 with the query results shown below. Notice the arrow on the line between the two tables that points toward the Orders tables. This is the way Access alerts you to the fact that the join is an outer join.

6. To get ready for the next exercise, return to the Query Design panel by clicking the View icon just below the Office button.

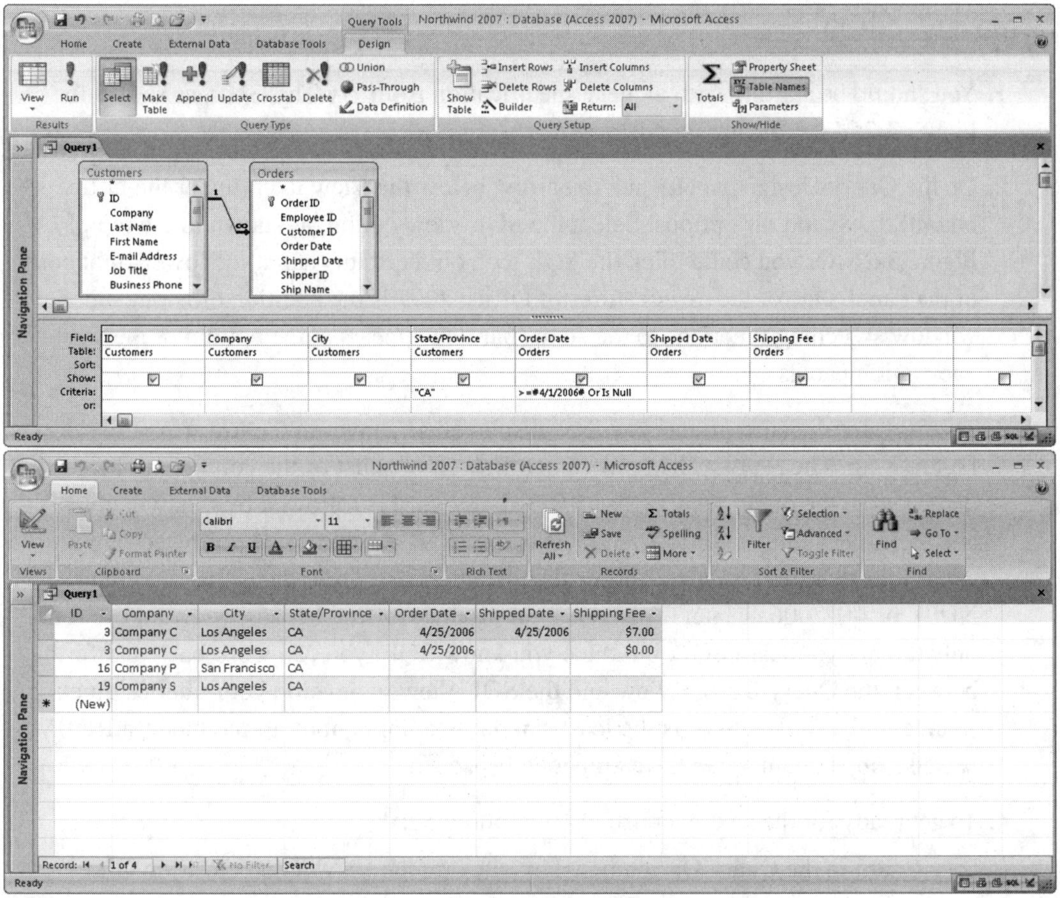

Figure 3-25 Try This 3-10 (Outer Joins), query design (top) and query results (bottom)

Try This 3-11 Microsoft Access SQL

SQL is discussed in Chapter 4; however, since Microsoft Access automatically generates SQL for queries defined on the Query Design panel, a quick preview of SQL is in order. In this Try This exercise, you will display the SQL for the query created in Try This 3-10.

(continued)

Step by Step

1. You should be starting with a query specification from Try This 3-10, as shown in Figure 3-25.

2. On the Query Design panel, click the arrow below the View icon (under the Office button) to expand the options. Select the SQL View option, as shown in the top of Figure 3-26. Or you could click the SQL icon on the status bar at the lower-right corner of the panel. One of the new features of Office 2007 is the addition of zoom and view/ window switching functions to the status bar that appears at the bottom of the various application panels.

3. The SQL for the current query will be displayed as shown in the lower part of Figure 3-26. The **SELECT** keyword is followed by a list of the columns to be displayed in the query results. The **FROM** keyword is followed by the two tables and their outer join condition. And last is the **WHERE** keyword, followed by the conditions that limit rows to California customers and order dates that are either NULL or 4/1/2006 or later. This is a great product feature because you can use it not only to help you learn SQL, but once you know SQL, you can work back and forth between the Query Design View and the SQL View to develop your queries quickly. (Incidentally, Access SQL is the least standards-compliant of all the modern RDBMSs because object names can have embedded spaces.)

4. To get ready for the next exercise, do the following:

   a. Return to the Query Design panel by clicking the View icon below the Office button.

   b. Clear all the selected columns and criteria by dragging your mouse pointer over the slim gray strips above each column (just above the Field: label). The columns will display as black (reverse video) as they are selected. Then press DELETE to remove them from the query.

   c. Change the join between the Customers and Orders tables back to an inner join. To do this, double-click the thin part of the line between the two tables displayed on the Query Design panel to display the Join Properties dialog box. Then select option 1 and click OK.

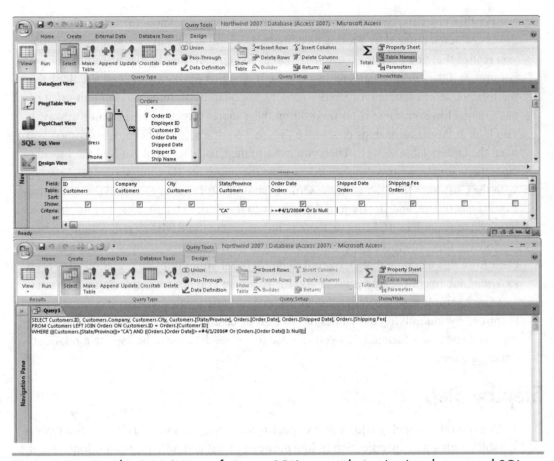

Figure 3-26   Try This 3-11 (Microsoft Access SQL), query design (top) and generated SQL query (bottom)

Try This 3-12   Multiple Joins and Calculated Columns

When you need information from more than two tables in the same query result, you can simply add more tables, and therefore more join operations, to the query. The beauty of relational databases is that you need not be concerned with which join is best processed first and other such implementation details. You can trust the RDBMS to make those decisions for you.

(continued)

For this Try This, consider another scenario: You want to know the total value in dollars of items ordered by Florida customers. Looking at the tables you have available, you realize that you need the Customers table, so you can filter by the State/Province column, and the Order Details table, because it contains the data you need to calculate the total value of each item ordered—namely, the quantity ordered and the unit price of each item. However, there is no way to join these tables directly in a meaningful way. If you look at the Relationships panel (see Figure 3-9), the solution becomes obvious: you need the Orders table as well. Then you can use the Customers table to find the Florida customers, join those rows to the Orders table matching the ID column (the primary key) with the Customer ID column in the Orders table (the foreign key) to find the orders for Florida customers, and finally join those rows to the Order Details table to find the line items on those orders. (Of course, there is no guarantee the RDBMS will actually process the joins in this sequence, but the end result will be the same regardless.) It should be clear from this example that an overall diagram of all your tables and relationships is an *essential* document because it gives you the roadmap you need when forming queries.

This example also requires a *calculated column* (also called a *derived* column), which is formed by multiplying the values in the Unit Price and Quantity columns in each row. Just about any formula that you can use in a spreadsheet can be used in a relational database query.

Step by Step

1. You should be starting with a query specification that joins the Customers and Orders tables with a join specification (a line between them) and not other conditions, like the one shown in Try This 3-8 (Figure 3-22). Be certain that the join between Customers and Orders is an inner join and that no columns are currently included in the query specification.

2. Add the Order Details table to the query by clicking the Show Table icon and selecting the table from the list in the Show Table dialog box.

3. In the Customers table, add the Company and State/Province columns to the query by double-clicking their names. Alternatively, you can drag-and-drop the column's name to the columns in the query specification.

4. In the Order Details table, add Unit Price and Quantity columns to the query.

5. To add the calculated column, enter the following into the Field row of the empty column to the right of the Quantity column: **Extended Price: [Unit Price] * Quantity**. The first part of the entry is a *label* for the new column. Every column in your results must have a unique name, and if you don't name it, Microsoft Access will. Default column names are usually not very meaningful and sometimes are just plain ugly, so it is *always* best to supply a column label (name) for calculated columns. Note that the spaces on each side of the multiplication operator (*) in field specifications do not matter, so you could have left them out. However, you must leave the space as is in the Unit Price column because that is the actual column name and, as a result, must also enclose the column name in square brackets as shown because of the embedded space. Chances are that Microsoft Access will rewrite your column specification by removing the spaces and placing square brackets around the other column name, so don't be surprised if you see what you entered change on the panel when you move the cursor to another location.

6. To limit the query only to customers in Florida (FL), enter **FL** in the Criteria row for the State/Province column.

7. Add an ascending sort to the Company column either by typing the letter **A** in the Sort row for the column and pressing ENTER, or by clicking in that location and selecting Ascending from the list.

8. Click the Run icon on the ribbon to run your query. The completed panel is shown at the top of Figure 3-27 with the query results shown below.

9. To get ready for the next exercise, return to the Query Design panel by clicking the View icon just below the Office button.

(continued)

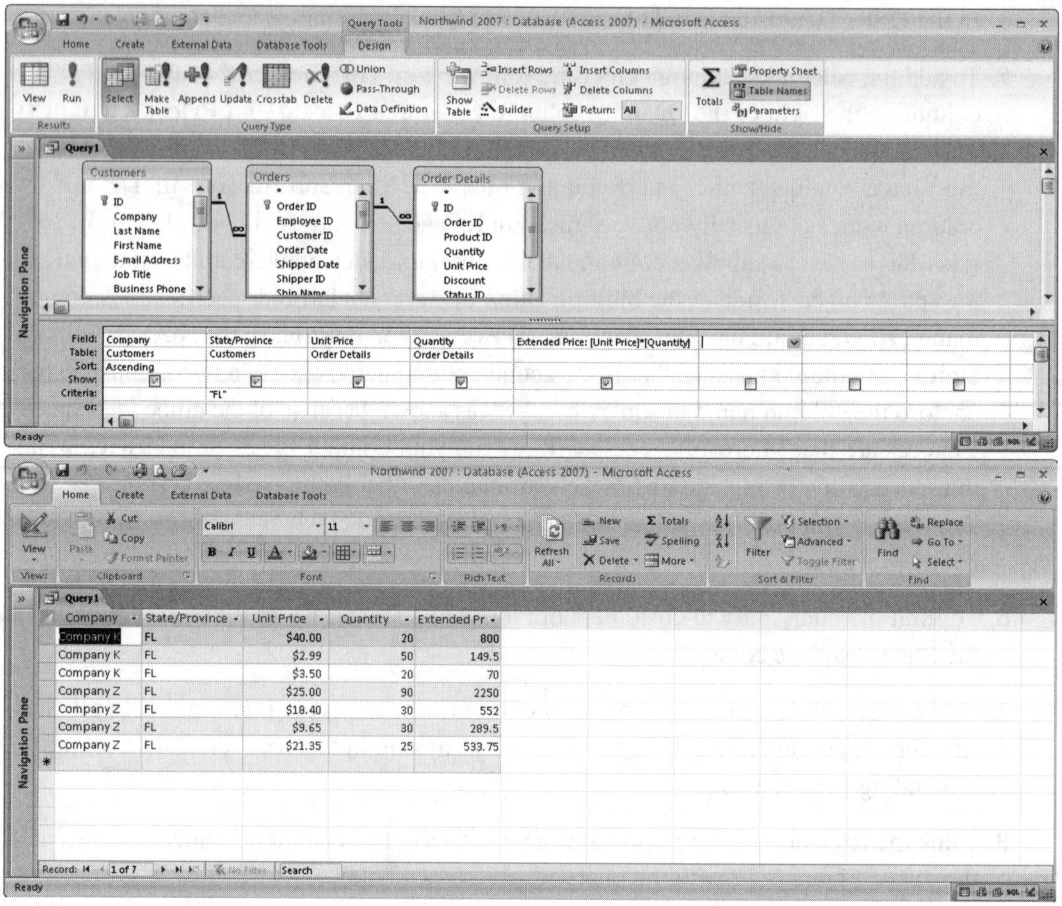

Figure 3-27 Try This 3-12 (Multiple Joins and Calculated Columns), query design (top) and query results (bottom)

Try This 3-13 Aggregate Functions

In reviewing the Try This 3-12 results, you probably noticed that seven rows were returned covering orders for two different customers in Florida. All the details are here, but at a glance, it is difficult to easily get a sense of the *total* amount that each customer has ordered from Northwind. What you really need to do is sum up the Extended Price column for each customer. In relational databases, this is done with the **SUM** function.

A *function* is a special type of program that returns a single value each time it is invoked, named for the mathematical concept of a function. Because you will use the function to operate on a column, it will be invoked for each row and therefore return a single value for each row the query handles. Sometimes the term *column function* is used to remind you that the function is being applied to a table or view column. An example of an ordinary column function is **ROUND**, which can be used to round numbers in various ways. Special classes of functions that combine multiple rows together into one row are called *aggregate* functions. The following table shows aggregate functions that are commonly used in relational databases:

Function Name	Description
AVG	Calculates the average value for a column
COUNT	Counts the number of values found in a column
MAX	Finds the maximum value in a column
MIN	Finds the minimum value in a column
SUM	Sums (totals up) the values in a column

If you use an aggregate function by itself in a query, you get one row back for the entire query. This makes sense, because there is no way for the RDBMS to know what other result you might want. So, if you want the aggregate result to be for *groups* of rows in the query, you need to include a **GROUP BY** specification to tell the RDBMS to group the rows by the values in one or more columns, and to apply the aggregate function to each group. This is much like asking for subtotals instead of a grand total for a list of numbers.

For this exercise, you want the RDBMS to provide a total of the calculated column Extended Price for each customer. In other words, you want to group the rows by customer, and for each group, display a single row containing the company name, state or province, and total order dollar amount.

The state/province is actually unnecessary because only Florida customers are included in the query. However, it remains here to illustrate an important concept that most newcomers to relational databases have a difficult time understanding: If you select the Company, State/Province, and calculated Total Price columns, telling the RDBMS the formula for calculating the total price and asking it to group the rows in the result by Company, there is a hidden logic problem that will cause an error to be returned by the RDBMS. You have essentially asked the RDBMS to return the value of State/Province for every row in the query results, but, at the same time, to aggregate rows by Company

(continued)

and provide the calculated total for each aggregate. It is illogical to ask for some rows to be aggregated and others not. To make matters worse, the resulting error message is rather cryptic. Small wonder that we often hear aggregate functions called "aggravating" functions. Remember this rule: Whenever a query includes an aggregate function, then *every* column in the query results must either be formed using an aggregate function or be named in the GROUP BY column list. In Microsoft Access, the Totals icon (the Greek letter Sigma) on the ribbon toggles (hides and exposes) a line called Total on the Query View panel. It is the total line that lets you specify aggregate functions and groupings for our query.

Step by Step

1. You should be starting with a query specification from Try This 3-12 as shown in Figure 3-27.

2. Remove the Unit Price and Quantity columns by clicking in the slim gray strip above the field name and pressing DELETE.

3. Change the label on the Extended Price column to Total Price. This column name will make more sense in the results.

4. Click the Totals icon on the ribbon to expose the Total line in the query specification. By default, each column will initially have Group By specified on that line.

5. In the Total Price column, click in the Total line and use the pull-down list to select the Sum function.

6. Click the Run icon on the ribbon to run your query. The completed panel is shown at the top of Figure 3-28 with the query results shown below.

7. To complete this exercise, close the Query Design panel either by clicking the Close button in the upper-right corner of the panel (being careful not to click the button at the upper-right of your Microsoft Access screen, because that will completely close the Access database), or right-clicking the tab that shows the query name (most likely Query1) and choosing Close. When asked about saving the query, click No.

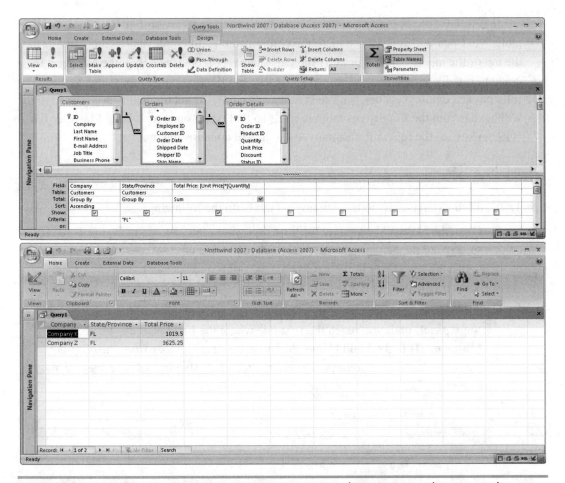

Figure 3-28 Try This 3-13 (Aggregate Functions), query design (top) and query results (bottom)

Try This 3-14 Self-Joins

When tables have a recursive relationship built in to them, you must use a *self-join* (joining a table to itself) to resolve the relationship. Unfortunately, the 2007 version of the Northwind database does not have a recursive relationship built in, so you will add one to help facilitate a demonstration of this important concept.

(continued)

In this Try This exercise, you will first add a Manager ID column in the Employees table. Next you will add some data to the column so that all employees except the one at the top of the management hierarchy have the manager's ID assigned in the Manager ID column. Finally, you will create a query that lists the ID, first name, last name, and job title for each employee along with the manager's name. To get the manager's name, you will have to join the Employees table to itself so that Access can match the Manager ID (foreign key) to the row in the Employees table that contains the manager's name.

Step by Step

1. To add the Manager ID to the Employees table, do the following:

   a. Open the Design View panel for the Employees table, shown in Figure 3-11. To do so, expand the Navigation Pane along the left edge of the Access main panel, find the Employees table in the list of objects, right-click its name, and click Design View on the pop-up menu.

   b. Scroll down through the field definitions (the rows in the upper part of the Design View panel) until you reach the first one where the Field Name is blank. Enter **Manager ID** in the Field Name column and select Number from the drop-down list in the Data Type column. The completed entry should look like the one shown in Figure 3-29.

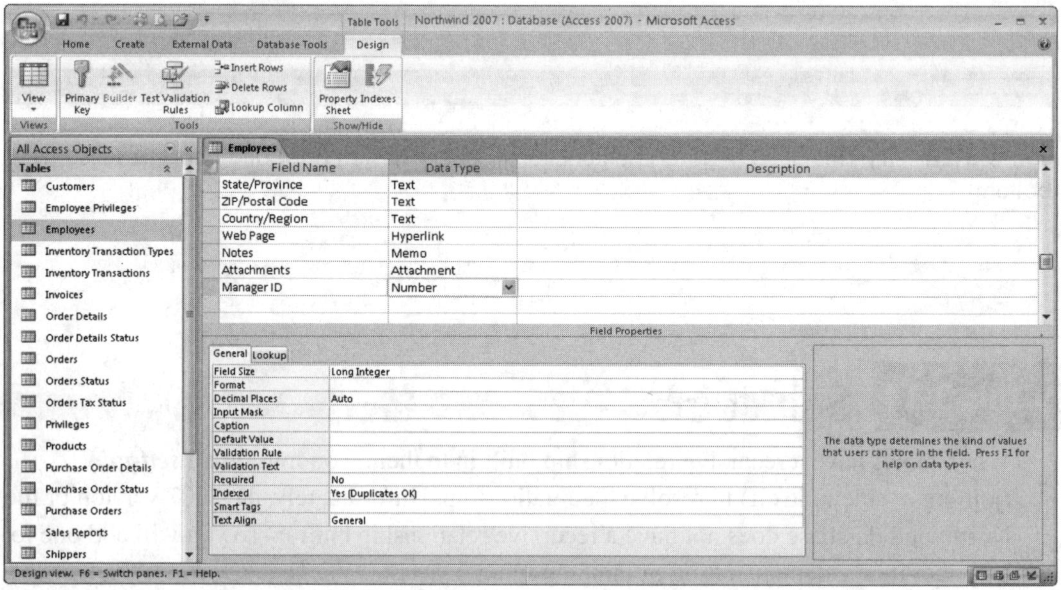

Figure 3-29 Employees table (design view) with Manager ID column added

2. To populate the newly added Manager ID column with data, do the following:

  a. Click the View icon in the ribbon to display the rows and columns of data in the Employees table, similar to the one shown in Figure 3-10.

  b. Scroll to the right using the scroll bar at the bottom of the panel so that the Manager ID column is visible. It should be the next to last one. (You may notice that the rightmost column displayed is for adding a new field [column] to the table. You could have added the new Manager ID column using this facility, but I very much prefer using the Design View to make table definition changes because many more options are available.)

  c. Type in the data values in the Manager ID column, as shown in Figure 3-30. Notice that no values are included in the second and last rows on the panel. The second row is for Sales Vice President Andrew Cencini, who is the most senior manager currently in the table (his manager is not currently in the table so you leave his manager's ID blank, which is actually a null value). The last row is for adding new employees to the table, and since you are not adding new employees, but merely updating the existing ones, you must leave all values in this last row blank.

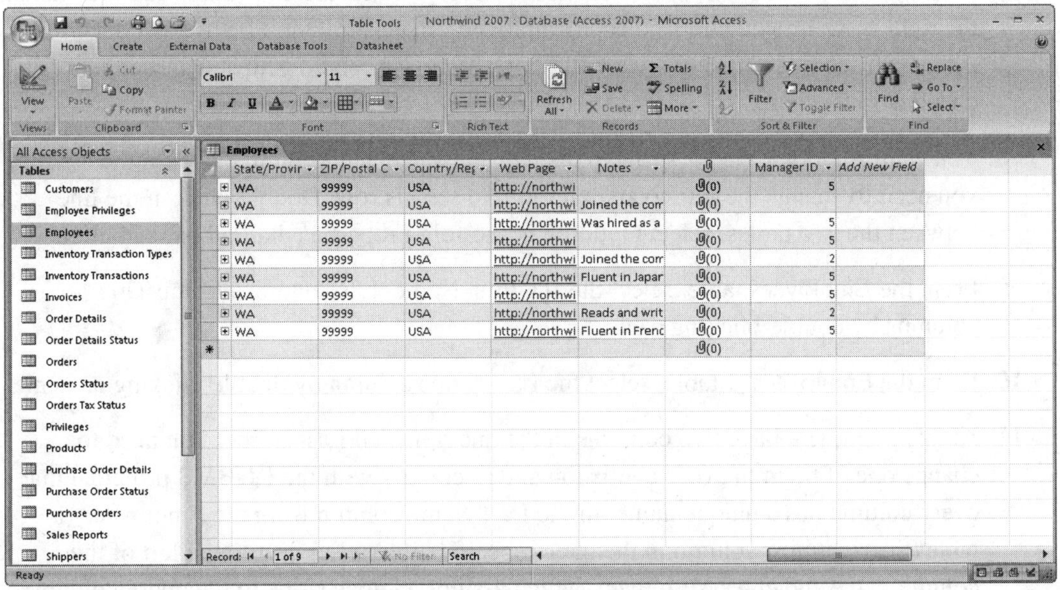

Figure 3-30 Employees table (Datasheet View) with Manager ID values added

(continued)

3. You could (and probably should) use the Relationships panel to add the relationship from the Manager ID column to the primary key column to define Manager ID as a foreign key, but since the column was added simply for the sake of a demonstration, you can skip that step.

4. Create a new query by opening the Create ribbon and then clicking the Query Design icon.

5. When the Show Table dialog box opens, add the Employees table to the query *twice*. This may seem odd at first, but this is the only way to tell Microsoft Access that you want to match each row in the Employees table with a different row (the manager's row) in the same table. Note that the tables are named Employees and Employees_1 on the panel, even though both are really two representations of the exact same table.

6. You can minimize the Navigation Pane and close the Employees table (Design View) if you want (to reduce the visual clutter on the screen).

7. In the Employees table (on the left), scroll down until the Manager ID column is visible. Click its name and (while holding down the mouse button) drag-and-drop the name on to the ID column in the Employees_1 table. This tells Access how to join the Employees table to itself. The table on the left represents the employees and the one on the right is where you will find each employee's manager. Don't be overly concerned if this still seems confusing—we will revisit recursive relationships in subsequent chapters in this book.

8. You want Andrew Cencini's row to display, but since he has no manager in the table, you need to change the join to an outer join to see his row. Double-click in the line between the two tables, select Option 2 in the Join Properties dialog box, and click OK.

9. From the Employees table, select the ID, First Name, Last Name, and Job Title columns by double-clicking each.

10. From the Employees_1 table, select the Last Name column by double-clicking its name.

11. At this point, you have two columns in the query named Last Name. You need to change one of them to avoid confusion and to comply with the RDBMS principal that every column has a unique name. In the Last Name column from the Employees_1 table (the rightmost column in the query specification), click just to the left of the column name and enter **Manager:**, which assigns an alias name to the query column.

12. Click the Run icon on the ribbon to run your query. The completed panel is shown at the top of Figure 3-31 with the query results shown below. Your results should be

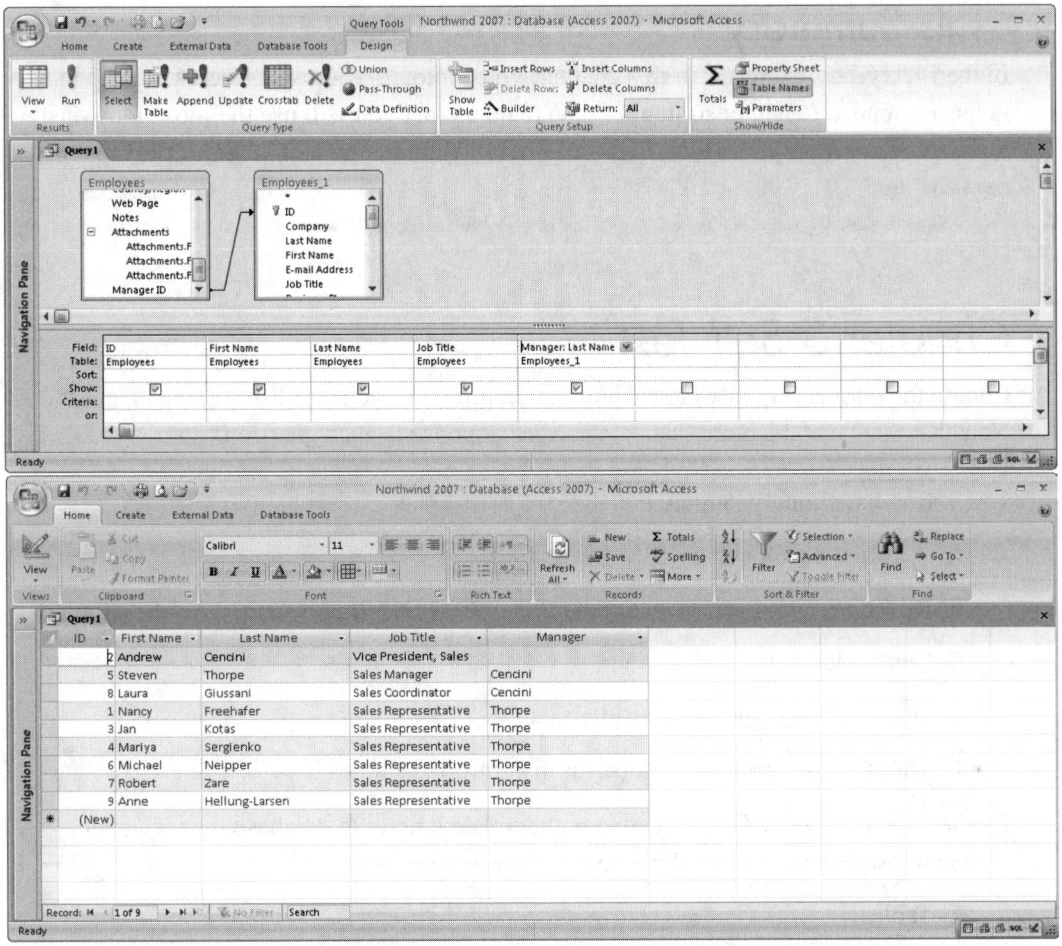

Figure 3-31   Try This 3-14 (Self-Joins), query design (top) and query results (bottom)

similar, but since you didn't specify a sort order, the order of rows in your results may be different.

13. To complete this exercise, close the Query Design panel by either clicking on the Close box in the upper-right corner of the panel, or right-clicking the tab that shows the query name (most likely Query1) and choosing Close. When asked about saving the query, click No. You can then close Microsoft Access if you want.

(continued)

Try This Summary

In the 14 Try This exercises in this chapter, you explored Microsoft Access queries in a manner intended to demonstrate the basic features that you will use the most. Obviously there are many more features to explore. But it is time to move on to SQL, the topic of the next chapter.

✔ Chapter 3 Self Test

Choose the correct responses to each of the multiple-choice and fill-in-the-blank questions. Note that there may be more than one correct response to each question.

1. A forms-based query language

    A Was first developed by IBM in the 1980s

    B Describes how a query should be processed rather than what the results should be

    C Resembles SQL

    D Uses a GUI (graphical user interface)

    E Was shown to be clearly superior in controlled studies

2. The object types in Microsoft Access that relate strictly to database management (as opposed to application development) are

    A Tables

    B Queries

    C Forms

    D Macros

    E Modules

3. When a table is deleted from the Microsoft Access Relationships panel, what happens next?

    A It is immediately deleted from the database.

    B It remains unchanged in the database and is merely removed from the Relationships panel.

C It remains in the database, but all data rows are deleted.

D Relationships belonging to the table are also deleted.

4. Relationships on the Microsoft Access Relationships panel represent _____ in the database.

5. A column in the results of a Microsoft Access query can be formed from

    A A table column

    B A query column

    C A constant

    D A calculation

    E All of the above

6. When a query with no criteria included is executed, the result is

    A An error message

    B No rows being displayed

    C All the rows in the table being displayed

    D None of the above

7. When sequencing (sorting) of rows is not included in a database query, the rows returned by the query are in _____ order.

8. In a query, the search criteria REGION NOT = "CA" OR REGION NOT ="NV" will display

    A An error message

    B All the rows in the table

    C Only the rows in which Region is equal to "CA" or "NV"

    D All the rows in the table except those in which Region is NULL

    E All the rows in the table except those in which the Region is "CA" or "NV"

9. Criteria on different lines in a Microsoft Access query are connected with the _____ logical operator.

10. The join connector between tables in a Microsoft Access query may

   A Be manually created by dragging a column from one table or view to a column of another table or view

   B Be inherited from the metadata defined on the Relationships panel

   C Be altered to define left, right, and full outer joins

   D Cause a Cartesian product if not defined between two tables or views in the query

   E All of the above

11. When an outer join is used, column data from tables (or views) in which no matching rows were found will contain _____.

12. An aggregate function

   A Combines data from multiple columns together

   B Combines data from multiple rows together

   C May be applied to table columns but not to calculated columns

   D Requires that every column in a query be either an aggregate function or named in the GROUP BY list for the query

   E All of the above

13. Self-joins in a query are a method of resolving a _____.

14. The column name of a calculated column in the query results is _____ when not provided in the query definition.

15. Tables may be joined

   A Using only the primary key in one table and a foreign key in another

   B Using any column in either table (theoretically)

   C Only to themselves

   D Only to other tables

   E Only using the Cartesian product formula

Chapter 4

Introduction to SQL

Key Skills & Concepts

- A Brief History of SQL

- Getting Started with Oracle SQL

- Where's the Data?

- Data Query Language (DQL): The SELECT Statement

- Data Manipulation Language (DML) Statements

- Data Definition Language (DDL) Statements

- Data Control Language (DCL) Statements

This chapter introduces Structured Query Language (SQL), which has become the universal language for relational databases in that nearly every DBMS in modern use supports it. The reason for this wide acceptance is clearly the time and effort that went into the development of language features and standards, making SQL highly portable across different RDBMS products.

In this chapter I use Oracle and its sample HR (Human Resources) schema to demonstrate SQL. A *schema* is the collection of database objects that belong to a particular database user (the HR user in this case). Oracle Database 10*g* Express Edition (10*g* XE), which requires no license fee, can be downloaded at no charge from www.oracle.com/technology/software/products/database/index.html. Oracle 10*g* XE includes a human resources (HR) sample schema that I use in the examples and Try This exercises in this chapter. You will learn more if you try the SQL statements yourself, so it should be well worth your effort to download and install the software. Documentation specific to 10*g* XE can be found at www.oracle.com/pls/xe102/homepage.

NOTE

Because Oracle provides 10*g* XE without charging a license fee, significant restrictions are imposed regarding how the product may be used. If you plan to use it for purposes beyond merely learning SQL and trying out Oracle, you should carefully read the licensing information provided with the product.

Except as noted, every command and feature demonstrated in this chapter meets current SQL standards and therefore should work correctly in any DBMS that supports SQL.

However, without the Oracle HR sample schema, you will have to create sample tables like the ones Oracle provides and populate them with data to run the exact statements included in this chapter. By convention, all the SQL statements are shown in uppercase. However, Oracle is not case sensitive for either SQL commands or database object names, so you can type the commands in uppercase, lowercase, or mixed case as you follow along on your own computer. But do keep in mind that data in Oracle *is* case sensitive, so whenever you type a data value that is to be stored in the database or is to be used to find data in the database, you must type it in the proper case.

NOTE
Oracle has released Database 11*g*. However, as of this writing, the Express Edition (XE) is available only in the Database 10*g* version, and that is the version available on the Oracle Database Software Downloads web page. If a newer version of XE becomes available, you may find it listed on the web page, and it will most likely work just fine for the purposes of following along with the examples and Try This exercises in this book—although, of course, the user interface might be different.

As stated in the previous chapter, SQL is a command-based language. SQL statements are formed in clauses using *keywords* and *parameters*. The keywords used are usually reserved words for the DBMS, meaning they cannot be used for the names of database objects. The clauses usually have to appear in a prescribed sequence. SQL statements should be terminated with a semicolon (;). The program you use to connect to the database and interact with it is called an *SQL client*. Other clients are available from Oracle, including SQL*Plus, iSQL*Plus, and SQL Developer, but I use Oracle Application Express in this chapter because it comes with Oracle 10*g* XE and therefore is ready for use as soon as 10*g* XE is installed.

Some SQL clients will not run an SQL statement unless it ends with a semicolon or a slash (the slash being an Oracle extension to the standard). But, most of the GUI or web-based clients such as Oracle Application Express do not require a termination character, because a button or icon is clicked to tell the client when you are ready to run the statement. Beyond the restrictions I have mentioned, SQL is freeform, with one or more spaces separating language elements and line breaks permitted between any two elements (but not in the middle of an element).

SQL statements can be divided into the following categories:

- **Data Query Language (DQL)**   Statements that query the database but do not alter any data or database objects. This category contains the SELECT statement. Not all vendors make a distinction here; many lump DQL into DML, as defined next.

- **Data Manipulation Language (DML)**   Statements that modify data stored in database objects (that is, tables). This category contains the INSERT, UPDATE, and DELETE statements.

- **Data Definition Language (DDL)** Statements that create and modify database objects. Whereas DML and DQL work with the data in the database objects, DDL works with the database objects themselves. In other words, DDL manages the data *containers* whereas DML manages the data *inside* the containers. This category includes the CREATE, ALTER, and DROP statements.

- **Data Control Language (DCL)** Statements that manage privileges that database users have regarding the database and objects stored in it. This category includes the GRANT and REVOKE statements.

Representative statements in each of these categories are presented in the sections that follow. But first, we'll cover a little bit of the history of the language.

A Brief History of SQL

The forerunner of SQL, which was called QUEL, first emerged in the specifications for System/R, IBM's experimental relational database, in the late 1970s. However, two other products, with various names for their query languages, beat IBM to the marketplace with the first commercial relational database products: Relational Software's Oracle and Relational Technology's Ingres. IBM released SQL/DS in 1982, with the query language named Structured English Query Language (SEQUEL). However, when IBM learned that SEQUEL was a trademark owned by Hawker Siddeley Aircraft Company of the UK, the name was changed to SQL. As a result of the name change, you will hear the name pronounced both as a word (*sequel*) and as a string of letters (*S-Q-L*), and while the later is generally preferred, both are considered correct.

SQL standards committees were formed by ANSI (American National Standards Institute) in 1986 and ISO (International Organization for Standardization) in 1987. Two years later, the first standard specification, known as SQL-89, was published. The standard was expanded three years later into SQL-92, which weighed in at roughly 600 pages. The third generation, published in 1999, was called SQL-99, or SQL3. Additional revisions were published in 2003 (SQL:2003) and 2006 (SQL:2006), and work continues on the SQL standard. The revisions published in 1999 and later incorporate many of the object features required for SQL to operate on an object-relational database, as well as language extensions to make SQL computationally complete (adding looping, branching, and case constructs) and additional features such as Extensible Markup Language (XML). Most current RDBMS products comply with the standard to one degree or another.

Nearly every vendor has added extensions to SQL, partly because they wanted to differentiate their products, and partly because market demands pressed them into implementing features before standards existed for them. One case in point is support for the DATE and TIMESTAMP data types. Dates are highly important in business data processing, but the developers of the original RDBMS products were computer scientists and academics, not business computing specialists, so such a need was unanticipated. As a result, the early SQL dialects did not have any special support for dates. As commercial products emerged, vendors responded to pressure from their biggest customers by hurriedly adding support for dates. Unfortunately, this led to each doing so in its own way. Whenever you migrate SQL statements from one vendor to another, beware of the SQL dialect differences. SQL is highly compatible and portable across vendor products, but complete database systems can seldom be moved without some adjustments.

Getting Started with Oracle SQL

As mentioned, Oracle provides several different client tools (SQL clients) for managing the formation and execution of SQL statements and the presentation of results. These are called *client* tools because they normally run on the database user's workstation and are capable of connecting remotely to databases that run on other computer systems, which are often shared servers. It is not unusual for the client tools also to be installed on the server alongside the database for easy administration, allowing the DBA logged in to the server to access the database without the need for a client workstation. However, for the Personal and Express editions of Oracle, the database itself, along with the client tools, is installed on an individual user's workstation or handheld device.

The examples and Try This exercises in this chapter focus on Oracle. However, if you use a different RDBMS, client tools will be available for it as well, usually provided by the RDBMS vendor. For example, Microsoft SQL Server has both a GUI tool (SQL Server Management Studio) and a command-line tool (OSQL) available. Most commercial DBMS products have express editions that you can install and use without purchasing a license, and open source products, such as MySQL and PostgreSQL (a derivative of Ingres) also exist. However, as mentioned, if you use a different product, you will be on your own to create tables resembling the Oracle HR sample schema and to populate them with data.

Once you have installed Oracle 10*g* XE, you can start Application Express by choosing Start | Programs | Oracle Database 10g Express Edition | Go To Database Home Page. (If you are using Windows Vista, the Programs option will appear as All Programs.) Your default web browser (usually Microsoft Internet Explorer, but you may have another default such as Mozilla Firefox) will launch and a login page like the one shown in Figure 4-1 will be displayed.

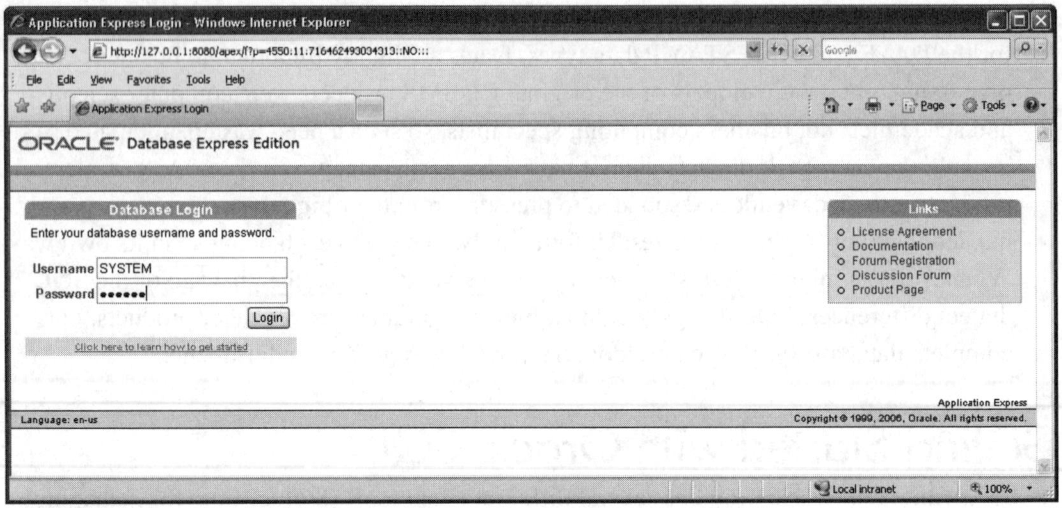

Figure 4-1 Oracle Application Express Login page

Try This 4-1 Unlock the HR Account and Log in as HR

The HR user account is locked by default, so you will need to log in as SYSTEM (the master account for an Oracle database) and unlock it before you can use it. You will need the password you provided when you installed Oracle 10g XE in order to log in as SYSTEM. Keep in mind that while Oracle user accounts are not case sensitive, Oracle passwords are. In this Try This exercise you will unlock the HR account and assign a password to it, and then log in as the HR user.

Step by Step

1. If you do not already have Oracle Application Express running, launch it from your Start menu.

2. Enter **SYSTEM** in the Username field on the Login page.

3. In the Password field, enter the password you chose for the SYSTEM account when you installed 10g XE.

4. Click the Login button to open the main Application Express page, shown in Figure 4-2. The options available are explained later in this section.

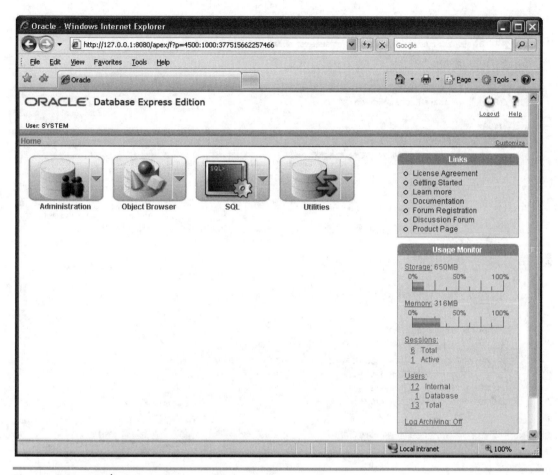

Figure 4-2 Application Express main page

5. Click the arrow next to the Administration icon and choose Database Users. The list of current database user accounts will display next, and in all likelihood, the only one listed will be HR.

6. Click the icon for the HR user to display the Manager Database User page for that account, as shown in Figure 4-3.

7. Choose a password for the HR account and enter it in the Password and Confirm Password fields.

8. Using the pull-down menu in the Account Status field, choose Unlocked.

(continued)

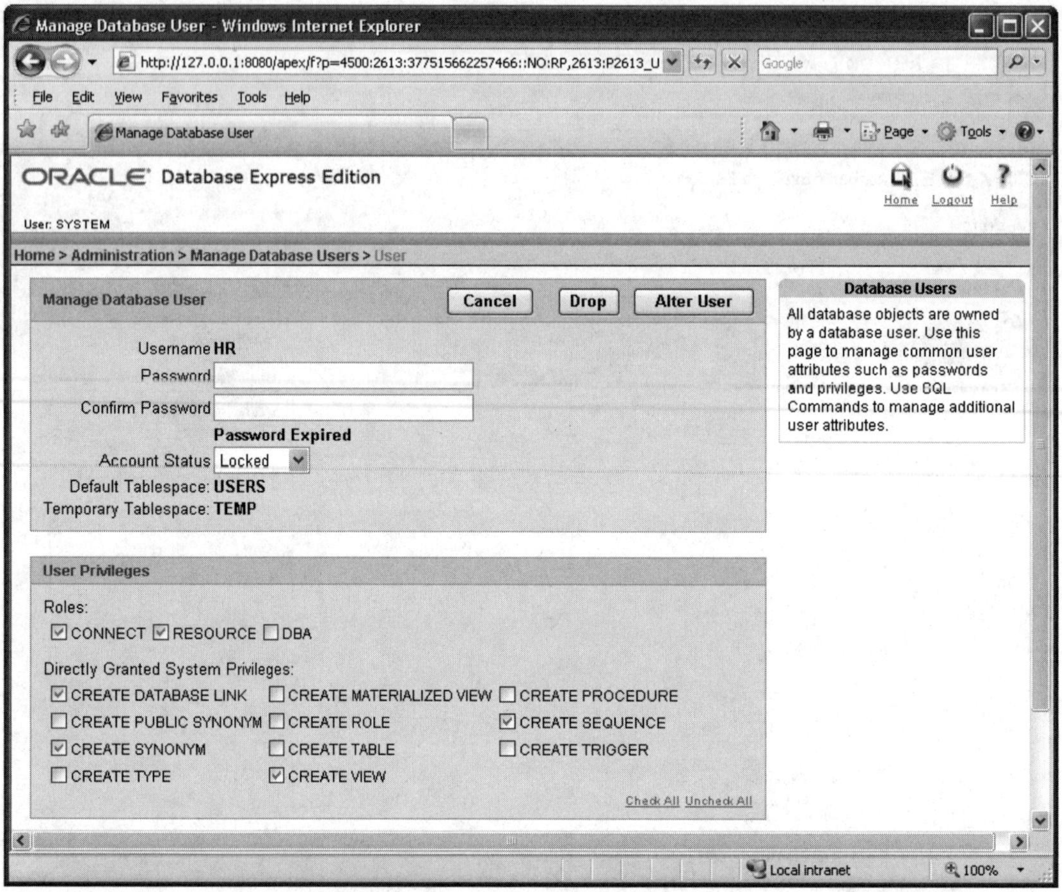

Figure 4-3 Manage Database User page

9. Click the Alter User button. You will be returned to the previous page (the list of user accounts) with a confirmation message displayed across the page in a gray box.

10. Click the Logout link near the upper-right corner of the page. A page confirming the logout will be displayed.

11. Click the Login link to return to the Login page shown in Figure 4-1.

12. Enter the Username (**HR**) and the password you selected in the appropriate fields and click the Login button. The Applications Express main page, shown in Figure 4-2, will again be displayed.

Try This Summary

In this Try This exercise you unlocked the HR user account that came with your Oracle 10*g* XE database, assigned a password to it, and then logged in as the HR user. You are now prepared to use the HR sample schema to explore SQL.

On the Application Express main page (Figure 4-2), you should see four (or perhaps five) icons, each of which provides a set of functions. Here is a brief overview of each option:

- **Administration**   This option provides tools for administering the DBMS (including storage and memory settings), for managing user accounts (as you already used in unlocking the HR account), and for monitoring the database to identify and deal with performance issues.

- **Object Browser**   This option provides tools to create and browse database objects (tables, views, indexes, and so forth). The Object Browser is used in the next topic in this chapter to explore the objects in the HR schema.

- **SQL**   The SQL option provides three SQL tools: SQL Commands, which is used extensively in this chapter to edit and submit SQL statements and view the results; SQL Scripts, which lets you edit, save, and execute scripts containing multiple SQL commands; and Query Builder, a graphical query tool similar in concept to the Access Query tool that was discussed in detail in Chapter 3.

- **Utilities**   This option provides tools for moving data between database tables and external files, generating DDL statements for existing database objects, generating a variety of reports, and managing the recycle bin that 10*g* XE provides for dropped database objects.

- **Application Builder**   This option is not shown in Figure 4-2 because it is not available to all users. However, it has been enabled for the HR user, so you will likely see it on the main page. The Application Builder provides tools for the development and management of web-based applications that use the database. Since this option is about application programming instead of database management, it is beyond the scope of this book.

Of all the tools provided in 10*g* XE, the SQL Commands tool is used almost exclusively in this chapter. From the main page, select the arrow next to the SQL icon and then choose SQL Commands to open the page shown in Figure 4-4. The page is quite

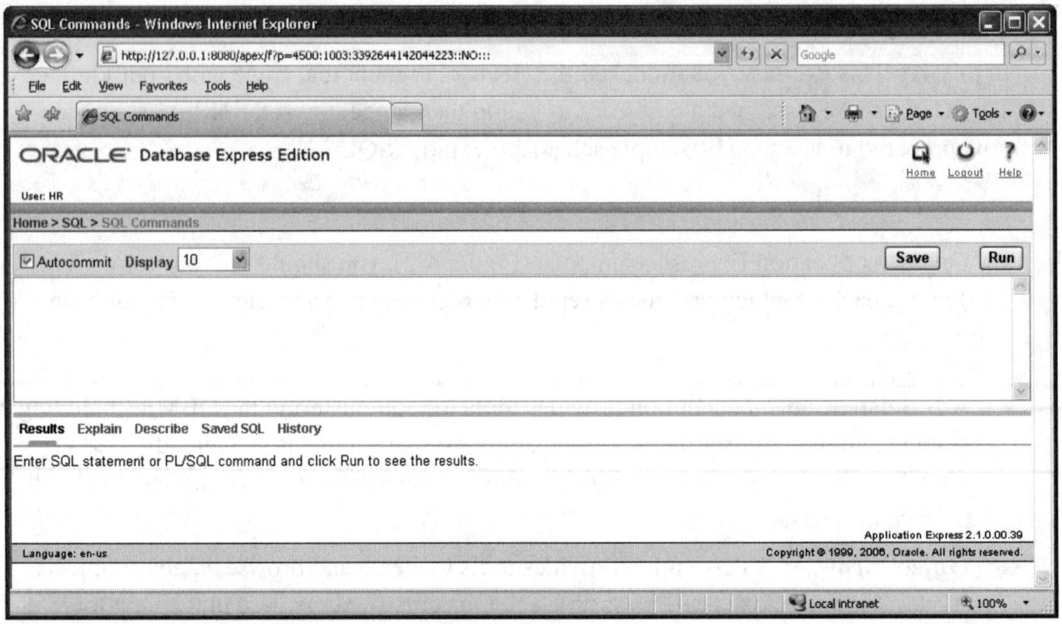

Figure 4-4 Oracle 10g XE SQL Commands page

simple to use. You type SQL commands in the empty area in the upper half of the page, click the Run button and the query results are displayed in the lower half of the page.

You should, however, be aware of some other options on the page:

● *The Autocommit check box* (above the area where SQL commands are entered) determines whether or not changes to the database are automatically committed. Autocommit is covered in more detail in the "Transaction Support (COMMIT and ROLLBACK)" section later in this chapter.

● *The Display setting* (next to the Autocommit box) determines the maximum number of rows that will appear in the result sets displayed in the lower half of the page. The default is 10, which means you will see only the first 10 rows of the results of any SQL command that you run. You will need to set this value higher for some of the examples presented later in this chapter.

● *The Save button* allows you to save a query, giving it a name that can be used to find it at a later time when you want to reuse it.

- *The Explain option* provides an explanation of how the SQL engine will run the query. We will look at it further in the "Performance Tuning" section in Chapter 11.

- *The Describe option* tells you how to use the Oracle **DESCRIBE** command to view the definition of objects stored in the database. The next section looks at the **DESCRIBE** command.

- *The Saved SQL option* allows you to find and retrieve SQL commands that you stored using the Save button.

- *The History option* provides a list of SQL statements you have previously run, allowing you to select one of them for reuse.

Where's the Data?

Although the focus of this chapter is SQL, you cannot write SQL statements without having at least a basic understanding of the tables that hold the data you want to access. When using a graphical query tool such as the Access Query tool or the Oracle 10*g* XE Query Builder, database objects and definitions are presented to you graphically as you create the query. However, when you are using SQL commands and you need to reference the database object definitions, you must do so using a separate tool. The basic methods for doing this are either by using *catalog views* (special views provided by the RDBMS that present database metadata that documents the database contents), or by using a graphical tool specifically designed to present the database metadata. I discuss each of these in the sections that follow.

Finding Database Objects Using Catalog Views

Oracle provides a comprehensive set of catalog views that can be queried to show the names and definitions of all database objects available to a database user. Most other RDBMSs have a similar capability, but of course the names of the views vary. By issuing a SELECT statement against any of these views, you can display information about your database objects. For complete information on the available catalog views, consult the *Oracle 10*g *Database Reference*, available via the "Reference" link at www.oracle.com/pls/db102/homepage. Here are the most useful views:

- **USER_TABLES**   Contains one row of information for each table in the user schema. This view contains a lot of columns, but the one of most interest, TABLE_NAME, is the first column in the view. Once you know the table names, the **DESCRIBE** command can be used on each to reveal more information about the table definitions.

Figure 4-5 shows an example of selecting everything from the USER_TABLES view. Here is the SQL statement:

```
SELECT *
  FROM USER_TABLES;
```

NOTE
The SQL SELECT statement, shown in Figure 4-5, is described in more detail a little further along in this chapter.

● **USER_TAB_COLUMNS**   Contains one row of information for each column of the tables contained in the current user schema. Like the USER_TABLES view, it contains a lot of columns, but the most useful ones are TABLE_NAME, COLUMN_NAME, DATA_TYPE, DATA_LENGTH, DATA_PRECISION, DATA_SCALE, NULLABLE, and DATA_DEFAULT. If you read the discussion of data types in Chapter 2, the contents of these columns should be self-evident based on their names.

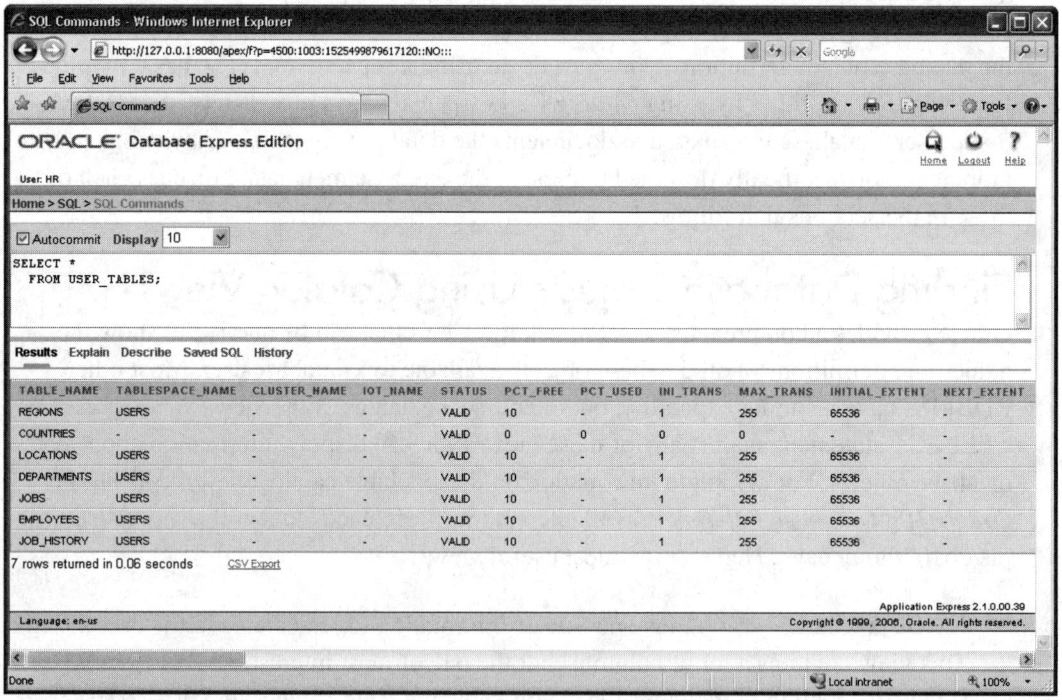

Figure 4-5   Selecting all columns from USER_TABLES

● **USER_VIEWS** Contains one row of information for each view in the user schema, containing, among other things, the name of the view and the text of the SQL statement that forms the view. Note that catalog views are not included because they belong to a different schema called SYS.

As an alternative to wading through the USER_TAB_COLUMNS view to find the definition of an individual table or view, Oracle provides the **DESCRIBE** command. The syntax is very simple: just type the keyword **DESCRIBE** followed by the table or view name and run the command. This command is particular to Oracle, but it works on all of Oracle's SQL clients. Figure 4-6 shows the **DESCRIBE** command run (using the SQL Commands page) for the EMPLOYEES table in the HR schema. The command is very simple:

```
DESCRIBE EMPLOYEES
```

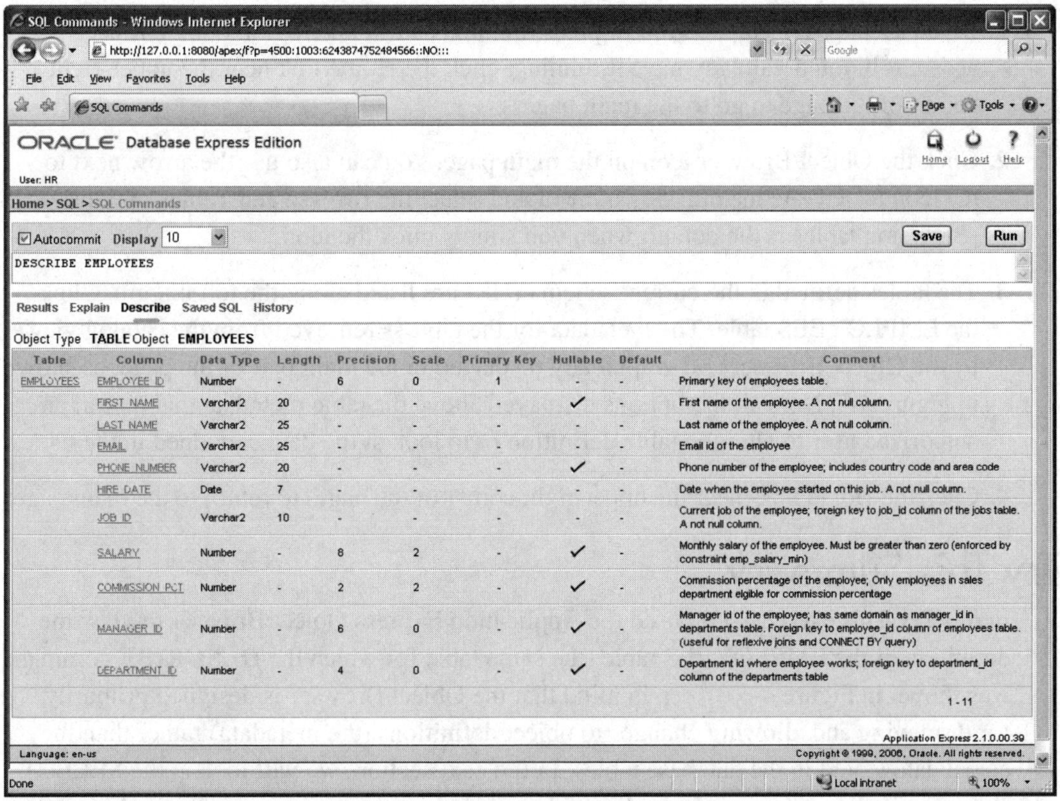

Figure 4-6 DESCRIBE command run for the EMPLOYEES table

Viewing Database Objects Using the Object Browser

For those less inclined to type SQL commands, Oracle provides several GUI tools, including the Object Browser included in 10*g* XE's Application Express. For other editions of Oracle, the SQL Developer product provides similar capabilities, and a number of tools are also available from third-party software vendors. Most other RDBMS vendors also provide graphical tools, such as the SQL Server Management Studio from Microsoft.

Try This 4-2 **Using the Application Express Object Browser**

In this Try This exercise, you will use the Object Browser in Application Express.

Step by Step

1. If you do not have Application Express running, start it and log in to the HR user account; if you do already have it running, click the Home link near the upper-right corner of the page to go to the main page.

2. Click the Object Browser icon on the main page. You can also use the arrow next to the icon to activate the pull-down menu and select the Browse and Tables options. (Browsing tables is the default when you simply click the icon.)

3. The tables defined in the current schema (HR) are listed along the left margin. Click the EMPLOYEES table. The metadata for the table is retrieved from the catalog views by the Object Browser and graphically displayed in the main part of the page, as shown in Figure 4-7. Note all the options displayed above the table metadata that permit an authorized user to alter the table definition or to look at the data contained in the table.

4. Click the Home link (near the upper-right corner of the page) to return to the main page.

Try This Summary

In this Try This exercise, you used the Application Express Object Browser to view the definition of the EMPLOYEES table (the same table for which the **DESCRIBE** command was shown in Figure 4-6). Keep in mind that the Object Browser is designed primarily for displaying and allowing changes to object definitions (the metadata) rather than the actual data stored in the database tables. In the next section, we will look at the SELECT statement in detail and how it can be used to view the data stored in database tables.

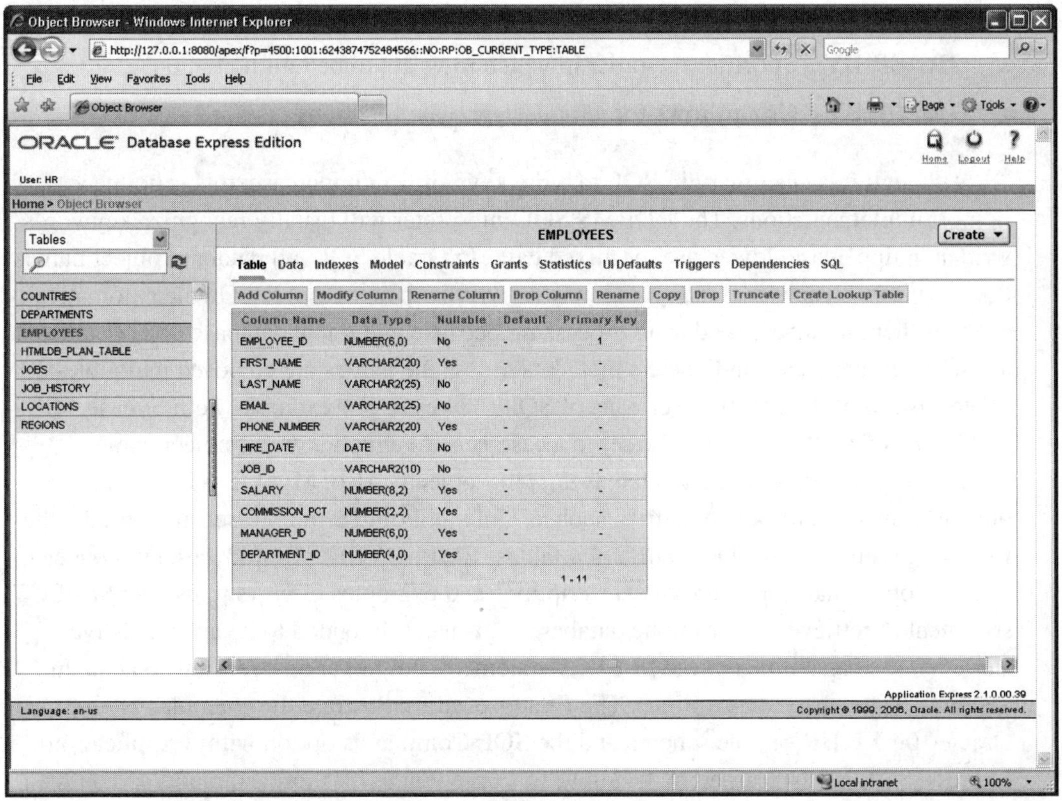

Figure 4-7 Application Express Object Browser with EMPLOYEES table metadata displayed

Data Query Language (DQL): The SELECT Statement

The SELECT statement retrieves data from the database. Following are the clauses of the statement, which are demonstrated in the following sections:

- **SELECT** Lists the columns that are to be returned in the results
- **FROM** Lists the tables or views from which data is to be selected

- **WHERE**   Provides conditions for the selection of rows in the results
- **ORDER BY**   Specifies the order in which rows are to be returned
- **GROUP BY**   Groups rows for various aggregate functions

Although it is customary in SQL to write keywords in uppercase, this is not necessary in most implementations. The RDBMS SQL interpreter will usually recognize keywords written in uppercase, lowercase, or mixed case. In Oracle SQL, all database object names (tables, views, synonyms, and so on) may be written in any case, but Oracle automatically changes them to uppercase during processing because all Oracle database object names are stored in uppercase in Oracle's metadata unless the names are enclosed in double-quotes. Be careful with other versions of SQL, however. For example, both Sybase ASE and Microsoft SQL Server can be set to a case-sensitive mode, where object names written in different cases are treated as *different* objects. Also, MySQL is case-sensitive on platforms that are case-sensitive, such as Unix and Linux. In case-sensitive mode, the following would be considered *different* tables: EMPLOYEES, Employees, employees.

The topics that follow provide descriptions and examples of ways to use the SELECT statement to retrieve data from the database. This is not intended to be an exhaustive survey of the capabilities of the SELECT statement, but rather an overview to acquaint you with its extensive capabilities. The figures used to illustrate the examples all use the Oracle 10*g* XE HR sample schema and the SQL Commands option within Application Express. SQL is best learned by trying it, so I urge you to try these examples as you read.

Listing All Rows and Columns

The asterisk (*) symbol may be used in place of a column list to select all columns in a table or view. This is a useful feature for listing data quickly, but it should be avoided in statements that will be reused, because any new column will be automatically selected the next time the statement is run, which compromises logical data independence. Note also that in SQL syntax, tables, views, and *synonyms* (an alias for a table or view) are all referenced in the same way. This is because the names of these come for the same *namespace,* meaning that a name of a table, for example, must be unique among all tables, views, and synonyms defined in particular schema. Figure 4-8 shows an SQL statement that uses the SELECT * clause to list all rows and columns in the EMPLOYEES table along with part of the query results. Here is the SQL statement:

```
SELECT *
  FROM EMPLOYEES;
```

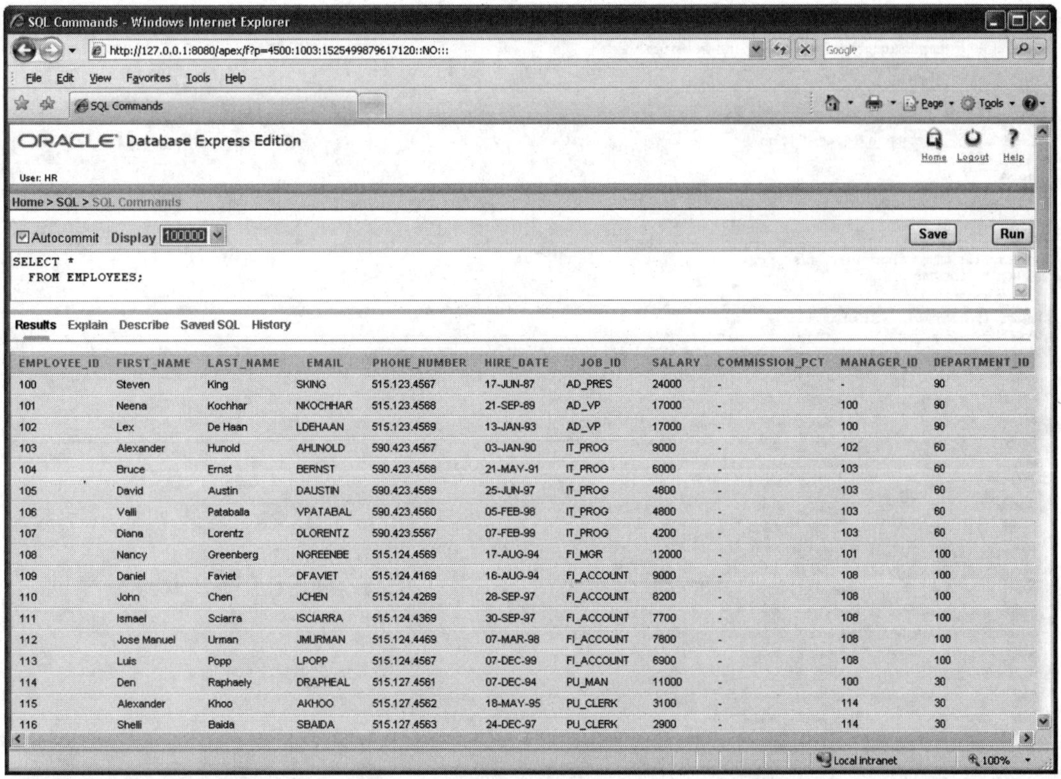

Figure 4-8 Using SELECT * to list all rows and columns of the EMPLOYEES table

This is the simplest form of the SELECT statement, using only the SELECT and FROM clauses. Note that I changed the Display setting on the SQL Commands page from the default of 10 to a much higher value (100,000) because the EMPLOYEES table contains 107 rows and, using the default, only the first 10 rows would appear in the query results. No computer screen is large enough to show a result set this large, so you'll have to use the scroll bar along the right edge of the page to scroll through all the rows in the result set.

Limiting Columns to Display

To specify the columns to be selected, provide a comma-separated list following the **SELECT** keyword instead of an asterisk. Keep in mind that the list in the SELECT clause actually provides *expressions* that describe the columns desired in the query results, and although many times these expressions are merely column names from tables or views,

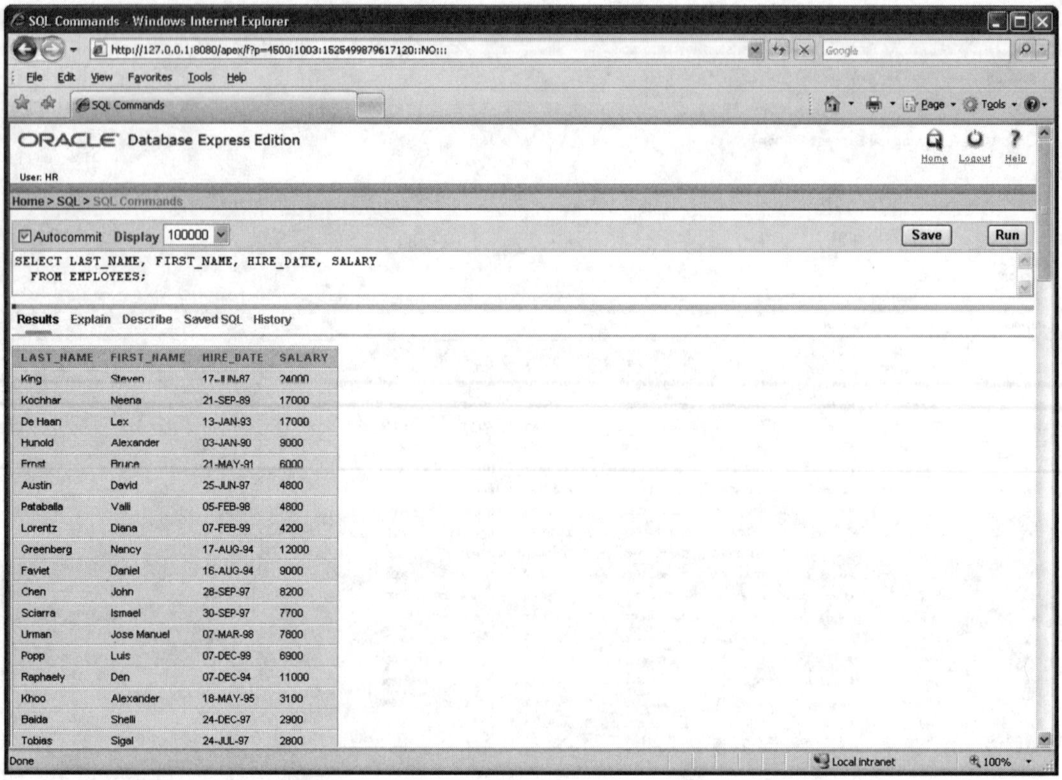

Figure 4-9   Selecting four columns from the EMPLOYEES table

they may also be any constant or formula that SQL can interpret and form into data values for the column. Examples later in this chapter show you how to use formulas and constants to form query columns. Figure 4-9 shows the SQL for selecting the LAST_NAME, FIRST_NAME, HIRE_DATE, and SALARY columns from the EMPLOYEES table along with partial query results. Here is the SQL statement:

```
SELECT LAST_NAME, FIRST_NAME, HIRE_DATE, SALARY
  FROM EMPLOYEES;
```

Sorting Results

Just as with Microsoft Access queries, with SQL there is no guarantee as to the sequence of the rows in the query results unless the desired sequence is specified in the query. In SQL, providing a comma-separated list following the **ORDER BY** keyword does this.

Figure 4-10 shows the SQL from the preceding example with row sequencing added. Here is the SQL statement:

```
SELECT LAST_NAME, FIRST_NAME, HIRE_DATE, SALARY
  FROM EMPLOYEES
 ORDER BY LAST_NAME, FIRST_NAME;
```

Note the following points:

- Ascending sequence is the default for each column, but the keyword **ASC** can be added after the column name for ascending sequence, and **DESC** can be added for descending sequence.

- The column(s) named in the **ORDER BY** list do not have to be included in the query results (that is, the **SELECT** list). However, this is not the best human engineering.

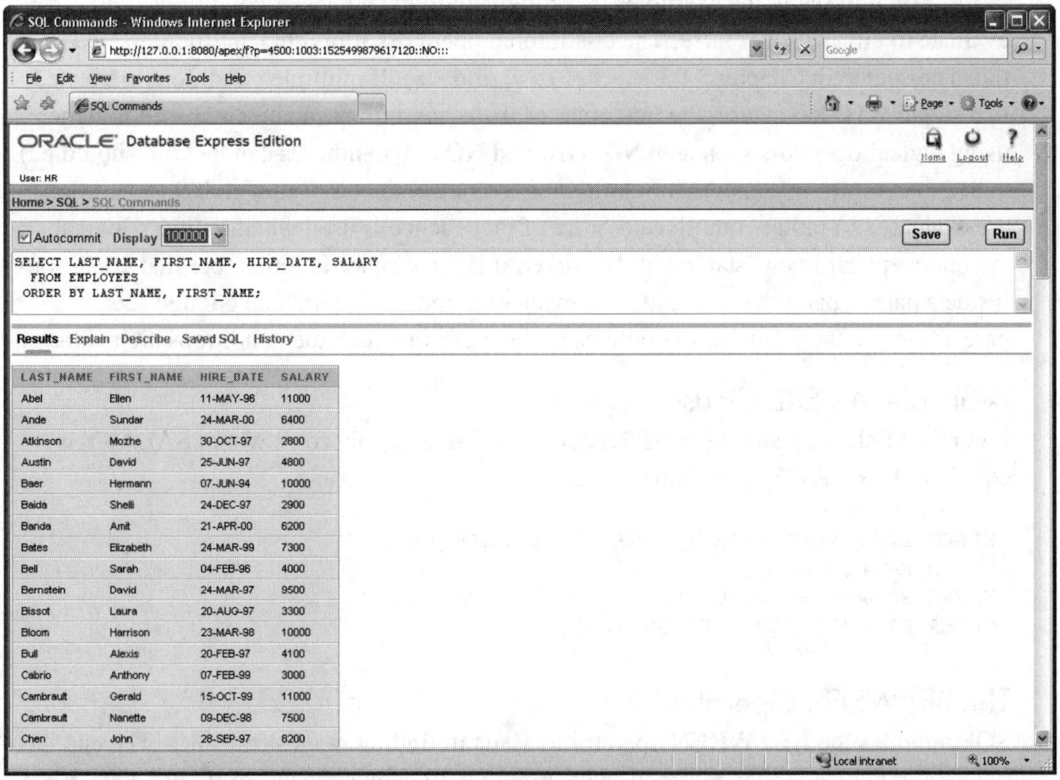

Figure 4-10   EMPLOYEES table query with ORDER BY clause added

● Instead of column names, the relative position of the columns in the results can be listed. The number provided has no correlation with the column position in the source table or view, however. This option is frowned upon in formal SQL because someone changing the query at a later time might shuffle columns around in the SELECT list and not realize that, in doing so, they are changing the columns used for sorting results. In this example, another ORDER BY clause can be used to achieve the same query results: ORDER BY 1,2.

Choosing Rows to Display

SQL uses the WHERE clause for the selection of rows to display. Without a WHERE clause, all rows found in the source tables and/or views are displayed. When a WHERE clause is included, the rules of Boolean algebra, named for logician George Boole, are used to evaluate the WHERE clause for each row of data. Only rows for which the WHERE clause evaluates to a logical *true* are displayed in the query results.

As you will see in the examples that follow, individual tests of conditions must evaluate to either *true* or *false*. The conditional operators supported are the same as those presented in Chapter 3 (**=, <, <=, >, >=, and <>**). If multiple conditions are tested in a single WHERE clause, the outcomes of these conditions can be combined together using logical operators such as **AND**, **OR**, and **NOT**. Parentheses can be (and should be) added to complex statements for clarity and to control the order in which the conditions are evaluated. A rather complicated order of precedence is used when multiple logical operators appear in one statement. However, it is far simpler to remember that conditions inside a pair of parentheses are always evaluated first, and to include enough sets of parentheses so there can be no doubt as to the order in which the conditions are evaluated.

A Simple WHERE Clause

Figure 4-11 shows a simple WHERE clause that selects only rows where SALARY is equal to 11000. The SQL statement used is

```
SELECT LAST_NAME, FIRST_NAME, HIRE_DATE, SALARY
  FROM EMPLOYEES
 WHERE SALARY = 11000
 ORDER BY LAST_NAME, FIRST_NAME;
```

The BETWEEN Operator

SQL provides the **BETWEEN** operator to assist in finding ranges of values. The end points *are* included in the returned rows. Figure 4-12 shows the use of the **BETWEEN**

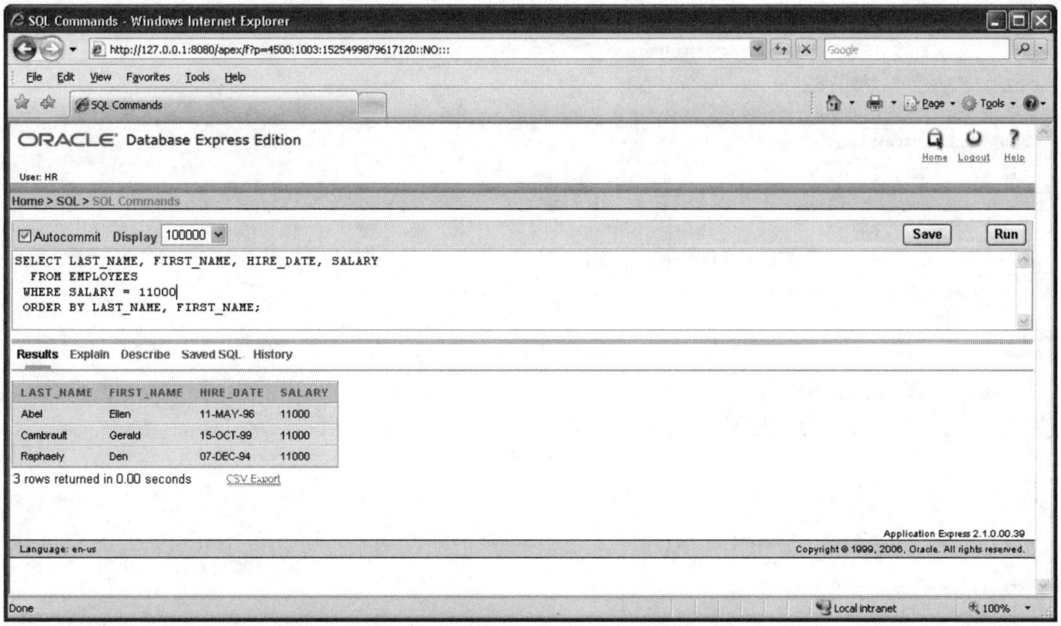

Figure 4-11 SELECT with a simple WHERE clause

operator to find all rows where SALARY is greater than or equal to 10000 and SALARY is less than or equal to 11000. Here is the SQL statement:

```
SELECT LAST_NAME, FIRST_NAME, HIRE_DATE, SALARY
  FROM EMPLOYEES
 WHERE SALARY BETWEEN 10000 AND 11000
 ORDER BY LAST_NAME, FIRST_NAME;
```

Here's an alternative way to write an equivalent WHERE clause:

```
        WHERE SALARY >= 10000
          AND SALARY <= 11000
```

The LIKE Operator

For searching character columns, SQL provides the **LIKE** operator, which compares the character string in the column to a pattern, returning a logical *true* if the column matches the pattern, and *false* if not. The underscore character (_) can be used as a positional *wildcard*, meaning it matches any character in that position of the character string being evaluated. The percent sign (%) can be used as a nonpositional wildcard, meaning it matches any

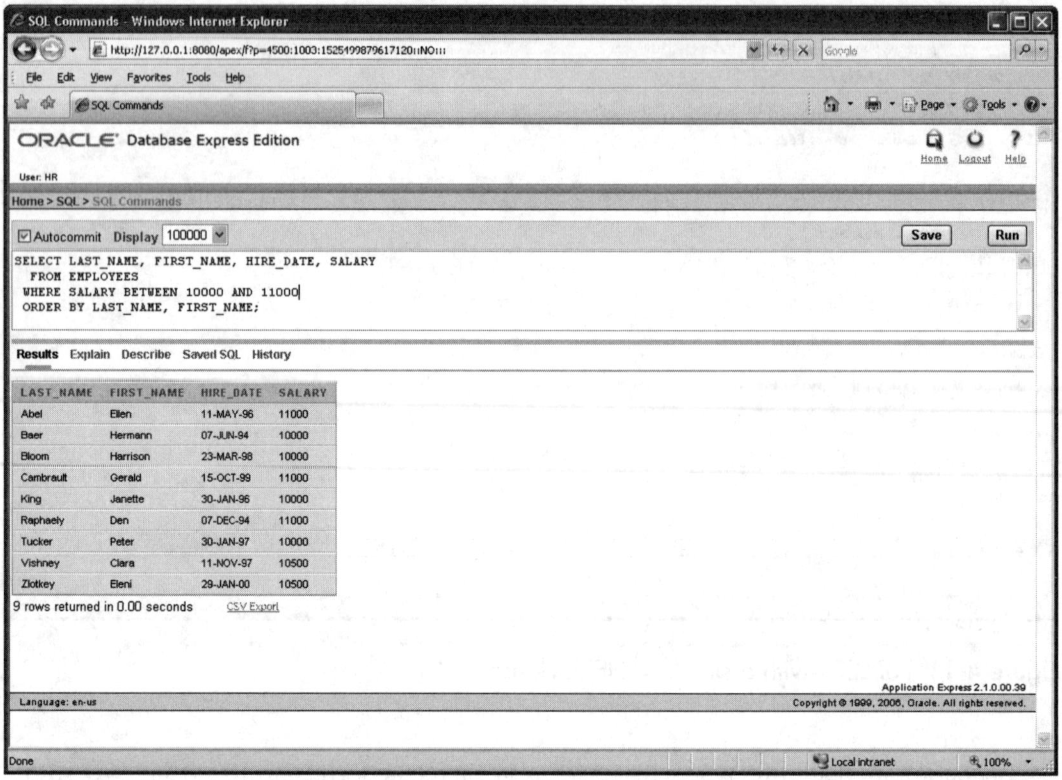

Figure 4-12   SELECT using the BETWEEN operator

number of characters for any length. Note that Microsoft Access uses a similar feature, but the wildcard characters are different (they match those in DOS and Visual Basic): The question mark (?) is the positional wildcard, and the asterisk (*) is the nonpositional wildcard. The following table provides some examples:

Pattern	Interpretation
%Now	Matches any character string that ends with *Now*
Now%	Matches any character string that begins with *Now*
%Now%	Matches any character string that contains *Now* (whether at the beginning, the middle, or the end)
N_w	Matches any string of exactly three characters, where the first character is *N* and the third character is *w*
%N_w%	Matches any string that contains the character *N* followed by any character, which is in turn followed by the character *w* and continues with any number of characters

Figure 4-13 shows the use of the **LIKE** operator to display only rows where the FIRST_NAME column starts with the text *Pete*. Here is the SQL statement:

```
SELECT LAST_NAME, FIRST_NAME, HIRE_DATE, SALARY
  FROM EMPLOYEES
 WHERE FIRST_NAME LIKE 'Pete%'
 ORDER BY LAST_NAME, FIRST_NAME;
```

Compound Conditions Using OR

As stated earlier, multiple conditions can be combined using the **OR** operator. Figure 4-14 shows a WHERE clause that selects rows having either a FIRST_NAME column beginning with *Pete* or a SALARY column that is between 10000 and 20000 inclusive. The SQL statement is:

```
SELECT LAST_NAME, FIRST_NAME, HIRE_DATE, SALARY
  FROM EMPLOYEES
 WHERE FIRST_NAME LIKE 'Pete%'
    OR SALARY BETWEEN 10000 AND 11000
 ORDER BY LAST_NAME, FIRST_NAME;
```

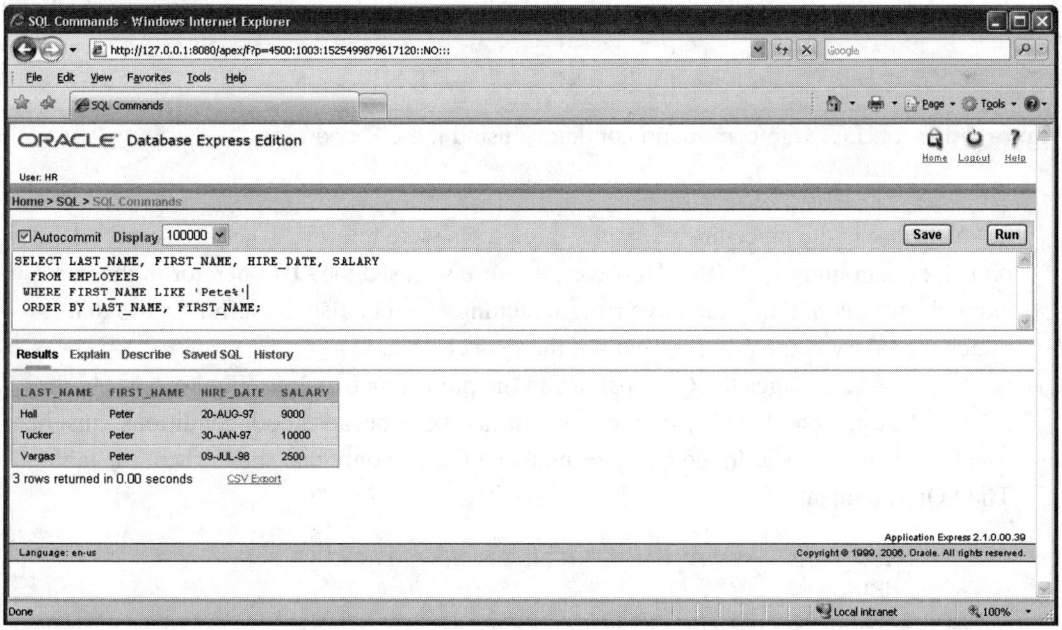

Figure 4-13 SELECT using the LIKE operator

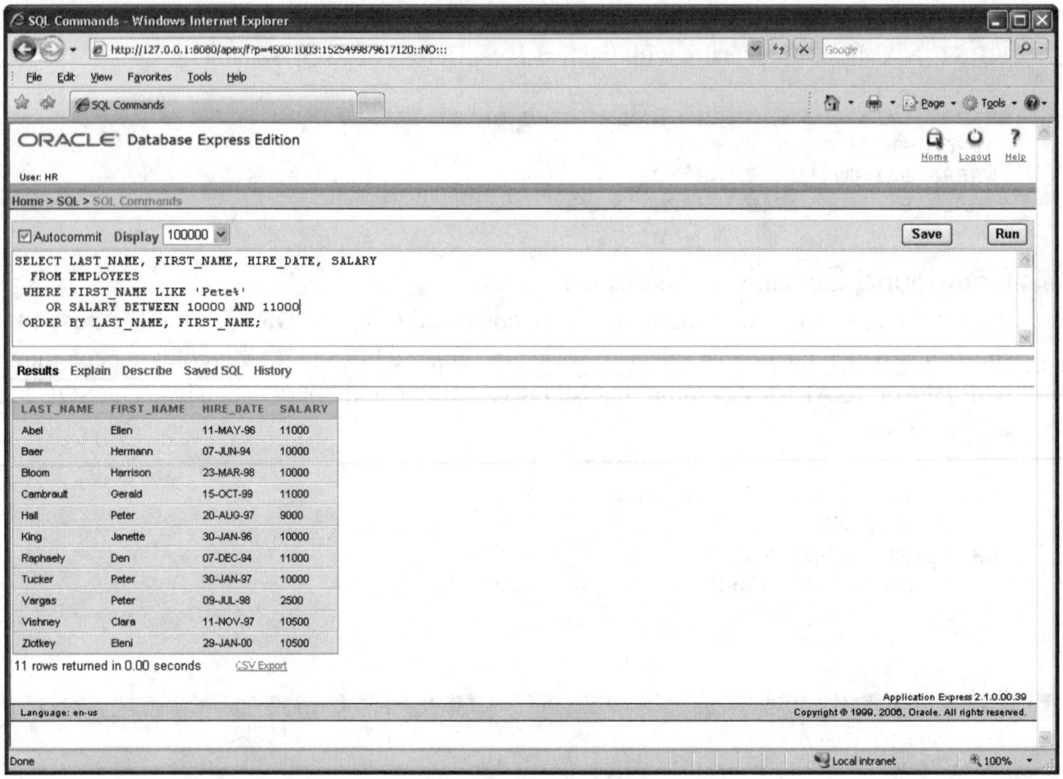

Figure 4-14 SELECT with compound conditions using the OR operator

Note that in the preceding example, three rows were returned when we searched only on names beginning with *Pete*. However, because we used the **OR** operator in the latest example, we get not only the three rows matching *Pete* but also eight more rows that match the salary range provided but not the *Pete* criteria.

Figure 4-15 changes the **OR** operator in the preceding example (Figure 4-14) to the **AND** operator. Note that only one row is returned now, because both conditions must be true for a row to appear in the query results, and there is only one such row in the table. The SQL statement is:

```
SELECT LAST_NAME, FIRST_NAME, HIRE_DATE, SALARY
  FROM EMPLOYEES
 WHERE FIRST_NAME LIKE 'Pete%'
   AND SALARY BETWEEN 10000 AND 11000
 ORDER BY LAST_NAME, FIRST_NAME;
```

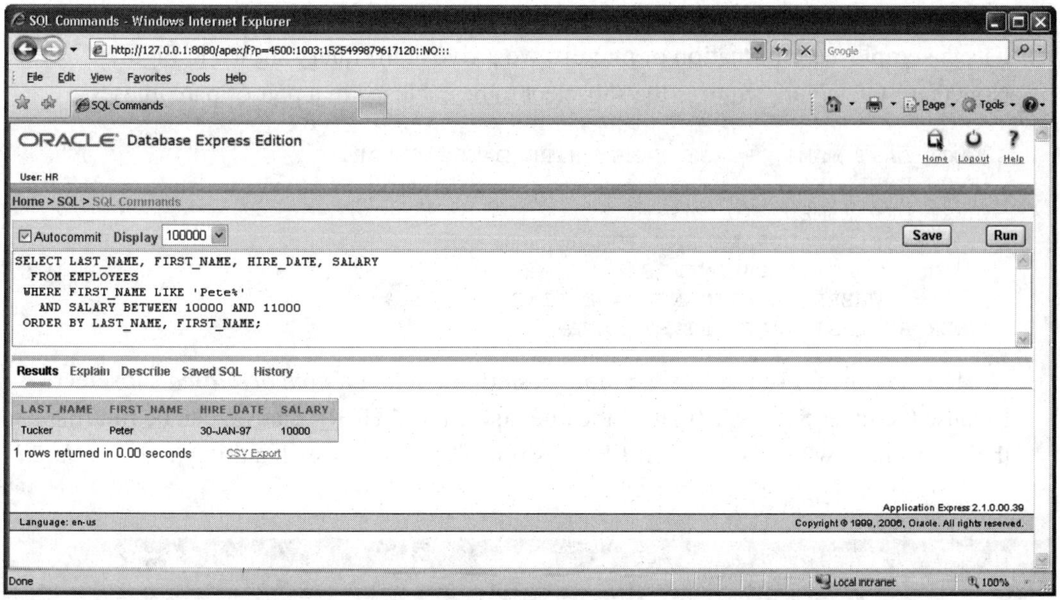

Figure 4-15 SELECT with compound conditions using the AND operator

The Subselect

A very powerful feature of SQL is the *subselect* (or *subquery),* which, as the name implies, refers to a SELECT statement that contains a subordinate SELECT statement. This can be a very flexible way of selecting data.

Let's assume that we want to list all employees who work in sales. The dilemma is that the DEPARTMENTS table in the sample HR schema contains several sales departments, including Sales, Government Sales, and Retail Sales. We could place literals for those three department names or their corresponding department IDs in the WHERE clause of our SELECT statement. However, the problem we then face is maintenance of the query if a sales-related department is subsequently added or eliminated. A safer approach is to use an SQL query to find the applicable department IDs when the query is run and then use that list of IDs to find the employees. The query to find the department IDs is simple enough:

```
SELECT DEPARTMENT_ID
  FROM DEPARTMENTS
 WHERE DEPARTMENT_NAME LIKE '%Sales%';
```

If we place the preceding SELECT statement in the WHERE clause of a query that lists the employee information of interest, we arrive at the query shown in Figure 4-16. Note that SQL syntax requires the subselect to be enclosed in a pair of parentheses:

```
SELECT LAST_NAME, FIRST_NAME, HIRE_DATE, SALARY
  FROM EMPLOYEES
 WHERE DEPARTMENT_ID IN
       (SELECT DEPARTMENT_ID
          FROM DEPARTMENTS
         WHERE DEPARTMENT_NAME LIKE '%Sales%')
 ORDER BY LAST_NAME, FIRST_NAME;
```

The statement used in this example is said to contain a *noncorrelated* subselect because the inner SELECT (that is, the one inside the WHERE clause) can be run first and the results used when the outer SELECT is run. There also is such a thing as a *correlated*

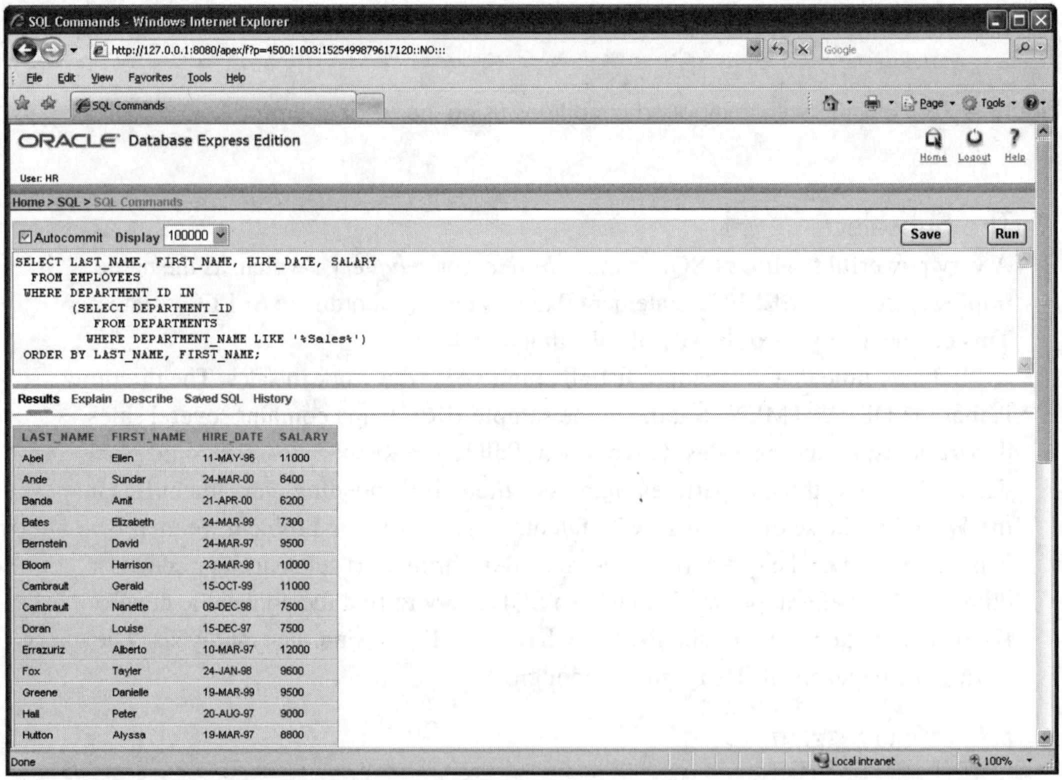

Figure 4-16 SELECT with a subselect

subselect (or subquery), where the outer query must be invoked multiple times—once for each row found in the inner query. Consider this example:

```
SELECT LAST_NAME, FIRST_NAME, SALARY, DEPARTMENT_ID
  FROM EMPLOYEES A
 WHERE SALARY >
         (SELECT AVG(SALARY)
            FROM EMPLOYEES B
           WHERE A.DEPARTMENT_ID = B.DEPARTMENT_ID);
```

This query finds all employees whose salary is above the average salary for their department. The inner SELECT finds the average salary for each department. The outer SELECT is then executed for each row returned from the inner SELECT (that is, for each department) to find all employees for that department whose salary is above the average for that department. You may recognize the **AVG** function, which was introduced back in Chapter 3. We will review using aggregate functions in an upcoming SQL example.

Joining Tables

As you learned in Chapter 3, you need to join tables (or views) whenever you need data from more than one table in your query results. In SQL, you specify joins either by listing the tables or views to be joined in a comma-separated list in the FROM clause of the SELECT statement or by using the newer JOIN clause in conjunction with the FROM clause. In this section, you will explore those options in detail.

The Cartesian Product

When specifying joins, it is important to tell the RDBMS how to match rows in the tables (or views) being joined. However, SQL does not remind you to do so. If you forget,

Ask the Expert

Q: Are any performance issues associated with subselects?

A: Yes, performance issues can be associated with subselects. In general, the more rows the inner SELECT returns, the higher the risk of a performance problem. This is especially true with correlated subselects because the outer SELECT must be run for every row returned by the subselect.

you will get a Cartesian product (named for French mathematician René Descartes), as shown in this SQL statement and Figure 4-17:

```
SELECT EMPLOYEE_ID, LAST_NAME, FIRST_NAME, DEPARTMENT_NAME
    FROM EMPLOYEES, DEPARTMENTS;
```

Whenever you write a new query, you should apply a "reasonableness" test to the results. The SQL query in Figure 4-17 looks fine on the surface, but if you scroll to the bottom of the result set, you will see that 2889 rows are returned by the query. When you consider that there are only 107 employees, you realize something is horribly wrong. How could the query possibly result in 2889 rows simply by joining employees and departments? The answer: this query failed to include a join specification in either the WHERE clause or JOIN clause, so the RDBMS created a Cartesian product, joining each employee with *every* department, and 27 departments times 107 employees yields 2889 (27 * 107) rows. Oops!

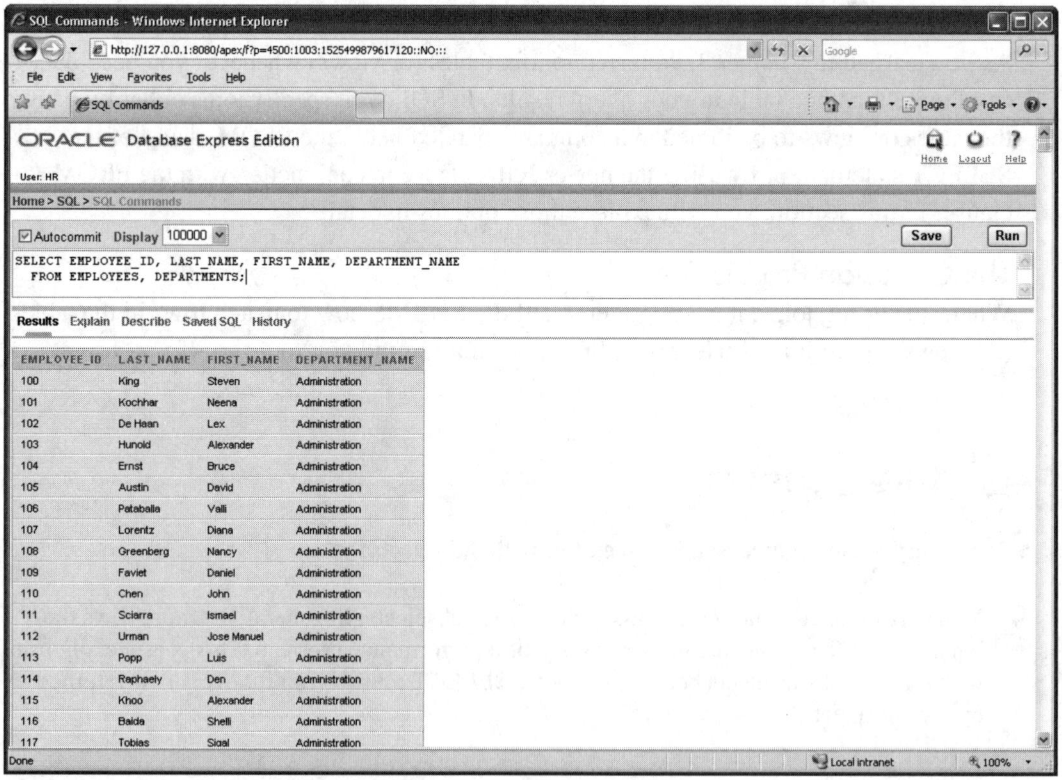

Figure 4-17   Join resulting in a Cartesian product

The Inner Join of Two Tables

Figure 4-18 shows the correction, which involves adding a WHERE clause that tells the DBMS to match the DEPARTMENT_ID column in the EMPLOYEES table (the foreign key) to the DEPARTMENT_ID column in the DEPARTMENTS table (the primary key). The corrected SQL statement is shown here:

```
SELECT EMPLOYEE_ID, LAST_NAME, FIRST_NAME, DEPARTMENT_NAME
  FROM EMPLOYEES, DEPARTMENTS
 WHERE EMPLOYEES.DEPARTMENT_ID = DEPARTMENTS.DEPARTMENT_ID;
```

This gets a much more reasonable result, with 106 rows. If you scroll through the results, you can see that each employee is only listed once. You may notice that one row is missing, since 107 employees exist. The reason for this and the modification to the query so that all 107 employees are displayed is covered in next topic, "The Outer Join."

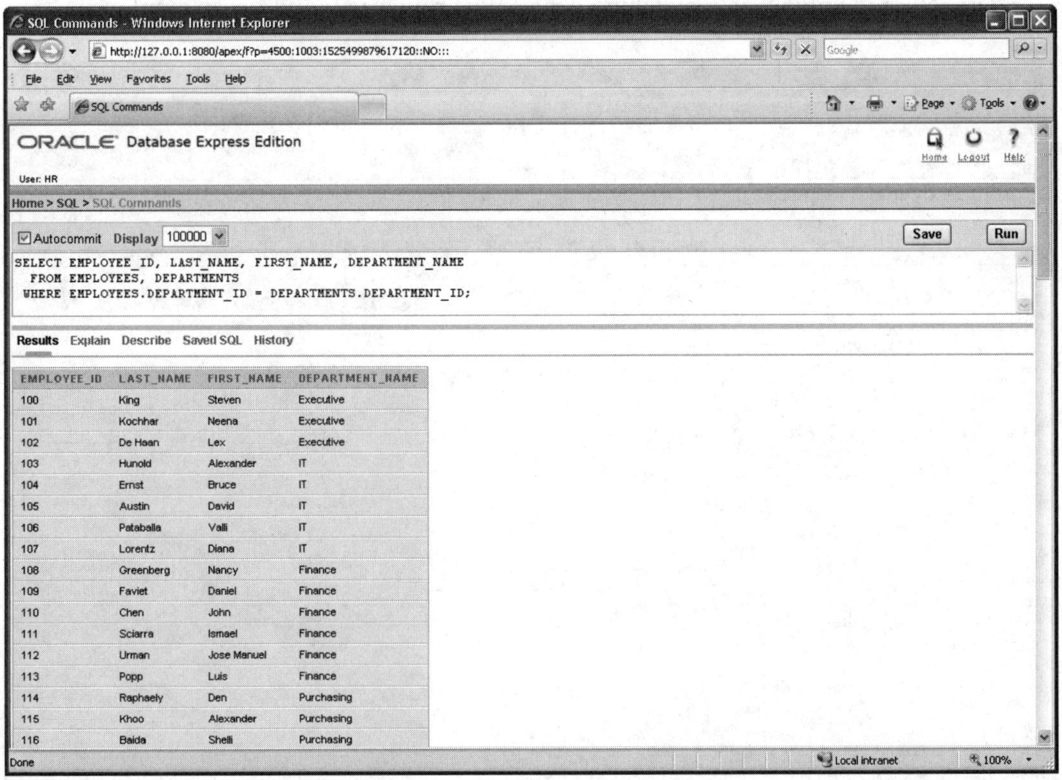

Figure 4-18   Inner join of two tables using the WHERE clause

Placing the join condition in the WHERE clause was the original join method in SQL. However, a JOIN clause has been added to the SQL standard and is now the preferred method for writing join conditions. The JOIN clause not only improves readability by separating the join condition from conditions intended to filter unwanted rows out of the result set, but it is also more flexible, as you will see in upcoming examples. Figure 4-19 shows the SQL statement from Figure 4-18 rewritten to use the JOIN clause. Note that the query results are exactly the same. Here is the modified SQL statement:

```
SELECT EMPLOYEE_ID, LAST_NAME, FIRST_NAME, DEPARTMENT_NAME
   FROM EMPLOYEES JOIN DEPARTMENTS
      ON EMPLOYEES.DEPARTMENT_ID = DEPARTMENTS.DEPARTMENT_ID;
```

The Outer Join

The queries shown in Figures 4-18 and 4-19 returned only 106 employees, and yet 107 rows exist in the EMPLOYEES table. This result is because we performed an inner join. Rows were returned only when a matching department row was found for an employee—and

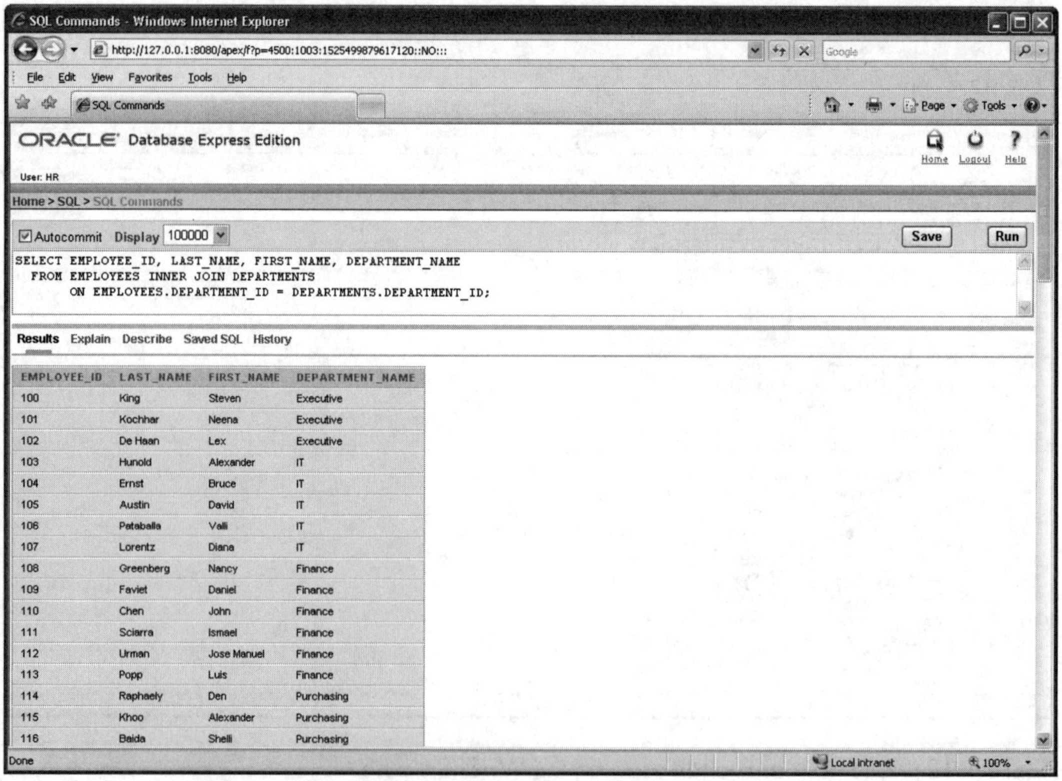

Figure 4-19 Inner join of the two tables using the JOIN clause

there is one employee (Kimberely Grant) who is not assigned to a department. We can correct this problem by changing our inner join to an outer join. Using an outer join, we can retrieve all rows from the EMPLOYEES table, even if no matching row is found in the DEPARTMENTS table for some employees.

The syntax for outer joins can be a little confusing, because three variations exist: left, right, and full outer joins. However, if you remember that the modifier merely indicates which table in the JOIN clause is to have all rows returned (regardless of whether there are matching rows in the other table), you will no longer be confused. A left outer join (the most common form) returns all rows from the table named to the left of (before) the **JOIN** keyword; a right outer join returns all rows from the table named to the right of (after) the **JOIN** keyword; and a full outer join returns all rows from both tables. Figure 4-20 shows the join used in Figure 4-19 changed into a left outer join so that all employees are

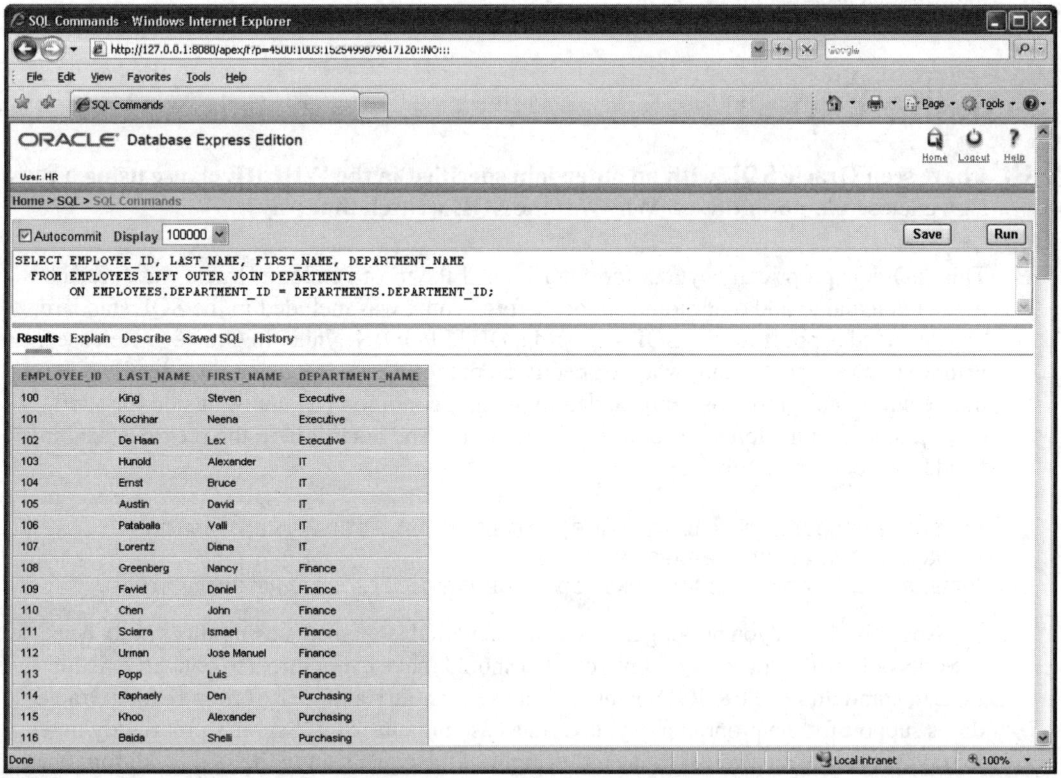

Figure 4-20   Left outer join of the EMPLOYEES and DEPARTMENTS tables

included in the results, including those for which no department has been assigned using this SQL statement:

```
SELECT EMPLOYEE_ID, LAST_NAME, FIRST_NAME, DEPARTMENT_NAME
  FROM EMPLOYEES LEFT OUTER JOIN DEPARTMENTS
    ON EMPLOYEES.DEPARTMENT_ID = DEPARTMENTS.DEPARTMENT_ID;
```

Limiting Join Results

The WHERE clause can be easily used to add conditions to limit rows returned from a query that also involves joins. Figure 4-21 shows a modification to the query from Figure 4-20 such that only employees who work in departments with *Sales* in the department name are returned. Here is the modified SQL:

```
SELECT EMPLOYEE_ID, LAST_NAME, FIRST_NAME, DEPARTMENT_NAME
  FROM EMPLOYEES LEFT OUTER JOIN DEPARTMENTS
    ON EMPLOYEES.DEPARTMENT_ID = DEPARTMENTS.DEPARTMENT_ID
 WHERE DEPARTMENT_NAME LIKE '%Sales%';
```

Ask the Expert

Q: I have seen Oracle SQL with an outer join specified in the WHERE clause using a plus sign enclosed in parentheses. Why was the SQL written that way?

A: This is Oracle proprietary syntax for outer joins. Like most vendors, Oracle was forced by market demand to add outer join support before syntax was included in the SQL standard. Oracle added support for the SQL standard's OUTER JOIN syntax in Oracle 9*i* Release 2. Prior to that release, the only way to specify an outer join was by using proprietary syntax that required the symbol (+) to be added to the join condition (on the right side for a left outer join and on the left side for a right outer join). The outer join in the previous example would thus be written this way:

```
SELECT EMPLOYEE_ID, LAST_NAME, FIRST_NAME, DEPARTMENT_NAME
  FROM EMPLOYEES, DEPARTMENTS
 WHERE EMPLOYEES.DEPARTMENT_ID = DEPARTMENTS.DEPARTMENT_ID(+);
```

Not only should you no longer be writing new SQL statements using this syntax because it works only with Oracle SQL, but you also should make every effort to convert existing SQL to standard OUTER JOIN syntax because it is only a matter of time before Oracle drops support for the proprietary syntax. As a case in point, SQL Server's proprietary outer join syntax (using an asterisk to the left or right of the equal sign in the join condition) was deprecated as of SQL Server 2005, causing lots of problems for those wanting to convert to the newer release, unless they ran the new database in compatibility mode.

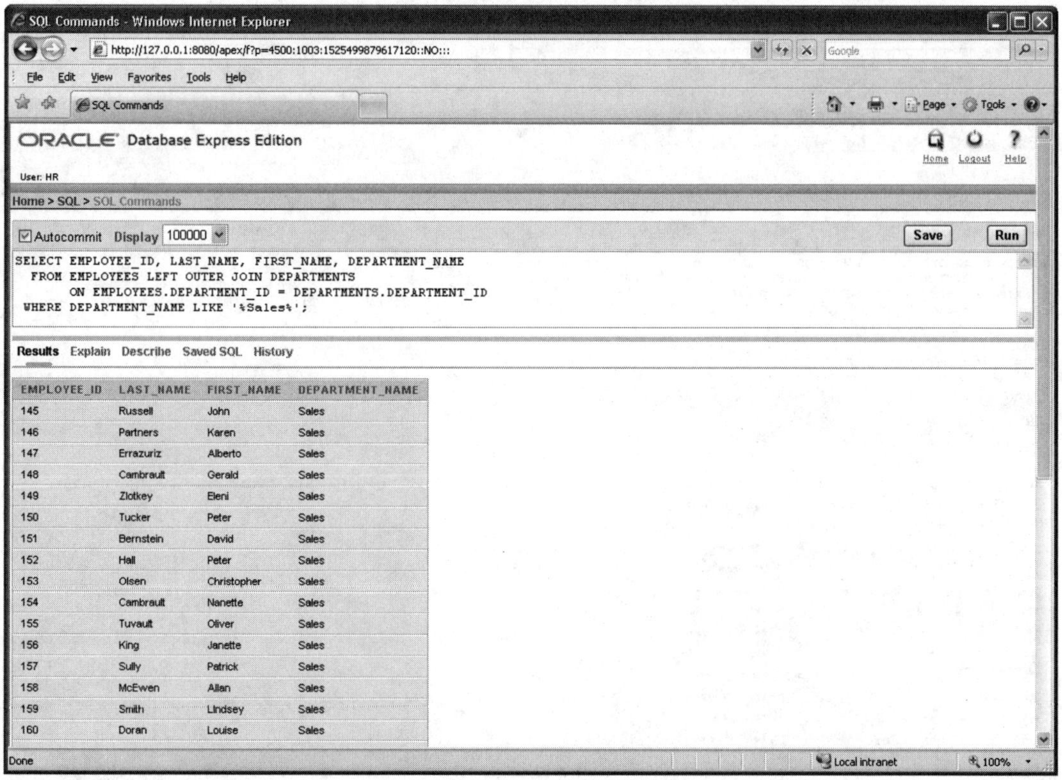

Figure 4-21 Outer join with WHERE clause condition added

The Self-Join

When a table has a recursive relationship, you need to join the table to itself in order to follow the relationship in your query results. The EMPLOYEES table has such a relationship in that the MANAGER_ID column contains the EMPLOYEE_ID value of the employee to whom each employee reports. In our example, every employee has a manager in the table except for the owner of the company (Steven King), so the query is written using an outer join, as shown in Figure 4-22. By the way, it is very common in recursive relationships for some rows not to have parents; otherwise, you would never be able to insert the first row into the table. Here is the SQL statement:

```
SELECT A.EMPLOYEE_ID, A.LAST_NAME, A.FIRST_NAME,
       B.FIRST_NAME || ' ' || B.LAST_NAME AS MANAGER_NAME
  FROM EMPLOYEES A LEFT OUTER JOIN EMPLOYEES B
       ON A.MANAGER_ID = B.EMPLOYEE_ID;
```

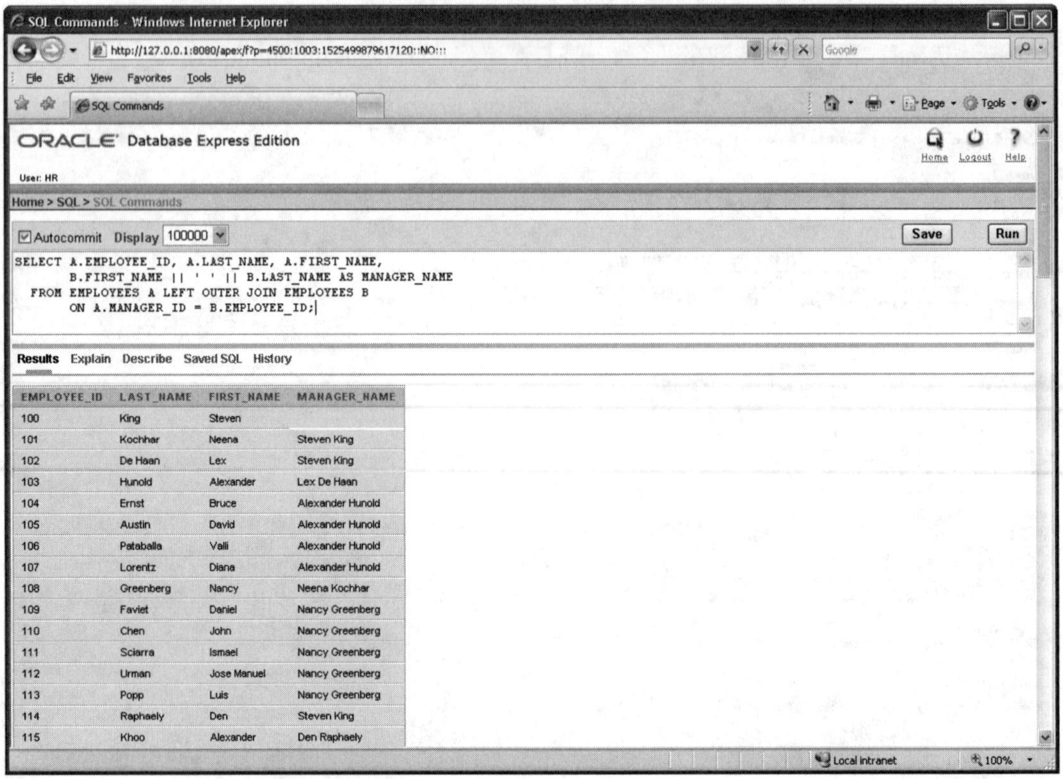

Figure 4-22 SELECT containing a self-join

Note that we added another wrinkle to this example by concatenating the first and last names of the manager with a space in between to form the MANAGER_NAME column in the results. The SQL standard concatenation operator is ||, but SQL Server requires + instead. The column name is assigned using the keyword **AS** followed by the desired name. (Actually the keyword **AS** is optional in Oracle SQL, so you can just leave a space after the column expression and add the desired column name. However, it's better to include it always, because some SQL implementations require it.) If a column name were not assigned in this manner, the RDBMS would have to make one up (every column in the result set must have a valid column name), so it is better to assign one any time a column in a query is formed using an expression instead of a simple column name.

Aggregate Functions

As you will recall from Chapter 3, aggregate functions combine the values in multiple rows. In this section, you will explore them in detail.

Simple Aggregate Functions

In Figure 4-23, aggregate functions are used to find the minimum, maximum, and average salaries for all employees along with a count of the total number of employees. Here is the SQL statement used:

```
SELECT MIN(SALARY), MAX(SALARY), AVG(SALARY), COUNT(*)
  FROM EMPLOYEES;
```

Because no GROUP BY clause is used to group rows, the entire table is considered one group, so only one row is returned in the result set. You may have noticed the value returned by the **AVG(SALARY)** function—the SQL engine does not round results unless you ask it to, so a **ROUND** function is added to it in the next example to improve the readability of the results.

Mixed Aggregate and Normal Columns (Error)

If you add DEPARTMENT_ID to the query without adding a GROUP BY clause, the query returns an error message, as shown in Figure 4-24, (not a single-group group function) which is rather cryptic. What it is trying to point out is that the query contains only a single group (the entire table) because there is no GROUP BY clause, and it also

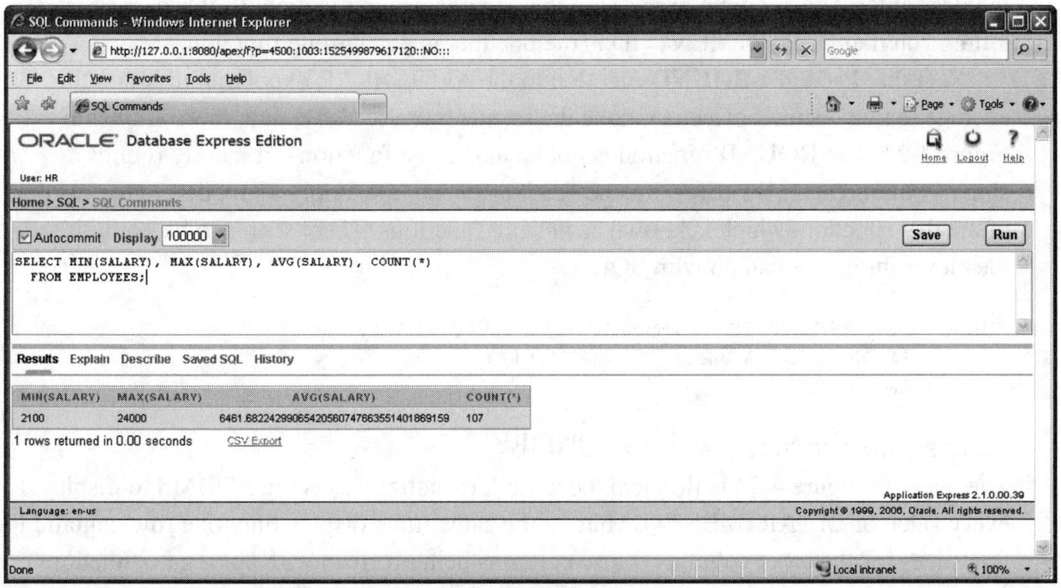

Figure 4-23   SELECT with simple aggregate functions

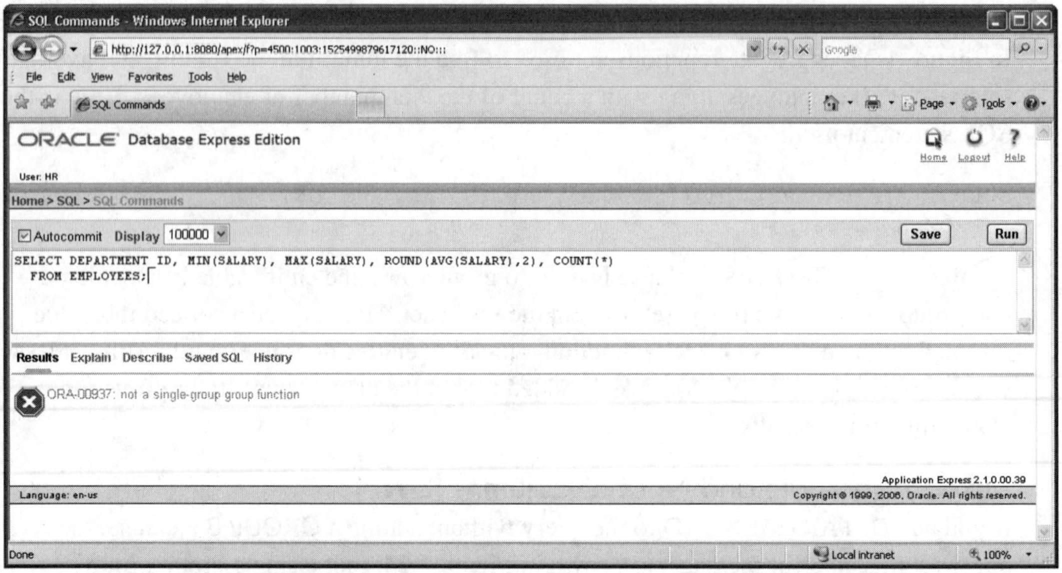

Figure 4-24   Error caused by mixing aggregate functions and normal columns without grouping

includes at least one column expression that is not a group function. In this case, it is telling you that DEPARTMENT_ID is the one that is not a group function.

Note that I added a **ROUND** function to the AVG(SALARY) column to round the average to two decimal places to make the results more readable than those shown in Figure 4-23. The **ROUND** function is *not* an aggregate function—it merely rounds a single column value. However, it is perfectly acceptable to apply a function to the results of another function, which is known as *nesting* functions. There seems to be no limit to the clever things we can do with SQL:

```
SELECT DEPARTMENT_ID, MIN(SALARY), MAX(SALARY),
       ROUND(AVG(SALARY),2), COUNT(*)
  FROM EMPLOYEES;
```

Aggregate Functions with GROUP BY

The query in Figure 4-24 is illogical, because it essentially asks the RDBMS to display every value of DEPARTMENT_ID but, at the same time, display only one row containing the values for the other columns (those columns being formed with aggregate functions). To remedy the situation, we must tell the RDBMS that we want to *group* the rows by DEPARTMENT_ID, and for each *group* display the DEPARTMENT_ID along with the aggregate column results (the minimum, maximum, and average salaries for the department and the count of the number of employees in the department). The corrected query is shown here and in Figure 4-25:

```
SELECT DEPARTMENT_ID, MIN(SALARY), MAX(SALARY),
       ROUND(AVG(SALARY),2), COUNT(*)
  FROM EMPLOYEES
 GROUP BY DEPARTMENT_ID;
```

The GROUP BY clause returns only one row per department, but those rows will not necessarily be in department ID sequence—and looking at Figure 4-25, you can see that the rows are not in any particular sequence. The lesson here is always to include an ORDER BY when you want the rows in the query results returned in a particular sequence.

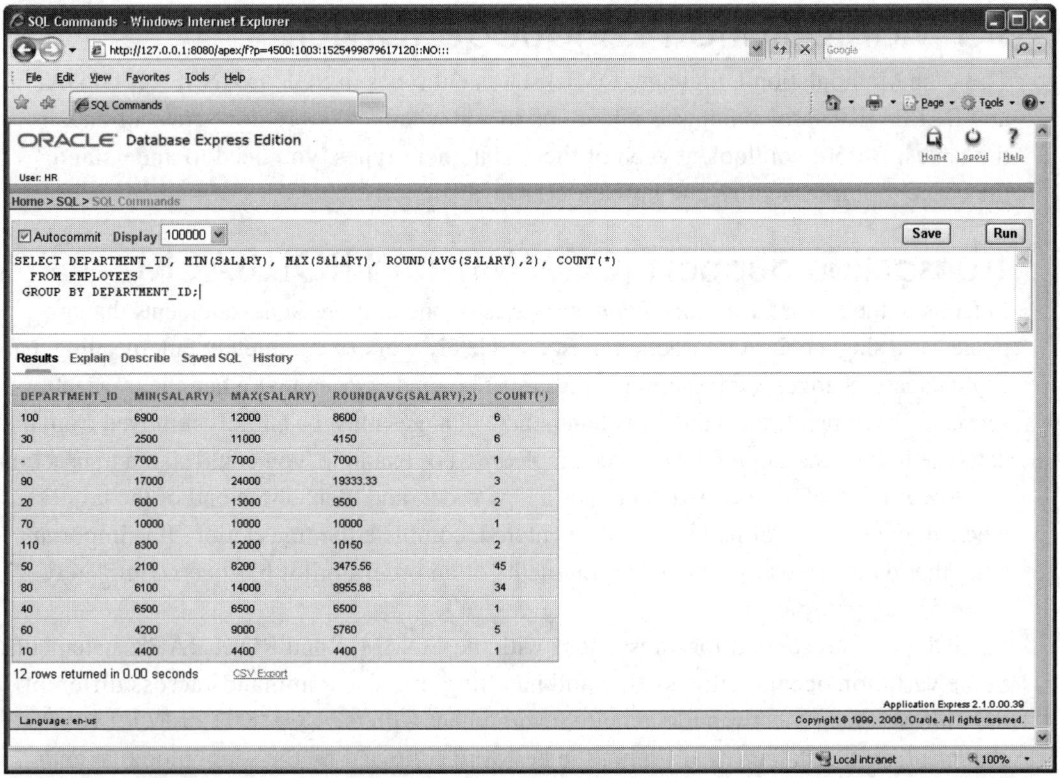

Figure 4-25 SELECT with aggregate functions and a GROUP BY clause

Ask the Expert

Q: I recall that the ORDER BY clause provides a list of column names to be used in sequencing the rows in a query's result set. Can I use it to sort on columns formed using functions and other expressions?

A: Yes, you can use result set columns formed using expressions in the ORDER BY clause. Simply repeat the entire expression in the ORDER BY clause. For example, if you wanted to change the query shown in Figure 4-25 to display the rows in descending sequence by the maximum salary in the department, you can do so by adding this ORDER BY clause:

```
ORDER BY MAX(SALARY) DESC
```

Data Manipulation Language (DML)

The Data Manipulation Language (DML) statement types in SQL are INSERT, UPDATE, and DELETE. These commands allow you to add, change, and remove rows of data in the tables. Before you look at each of these statement types, you need to understand the concept of transactions and how the RDBMS supports them.

Transaction Support (COMMIT and ROLLBACK)

In terms of the RDBMS, a *transaction* is a series of one or more SQL statements that are treated as a single unit. A transaction must completely work or completely fail, meaning that any database changes a transaction makes must be made permanent when the transaction successfully completes. On the other hand, these changes must be entirely removed from the database if the transaction fails before completion. For example, you could start a transaction at the beginning of a process that creates a new order, and then, at the end of the process when all the order information has been entered, complete the transaction. It is important that other database users do not see fragments of an order until it has been completely entered and confirmed.

SQL provides support for transactions with the COMMIT and ROLLBACK statements. Some variation occurs in the syntax and handling of these commands across different RDBMS vendors. Most vendors require no argument with the COMMIT or ROLLBACK statement, so the statement is simply the keyword followed by the semicolon that ends every SQL statement.

In Oracle, a transaction is implicitly started for a database user session as soon as the user submits a statement that changes any data (that is, an INSERT, UPDATE or DELETE statement, but not a SELECT statement). At any time, the database user can issue a COMMIT, which makes all the database changes completed up to that point permanent and therefore visible to any other database user. The user can also issue a ROLLBACK, which reverses any changes made to the database. The COMMIT and ROLLBACK statements not only end one transaction, but they also set the stage for a new one. There is one more wrinkle to remember: In Oracle, an *automatic* commit occurs when the user disconnects from the database and before any DDL statement (covered later in this chapter).

An alternative to implicit transactions is *autocommit* mode, which essentially puts each SQL statement in its own transaction. When autocommit is active, any statement that modifies data is automatically committed as soon as the statement is successfully completed. Earlier in the chapter I described the Autocommit check box in the Application Express client that toggles the database session in or out of autocommit mode. Another way to change the mode in Oracle is by running the **SET AUTOCOMMIT ON** and **SET AUTOCOMMIT OFF** commands. However, these commands are not supported in the Oracle Application Express client, presumably because of explicit support using the Autocommit check box.

By contrast, in Sybase ASE and Microsoft SQL Server, autocommit is the default mode. The database user must issue a BEGIN TRANSACTION statement to explicitly start a transaction. Once a transaction is started, changes made to the database can be made permanent with a COMMIT TRANSACTION statement or they can be reversed using a ROLLBACK TRANSACTION statement. Some RDBMSs, such as Microsoft Access and MySQL, do not provide transaction support at all.

The INSERT Statement

The INSERT statement in SQL is used to add new rows of data to tables. An INSERT statement can also insert rows via a view, provided the following conditions are met:

- If the view joins multiple tables, the columns referenced by the INSERT statement must all be from the same table. Said another way, an INSERT can affect only one table.

- The view must include all the mandatory table columns in the base table. If columns with NOT NULL constraints do not appear in the view, it is impossible to provide values for those columns and therefore impossible to use the view to perform an INSERT.

The INSERT statement takes two basic forms: one where column values are provided in the statement itself, and the other where values are selected from a table or view using a subselect. Let's have a look at those two forms.

INSERT with VALUES Clause

The form of the INSERT statement that includes the VALUES clause can create only one row each time it is run, because the values for that one row of data are provided in the statement itself. Figure 4-26 shows an example that adds a new row to the EMPLOYEES table. Here is the SQL statement:

```
INSERT INTO EMPLOYEES
   (EMPLOYEE_ID, FIRST_NAME, LAST_NAME, EMAIL, PHONE_NUMBER, HIRE_DATE,
    JOB_ID, SALARY, COMMISSION_PCT, MANAGER_ID, DEPARTMENT_ID)
VALUES (921, 'Werdna', 'Leppo', 'leppo@whatever.com', null, SYSDATE,
        'IT_PROG', 15000, 0.0, 103, 60);
```

Note the column list following the **INSERT** keyword. This comma-separated list is optional, but if provided, it must always be enclosed in a pair of parentheses. If you omit the list, the column values must be provided in the correct order (that is, the same as the order in which the columns are physically ordered in the table), and you cannot skip any

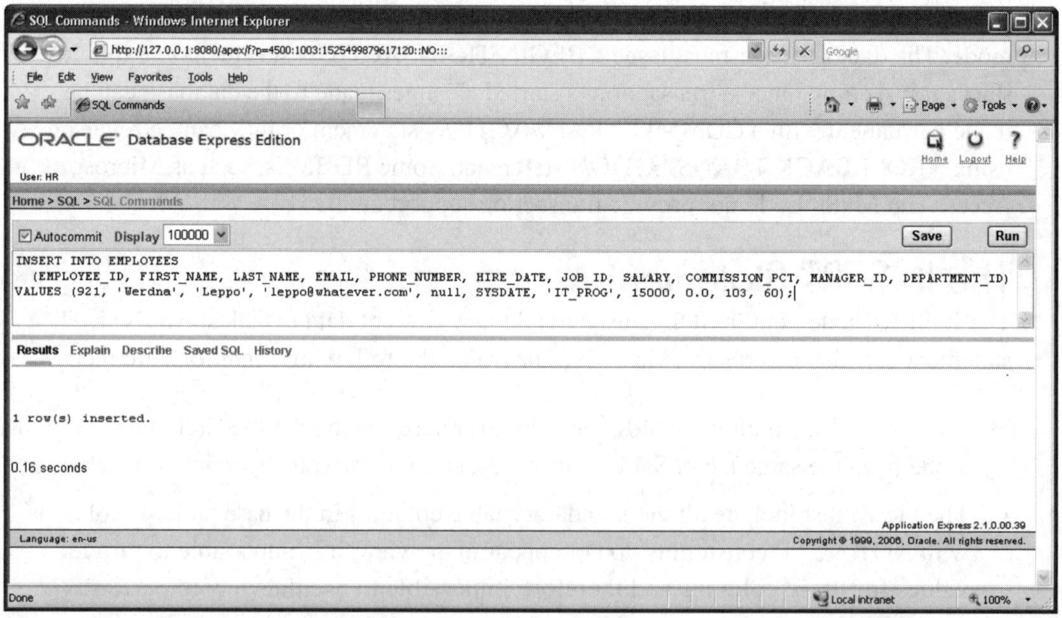

Figure 4-26   INSERT using the VALUES clause

column values. The statement may malfunction if anyone adds columns to the table, even optional ones, so it is *always* a good idea to provide the column list, even though it is more work to create one. Following the column list is the keyword **VALUES** and then a list of the values for the columns. This comma-separated list must also be enclosed in a pair of parentheses. The items in the VALUES list have a one-to-one correspondence with the column list (if one was provided) or with the columns defined in the table or view (if a column list was not provided). The keyword **null** (or **NULL**) may be used to assign null values to columns in the list. SYSDATE is a pseudo-column provided in Oracle databases that always contains the current date and time.

INSERT with Subquery

The form of INSERT statement that includes a subquery creates one row in the target table for each row retrieved from the source table or view. A subquery is used to retrieve the information that will be inserted. In the example that follows, rows in an imaginary table called EMPLOYEE_INPUT are used to insert data into the EMPLOYEES table:

```
INSERT INTO EMPLOYEES
    (EMPLOYEE_ID, FIRST_NAME, LAST_NAME, EMAIL, PHONE_NUMBER,
    HIRE_DATE, JOB_ID)
        SELECT EMPLOYEE_ID, FIRST_NAME, LAST_NAME,
                EMAIL, PHONE_NUMBER, SYSDATE, JOB_ID
        FROM EMPLOYEE_INPUT;
```

If you want to try this INSERT statement, you can find the statements used to create the EMPLOYEE_INPUT table in the "Data Definition Language (DDL) Statements" section a bit further along in this chapter.

The UPDATE Statement

The UPDATE statement in SQL is used to update the data values for table (or view) columns listed in the statement. A WHERE clause can be included to limit the scope of the statement to rows matching its conditions; otherwise, the statement attempts to update every row in the table (or view) named in the statement. Figure 4-27 shows an example of the UPDATE statement that changes the phone number for employee 921. Here is the SQL statement:

```
UPDATE EMPLOYEES
    SET PHONE_NUMBER = '301.555.1212'
WHERE EMPLOYEE_ID = 921;
```

For each column to be updated, a SET clause is used to name the column and the new value for the column. The new value provided can be a constant, another column

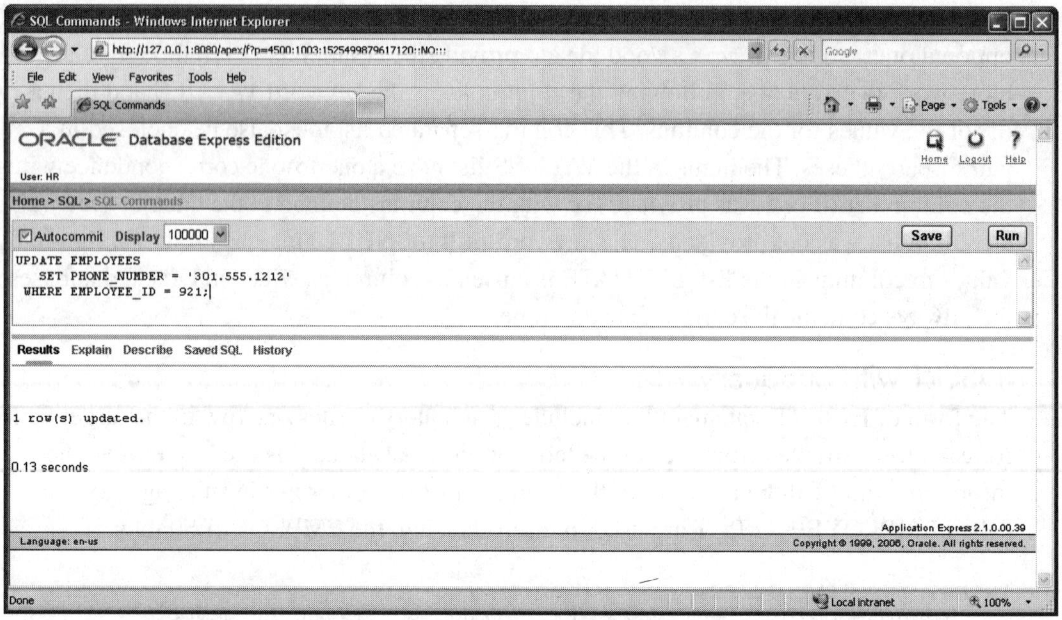

Figure 4-27 UPDATE statement for the EMPLOYEES table

name, or any other expression that SQL can resolve to a column value. If the SET clause references multiple columns, the column names and values must be in a comma-separated list. The UPDATE statement may include a WHERE clause to limit the rows affected by the statement. If the WHERE clause is omitted, the UPDATE statement will attempt to update every row in the table (or view). If you forget this key point, remember our friend the ROLLBACK statement, which can back out the results of the update (unless you are in autocommit mode, of course).

The DELETE Statement

The DELETE statement removes one or more rows from a table. The statement can also reference a view, but only if the view is based on a single table (in other words, views that join multiple tables cannot be referenced). A DELETE statement does not reference columns because the statement automatically clears all column data for any rows deleted. A WHERE clause can be included to limit the rows affected by the DELETE statement; if the WHERE clause is omitted, the statement attempts to delete all the rows in

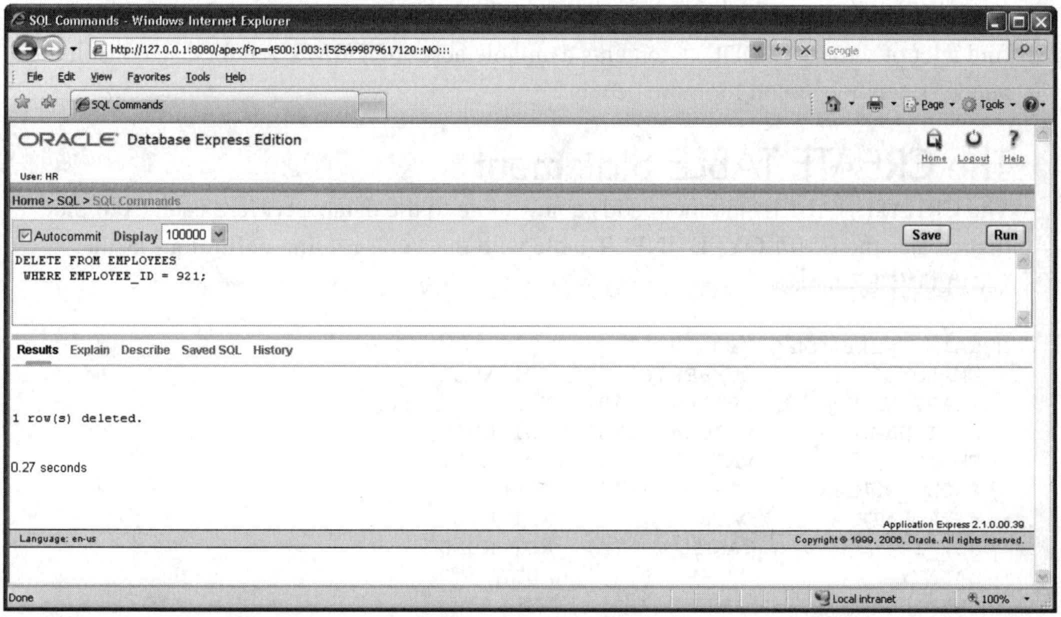

Figure 4-28   DELETE statement for the EMPLOYEES table

the referenced table. Figure 4-28 shows an example of a DELETE statement that deletes employee 921 from the EMPLOYEES table. Here is the SQL statement:

```
DELETE FROM EMPLOYEES
 WHERE EMPLOYEE_ID = 921;
```

Data Definition Language (DDL) Statements

Data Definition Language (DDL) statements define the database objects but do not insert or update any data stored within those objects. (DML statements serve that purpose.) In SQL, three basic commands are used within DDL:

- **CREATE**   Creates a new database object of the type named in the statement
- **DROP**   Drops (destroys) an existing database object of the type named in the statement
- **ALTER**   Changes the definition of an existing database object of the type named in the statement

The sections that follow examine the most commonly used DDL statement types. You'll find a lot of variety in DDL statements available across RDBMS vendors, so consult the vendor's documentation for more details.

The CREATE TABLE Statement

The CREATE TABLE statement adds a new table to the database. Here is an example that creates the EMPLOYEE_INPUT table with the same column definitions as the EMPLOYEES table:

```
CREATE TABLE EMPLOYEE_INPUT (
    EMPLOYEE_ID      NUMBER(6)        NOT NULL,
    FIRST_NAME       VARCHAR2(20)     NULL,
    LAST_NAME        VARCHAR2(25)     NOT NULL,
    EMAIL            VARCHAR2(25)     NOT NULL,
    PHONE_NUMBER     VARCHAR2(20)     NULL,
    HIRE_DATE        DATE             NOT NULL,
    JOB_ID           VARCHAR2(10)     NOT NULL,
    SALARY           NUMBER(8,2)      NULL,
    COMMISSION_PCT   NUMBER(2,2)      NULL,
    MANAGER_ID       NUMBER(6)        NULL,
    DEPARTMENT_ID    NUMBER(4)        NULL)
;
```

Note that a comma-separated list of columns is provided, along with the data type and NULL or NOT NULL specification for each. You may recall from Chapter 2 that a wide variety of data types is supported across RDBMS vendors. The data types shown here apply to Oracle. Be careful with NULL and NOT NULL specifications. In most RDBMSs, including Oracle, NULL is the default. However, in others, the default might be NOT NULL. It is therefore safer, but of course more work, always to specify either NULL or NOT NULL. Incidentally, most RDBMSs require that primary key columns be specified as NOT NULL. You'll see how to create a primary key constraint on the EMPLOYEE_ID column of this table in the "Primary Key Constraints" section a little further along in this chapter.

Many vendor extensions to the CREATE TABLE statement exist beyond the basic column list used in our example. For example, in Oracle, the STORAGE clause can be included to specify the amount of physical space that is to be allocated to the table, and a TABLESPACE clause can be included to specify the tablespace that will hold the table's data.

The ALTER TABLE Statement

The ALTER TABLE statement can be used to change many aspects of the definition of a database table. Again, a wide variation in implementation exists across RDBMS vendors, but generally speaking, the following types of changes can be made using the ALTER TABLE statement:

- Adding columns to the table
- Removing columns from the table
- Altering the data type for existing table columns
- Changing physical storage attributes of the table
- Adding, removing, or altering constraints

Because the implementation of constraints is the way we enforce business rules in the database, we will take a closer look at them here. It is important that you name the constraints, because in most SQL implementations the names appear in the error messages generated when constraint violations take place.

Referential Constraints

Here is an example of a referential constraint definition using the ALTER TABLE statement:

```
ALTER TABLE EMPLOYEE_INPUT
  ADD CONSTRAINT EMP_INPUT_DEPT_FK
      FOREIGN KEY (DEPARTMENT_ID)
      REFERENCES DEPARTMENTS (DEPARTMENT_ID);
```

In this example, a referential constraint named EMP_DEPT_FK is added to the EMPLOYEES table to define the DEPARTMENT_ID column as a foreign key to the primary key column (DEPARTMENT_ID) of the DEPARTMENTS table. This is the way you implement the relationships you've identified in the logical database design.

Primary Key Constraints

Primary key constraints ensure that the column(s) designated as the primary key for the table never have duplicate values. Most RDBMSs, Oracle included, create a unique index to assist in enforcement of primary key constraints. An *index* is a special database object containing the key value from one or more table columns and pointers to the table rows that match the key value. Indexes can be used for fast searching of a table based on the key value. Here is the definition of the primary key constraint for the EMPLOYEES table:

```
ALTER TABLE EMPLOYEE_INPUT
  ADD CONSTRAINT EMPLOYEES_PK
      PRIMARY KEY (EMPLOYEE_ID)
      USING INDEX;
```

Unique Constraints

In addition to enforcing primary keys, you can force uniqueness of other column(s) in a table using a unique constraint. A table may have only one primary key constraint, but in addition it may have as many unique constraints as necessary. Most RDBMSs, including Oracle, use a unique index to assist with the enforcement of unique constraints. For example, you can use a unique constraint to ensure that no two employees have the same e-mail address as follows:

```
ALTER TABLE EMPLOYEE_INPUT
  ADD CONSTRAINT EMPLOYEES_UNQ_EMAIL
      UNIQUE (EMAIL);
```

The same constraint can be removed using this statement:

```
ALTER TABLE EMPLOYEE_INPUT
 DROP CONSTRAINT EMPLOYEES_UNQ_EMAIL;
```

Check Constraints

Check constraints can be used to enforce any business rule that can be applied to a single column in a table. The condition included in the constraint must always be true whenever the column data in the table is changed or else the SQL statement fails and an error message is displayed. The following example implements a check constraint that ensures that the SALARY column in the EMPLOYEES table is always greater than zero:

```
ALTER TABLE EMPLOYEES
  ADD CONSTRAINT EMPLOYEES_CHK_SALARY_MIN
      CHECK (SALARY > 0);
```

The same constraint can be removed with this statement:

```
ALTER TABLE EMPLOYEES
 DROP CONSTRAINT EMPLOYEES_CHK_SALARY_MIN;
```

The CREATE VIEW Statement

Because a view is merely a stored query, any query that can be run using a SELECT statement can be saved as a view in the database. View names must be unique among all the tables, views, and synonyms in the database schema. In Oracle, the **OR REPLACE** option can be included so that an existing view of the same name will be replaced. The following example creates a view for the query shown in Figure 4-21:

```
CREATE OR REPLACE VIEW SALES_EMPLOYEES AS
   SELECT EMPLOYEE_ID, LAST_NAME, FIRST_NAME, DEPARTMENT_NAME
     FROM EMPLOYEES LEFT OUTER JOIN DEPARTMENTS
         ON EMPLOYEES.DEPARTMENT_ID = DEPARTMENTS.DEPARTMENT_ID
    WHERE DEPARTMENT_NAME LIKE '%Sales%';
```

Running the following SQL statement will select the data from the view, which will yield the exact same results as those shown in Figure 4-21:

```
SELECT *
  FROM SALES_EMPLOYEES;
```

The CREATE INDEX Statement

The CREATE INDEX statement creates an index on one or more table columns. As mentioned, indexes provide fast searching of a table based on one or more key columns. Indexes on foreign keys can also greatly improve the performance of joins. The RDBMS automatically maintains the index when rows are added to or deleted from the database, or when indexed column values are updated. However, indexes take storage space and their maintenance takes processing resources. The following example creates an index on the DEPARTMENT_ID column in the EMPLOYEE_INPUT table:

```
CREATE INDEX EMPLOYEE_INPUT_IX_DEPT_ID
    ON EMPLOYEE_INPUT (DEPARTMENT_ID);
```

If the column values in the index will always be unique, the **UNIQUE** keyword can be placed between the **CREATE** and **INDEX** keywords. As an alternative, a unique constraint can be added to the table, which indirectly creates the unique index. Unique indexes are usually more efficient than nonunique ones.

The DROP Statement

The DROP statement is used to remove database objects from the database when they are no longer necessary. For table deletions, the CASCADE CONSTRAINTS clause (shortened to CASCADE in some SQL implementations) can be added to remove automatically any referential constraints in which the table participates. When a table is dropped, most objects depending on the table (indexes and constraints) are also dropped.

In most RDBMSs, however, views dependent on a dropped table remain but are marked invalid so they cannot be used until the table is re-created. Here are the DROP statements that remove the objects created in the preceding examples:

```
DROP VIEW SALES_EMPLOYEES;
DROP INDEX EMPLOYEE_INPUT_IX_DEPT_ID;
DROP TABLE EMPLOYEE_INPUT CASCADE CONSTRAINTS;
```

NOTE
You may find that you have to run these statements one at a time. This appears to be a quirk in the Oracle XE client.

Data Control Language (DCL) Statements

A database *privilege* is the authorization to do something in the database. The database user granting the privilege is called the *grantor*, and the database user receiving the privilege is called the *grantee*. Privileges fall into two broad categories:

- **System privileges**   Permit the grantee to perform a general database function, such as creating new user accounts or connecting to the database
- **Object privileges**   Permit the grantee to perform specific actions on specific objects, such as selecting from the EMPLOYEES table or updating the DEPARTMENTS table

To reduce the tedium of managing privileges, most RDBMSs support storing a group of privilege definitions as a single named object called a *role*. Roles may then be granted to individual users, who inherit all the privileges contained in the role. RDBMSs that support roles also typically come with a number of predefined roles. Oracle, for example, has a role called DBA that contains all the high-powered system and object privileges a database user needs in administering a database.

The GRANT Statement

Privileges are given to users in SQL using the GRANT statement. The following examples show the syntax for granting a system privilege and an object privilege to database users. The user account granting the privilege must possess the privilege, so many of the examples here will not run unless you are connected to the database using the SYSTEM account.

The following statement grants the CREATE VIEW privilege to user HR:

```
GRANT CREATE VIEW TO HR;
```

The following statement grants the select, insert, and update privileges on the EMPLOYEES table in the HR schema to user HR_ADMIN. Note that you must qualify the table name with the schema name if you are logged in as a different user, such as SYSTEM. You must always qualify objects that belong to another schema (user) when you reference them in SQL. Here's the statement:

```
GRANT SELECT, INSERT, UPDATE
   ON HR.EMPLOYEES TO HR_ADMIN;
```

NOTE
User account HR_ADMIN must exist for this statement to run. If you want to try it out, you may use the Administration icon on the main page and choose Database Users | Create User to create the account. I do not cover creating user accounts in this chapter because no standard SQL syntax exists for doing so, which means that every vendor offers a proprietary solution.

Most RDBMSs that support privileges also allow for giving the grantee permission to grant the privilege to others. In Oracle, the clause for doing so is WITH ADMIN OPTION for system privileges and WITH GRANT OPTION for object privileges. However, I *strongly* recommend *against* doing so. It is simply too easy to lose control of privileges when you allow people who have a privilege to in turn grant it to others.

The REVOKE Statement
Granted privileges can be withdrawn using the REVOKE statement. For object privileges, if WITH GRANT OPTION is exercised by the user, the revoke cascades and everyone downstream loses the privilege as well. This is not necessarily true for system privileges— consult your RDBMS manuals for details. Better yet, if you never use WITH GRANT OPTION and WITH ADMIN OPTION, you will never have to worry about this problem. The privileges shown in the preceding section can be revoked with these commands:

```
REVOKE CREATE VIEW FROM HR;

REVOKE SELECT, INSERT, UPDATE
   ON HR.EMPLOYEES FROM HR_ADMIN;
```

✓ Chapter 4 Self Test

Choose the correct responses to each of the multiple-choice and fill-in-the-blank questions.
Note that there may be more than one correct response to each question.

1. SQL may be divided into the following subsets:

    A Data Selection Language (DSL)

    B Data Control Language (DCL)

    C Data Query Language (DQL)

    D Data Definition Language (DDL)

2. SQL was first developed by _____.

3. A program used to connect to the database and interact with it is called a(n) _____.

4. A SELECT without a WHERE clause

    A Selects all rows in the source table or view

    B Returns no rows in the result set

    C Results in an error message

    D Lists only the definition of the table or view

5. In SQL, row order in query results

    A Is specified using the SORTED BY clause

    B Is unpredictable unless specified in the query

    C Defaults to descending when sequence is not specified

    D May be specified only for columns in the query results

6. The **BETWEEN** operator

    A Includes the end-point values

    B Selects rows added to a table during a time interval

    C Can be rewritten using the <= and **NOT** = operators

    D Can be rewritten using the <= and >= operators

7. The **LIKE** operator uses _____ as positional wildcards and _____ as nonpositional wildcards.

8. A subselect

   A May be corrugated or noncorrugated

   B Allows for the flexible selection of rows

   C Must not be enclosed in parentheses

   D May be used to select values to be applied to WHERE clause conditions

9. A join without a WHERE clause or JOIN clause

   A Results in an error message

   B Results in an outer join

   C Results in a Cartesian product

   D Returns no rows in the result set

10. A join that returns all rows from both tables whether or not matches are found is known as a(n) _____.

11. A self-join

   A Involves two different tables

   B Can be either an inner or outer join

   C Resolves recursive relationships

   D May use a subselect to further limit returned rows

12. An SQL statement containing an aggregate function

   A Must contain a GROUP BY clause

   B May also include ordinary columns

   C May not include both GROUP BY and ORDER BY clauses

   D May also include calculated columns

13. A(n) _____ causes changes made by a transaction to become permanent.

14. An INSERT statement

   A Must contain a column list

   B Must contain a VALUES list

C May create multiple table rows

D May contain a subquery

15. An UPDATE statement without a WHERE clause

   A Results in an error message

   B Updates no rows in a table

   C Updates every row in a table

   D Results in a Cartesian product

16. A DELETE statement with a column list

   A Results in an error message

   B Deletes data only in the listed columns

   C Deletes every column in the table

   D Can be used to delete from a view

17. A CREATE statement

   A Is a form of DML

   B Creates new user privileges

   C Creates a database object

   D May be reversed later using a DROP statement

18. An ALTER statement

   A May be used to add a constraint

   B May be used to drop a constraint

   C May be used to add a view

   D May be used to drop a table column

19. The _____ mode causes each SQL statement to commit as soon as it completes.

20. Database privileges

   A May be changed with an ALTER PRIVILEGE statement

   B May be either system or object privileges

   C Are best managed when assembled into groups using GROUP BY

   D Are managed using GRANT and REVOKE

Part II

Database Development

Chapter 5
The Database Life Cycle

Key Skills & Concepts

● The Traditional Life Cycle

● Nontraditional Life Cycles

● The Project Triangle

Before delving into the particulars of database design, you'll find it useful to understand the framework in which the design takes place. The *life cycle* of a database (or computer system) comprises all the events that occur from the time you first recognize the need for a database, through its development and deployment, and finally ending with the day the database is retired from service.

Most businesses that develop computer systems follow a formal process that ensures that development runs smoothly, that it is cost effective, and that the outcome is a complete computer system that meets expectations. Databases are never designed and implemented in a vacuum—other components of the complete system are always developed along with the database, such as the user interface, application programs, and reports. All the work to be accomplished over the long term is typically divided into *projects*, with each project having its own finite list of goals (sometimes called *deliverables*), an expected timeframe for completion, and a project manager or leader who will be held accountable for delivery of the project. To understand the database life cycle, you must also understand the life cycle of the entire systems-development effort and the way projects are organized and managed. This chapter takes a look at both traditional and nontraditional systems-development processes.

Not all databases are built by businesses using formal projects and funding. However, the disciplines outlined in this chapter can assist you in thinking through your database project and asking the tough questions before you embark on an extended effort.

The Traditional Life Cycle

The traditional method for developing computer systems follows a process called the *system development life cycle (SDLC)*, which divides the work into the phases shown in Figure 5-1. There are perhaps as many variations of the SDLC as there are authors, project management software vendors, and companies that have elected to create their own methodologies. However, they all have the basic components, and in that sense, are all cut from the same cloth. I could argue the merits of one variation versus another, but that

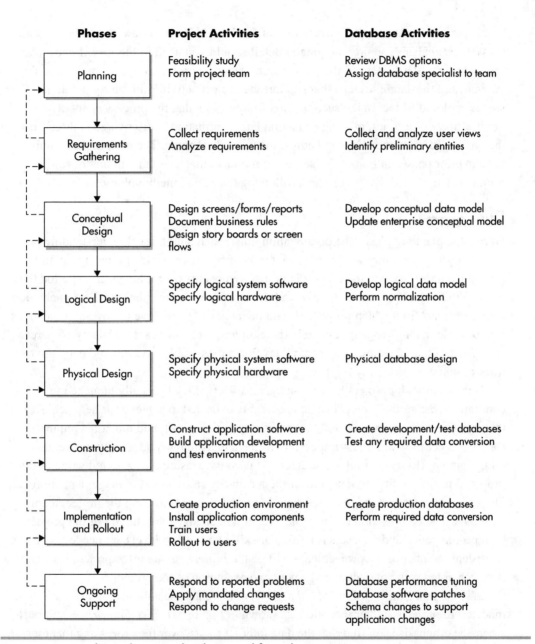

Phases	Project Activities	Database Activities
Planning	Feasibility study Form project team	Review DBMS options Assign database specialist to team
Requirements Gathering	Collect requirements Analyze requirements	Collect and analyze user views Identify preliminary entities
Conceptual Design	Design screens/forms/reports Document business rules Design story boards or screen flows	Develop conceptual data model Update enterprise conceptual model
Logical Design	Specify logical system software Specify logical hardware	Develop logical data model Perform normalization
Physical Design	Specify physical system software Specify physical hardware	Physical database design
Construction	Construct application software Build application development and test environments	Create development/test databases Test any required data conversion
Implementation and Rollout	Create production environment Install application components Train users Rollout to users	Create production databases Perform required data conversion
Ongoing Support	Respond to reported problems Apply mandated changes Respond to change requests	Database performance tuning Database software patches Schema changes to support application changes

Figure 5-1 Traditional system development life cycle (SDLC)

would merely confuse matters when all you need is a basic overview. A good textbook on systems analysis can provide greater detail should you need it. Figure 5-1 shows the traditional SDLC steps in the left column, the basic project activities in the middle column, and the database steps that support the project activities in the right column. Each step is explored further in the sections that follow. Note that the process is not always unidirectional—at times, missing or incomplete information is discovered and requires that you to go back one phase and adjust the work done there. The dotted lines pointing back to prior phases in Figure 5-1 serve as reminders that a certain amount of rework is normal and expected during a project following the SDLC methodology.

Planning

During the planning phase, the organization must reach a high-level understanding of where they currently are, where they want to be, and a reasonable approach or plan for getting from one place to the other. Planning often occurs over a longer time period than any one individual project, and the overall information systems plan for the organization forms the basis from which projects should be launched to achieve the overall objectives. For example, a long-range objective in the plan might be "Increase profits by 15 percent." In support of that objective, a project to develop an application system and database to track customer profitability might be proposed.

Once a particular project is proposed, a *feasibility study* is usually launched to determine whether the project can be reasonably expected to achieve (or help achieve) the objective and whether preliminary estimates of time, staff, and materials required for the project fit within the required timeframe and available budget. Often a return on investment (ROI) or similar calculation is used to measure the expected value of the proposed project to the organization. If the feasibility study meets management approval, the project is placed on the overall schedule for the organization and the project team is formed. The composition of the project team will change over the life of the project, with people added and released as particular skill and staffing levels are needed. The one consistent member of the project team will be the *project manager* (or project leader), who is responsible for the overall management and execution of the project.

Many organizations assign a *database specialist* (database administrator or data modeler) to projects at their inception, as shown in Figure 5-1. In a *data-driven* approach, where the emphasis is on studying the data in order to discover the processing that must take place to transform the data as required by the project, early assignment of someone skilled at analyzing the data is essential. In a *process-driven* approach, where the emphasis is on studying the processes required to discover what the data should be, a database specialist is less essential during the earliest phases of the project. Industry experience suggests that the very best results are obtained by applying *both* a process-driven and a data-driven approach. However, there is seldom time and staff to do so, so the next-best results for a project involving databases come from the data-driven approach. Processes still need to be designed, but if we study the data first, the required processes become apparent. For example, in designing our customer profitability system, if we have customer sales data and know that customers who place fewer, larger orders are more profitable, then we can conclude that we need a process to rank customers by order volume and size. On the other hand, if all we know is that we need a process that ranks customers, it may take considerably more work to arrive at the criteria we should use to rank them.

The database activities in this phase involve reviewing DBMS options and determining whether the technologies currently in use meet the overall needs of the project. Most organizations settle on one, or perhaps two, standard DBMS products that they use for all projects. At this point, the goals of the project should be compared with the current technology to ensure that the project can reasonably be expected to be successful using that technology. If a newer version of the DBMS is required, or if a completely different DBMS is required, the planning phase is the time to find out, so the acquisition and installation of the DBMS can be started.

Requirements Gathering

During the requirements-gathering phase, the project team must gather and document a high-level, yet precise, description of what the project is to accomplish. The focus must be on *what* rather than *how*; the how is developed during the subsequent design phases. It is important for the requirements to include as much as can be known about the existing and expected business processes, business rules, and entities. The more work that is done in the early stages of a project, the more smoothly the subsequent stages will proceed. On the other hand, without some tolerance for the unknown (that is, those gray areas that have no solid answers), *analysis paralysis* can occur, wherein the entire project stalls while analysts spin their wheels looking for answers and clarifications that are not forthcoming.

From a database design perspective, the items of most interest during requirements gathering are user views. Recall that a *user view* is the method employed for presenting a set of data to the database user in a manner tailored to the needs of that person or application. At this phase of development, user views take the form of existing or proposed reports, forms, screens, web pages, and the like.

Many techniques can be used in gathering requirements. The more commonly used techniques are compared and contrasted here: conduct interviews, conduct survey, observation, and document review. No particular technique is clearly superior to another, and it is best to find a blend of techniques that works well for the particular organization rather than rely on one over the others. For example, whether it is better to conduct a survey and follow up with interviews with key people, or to start with interviews and use the interview findings to formulate a survey, is often a question of what works best given the organization's culture and operating methods. With each technique detailed in the following subsections, some advantages and disadvantages are listed to assist in decision-making.

Conduct Interviews

Interviewing key individuals who have information about what the project is expected to accomplish is a popular approach. One of the common errors, however, is to interview only management. If you do not include those who are actually going to use the new application(s) and database(s), the project may end up delivering something that is not practical, because management may not fully understand all the details of the requirements necessary to run the business of the organization. In particular, you need to start a dialog with one or more *subject matter experts (SMEs)*—professionals who have expertise in the field of the application but who usually do not have technical computer system knowledge.

The advantages of requirements gathering using interviews include the following:

- The interviewer can get answers to questions that were not asked. Side topics often come up that provide additional useful information.

- The interviewer can learn a lot from the body language of the interviewee. It is far easier to detect uncertainty and attempts at deception in person rather than in written responses to questions.

   The disadvantages include the following:

- Interviews take considerably more time than other methods.

- Poorly skilled interviewers can "telegraph" the answers they are expecting by the way they ask the questions or by their reactions to the answers received.

Conduct a Survey

Another popular approach is to write a survey seeking responses to key questions regarding the requirements for a project. The survey is sent to all the decision-makers and potential users of the application(s) and database(s) the project is expected to deliver, and responses are analyzed for items to be included in the requirements.

The advantages of requirements gathering using surveys include the following:

- A lot of ground can be covered in a short time. Once the survey is written, it takes little additional effort to distribute it to a wider audience if necessary.

- Questions are presented in the same manner to every participant.

The disadvantages include the following:

- Surveys typically have very poor response rates. Consider yourself fortunate if 10 percent respond without having to be prodded or threatened with consequences.

- Unbiased survey questions are much more difficult to compose than you might imagine.

- The project team does not get the benefit of the nonverbal clues that an interview provides.

Observation

Observing the business operation and the people who will be using the new application(s) and database(s) is another popular technique for gathering requirements.

The advantages of requirements gathering using observation include the following:

- Assuming you watch in an unobtrusive manner, you get to see people following normal processes in everyday use. Note that these may not be the processes that management believes are being followed, or even those in existing documentation. Instead, you may observe adaptations that were made so that the processes actually work or so they are more efficient.

- You may observe events that people would not think (or dare) to mention in response to questionnaires or interview questions.

The disadvantages include the following:

- If the people know they are being watched, their behaviors change, and you may not get an accurate picture of their business processes. This is often termed the *Hawthorne effect* after a phenomenon first noticed in the Hawthorne Plant of Western Electric, where production improved not because of improvements in working conditions but rather because management demonstrated interest in such improvements.

- Unless enormous periods of time are dedicated to observation, you may never see the exceptions that subvert existing business processes. To bend an old analogy, you end up paving the cow path while cows are wandering on the highway on the other side of the pasture due to a hole in the fence.

- Travel to various business locations can add considerably to project expense.

Document Review

This technique involves locating and reviewing all available documents for the existing business units and processes that will be affected by the new program(s) and database(s).

The advantages of requirements gathering using document review include the following:

- Document review is typically less time consuming than any of the other methods.

- Documents often provide an overview of the system that is better thought out compared with the introductory information you receive in an interview.

- Pictures and diagrams really are worth a thousand words each.

The disadvantages are the following:

- The documents may not reflect actual practices. Documents often deal with what *should* happen rather than what *really* happens.

- Documentation is often out of date.

Conceptual Design

The conceptual design phase involves designing the externals of the application(s) and database(s). In fact, many methodologies use the term *external design* for this project phase. The layout of reports, screens, forms, web pages, and other data entry and presentation vehicles are finalized during this phase. In addition, the flow of the external application is documented in the form of a flow chart, storyboard, or screen flow diagram. This helps the project team understand the logical flow of the system. Process diagramming techniques are discussed further in Chapter 7.

During this phase, the database specialist (DBA or data modeler) assigned to the project updates the enterprise conceptual data model, which is usually maintained in the form of an entity-relationship diagram (ERD). New or changed entities discovered are added to the ERD, and any additional or changed business rules are also noted. The user views, entities, and business rules are essential for the successful logical database design that follows in the next phase.

Logical Design

During logical design, the bulk of the technical design of the application(s) and database(s) included in the project is carried out. Many methodologies call this phase *internal design,* because it involves the design of the internals of the project that the business users will never see.

The work to be accomplished by the application(s) is segmented into *modules* (individual units of application programming that will be written and tested together), and a detailed specification is written for each unit. The specification should be complete enough that any programmer with the proper programming skills can write the module and test it with little or no additional information. Diagrams such as data flow diagrams or flow charts (an older technique) are often used to document the logic flow between modules. Process modeling is covered in more detail in Chapter 7.

From the database perspective, the major effort in this phase is *normalization*, a technique developed by E.F. (Ted) Codd for designing relational database tables that are best for transaction-based systems (that is, those that insert, update, and delete data in the relational database tables). Normalization, the single most important topic in this entire book, is covered in great detail in Chapter 6. Once normalization is completed, the overall logical data model for the enterprise (assuming one exists) is updated to reflect any newly discovered entities.

Physical Design

During the physical design phase, the logical design is mapped or converted to the actual hardware and systems software that will be used to implement the application(s) and database(s). From the process side, little or nothing needs to be done if the application specifications were written in a manner that can be directly implemented. However, much work is required to specify the hardware on which the application(s) and database(s) will be installed, including capacity estimates for the processors, disk devices, and network bandwidth on which the system will run.

On the database side, the normalized relations that were designed in the prior logical design phase are implemented in the relational DBMS(s) to be used. In particular, Data Definition Language (DDL) is coded or generated to define the database objects, including the SQL clauses that define the physical storage of the tables and indexes. Preliminary analyses of required database queries are conducted to identify any additional indexes that may be necessary to achieve acceptable database performance. An essential outcome of this phase is the DDL for creation of the development database objects that the developers will need for testing the application programs during the construction phase that follows. Physical database design is covered in more detail in Chapter 8.

Construction

During the construction phase, the application developers code and test the individual programming units. Tested program units are promoted to a system test environment, where the entire application and database system is assembled and tested from end to end. Figure 5-2 shows the environments that are typically used as an application system is developed, tested, and implemented. Each environment is a complete hardware and software environment that includes all the components necessary to run the application system. Once system testing is completed, the system is promoted to a quality assurance

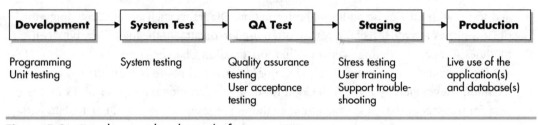

Figure 5-2 Development hardware/software environments

(QA) environment. Most medium- and large-size organizations have a separate QA department that tests the application system to ensure that it conforms to the stated requirements. Some organizations also have business users test the system to make sure it also meets their needs. The sooner errors are found in a computer system, the less expensive they are to repair. After QA has passed the application system, it is promoted to a staging environment. The staging environment must be as near a duplicate of the production environment as possible. In this environment, stress testing is conducted to ensure that the application and database will perform reasonably when deployed into live production use. Often final user training is conducted here as well, because it will be most like the live environment users will soon use.

The major work of the DBA is already complete by the time construction begins. However, as each part of the application system is migrated from one environment to the next, the database components needed by the application must also be migrated. Hopefully, a script is written that deploys the database components to the development environment, and that script is reused in each subsequent environment. However, complications can occur when an existing database is being enhanced or an older data storage system is being replaced, because data must be converted from the old storage structures to the new. Data transcends systems. Therefore, data conversion between old and new versions of systems is quite commonplace, ranging from simply adding new tables and columns to complex conversions that require extensive programming efforts in and of themselves.

Implementation and Rollout

Implementation is the process of installing the new application system's components (application programs, forms or web pages, reports, database objects, and so on) into the live system and carrying out any required data conversions. *Rollout* is the process of placing groups of business users on the new application. Sometimes a new project is implemented *cold turkey*, meaning every user starts on the new version at the same time. However, with more complicated applications or those involving large numbers of users, a *phased* implementation is often used to reduce risk. The old and new versions of the application must run in parallel for a time while groups of users—often partitioned by physical work location or by department—are trained and migrated over to the new application. This method is often humorously referred to as the *chicken method* (in contrast to the cold turkey method).

Ongoing Support

Once a new application system and database have been implemented in a production environment, support of the application is often turned over to a production support team. This team must be prepared to isolate and respond to any issues that may arise, which could include performance issues, abnormal or unexpected results, complete failures, or the inevitable requests for enhancements. With enhancements, it is best to categorize and prioritize them and then fold them into future projects. However, genuine errors found in the existing application or database (called *bugs* in IT slang) must be fixed more immediately. Each bug fix becomes a mini-project, where all the SDLC phases must be revisited. At the very least, documentation must be updated as changes are made. As noted in Figure 5-2, the staging environment provides an ideal place for the validation of errors and their fixes and makes it possible to fix errors in parallel with the next major enhancement to the application system, which may have already been started in the development environment.

Assuming no gross errors were made during database design, the database support required during this phase is usually minor. Here are some of the tasks that may be required:

- Patches must be applied when the problems turn out to be bugs in the vendor's RDBMS software.

- Performance tuning, such as moving data files or adding indexes, may be necessary to circumvent performance problems.

- Space must be monitored and storage added as the database grows.

- Some application bug fixes may require new table columns or alterations to existing columns. If testing was done well, gross errors that require extensive database changes simply do not occur. Some application changes are required by statutory or regulatory changes beyond the control of the organization, and those changes can lead to extensive modifications to application(s) and database(s).

Ask the Expert

Q: I've been hearing about the Rational Unified Process (RUP) lately. How does that fit in with SDLC?

A: The Rational Unified Process is an iterative software development process framework originally developed by the Rational Software Corporation, which became a division of IBM in 2003. Organizations that use the Rational toolset for application development usually also use the companion process framework. RUP is intended to be tailored by the organization using it, so no two implementations are the same. Unlike an SDLC, RUP has iterations designed into the framework. While the phases in RUP (Inception, Elaboration, Construction, and Transition) have somewhat different names than SDLC phases, the tasks are categorized into six engineering disciplines that align nicely with the classic SDLC (Business Modeling, Requirements, Analysis and Design, Implementation, Test, and Deployment).

Nontraditional Life Cycles

In response to the belief that SDLC projects take too much time and consume too many resources, some nontraditional methods have come into routine use in some organizations. The two most prevalent of these are *prototyping* and *Rapid Application Development (RAD)*.

Prototyping

Prototyping involves rapid development of the application using iterative sets of design, development, and implementation steps as a method of determining user requirements. Extensive business user involvement is required throughout the development process. In its extreme form, the prototyping process starts with a meeting conducted during the business day to review the latest iteration of the application, followed by the development team working through the evening and often late into the night. The next iteration is then reviewed during the following workday.

Some prototyping techniques carry all the way through to a production version of the application and database. In this variation, iterations have increasing levels of detail added to them until they become completely functional applications. If you choose this path, keep in mind that prototyping never ends, and even after implementation and rollout, any future enhancements fall right back into more prototyping. The most common downside to this implementation technique is development team burnout.

Another variation of prototyping restricts the effort to the definition of requirements. Once requirements and the user-facing parts of the conceptual design (that is, user views) are determined, a traditional SDLC methodology is used to complete the project. IBM introduced a version of this methodology called *Joint Application Design (JAD)*, which was highly successful in situations where user requirements could not be determined using more traditional techniques. The biggest exposure for this variant of prototyping is in not setting and maintaining expectations with the business sponsors of the project. The prototype is more or less a façade, much like a movie set where the buildings look real from the front but have no substance beyond that. Nontechnical audiences have no understanding of what it takes to develop the logic and data storage structures that form the inner workings of the application, and they become most disappointed when they realize that what looked like a complete, functional application system was really just an empty shell. However, when done correctly, this technique can be remarkably successful in determining user requirements that describe precisely the application system the business users want and need.

Rapid Application Development

Rapid Application Development (RAD) is a software development process that allows functioning application systems to be built in as little as 60 to 90 days. Compromises are often made using the *80/20 rule*, which assumes that 80 percent of the required work can be completed in 20 percent of the time. Complicated exception handling, for example, can be omitted in the interest of delivering a working system sooner. If the process is repeated on the same set of requirements, the system is ultimately built out to meet 100 percent of the requirements in a manner similar to prototyping.

RAD is not useful in controlling project schedules or budgets, and in fact it requires a project manager who is highly skilled at managing schedules and controlling costs. It is most useful in situations for which a rapid schedule is more important than product quality (measured in terms of conforming to all known requirements).

The Project Triangle

The motivation behind the growth of nontraditional development processes is pressure from business management to develop better business applications more quickly and at less expense. Said simply, they want fast delivery of high quality and inexpensive application software systems. However, despite the claims of some of the vendors selling development tools and methodologies, all three objectives simply cannot be maximized.

Figure 5-3 The project triangle

Figure 5-3 shows a graphical representation of the dilemma using the *project triangle*. The three points of the triangle represent the three objectives: quality, delivery time, and cost (often known as good, fast, and cheap). The lines between the points remind us that the objectives are interrelated. In fact, most experts agree only two of the objectives can be optimized, and when they are, the third objective always suffers. The commonly understood rule is that you must pick two and optimize your project accordingly. It has also been generally proven that the rule applies to human endeavors and not to matters of pure technology. For example, you can create a new video format that renders higher quality images faster and less expensively. However, if you launched a project to design such a new format, the project tasks could not be optimized for all three objectives.

This rule didn't start with the software industry. In fact, some claim that it is an old Hollywood maxim about filmmaking. While every producer wants a high-quality film, made quickly, and finished on budget, it simply cannot be done. A good movie made quickly isn't cheap. A movie made quickly and cheaply won't be good. And a movie that is good and cheaply made can't be made quickly. Applying the analogy to application development projects, three choices emerge:

- Design and develop the system quickly and to a high standard, but expect higher costs.

- Design and develop the system quickly while minimizing costs, but expect the outcome to meet a lower standard of quality.

- Design and develop the system to a high standard while minimizing costs, but expect the project to take much longer.

Try This 5-1 Project Database Management Tasks

In this Try This exercise, you will assign typical project management database management tasks to SDLC project phases. You may have to do a little research on your own to understand the particulars of one or more tasks, but that will only enhance your learning experience.

Step by Step

1. Make a list of the SDLC project phases:

    a. Planning

    b. Requirements Gathering

    c. Conceptual Design

    d. Logical Design

    e. Physical Design

    f. Construction

    g. Implementation and Rollout

    h. Ongoing Support

2. Using what you learned in this chapter along with what you are able to find out using other sources, assign each of the following tasks to one of the project phases. Note that some may apply to more than one phase. Also, methodologies are usually tailored to fit the organization in which they are used, so there are no absolute correct or incorrect answers for some of the tasks.

    a. Normalization.

    b. Add foreign keys to the database.

    c. Specify the physical placement of database objects on storage media.

    d. Specify the unique identifier for each relation.

    e. Specify the primary key for each table.

    f. Determine the views required by the business users.

    g. Remove data that is easily derived.

    h. Resolve many-to-many relationships.

    i. Define views in the database.

    j. Modify the database to meet business requirements.

    k. Denormalize the database for performance.

    l. Specify a logical name for each entity and attribute.

    m. Specify a physical name for each table and column.

    n. Add derivable data to improve performance.

(continued)

   o. Specify database indexes.

   p. Translate the conceptual data model into a logical model.

   q. Document business rules that cannot be represented in the data model.

   r. Identify the attributes required by the business users.

   s. Identify the relationships between the entities.

   t. Identify and document business data requirements.

   u. Ensure that user data requirements are met.

   v. Tune the database to improve performance.

   w. Evaluate available DBMS options.

Try This Summary

In this Try This exercise, you assigned project tasks to SDLC phases using information in this chapter, as well as independent research. My solution can be found in Appendix B, but as already stated, there is no single correct solution to this exercise.

✔ Chapter 5 Self Test

Choose the correct responses to each of the multiple-choice and fill-in-the-blank questions. Note that there may be more than one correct response to each question.

1. The phases of a systems development life cycle (SDLC) methodology include which of the following?

   A Physical design

   B Logical design

   C Prototyping

   D Requirements gathering

   E Ongoing support

2. During the requirements phase of an SDLC project,

   A User views are discovered.

   B The quality assurance (QA) environment is used.

   C Surveys may be conducted.

   D Interviews are often conducted.

   E Observation may be used.

3. The advantages of conducting interviews are

   A Interviews take less time than other methods.

   B Answers may be obtained for unasked questions.

   C A lot can be learned from nonverbal responses.

   D Questions are presented more objectively compared to survey techniques.

   E Entities are more easily discovered.

4. The advantages of conducting surveys include

   A A lot of ground can be covered quickly.

   B Nonverbal responses are not included.

   C Most survey recipients respond.

   D Surveys are simple to develop.

   E Prototyping of requirements is unnecessary.

5. The advantages of observation are

   A You always see people acting normally.

   B You are likely to see lots of situations in which exceptions are handled.

   C You may see the way things really are instead of the way management and/or documentation presents them.

   D The Hawthorne effect enhances your results.

   E You may observe events that would not be described to you by anyone.

6. The advantages of document reviews are

   A Pictures and diagrams are valuable tools for understanding systems.

   B Document reviews can be done relatively quickly.

   C Documents will always be up to date.

   D Documents will always reflect current practices.

   E Documents often present overviews better than other techniques can.

7. Application program modules are specified during the SDLC _____ phase.

8. A feasibility study is often conducted during the _____ phase of an SDLC project.

9. Normalization takes place during the _____ phase of an SDLC project.

10. DDL is written to define database objects during the _____ phase of an SDLC project.

11. Program specifications are written during the _____ phase of an SDLC project.

12. During implementation and rollout,

    A Users are placed on the live system.

    B Enhancements are designed.

    C The old and new applications may be run in parallel.

    D Quality assurance testing takes place.

    E User training takes place.

13. During ongoing support,

    A Enhancements are immediately implemented.

    B Storage for the database may require expansion.

    C The staging environment is no longer required.

    D Bug fixes may take place.

    E Patches may be applied if needed.

14. When requirements are sketchy, _____ can work well.

15. Rapid Application Development develops systems rapidly by skipping _____.

16. The three objectives depicted in the application triangle are _____, _____, and _____.

17. The database is initially constructed in the _____ environment.

18. Database conversion is tested during the _____ phase of an SDLC project.

19. User views are analyzed during the _____ phase of an SDLC project.

20. The relational database was invented by _____.

Chapter 6
Database Design Using Normalization

Key Skills & Concepts

- The Need for Normalization
- Applying the Normalization Process
- Denormalization

In this chapter, you will learn how to perform logical database design using a process called *normalization*. In terms of understanding relational database technology, this is the most important topic in this book, because normalization teaches you how best to organize your data into tables.

Normalization is a technique for producing a set of *relations* (data represented logically in a two-dimensional format using rows and columns) that possesses a certain set of properties. You'll remember from previous chapters that E.F. (Ted) Codd is the father of the relational database, and that he developed the process in 1972, using three normal forms. The name was a bit of a political gag at the time. President Nixon was "normalizing" relations with China, so Codd figured if you could normalize relations with a country, you should be able to "normalize" data relations as well. Additional normal forms were added later, as discussed toward the end of this chapter.

The normalization process is shown in Figure 6-1. On the surface, it is quite simple and straightforward, but it takes considerable practice to execute the process consistently and correctly. Briefly, we take any relation and choose a unique identifier for the entity that the relation represents. Then, through a series of steps that apply various rules, we reorganize the relation into continuously more progressive normal forms. The definitions of each of these normal forms and the process required to arrive at each one are covered in the sections that follow.

Throughout the normalization process, I consistently use the *logical terms* whenever possible. The only exception is the term *primary key*, which I use in lieu of *unique identifier* for consistency with current industry practice. Beginners may find it easier to think in terms of the physical objects that will eventually be created from the logical design. This is because learning to think of databases at the conceptual and logical levels of abstraction instead of the physical level is, in fact, a very difficult discipline for your mind to master. If you find yourself thinking of tables instead of relations, and columns instead of attributes, you need to break the habit as soon as possible. Those who think

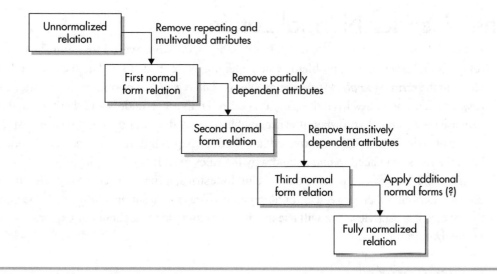

Figure 6-1   The normalization process

only physically while attempting to normalize tables run into difficulties later, because a one-to-one correspondence does not necessarily exist between normalized relations and tables. In fact, it is physical database design that transforms the normalized relations into relational tables, and there is some latitude in mapping normalized relations to physical tables. The following table may help you remember the correspondence between the logical and physical terms:

Logical Term	Physical Term
Relation or Entity	Table
Unique identifier	Primary key
Attribute	Column
Tuple	Row

NOTE

Relation was Codd's original name for a data structure made of rows and columns, and it is the basis for the name *relational database*. However, over time the term *entity* became more popular, even though the definitions of the two are not exactly the same. Be careful not to confuse *relation* (a data structure) with *relationship* (how one structure is related to another). If fact, it may be this confusion that has driven people away from using the term *relation*.

The Need for Normalization

In his early work with relational database theory, Codd discovered that unnormalized relations presented certain problems when attempts were made to update the data in them. He used the term *anomalies* for these problems. The reason we normalize the relations is to *remove* these anomalies from the data. It is essential that you understand these anomalies, because they also tell you when it is acceptable to bend the rules during physical design by "denormalizing" the relations (covered later in this chapter). It makes sense that in order to bend the rules, you need to understand why the rules exist in the first place.

Figure 6-2 shows an invoice from Acme Industries, a fictitious company. The invoice contains attributes that are typical for a printed invoice from a supply company. Conceptually, the invoice is a user view. We will use this invoice example throughout our exploration of the normalization process.

Insert Anomaly

The *insert anomaly* refers to a situation in which you cannot insert a new tuple into a relation because of an artificial dependency on another relation. (A *tuple* is a collection of data values that form one occurrence of an entity. In a physical database, a tuple is called a row of data.) The error that has caused the anomaly is that attributes of two different entities are mixed into the same relation. Referring to Figure 6-2, we see that the ID, name, and address of the customer are included in the invoice view. Were you merely to make a relation from this view as it is, and eventually a table from the relation, you would soon

Acme Industries
INVOICE

Customer Number: 1454837
Customer: W. Coyote
      General Delivery
      Falling Rocks, AZ 84211
      (599) 555-9345

Terms: Net 30
Ship Via: USPS

Order Date: 12/01/2008

Product No.	Description	Quantity	Unit Price	Extended Amount
SPR-2290	Super Strength Springs	2	24.00	$48.00
STR-67	Foot Straps, leather	2	2.50	$5.00
HLM-45	Deluxe Crash Helmet	1	67.88	$67.88
SFR-1	Rocket, solid fuel	1	128,200.40	$128,200.40
ELT-1	Emergency Location Transmitter	1	79.88	**FREE GIFT**

TOTAL ORDER AMOUNT: $128,321.28

Figure 6-2   Invoice from Acme Industries

discover that you could not insert a new customer into the database unless the customer had bought something. This is because all the customer data is embedded in the invoice.

Delete Anomaly

The *delete anomaly* is the opposite of the insert anomaly. It refers to a situation wherein a deletion of data about one particular entity causes unintended loss of data that characterizes another entity. In the case of the Acme Industries invoice, if we delete the last invoice that belongs to a particular customer, we lose all the data related to that customer. Again, this is because data from two entities (customers and invoices) would be incorrectly mixed into a single relation if we merely implemented the invoice as a table without applying the normalization process to the relation.

Update Anomaly

The *update anomaly* refers to a situation in which an update of a single data value requires multiple tuples (rows) of data to be updated. In our invoice example, if we wanted to change the customer's address, we would have to change it on every single invoice for the customer. This is because the customer address would be redundantly stored in every invoice for the customer. To make matters worse, redundant data provides a golden opportunity to update many copies of the data but miss a few of them, resulting in inconsistent data. The mantra of the skilled database designer is this: For each attribute, capture it once, store it once, and use that one copy everywhere.

Applying the Normalization Process

The normalization process is applied to each user view collected during earlier design stages. Some people find it easier to apply the first step (choosing a primary key) to each user view, and then to apply the next step (converting to first normal form), and so forth. Other people prefer to take the first user view and apply all the normalization steps to it, and then the next user view, and so forth. With practice, you'll know which process works best for you, but whichever you choose, you must be *very* systematic in your approach, lest you overlook something. Our example has only one user view (the Acme Industries invoice), so this may seem a moot point, but two practice problems toward the end of the chapter contain several user views each, so you will be able to try this out soon enough. Using dry-erase markers or chalk on a wall-mounted board is most helpful because you can easily erase and rewrite relations as you go.

Start with each user view being a relation, which means you represent it as if it is a two-dimensional table. As you work through the normalization process, you will be rewriting existing relations and creating new ones. Some find it useful to draw the relations with sample tuples (rows) of data in them to assist in visualizing the work. If you take this approach, be certain that your data represents real-world situations. For example, you might not realize that two customers have exactly the same name in the invoice example—as a result, your normalization results might be incorrect. Therefore, you should *always* think of as many possibilities as you can when using this approach. Figure 6-3 shows the information from the invoice example (Figure 6-2) represented in tabular form. Only one invoice is shown here, but many more could be filled in to show examples of multiple invoices per customer, multiple customers, the same product on multiple invoices, and so on.

You probably noticed that each invoice has many line items. This will be essential information when we get to first normal form. In Figure 6-3, multiple values are placed in the cells for the columns that hold data from the line items. These are called *multivalued attributes* because they have multiple values for at least some tuples (rows) in the relation. If you were to construct an actual database table in this manner, your ability to use a language such as SQL to query those columns would be limited. For example, finding all orders that contain a particular product would require you to parse the column data with a **LIKE** operator. Updates would be equally awkward because SQL was not designed to handle multivalued columns. Worst of all, a delete of one product from an invoice would require an SQL UPDATE instead of a DELETE because you would not want to delete the entire invoice. As you consider the first normal form later in this chapter, you will see how to mitigate this problem.

Figure 6-4 shows another way a relation could be organized using the invoice shown in Figure 6-2. Here, the multivalued column data has been placed in separate rows and the other columns' data has been repeated to match. The obvious problem here is all the

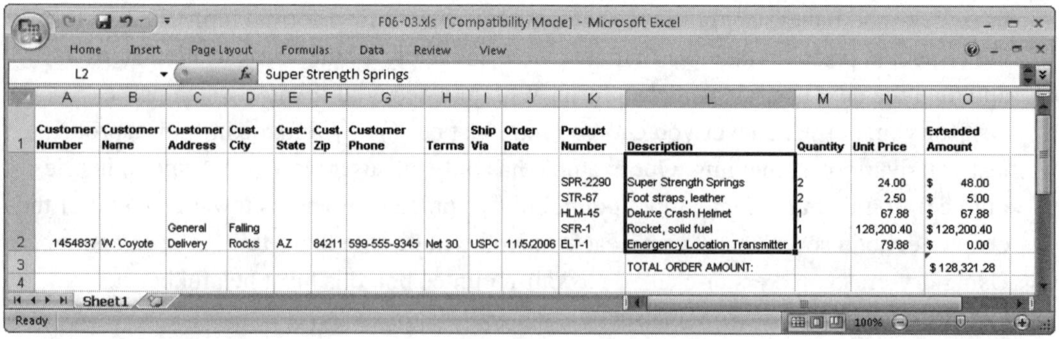

F06-03.xls [Compatibility Mode] - Microsoft Excel

L2 Super Strength Springs

	A	B	C	D	E	F	G	H	I	J	K	L	M	N	O
1	Customer Number	Customer Name	Customer Address	Cust. City	Cust. State	Cust. Zip	Customer Phone	Terms	Ship Via	Order Date	Product Number	Description	Quantity	Unit Price	Extended Amount
2	1454837	W. Coyote	General Delivery	Falling Rocks	AZ	84211	599-555-9345	Net 30	USPC	11/5/2006	SPR-2290 STR-67 HLM-45 SFR-1 ELT-1	Super Strength Springs Foot straps, leather Deluxe Crash Helmet Rocket, solid fuel Emergency Location Transmitter	2 2 1 1 1	24.00 2.50 67.88 128,200.40 79.88	$ 48.00 $ 5.00 $ 67.88 $ 128,200.40 $ 0.00
3												TOTAL ORDER AMOUNT:			$ 128,321.28
4															

Sheet1

Figure 6-3 Acme Industries invoice represented in tabular form

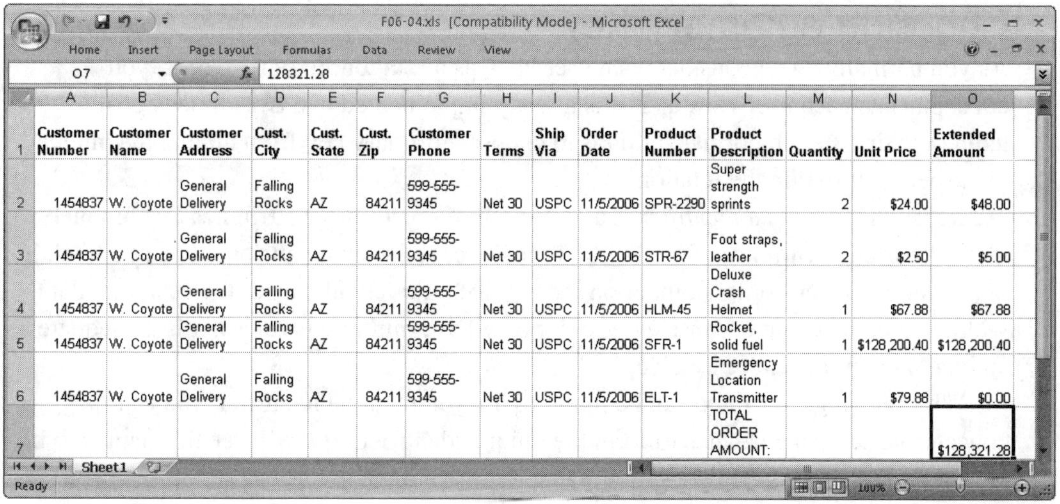

	Customer Number	Customer Name	Customer Address	Cust. City	Cust. State	Cust. Zip	Customer Phone	Terms	Ship Via	Order Date	Product Number	Product Description	Quantity	Unit Price	Extended Amount
2	1454837	W. Coyote	General Delivery	Falling Rocks	AZ	84211	599-555-9345	Net 30	USPC	11/5/2006	SPR-2290	Super strength sprints	2	$24.00	$48.00
3	1454837	W. Coyote	General Delivery	Falling Rocks	AZ	84211	599-555-9345	Net 30	USPC	11/5/2006	STR-67	Foot straps, leather	2	$2.50	$5.00
4	1454837	W. Coyote	General Delivery	Falling Rocks	AZ	84211	599-555-9345	Net 30	USPC	11/5/2006	HLM-45	Deluxe Crash Helmet	1	$67.88	$67.88
5	1454837	W. Coyote	General Delivery	Falling Rocks	AZ	84211	599-555-9345	Net 30	USPC	11/5/2006	SFR-1	Rocket, solid fuel	1	$128,200.40	$128,200.40
6	1454837	W. Coyote	General Delivery	Falling Rocks	AZ	84211	599-555-9345	Net 30	USPC	11/5/2006	ELT-1	Emergency Location Transmitter	1	$79.88	$0.00
7												TOTAL ORDER AMOUNT:			$128,321.28

Figure 6-4 Acme Industries invoice represented without multivalued attributes

repeated data. For example, the customer's name and address are repeated for each line item on the invoice, which is not only wasteful of resources, but also exposes you to inconsistencies whenever the data is not maintained uniformly (for example, if you update the city for one line item but not all the others).

Rewriting user views into tables with representative data is a tedious and time-consuming process. For this reason, you can simply write the attributes as a list and visualize them in your mind as the two-dimensional tables they will eventually become. This takes some practice and some training of the mind, but once you master it, you'll find it considerably faster to visualize the data rather than writing out exhaustive examples. Here is the list for the invoice example from Figure 6-2:

```
INVOICE: Customer Number, Customer Name, Customer Address,
         Customer City, Customer State, Customer Zip Code,
         Customer Phone, Terms, Ship Via, Order Date,
         Product Number, Product Description, Quantity,
         Unit Price, Extended Amount, Total Order Amount
```

For clarity, a name for the relation has been added, with the relation name in uppercase letters and separated from the attributes with a colon. This is the convention I will use for the remainder of this chapter. However, if another technique works better for you, by all means use it. The best news of all is that no matter which representation you use (Figure 6-3, Figure 6-4, or the preceding list), if you properly apply the normalization process and its rules, you will create a comparable database design.

Choosing a Primary Key

As you normalize, you consider each user view as a relation. In other words, you conceptualize each user view as if it is already implemented in a two-dimensional table. The first step in normalization is to choose a primary key from among the unique identifiers you find in the relation.

Recall that a *unique identifier* is a collection of one or more attributes that uniquely identifies each occurrence of a relation. In many cases, a single attribute can be found. In our example, the customer number on the invoice uniquely identifies the customer data within the invoice, but because a customer may have multiple invoices, it is inadequate as an identifier for the entire invoice.

When no single attribute can be found to use for a unique identifier, you can concatenate several attributes to form the unique identifier. You will see this happen with our invoice example when we split the line items from the invoice as we normalize it. It is very important to understand that when a unique identifier is composed of multiple attributes, the attributes themselves are not combined—they still exist as independent attributes and will become individual columns in the table(s) created from our normalized relations.

In a few cases, no set of attributes in a relation can reasonably be used as the unique identifier. (You will find that many practitioners use the terms *identifier* and *key* interchangeably.) When this occurs, you must invent a unique identifier, often with values assigned sequentially or randomly as you add entity occurrences to the database. This technique (some might say "act of desperation") is the source of such unique identifiers as Social Security numbers, employee IDs, and driver's license numbers. Unique identifiers that have real-world meaning are called *natural* identifiers, and those that do not (which of course includes those we must invent) are called *surrogate* or *artificial* identifiers. In our invoice example, there appears to be no natural unique identifier for the relation. You could try using the customer number combined with the order date, but if a customer has two invoices on the same date, this would not be unique. Therefore, it would be much better to invent an identifier, such as an invoice number.

Whenever you choose a unique identifier for a relation, you must be *certain* that the identifier will *always* be unique. If even *one* case exists to render the identifier not unique, you cannot use it. People's names, for example, make lousy unique identifiers. You may have never met someone with exactly your name, but there are people out there with completely identical names. As an example of the harm poorly chosen unique identifiers cause, consider the case of the Brazilian government when it started registering voters in 1994 to reduce election fraud. Father's name, mother's name, and date of birth were chosen as the unique identifier. Unfortunately, this combination is unique only for siblings born on *different* dates, so as a result, when siblings born on the same date (twins, triplets, and so on) tried to register to vote, the first one that showed up was allowed to register and the rest were turned away. Sound impossible? It's not—this really happened. And to make matters worse, citizens are *required* to vote in Brazil and sometimes have to prove they voted in order to get a job. Someone should have spent more time thinking about the uniqueness of the chosen "unique" identifier.

Sometimes a relation will have more than one possible unique identifier. When this occurs, each possibility is called a *candidate*. Once you have identified all the possible candidates for a relation, you must choose one of them to be the primary key for the relation. Choosing a primary key is *essential* to the normalization process because all the normalization rules reference the primary key. The criteria for choosing the primary key from among the candidates is as follows (in order of precedence, most important first):

- *If only one candidate is available, choose it.*

- *Choose the candidate least likely to have its value change.* Changing primary key values once you store the data in tables is a complicated matter because the primary key can appear as a foreign key in many other tables. Incidentally, surrogate keys are almost always less likely to change compared with natural keys.

- *Choose the simplest candidate.* The one that comprises the fewest number of attributes is considered the simplest.

- *Choose the shortest candidate.* This is purely an efficiency consideration. However, when a primary key can appear in many tables as a foreign key, it is often worth it to save some space with each one.

For our invoice example, we have elected to add a surrogate primary identifier called Invoice Number. This gives us a simple primary key for the Acme Industries invoices that is guaranteed unique, because we can have the DBMS automatically assign sequential numbers to new invoices as they are generated. This will likely make Acme's accountants happy at the same time, because it gives them a simple tracking number for the invoices.

Many conventions can be used for signifying the primary key as you write the contents of relations. Using capitalized names causes confusion because most of us tend to write acronyms such as DOB (date of birth) that way, and those attributes are not always the primary key. Likewise, underlining and bolding the attribute names can be troublesome because these may not always display in the same way. Therefore, I use the letters *PK* enclosed in parentheses following the attribute name(s) of the primary key.

Rewriting the invoice relation in list form with the primary key added provides the following:

```
INVOICE: Invoice Number (PK), Customer Number, Customer Name,
         Customer Address, Customer City, Customer State,
         Customer Zip Code, Customer Phone, Terms,
         Ship Via, Order Date, Product Number,
         Product Description, Quantity, Unit Price,
         Extended Amount, Total Order Amount
```

First Normal Form: Eliminating Repeating Data

A relation is said to be in *first normal form* when it contains no multivalued attributes—that is, every intersection of a row and column in the relation must contain *at most* one data value (saying "at most" allows for missing or null values). Sometimes, you will find a group of attributes that repeat together, as with the line items on the invoice. Each attribute in the group is multivalued, but several attributes are so closely related that their values repeat together. This is called a *repeating group,* but in reality, it is just a special case of the multivalued attribute problem.

By convention, I enclose repeating groups and multivalued attributes in pairs of parentheses. Rewriting our invoice in this way to show the line item data as a repeating group, we get this:

```
INVOICE: Invoice Number (PK), Customer Number, Customer Name,
         Customer Address, Customer City, Customer State,
         Customer Zip Code, Customer Phone, Terms,
         Ship Via, Order Date, (Product Number,
         Product Description, Quantity, Unit Price,
         Extended Amount), Total Order Amount
```

It is essential that you understand that although you know that Acme Industries has many customers, only one customer exists for any given invoice, so the customer data on the invoice is *not* a repeating group. You may have noticed that the customer data for a given customer is repeated on every invoice for that customer, but this problem will be addressed when we get to third normal form. Because there is only one customer per invoice, the problem is not addressed when we transform the relation to first normal form.

To transform unnormalized relations into first normal form, you must move multivalued attributes and repeating groups to new relations. Because a repeating group is a set of attributes that repeat *together*, all attributes in a repeating group should be moved to the same new relation. However, a multivalued attribute (individual attributes that have multiple values) should be moved to its own new relation rather than combined with other multivalued attributes in the new relation. As you will see later, this technique avoids fourth normal form problems.

The procedure for moving a multivalued attribute or repeating group to a new relation is as follows:

1. Create a new relation with a meaningful name. Often, it makes sense to include all or part of the original relation's name in the new relation's name.

2. Copy the primary key from the original relation to the new one. The data depends on this primary key in the original relation, so it must still depend on this key in the new relation. This copied primary key now becomes a *foreign key* to the original relation. As you apply normalization to a database design, always keep in mind that eventually you will have to write SQL to reproduce the original user view from which you started. So the foreign keys used to join things back together are nothing less than essential.

3. Move the repeating group or multivalued attribute to the new relation. (The word *move* is used because these attributes are *removed* from the original relation.)

4. Make the primary key (as copied from the original relation) unique by adding attributes from the repeating group to it. If you move a multivalued attribute, which is basically a repeating group of only one attribute, that attribute is added to the primary key. This will seem odd at first, but the primary key attribute(s) that you copied from the original table is a *foreign key* in the new relation. It is quite normal for part of a primary key also to be a foreign key. One additional point: It is perfectly acceptable to have a relation in which all the attributes are part of the primary key (that is, where there are no "non-key" attributes). This is relatively common in intersection tables.

5. Optionally, you can choose to replace the primary key with a single surrogate key attribute. If you do so, you must keep the attributes that make up the natural primary key formed in Steps 2 and 4.

For our Acme Industries invoice example, here is the result of converting the original relation to first normal form:

```
INVOICE: Invoice Number (PK), Customer Number, Customer Name,
         Customer Address, Customer City, Customer State,
         Customer Zip Code, Customer Phone, Terms,
         Ship Via, Order Date, Total Order Amount

INVOICE LINE ITEM: Invoice Number (PK), Product Number (PK),
         Product Description, Quantity, Unit Price,
         Extended Amount
```

Note the following:

● The Invoice Number attribute was copied from INVOICE to INVOICE LINE ITEM and Product Number was added to it to form the primary key of the INVOICE LINE ITEM relation.

● The entire repeating group (Product Number, Product Description, Quantity, Unit Price, and Extended Amount) was removed from the INVOICE relation.

● Invoice Number is still the primary key in INVOICE, and it now also serves as a foreign key in INVOICE LINE ITEM as well as being *part* of the primary key of INVOICE LINE ITEM.

● There are no repeating groups or multivalued attributes in the relations, so they are therefore in first normal form.

Note an interesting consequence of composing a natural primary key for the INVOICE LINE ITEM relation: You cannot put the same product on a given invoice more than one time. This might be desirable, but it could also restrict Acme Industries. You have to understand their business rules to know. If Acme Industries wants the option of putting multiple line items on the same invoice for the same product (perhaps with different prices), you should make up a surrogate key instead. Moreover, there are those who believe that primary keys composed of multiple attributes are undesirable, along with software products that simply do not support them. The alternative is to make up a surrogate primary key for the INVOICE LINE ITEM relation. If you choose to do so, the relation can be rewritten this way:

```
INVOICE LINE ITEM: Invoice Line Item ID (PK),
                   Invoice Number, Product Number,
                   Product Description, Quantity,
                   Unit Price, Extended Amount
```

We are going to use the previous form (the one with the compound primary key made up of Invoice Number and Product Number, often called the *natural key*) as we continue with normalization.

Second Normal Form: Eliminating Partial Dependencies

Before you explore second normal form, you must understand the concept of *functional dependence.* For this definition, we'll use two arbitrary attributes, cleverly named "A" and "B." Attribute B is *functionally dependent* on attribute A if at any moment in time no more than one value of attribute B is associated with a given value of attribute A. Lest you wonder what planet I lived on before this one, I'll try to make the definition more understandable. First, suppose that attribute B is functionally dependent on attribute A; this is also saying that attribute A *determines* attribute B, or that A is a *determinant* (unique identifier) of attribute B. Second, let's look again at the first normal form relations in our Acme Industries example:

```
INVOICE: Invoice Number (PK), Customer Number, Customer Name,
         Customer Address, Customer City, Customer State,
         Customer Zip Code, Customer Phone, Terms,
         Ship Via, Order Date, Total Order Amount

INVOICE LINE ITEM: Invoice Number (PK), Product Number (PK),
         Product Description, Quantity, Unit Price,
         Extended Amount
```

In the INVOICE relation, you can easily see that Customer Number is functionally dependent on Invoice Number because at any point in time, there can be only one value of Customer Number associated with a given value of Invoice Number. The very fact that the Invoice Number uniquely identifies the Customer Number in this relation means that, in return, the Customer Number is *functionally dependent* on the Invoice Number.

In the INVOICE LINE ITEM relation, you can also say that Product Description is functionally dependent on Product Number because, at any point in time, there is only one value of Product Description associated with the Product Number. However, the fact that the Product Number is only part of the key of the INVOICE LINE ITEM is the very issue addressed by second normal form.

A relation is said to be in *second normal form* if it meets both the following criteria:

- The relation is in first normal form.
- All non-key attributes are functionally dependent on the *entire* primary key.

Look again at Product Description, and it should be easy to see that Product Number *alone* determines the value. Said another way, if the same product appears as a line item on many different invoices, the Product Description is the same *regardless* of the Invoice Number. Or you can say that Product Description is functionally dependent on only *part of* the primary key, meaning it depends only on Product Number and not on the *combination* of Invoice Number *and* Product Number.

It should also be clear by now that second normal form applies only to relations where we have concatenated primary keys (that is, those made up of multiple attributes). If a primary key is composed of only a single attribute, as is the case with the first normal form version of the Invoice relation, and the primary key is atomic (that is, has no subparts that make sense by themselves), as all attributes should be, then it is simply not possible for anything to depend on *part* of the primary key. It follows, then, that any first normal form relation that has only a single atomic attribute for its primary key is *automatically* in second normal form.

Looking at the INVOICE LINE ITEM relation, however, second normal form violations should be readily apparent: Product Description and Unit Price depend only on the Product Number instead of the *combination* of Invoice Number and Product Number. But not so fast! What about price changes? If Acme decides to change its prices, how could you possibly want that change to be retroactive for every invoice you have ever created? After all, an invoice is an official record that you must maintain for seven years, per current U.S. tax laws. This is a common dilemma with fast-changing attributes such as prices. Either you must be able to recall the price at any point in time or you must store the price with the invoice so you can reproduce the invoice as needed (that is, when the friendly tax auditors come calling).

For simplicity, let's store the price in two places—one being the current selling price and the other being the price at the time the sale was made. Because the latter is a snapshot at a point in time that is not expected to change, there are no anomalies to this seemingly redundant storage. An alternative would be to store a date-sensitive price history somewhere that you could use to reconstruct the correct price for any invoice. That is a practical alternative here, but you would never be able to do that with stock or commodities market transactions, for example. The point is that while the sales price *looks* redundant, there are no *anomalies* to the additional attribute, so it does no harm. Notice that the attribute names are adjusted so their meaning is abundantly clear.

Once you find a second normal form violation, the solution is to move any attributes that are partially dependent to a new relation where they depend on the *entire* key instead of *part* of the key. Here is our invoice example rewritten into second normal form:

```
INVOICE: Invoice Number (PK), Customer Number, Customer Name,
         Customer Address, Customer City, Customer State,
         Customer Zip Code, Customer Phone, Terms,
         Ship Via, Order Date, Total Order Amount

INVOICE LINE ITEM: Invoice Number (PK), Product Number (PK),
         Quantity, Sale Unit Price, Extended Amount

PRODUCT: Product Number (PK), Product Description,
         List Unit Price
```

The improvement from the first normal form solution is that maintenance of the Product Description now has no anomalies. You can set up a new product independent of the existence of an invoice for the product. If you want to change the Product Description, you may do so by merely changing one value in one row of data. Also, should the last invoice for a particular product be deleted from the database for whatever reason, you won't lose its description (it will still be in the row in the Product relation). *Always* remember that the reason you are normalizing is to eliminate these anomalies.

Third Normal Form: Eliminating Transitive Dependencies

To understand third normal form, you must first understand transitive dependency. An attribute that depends on another attribute that is not the primary key of the relation is said to be *transitively dependent*. Looking at our INVOICE relation in second normal form, you can clearly see that Customer Name is dependent on Invoice Number (each Invoice Number has only one Customer Name value associated with it), but at the same time Customer Name is also dependent on Customer Number. The same can be said of the rest of the customer attributes as well. The problem here is that attributes of another entity (Customer) have been included in our INVOICE relation.

A relation is said to be in *third normal form* if it meets both the following criteria:

- The relation is in second normal form.

- There is no transitive dependence (that is, all the non-key attributes depend *only* on the primary key).

To transform a second normal form relation into third normal form, simply move any transitively dependent attributes to relations where they depend only on the primary key. Be careful to leave the attribute on which they depend in the original relation as a foreign key. You will need it to reconstruct the original user view via a join.

If you have been wondering about easily calculated attributes such as Extended Amount in the INVOICE LINE ITEM relation, it is actually third normal form that forbids them, but it takes a subtle interpretation of the rule. Because the Extended Amount is calculated by multiplying Sale Unit Price × Quantity, it follows that Extended Amount is *determined by* the combination of Sale Unit Price and Quantity and therefore is *transitively dependent* on those two attributes. Thus, it is third normal form that tells you to remove easily calculated attributes. And in this case, they are simply removed. Using similar logic, you can also remove the Total Order Amount from the INVOICE relation because you can simply sum the INVOICE LINE ITEM relation to reproduce the value. A good designer will make a note in the documentation specifying the formula for the calculated attribute so that its value can be reproduced when needed. Another highly effective alternative is to write the SQL that reproduces the original views when you complete a normalization process. It's an excellent way to *test* your normalization because you can use the SQL to *prove* that the original user views can be easily reproduced.

Here is the Acme Industries invoice data rewritten into third normal form:

```
INVOICE: Invoice Number (PK), Customer Number, Terms,
       Ship Via, Order Date

INVOICE LINE ITEM: Invoice Number (PK), Product Number (PK),
       Quantity, Sale Unit Price

PRODUCT: Product Number (PK), Product Description,
       List Unit Price

CUSTOMER: Customer Number (PK), Customer Name,
       Customer Address, Customer City, Customer State,
       Customer Zip Code, Customer Phone
```

Ask the Expert

Q: In the CUSTOMER entity you just illustrated, aren't City and State transitively dependent on the Zip Code?

A: Not really. Even if you always have the *complete* nine-digit ZIP code (called "ZIP Plus 4" by the U.S. Postal Service), there is no absolute guarantee that the ZIP code will always contain only one city, county, and state. Yes, the Postal Service publishes a ZIP code list that provides a city, county, and state for each ZIP code, but that only tells you the location of the post office building that serves the ZIP code; it does not indicate that all the addresses within that ZIP code are in the listed city, county, and state. In the past, some ZIP codes in the United States have actually crossed state lines. Moreover, thousands of examples exist of different cities and towns sharing the same ZIP codes. Nor can you use ZIP codes to determine the county within the state—roughly 20 percent of U.S. five-digit ZIP codes contain parts of more than one county. So be careful when you assume things. The Postal Service will be the first to tell you that it is not responsible for aligning its zoning system with political boundaries. The only 100 percent reliable way to assign city, county, and state to a U.S. address is to use the complete street address in a ZIP code table that includes street names and ranges of street (building) numbers that apply to that ZIP code. By the way, ZIP is actually an acronym for Zoning Improvement Program, introduced in 1963. But I digress….

Should you then make a Zip Code relation and normalize the City and State out of all your addresses? Or would that be considered overdesign? The question can be answered by going back to the anomalies, because removal of the insert, update, and delete anomalies is the entire reason you normalize data in the first place:

- If a new city is formed, do you need to add it to the database even if you have no customers located there? (This is an insert anomaly.)

- If a city is dissolved, do you have a need to delete its information without losing other data? (This is a delete anomaly.)

- If a city changes its name (this rarely occurs, but it has happened), is it a burden to you to find all the customers in that city and change their addresses accordingly?

If you answered yes to any of the above, you should normalize the City and State attributes into a table with a primary key of Zip Code. (Note that the city and state names assigned will be the ones for the post office that serves the ZIP code, which are the names the post office prefers, but they may not be the ones preferred by those receiving the mail.) In fact, you can purchase ZIP code data on a regular basis from the U.S. Postal Service or other sources, or you can subscribe to an address cleansing service that will standardize addresses and provide accurate ZIP codes for each one. Furthermore, if you maintain other data by ZIP code, such as shipping rates, you have all the more reason to normalize it. But if not, the Zip Code example is a valuable lesson in why we normalize (or not) and when it may not be as important.

Another argument for not normalizing the Zip Code data is that the data is not stable. The post office is constantly adding and splitting ZIP codes, and whenever cities acquire new territory, the ZIP code list for the city can change. Common sense must prevail at all times.

NOTE

Here is an easy way to remember the rules of first, second, and third normal form: In a third normal form relation, every non-key attribute must depend on the key, the whole key, and nothing but the key, so help me Codd.

Beyond Third Normal Form

Since the original introduction of normalization, various authors have offered advanced versions. Third normal form will cover well over 90 percent of the cases you will see in business information systems, and it's considered the "gold standard" in business systems. Once you have mastered third normal form, additional normal forms are worth knowing.

Boyce-Codd Normal Form

Boyce-Codd Normal Form (BCNF) is a stronger version of third normal form. It addresses anomalies that occur when a non-key attribute is a *determinant* of an attribute that is part of the primary key (that is, when an attribute that is part of the primary key is functionally dependent on a non-key attribute).

As an example, assume that Acme Industries assigns multiple product support specialists to each customer, and each support specialist handles only one particular product line. Following is a relation that assigns specialists to customers. In reality, Customer ID and Support Specialist (Employee) ID could be used instead of the customer and support specialist names, but their names are used here for better illustration of the issue.

Customer	Product Line	Support Specialist
W. Coyote	Springs	R.E. Coil
W. Coyote	Straps	B. Brown
W. Coyote	Helmets	C. Bandecoot
W. Coyote	Rockets	R. Goddard
USAF	Rockets	R. Goddard
S. Gonzalez	Springs	R.E. Coil
S. Gonzalez	Straps	B. Brown
S. Gonzalez	Rockets	E. John
L. Armstrong	Helmets	S.D. Osborne

In this example, you must concatenate the Customer and Product Line attributes to form a primary key. However, because a given support specialist supports only one product line, it is also true that the Support Specialist attribute determines the Product Line attribute. If you had chosen a surrogate primary key instead of combining Customer and Product Line for the primary key, the third normal form violation—a non-key attribute determining another non-key attribute (Support Specialist determining Product Line in this case)—would be obvious. However, you masked the normalization error by making Product Line part of the primary key. This is why BCNF is considered a *stronger* version of third normal form.

The BCNF has two requirements:

- The relation must be in third normal form.

- No determinants exist that are not either the primary key or a candidate key for the table. That is, a non-key attribute may not uniquely identify (determine) any other attribute, including one that participates in the primary key.

The solution is to split the unwanted determinant to a different table, just as you would with a third normal form violation. The BCNF version of this relation is shown here:

```
SUPPORT SPECIALIST ASSIGNMENT: CUSTOMER ID (PK),
                               SUPPORT SPECIALIST ID

SUPPORT SPECIALIST SPECIALTY: SUPPORT SPECIALIST ID (PK),
                              PRODUCT LINE
```

In tabular form, the relations and data look like this (again, names have been substituted for the IDs to make the data easier to visualize):

Customer	Support Specialist
W. Coyote	R.E. Coil
W. Coyote	B. Brown
W. Coyote	C. Bandecoot
W. Coyote	R. Goddard
USAF	R. Goddard
S. Gonzalez	R.E. Coil
S. Gonzalez	B. Brown
S. Gonzalez	E. John
L. Armstrong	S.D. Osborne

Support Specialist	Product Line
B. Brown	Straps
C. Bandecoot	Helmets
E. John	Rockets
R.E. Coil	Springs
R. Goddard	Rockets
S.D. Osborne	Helmets

Fourth Normal Form

Once in BCNF, remaining normalization problems deal almost exclusively with relations where every attribute is part of the primary key. One such anomaly surfaces when two or more multivalued attributes are included in the same relation. Suppose, for example, you want to track both office skills and language skills for our employees. You might come up with a relation such as this one:

Employee ID	Office Skill	Language Skill
1001	Typing, 40 wpm	Spanish
1001	10 key	French
1002	Spreadsheets	Spanish
1002	10 key	German

You can form a primary key for this relation by choosing the combination of either Employee ID and Office Skill, or Employee ID and Language Skill. That leaves you with either of these two alternatives for third normal form relations:

```
EMPLOYEE SKILL: EMPLOYEE ID (PK), OFFICE SKILL (PK),
                LANGUAGE SKILL

EMPLOYEE SKILL: EMPLOYEE ID (PK), LANGUAGE SKILL (PK),
                OFFICE SKILL
```

Both the alternatives shown are in third normal form, and both pass BCNF as well. The problem, of course, is that an implied relationship exists between office skills and language skills. Does the first tuple for employee 1001 imply that he or she can type only in Spanish? And does the second tuple imply that he or she can work only on a French 10 Key pad?

Relations such as these are rare in real life because when experienced designers resolve multivalued attribute problems to satisfy first normal form, they move each multivalued attribute to its own relation rather than combining them as shown here. So, with some strict interpretation of first normal form procedures, this can be avoided altogether. Also, if you are going to apply the rules of fifth normal form, it covers the anomalies addressed by fourth normal form in terms that are much easier to understand, so you can skip this step altogether. However, should you encounter a fourth normal form violation, the remedy is simply to put each multivalued attribute in a separate relation, such as these:

```
EMPLOYEE OFFICE SKILL: EMPLOYEE ID (PK), OFFICE SKILL (PK)

EMPLOYEE LANGUAGE SKILL: EMPLOYEE ID (PK), LANGUAGE SKILL (PK)
```

Fifth Normal Form

Fifth normal form is very easy to understand. You simply keep splitting relations, stopping only when one of the following conditions is true:

- Any further splitting would lead to relations where the original view cannot be reconstructed with joins.

- The only splits left are trivial. *Trivial splits* occur when resulting relations have a primary key consisting only of the primary key or candidate key of the other relation.

While fifth normal form seems to forbid all three-way relationships, some of these are legitimate. Problems arise only when the entities can be split into simpler, more fundamental relationships.

To most practitioners, fifth normal form is synonymous with *fully normalized*. However, in recent years, database management guru C.J. (Chris) Date has proposed a sixth normal form that deals with temporal and interval data. It remains to be seen whether or not it will be widely adopted.

Domain-Key Normal Form (DKNF)

Ron Fagin introduced domain-key normal form (DKNF) in a research paper published in 1981. The theory is that a relation is in DKNF if and only if every constraint on the relation is a result of the definitions of domains and keys. Although Fagin was able to prove that relations in DKNF have no modification anomalies, he provided no procedure or step-by-step rules to achieve it. The dilemma then is that designers have no solid indication of when DKNF has been achieved for a relation. Nor is the notion that constraints are a consequence of keys obvious. This is likely why DKNF is not in widespread use and is not generally expected in the design of databases for business applications. Academic interest in it has also faded.

Denormalization

As you have seen, normalization leads to more relations, which translates to more tables and more joins. When database users suffer performance problems that cannot be resolved by other means, such as tuning the database or upgrading the hardware on which the RDBMS runs, denormalization may be required. Most database experts consider denormalization a last resort, if not an act of desperation. With continuous improvements in hardware and RDBMS efficiencies, denormalization has become far less necessary than in the earlier days of relational databases. The most essential point is that denormalization is not the same as not bothering to normalize in the first place. Once a normalized database design has been achieved, adjustments can be made with the potential consequences (anomalies) in mind.

Possible denormalization steps include the following:

- Recombining relations that were split to satisfy normalization rules
- Storing redundant data in tables
- Storing summarized data in tables

Note also that normalization is intended to remove anomalies from databases that are used for online transaction-processing systems. Databases that store historical data used solely for analytical purposes are not as subject to insert, update, and delete anomalies. Chapter 12 offers more information on databases that hold historical information.

Practice Problems

This section includes two practice problems (in the form of Try This exercises) with solutions so you can try normalization for yourself. These are very narrow, scaled-down case problems that most readers should be able to solve in about an hour each. As you work them, you will be more successful if you focus just on the views presented and don't worry about other business processes and data that might be needed. For each case problem, the intent is for you to produce third normal form relations that support the views presented and then draw an entity-relationship diagram (ERD) for the normalized relations. As you draw the ERDs, keep in mind that they are quite easy to create once normalization is complete—you simply create a rectangle for each normalized relation and then draw relationships everywhere a primary key in one relation is used as a foreign key in another (or the same) relation. These should all be one-to-many relationships, and the foreign key must always be on the *many* side of the relationship. My solution for each problem appears in Appendix B.

Try This 6-1 UTLA Academic Tracking

The University of Three Letter Acronyms (UTLA) is a small academic facility offering undergraduate and continuing adult education. Most of the recordkeeping is either manual or done by individuals using personal tools such as spreadsheets. A modernization effort is underway, which includes building integrated application and database systems to perform basic business functions.

The User Views

UTLA wishes to construct a system to track its academic activities, including course offerings, instructor qualifications for the courses, course enrollment, and student grades. The following illustrations show the desired output reports with sample data (these are the user views that should be normalized).

Student report:

Student Report:

ID	Name	Mailing Address				Home Phone
4567	Helen Wheels	127 Essex Drive	Hayward	CA	94545	510-555-2859
4953	Barry Bookworm	P.O. Box 45	Oakland	CA	94601	510-555-9403
6758	Carla Coed	South Hall #23	Berkeley	CA	94623	510-555-8742

Course report:

Course Report:

ID	Title	No. Credits	Prerequisite Courses	Description
X100	Concepts of Data Proc.	4	None	This course...
X301	C Programming I	4	X100	Students learn...
X302	C Programming II	6	X301	Continuation of...
X422	Systems Analysis	6	X301	Introduction to...
X408	Concepts of DBMS	6	X301, X422	The main focus...

Instructor report:

Instructor Report:

ID	Name	Home Address	Home Phone	Office Phone	Courses
756	Werdna Leppo	12 Main St. Alameda CA 94501	510-555-1234	x-7463	X408, X422
795	Cora Coder	32767 Binary Way Abend CA 21304	510-555-1010	x-5328	X301, X302
801	Tillie Talker	123 Forms Rd. Paperwork CA 95684	510-555-2829	408-555-2047	X100, X422

Section report:

Section Report:

Year: 2008   **Semester:** Spr   **Building:** Evans   **Room:** 70   **Day(s):** Tu   **Time(s):** 7-10
Instructor: 756, Werdna Leppo   **Course:** X408   **Credits:** 6

Student ID	Student Name	Grade
4567	Helen Wheels	A
6758	Carla Coed	B+

Year: 2008   **Semester:** Spr   **Building:** SFO   **Room:** 7   **Day(s):** We   **Time(s):** 7-10
Instructor: 756, Werdna Leppo   **Course:** X408   **Credits:** 6

Student ID	Student Name	Grade
4973	Barry Bookworm	B+
6758	Carla Coed	A-

Year: 2008   **Semester:** Spr   **Building:** Evans   **Room:** 70   **Day(s):** M,Fr   **Time(s):** 7-9
Instructor: 801, Tillie Talker   **Course:** X100   **Credits:** 4

Student ID	Student Name	Grade

(continued)

You cannot design a database without some knowledge of the business rules and processes of an organization. Here are a few such items to keep in mind:

● Only one mailing address and one contact phone number are kept for each student.

● Each course has a fixed number of credits (that is, no variable credit courses are offered).

● Each course may have one or more prerequisite courses. The list of all prerequisites for each course is shown in the Course report.

● Only one mailing address, one home phone number, and one office phone number are kept for each instructor.

● A qualifications committee must approve instructors before they are permitted to teach a particular course. The qualifications (that is, the courses that the committee has determined the instructor is qualified to teach) are then added to the instructor's records, as shown in the Instructor report. The list of qualified courses does not imply that the instructor has actually taught the course but only that he or she is qualified to do so.

● Based on demand, any course may be offered multiple times, even in the same year and semester. Each offering is called a "section," as shown in the Section report.

● Students enroll in a particular section of a course and receive a grade for their participation in that course offering. Should they take the course again at a later time, they receive another grade, and both grades are part of their permanent academic record.

● Although the day, time, building, and room for each section is noted in the Section report, this is done merely to facilitate registering students. The scheduling of classrooms is out of scope for this project.

● The day(s) and time(s) attributes on the Section report are merely text descriptions of the meeting schedule. The building of a meeting calendar for sections is out of scope for this project.

As a convenience, here are the attributes rewritten using the relation listing method, with repeating groups and multivalued attributes enclosed in parentheses:

```
STUDENT REPORT: ID, STUDENT NAME, STREET ADDRESS, CITY, STATE,
                ZIP CODE, HOME PHONE

COURSE REPORT: ID, TITLE, NUMBER OF CREDITS,
               (PREREQUISITE COURSES), DESCRIPTION
```

```
INSTRUCTOR REPORT: ID, INSTRUCTOR NAME, STREET ADDRESS,
                   CITY, STATE, ZIP CODE, HOME PHONE,
                   OFFICE PHONE, (QUALIFIED COURSES)

SECTION REPORT: YEAR, SEMESTER, BUILDING, ROOM, DAYS,
                TIMES, INSTRUCTOR ID, INSTRUCTOR NAME,
                COURSE ID, NUMBER OF CREDITS,
                (STUDENT ID, STUDENT NAME, GRADE)
```

Step by Step

1. Study each of the user views in the preceding description, along with the business rules. You may have to make some assumptions if you have questions that the description does not answer.

2. Apply the normalization process described in this chapter, normalizing each view to relations that are in at least third normal form. Be careful to consolidate the normalized relations you develop as you go. For the purposes of this exercise, no two relations should share the same primary key. (Exceptions to this rule are covered in subsequent chapters.)

3. Clearly indicate the primary key of each relation. Remember that a primary key can be one or more attributes within the relation.

4. Draw an ERD with one entity (rectangle) for each of your normalized relations and appropriate relationship lines with cardinality clearly noted. This should be quite easy to do once normalization is complete: simply draw a line from each foreign key to the matching primary key and mark the foreign key end of the line as "many" and the primary key end as "one."

Try This Summary

In this Try This exercise, you normalized four user views and drew an ERD of your design. My solution appears in Appendix B.

Try This 6-2 Computer Books Company

The Computer Books Company (CBC) buys books from publishers and sells them to individuals via mail and telephone orders. They are looking to expand their services by offering online ordering via the Internet, and in doing so CBC has a compelling need to build a database to hold its business information.

The User Views

Throughout these user views, "sale" and "price" are references to the retail sale of a book to a CBC customer, whereas "purchase" and "cost" are references to the purchase of books from a publisher (CBC supplier). Each user view is described briefly with a list of the attributes in the view following each description. Per our convention, multivalued attributes and repeating groups are enclosed in parentheses.

The Book Catalog lists all the books that CBC has for sale. Each book is uniquely identified by the International Standard Book Number (ISBN). Although an ISBN uniquely identifies a book, it is essentially a surrogate key, so there is no way to tell the edition of a particular book simply by looking at the ISBN. When new editions come out, CBC typically has leftover stock of prior editions and offers them at a reduced price. The previous edition ISBN in the Book Catalog is intended to help the buyer find the prior edition, if one exists. Books are organized by subject, with each book having only one subject. Any book can have multiple authors. (Although the catalog shows only author names, keep in mind that people's names are seldom unique, and nothing would stop two people with the same name from writing two different books.)

Here is the information in the Book Catalog:

```
BOOK CATALOG: SUBJECT CODE, SUBJECT DESCRIPTION, BOOK TITLE,
              BOOK ISBN, BOOK PRICE, PREVIOUS EDITION ISBN,
              PREVIOUS EDITION PRICE, (BOOK AUTHORS),
              PUBLISHER NAME
```

The Book Inventory Report helps the warehouse manager control the inventory in the warehouse. The Recommended Quantity is the reorder point, meaning when on-hand inventory falls below the recommended quantity, it is time to order more books of that title.

```
INVENTORY REPORT: BOOK ISBN, BOOK EDITION CODE, COST,
                  SELLING PRICE, QUANTITY ON HAND,
                  QUANTITY ON ORDER, RECOMMENDED QUANTITY
```

The Customer Book Orders view shows orders placed by CBC customers for purchases of books:

```
CUSTOMER BOOK ORDERS: CUSTOMER ID, CUSTOMER NAME,
                      STREET ADDRESS, CITY, STATE,
                      ZIP CODE (ISBN, BOOK EDITION CODE,
                      QUANTITY, PRICE), ORDER DATE,
                      TOTAL PRICE
```

CBC bills customers as books are shipped, so an unshipped order won't have an invoice. An invoice is created for each shipment. (An order can have zero, one, or more invoices, but each invoice belongs only to one order.) The Book Sales Invoice looks like this:

```
BOOK SALES INVOICE: SALES INVOICE NUMBER, CUSTOMER ID,
                    CUSTOMER NAME, CUSTOMER STREET ADDRESS,
                    CUSTOMER CITY, CUSTOMER STATE,
                    CUSTOMER ZIP CODE, (BOOK ISBN, TITLE,
                    EDITION CODE, (BOOK AUTHORS), QUANTITY,
                    PRICE, PUBLISHER NAME),
                    SHIPPING CHARGES, SALES TAX
```

The Master Billing Report helps the Collections and Customer Service departments manage customer accounts. A system for recording customer payments against invoices is out of scope for the current project, but the CBC project sponsors do want to keep a running balance showing what each customer owes CBC. As invoices are generated, a database trigger will be used to add invoice totals to the Balance Due. As payments are received, the CBC staff will manually adjust the Balance Due. The Master Billing Report attributes are as follows:

```
MASTER BILLING REPORT: CUSTOMER ID, CUSTOMER NAME, STREET ADDRESS,
                       STREET ADDRESS, CITY, STATE, ZIP CODE,
                       PHONE, BALANCE DUE
```

Each time CBC buys books from a publisher, the publisher sends an invoice to CBC. To assist in managing inventory cost, CBC wishes to store the Purchase Invoice information and report it using this view:

```
PURCHASE INVOICE: PUBLISHER ID, PUBLISHER NAME,
                  STREET ADDRESS, CITY, STATE, ZIP CODE,
                  PURCHASE INVOICE NUMBER, INVOICE DATE,
                  (BOOK ISBN, EDITION CODE, TITLE,
                  QUANTITY, COST EACH, EXTENDED COST),
                  TOTAL COST
```

Note that Extended Cost is calculated as Cost Each times Quantity.

(continued)

Step by Step

1. Study each of the user views in the preceding description, along with the business rules. You might have to make some assumptions if you have questions that the description does not answer.

2. Apply the normalization process described in this chapter, normalizing each view to relations that are in at least third normal form. Be careful to consolidate the normalized relations you develop as you go. For the purposes of this exercise, no two relations should share the same primary key. (Exceptions to this rule are covered in subsequent chapters.)

3. Clearly indicate the primary key of each relation. Remember that a primary key can be one or more attributes within the relation.

4. Draw an ERD with one entity (rectangle) for each of your normalized relations and appropriate relationship lines with cardinality clearly noted. This is actually quite easy once normalization is complete: simply draw a line from each foreign key to the matching primary key and mark the foreign key end of the line as "many" and the primary key end as "one."

Try This Summary

In this Try This exercise, you normalized six user views that were more complicated than the previous Try This exercise and drew an ERD of your design. My solution appears in Appendix B.

✓ *Chapter 6 Self Test*

Choose the correct responses to each of the multiple-choice and fill-in-the-blank questions. Note that there may be more than one correct response to each question.

1. Normalization

   A Was developed by E.F. Codd

   B Was first introduced with five normal forms

   C First appeared in 1972

   D Provides a set of rules for each normal form

   E Provides a procedure for converting relations to each normal form

2. The purpose of normalization is

   A To eliminate redundant data

   B To remove certain anomalies from the relations

   C To provide a reason to denormalize the database

   D To optimize data-retrieval performance

   E To optimize data for inserts, updates, and deletes

3. When implemented, a third normal form relation becomes a(n) _____.

4. The insert anomaly refers to a situation in which

   A Data must be inserted before it can be deleted.

   B Too many inserts cause the table to fill up.

   C Data must be deleted before it can be inserted.

   D A required insert cannot be done due to an artificial dependency.

   E A required insert cannot be done due to duplicate data.

5. The delete anomaly refers to a situation in which

   A Data must be deleted before it can be inserted.

   B Data must be inserted before it can be deleted.

   C Data deletion causes unintentional loss of another entity's data.

   D A required delete cannot be done due to referential constraints.

   E A required delete cannot be done due to lack of privileges.

6. The update anomaly refers to a situation in which

   A A simple update requires updates to multiple rows of data.

   B Data cannot be updated because it does not exist in the database.

   C Data cannot be updated due to lack of privileges.

   D Data cannot be updated due to an existing unique constraint.

   E Data cannot be updated due to an existing referential constraint.

7. The roles of unique identifiers in normalization are

    A They are unnecessary.

    B They are required once you reach third normal form.

    C All normalized forms require designation of a primary key.

    D You cannot normalize relations without first choosing a primary key.

    E You cannot choose a primary key until relations are normalized.

8. Writing sample user views with representative data in them is

    A The only way to normalize the user views successfully

    B A tedious and time-consuming process

    C An effective way to understand the data being normalized

    D Only as good as the examples shown in the sample data

    E A widely used normalization technique

9. Criteria useful in selecting a primary key from among several candidate keys are

    A Choose the simplest candidate.

    B Choose the shortest candidate.

    C Choose the candidate most likely to have its value change.

    D Choose concatenated keys over single attribute keys.

    E Invent a surrogate key if that is the best possible key.

10. First normal form resolves anomalies caused by _____.

11. Second normal form resolves anomalies caused by _____.

12. Third normal form resolves anomalies caused by _____.

13. In general, violations of a normalization rule are resolved by

    A Combining relations

    B Moving attributes or groups of attributes to a new relation

    C Combining attributes

    D Creating summary tables

    E Denormalization

14. A foreign key in a normalized relation may be

   A The entire primary key of the relation

   B Part of the primary key of the relation

   C A repeating group

   D A non-key attribute in the relation

   E A multivalued attribute

15. Boyce-Codd Normal Form deals with anomalies caused by _____.

16. Fourth normal form deals with anomalies caused by _____.

17. Fifth normal form deals with anomalies caused by _____.

18. Domain key normal form deals with anomalies caused by _____.

19. Most business systems require that you normalize only as far as _____.

20. Proper handling of multivalued attributes when converting relations to first normal form usually prevents subsequent problems with _____.

Chapter 7
Data and Process Modeling

Key Skills & Concepts

- Entity Relationship Modeling
- Process Models
- Relating Entities and Processes

A s you saw in Chapter 5, data and process modeling are major undertakings that are part of the logical design stage of an application system development project. You have already seen the rudiments of data modeling when you used entity relationship diagrams (ERDs) in preceding chapters. In this chapter, we will look at ERDs and data modeling in more detail. Process modeling, on the other hand, is less important to a database designer because application processes are designed by application designers and seldom directly involve the database designer. However, because the database designer must work closely with the application designer in gathering data requirements and in supplying a database design that will support the processes being designed, the database designer should at least be familiar with the basic concepts. For this reason, the second part of this chapter includes a high-level survey of process design concepts and diagramming techniques.

Entity Relationship Modeling

Entity relationship modeling is the process of visually representing entities, attributes, and relationships to produce the ERD. The process is iterative in nature because entities are discovered throughout the design process. The chief advantage of ERDs is that they can be understood by nontechnical people while still providing great value to technical people. Done correctly, ERDs are platform independent and can even be used for nonrelational databases if desired.

ERD Formats

Peter Chen developed the original ERD format in 1976. Since then, vendors, computer scientists, and academics have developed many variations, all of them conceptually the same. You should understand the most commonly used variations because you are likely to encounter them in active use in IT organizations. Here are the elements common to all ERD formats:

- Entities are represented as rectangles or boxes.

- Relationships are represented as lines.

- Line ends (or symbols next to them) indicate the maximum cardinality of the relationship (that is, one or many).

- Symbols near the line ends (in most ERD formats) indicate the minimum cardinality of the relationship (that is, whether participation in the relationship is mandatory or optional).

- Attributes may be optionally included (the format for displaying attributes varies quite a bit).

Chen's Format

For simplicity, we'll use the normalized solution for the Acme Industries invoice application from Chapter 6 for the examples in this chapter. Figure 7-1 shows the ERD using Chen's format.

Here are the particulars of the Chen format:

- Relationship lines contain a diamond in which is written a word or short phrase that describes the relationship. For example, the relationship between Invoice and Product may be read as "An invoice *contains* many products." Some variations permit another word or phrase to be used in reading the relationship in the other direction, separated with a slash. If the diamond read "Contains/Appears on," then the relationship from Product to Invoice would be read as "A product *appears on* many invoices."

- For many-to-many relationships that require an intersection table in an RDBMS, such as the one between Invoice and Product, a rectangle is often drawn around the diamond.

- Maximum cardinality of each relationship is shown using the symbol *1* for "one" or *M* for "many."

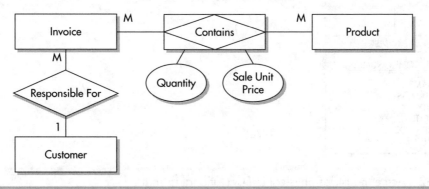

Figure 7-1   Acme Industries logical ERD format in Chen's format

- Minimum cardinality is not shown.

- Attributes, when shown, appear in ellipses (elongated circles), connected to the entity or relationship to which they belong with a line.

In practice, Chen ERDs are cumbersome for complicated data models. The diamonds take up a lot of space on the diagrams for the little added value they provide. Also, any ERD that includes many attributes becomes very difficult to read. Notwithstanding, we owe Chen a lot for his pioneering work, which laid the foundation for the techniques that followed.

The Relational Format

Over time, an ERD format known generically as the *relational format* evolved. It is available as an option in several of the better-known data modeling software tools, including PowerDesigner from Sybase and ER/Studio from Embarcadero Technologies, and in popular general drawing tools such as Visio from Microsoft. Figure 7-2 shows the ERD from Figure 7-1 converted to the relational format. In this example, the ERD is represented at a physical level, meaning that physical table names are shown instead of logical entity names, and physical column names are shown instead of logical attribute names. Also, intersection tables are shown to resolve many-to-many relationships. As the logical data model is transformed into a physical database design, it is essential to have a physical ERD that the project team can use in developing the application system. The beginnings of the physical model are shown here to help make that point.

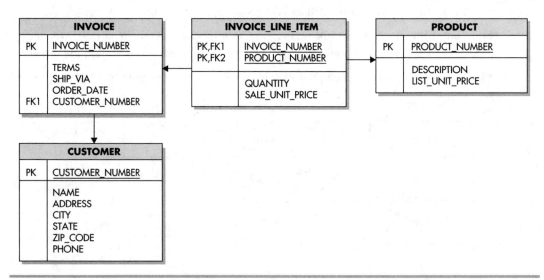

Figure 7-2 Acme Industries physical ERD, relational format

Here are the particulars of the relational ERD format:

- Relationship cardinality is shown with an arrowhead on the line end to signify "one" and nothing on the line end to signify "many." This will seem odd at first, but it aligns nicely with object diagrams, so this format is favored by object-oriented designers and developers.

- Attributes are shown inside the rectangle that represents each entity.

- Unique identifier attributes are shown above a horizontal line within the rectangle and are usually also shown with **PK** in bold type (for primary key) in the margin to the left of the attribute name.

- Attributes that are foreign keys are shown with FK and a number in the margin to the left of the attribute name.

The Information Engineering Format

The information engineering (IE) format was originally developed by Clive Finkelstein in Australia in the late 1970s. In the early 1980s he collaborated with James Martin to publicize it in the United States and Europe, including co-authoring the Savant Institute Report titled *Information Engineering*, published in 1981. Martin went on to be highly associated with the format and, in collaboration with Carma McClure, published a book on the subject in 1984 (*Diagramming Techniques for Analysis and Programmers*, Prentice-Hall). Finkelstein later published his own version in 1989 (*An Introduction to Information Engineering*, Addison-Wesley), which has some minor notation variations compared with Martin's version. Figure 7-3 shows our sample ERD converted to IE notation. You will notice that except for relationship lines, it is strikingly similar to the relational format.

Here are some of the ways that IE notation varies from the relational format:

- **Identifying relationships**   Shown with a solid line, are those for which the foreign key is part of the child entity's primary key.

- **Non-identifying relationships**   Shown with a dotted line, are those for which the foreign key is a non-key attribute in the child entity. In Figure 7-3, the relationship between PRODUCT and INVOICE_LINE_ITEM is identifying, but the one between CUSTOMER and INVOICE is non-identifying.

- **Maximum relationship cardinality**   Shown with a short perpendicular line across the relationship near its line end to signify "one" and a "crow's foot" on the line end to signify "many." This is best understood in combination with minimum cardinality, described next.

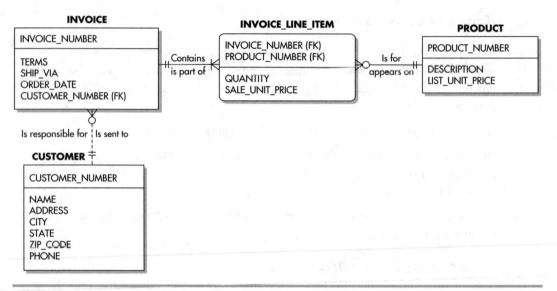

Figure 7-3 Acme Industries physical ERD, IE format

- **Minimum relationship cardinality** Shown with a small circle near the end of the line to signify "zero" (participation in the relationship is optional) or a short perpendicular line across the relationship line to signify "one" (participation in the relationship is mandatory). Figure 7-3 notes a few combinations of minimum and maximum cardinality. For example:

  - **A PRODUCT** May have zero to many associated INVOICE_LINE_ITEM occurrences (shown as a circle and a crow's foot); an INVOICE_LINE_ITEM must have one and only one associated PRODUCT (shown as two vertical bars).

  - **An INVOICE** Must have one or more associated INVOICE_LINE_ITEM occurrences (shown as a vertical bar and a crow's foot); an INVOICE_LINE_ITEM must have one and only one associated INVOICE (shown as two vertical bars).

- **Dependent entities** Shown with the corners of the rectangle rounded, have an existence dependency on one or more other entities (that is, those that cannot exist without the existence of another). For example, the INVOICE_LINE_ITEM entity depends on both the PRODUCT and INVOICE entities. Therefore, you cannot delete either an invoice or a product unless you somehow deal with any related invoice line items. This is valuable information during physical database design because you must consider the options for handling situations when the application attempts to delete table rows when dependent entities exist.

The IE format is by far the most popular. Therefore, I use it for the majority of the diagrams in this book.

The IDEF1X Format

The Computer Systems Laboratory of the National Institute of Standards and Technology released the IDEF1X standard for data modeling in FIPS Publication 184, first published in December 1993. The standard covers both a method for data modeling as well as the format for the ERDs produced during the modeling effort. It is widely used and understood across the information technology industry and the mandatory standard for many branches of the U.S. government. Thanks to its underlying standard, it has few variants. Figure 7-4 shows our sample ERD converted to the IDEF1X standard format.

The differences between IE and IDEF1X notation are largely isolated to relationships. Unlike other formats, relationship symbols in IDEF1X are asymmetrical. Each set of symbols describes a combination of optionality and cardinality, and thus the symbols used for optionality vary depending on the cardinality of the relationship. Said another way, optionality is shown differently for the "many" and "one" sides of a relationship. Here are some key points:

● Like the IE format, a solid line indicates that the foreign key is part of the dependent entity's primary key, while a broken line indicates that the foreign key will be a non-key attribute.

● A solid circle next to an entity generally means zero, one, or more occurrences of that entity as shown on the "many" end of the line between PRODUCT and INVOICE_LINE_ITEM. However, there are exceptions:

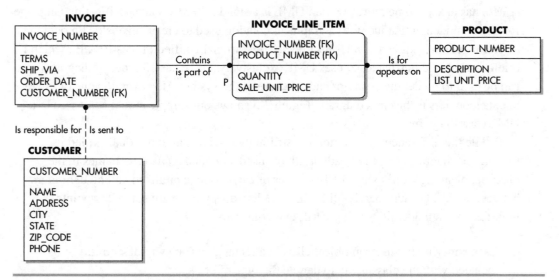

Figure 7-4 Acme Industries physical ERD, IDEF1X format

- Adding the symbol *P* near the solid circle makes the relationship mandatory, signifying that the cardinality must be one or more. In Figure 7-4, the relationship from INVOICE to INVOICE_LINE_ITEM is one-to-many and mandatory, meaning that every invoice must have at least one line item.

- Adding the symbol *1* also makes the relationship mandatory. However, this changes the cardinality of the relationship to one. Said another way, it changes the meaning of the solid circle from "may be one or more" to "must be one and only one."

- Absence of a solid circle at the end of the relationship line means that only one occurrence of the entity is involved. For example, the absence of any symbol on the end of the line next to CUSTOMER means "one and only one." It may be modified for optionality as well:

  - If no symbol appears next to the entity at that end of the line, the entity is mandatory in the relationship. Therefore, an INVOICE_LINE_ITEM must be related to one and only one PRODUCT.

  - If a small diamond symbol appears next to the entity, the entity is optional. Were we to add a diamond next to the CUSTOMER end of the relationship between INVOICE and CUSTOMER, it would mean that each INVOICE *may* have zero or one related CUSTOMER occurrences.

Entity Relationship Modeling with Unified Modeling Language

With the rising popularity of object programming languages, the *Unified Modeling Language (UML)* has also become more popular. UML is a standardized visual specification language for object modeling that includes a graphical notation used to create an abstract model of a system, which is known as a UML model. The Rational Unified Process (RUP), which I briefly introduced in Chapter 5, uses UML exclusively. UML has 13 types of diagrams that can be used to model the behavior and structure of the system. However, the one of interest to data modelers is the class diagram. Figure 7-5 shows our sample model converted to a UML class diagram.

While the differences in notation are strikingly obvious, an individual skilled in reading ER diagrams can easily adapt. I have used so-called *camelcase* names in the diagram, meaning names with the first letter of each word capitalized and no delimiters between words, because nearly all UML modelers do so. Here are some key points regarding modeling entities using UML class diagrams:

- Each entity is shown as an object class in a rectangle. The symbol <<Entity>> is included with the class name to denote the type of class.

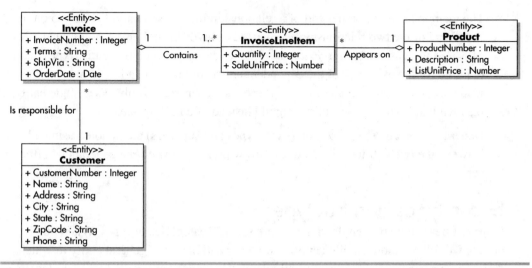

Figure 7-5 UML class diagram for Acme Industries

- Unique identifiers (primary keys) are not shown in class diagrams; they are specified elsewhere within the UML model.

- Foreign keys are not shown because they are not used in object-oriented systems. I discuss object-oriented technology in Chapter 13.

- Attributes are shown with a name and a type (separated with a colon). The type is very much like a relational data type. Attributes in entities are preceded by the symbol +, which means they are public (visible throughout the entire model).

- Relationships are shown with lines.

- Cardinality and optionality are shown with a combined symbol near the end of the line. Available symbols include those shown in the following table:

Symbol	Meaning
1	One and only one
*	Zero, one, or more
1..*	One or more
x..y	Between x and y occurrences. Also · x can be 0 or any positive integer · y can be any positive integer or * to denote "or more" · y must be greater than x (if y and x are the same, then y is simply omitted)

- The diamond symbol on the end of a relationship line, as shown in Figure 7-5 on the "one" end of the two relationships connected to InvoiceLineItem, denotes what UML calls an aggregation. An *aggregation* is a dependency between two entity types that is required for the existence of the dependent entity. In this case, a line item cannot exist without both the product and the invoice. If the dependency is always a single entity, the diamond is shown as a solid diamond instead of a hollow one.

- Generalization and specialization (super types and subtypes) are denoted using a line between the two entities with a hollow arrow pointing toward the general class (the super type).

Super Types and Subtypes

Some entities can be broken down into more specific categories or types. When this occurs, we call the more detailed entities *subtypes* and the more general entity to which they belong a *super type*. In object terminology, the super type is called a *super class* or *base class* and the subtypes are called *subclasses* of the super class. It is essential that you understand that subtypes break down entities by type rather than by *state,* meaning their mode or condition. An easy way to distinguish between the two is to realize that existing entities can change state, but they seldom, if ever, change type. For example, a motor vehicle entity can logically be broken down by type into automobile, bus, truck, motorcycle, and so on. However, the distinction between vehicles that are new or used, or between those that are operable or inoperable, is one of *state* rather than *type* because new vehicles become used once they are sold, and vehicles change between inoperable and operable states as they break down and are subsequently repaired.

The decisions involved in which entities should be broken down into subtypes and how detailed the subtypes should be revolve around the tradeoff between specialization and generalization. Unfortunately, there are no firm rules for resolving the tradeoff. Therefore, generalization versus specialization becomes one of the topics that prevent database design from becoming an exact science. The general guideline to follow (in addition to common sense) is that the more the various subtypes share common attributes and relationships, the more the designer should be inclined to combine the subtypes into the super type. The physical design tradeoffs involved are addressed in Chapter 8. Here we will focus on the logical design tradeoffs.

Let's look at an example. Assume for a moment that the database design shown in Figure 7-3 has been implemented, and now the Customer Service Department at Acme Industries has requested database and application enhancements that will allow it to record and track more information about customers. In particular, the department is interested in knowing the type of customer (such as individual person, sole proprietorship, partnership, or corporation) so that correspondence can be addressed appropriately for each type. Figure 7-6 shows the logical data model that was developed based on the new requirements.

In IE notation, the type or category is shown using a symbol that looks like a circle with a line under it. Therefore, you know that Individual Customer and Commercial Customer are subtypes of Customer because of the symbol that appears in the line that connects them. Also note that they share the exact same primary key and that in the subtypes, the primary key of the entity is also a foreign key to the super type entity. This makes perfect sense when you consider the fact that an Individual Customer entity *is a* Customer, meaning that any occurrence of the Individual Customer entity would have a tuple in the Customer relation as well as a matching tuple in the Individual Customer entity.

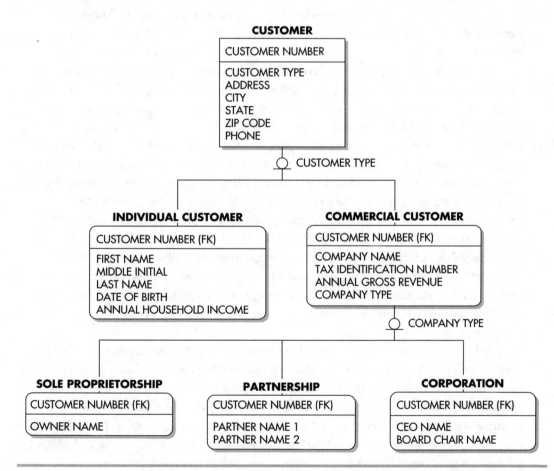

Figure 7-6   Customer subclasses

Usually an attribute in the super type entity indicates which subtype is assigned to each entity occurrence (tuple). Once this is implemented in tables, database users can use the type attribute to know where to look for (that is, which subtype table contains) the remainder of the information about each entity occurrence (each row). Such an attribute is called the *type discriminator* and is named next to the type symbol on the ERD. Therefore, Customer Type is the type discriminator that indicates whether a given Customer is an Individual Customer or a Commercial Customer. Similarly, Company Type is the type discriminator that indicates whether a given Commercial Customer is a sole proprietorship, partnership, or corporation.

As you might imagine, this IE notation is not the only format used in ERDs for super types and subtypes. However, it is the most commonly used method. Another popular format is to draw the subtype entities within the super type entity (that is, subtype entity rectangles drawn inside the corresponding super type entity's rectangle). Although this format makes it visually clear that the subtypes really are just a part of the super type, it has practical limitations when the entities are broken down into many levels.

As mentioned, finding the right level of specialization is a significant database design challenge. In reviewing the logical design as proposed in Figure 7-6, the database design team noticed something: The only difference among the Sole Proprietorship, Partnership, and Corporation subtypes is in the way that the names of key people in those types of companies appear as attributes. Moreover, the use of two nearly identical attributes for the names of the co-owners in the Partnership subtype could be considered a repeating attribute, and therefore a first normal form violation. The design team elected to generalize these names into the Commercial Customer entity, but in doing so, they recognized the first normal form problems and decided to place them into a separate relation called Commercial Customer Principal. This led to the ERD shown in Figure 7-7.

Clearly this is a simpler design that will result in fewer tables when it is physically implemented. It offers a very big win, because not only is there no loss of function when you consolidate the subtypes into the super type, but you actually have *more* function available because you can add as many names as you want to any type of commercial customer.

Further study by the design team helped them realize the similarity between the name attributes now contained in the Commercial Customer Principal entity and those contained in the Individual Customer entity. In discussing options further with the Customer Service Department, the design team uncovered a few cases for which it would be desirable for multiple contact names to be recorded for individual customers as well as for commercial customers. For example, customers that have legal disputes often request that all contact go through an attorney. With that information, the design team decided to generalize

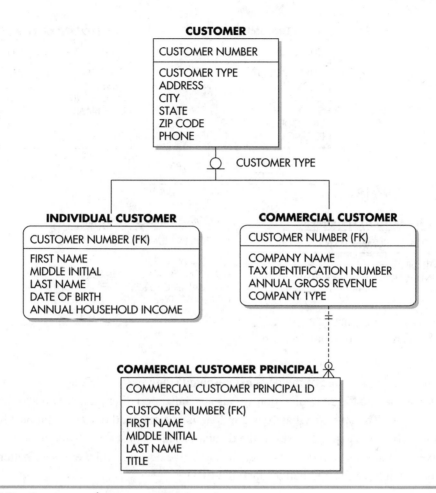

Figure 7-7   Customer subtypes, version 2

these names and move Commercial Customer Principal up to be a child of Customer and name it Customer Contact so that it could be used to hold the information about either a principal (owner, co-owner, partner, officer) of the customer or any other contact person for the customer that the Customer Service Department might find useful. The design team further realized that contact names would be more useful if a phone number was included. The Phone attribute was left in the Customer entity because it is intended to hold the general phone number for the customer. The phone number in the Customer Contact entity is intended to hold the phone for an individual contact person. The resultant logical design is shown in Figure 7-8.

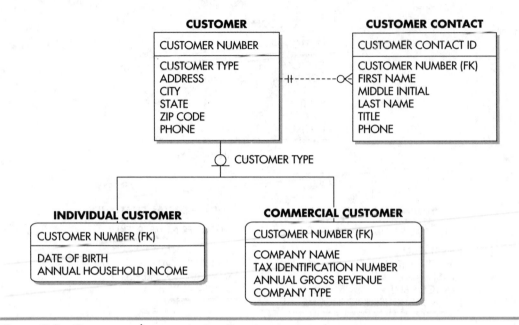

Figure 7-8 Customer subtypes, version 3

The fact that all three of the designs presented (Figures 7-6, 7-7, and 7-8) are workable should underscore the generalization versus specialization dilemma: No one "right" answer exists. The art to database design, then, is to arrive at the design that best fits what is known about the expected uses of the database. This is best done by comparing the relative strengths and weaknesses of each alternative design. And there is no better vehicle for communicating the alternatives than the ERD.

Ask the Expert

Q: In the discussion of UML in the chapter, you mentioned that generalization is shown using lines and arrows. How would you convert the super type and subtypes in Figure 7-8 to UML notation?

A: First, you remove the existing symbols (the lines, type symbol, and discriminator attribute name). Then you draw a line between each subtype and its super type, placing a hollow arrowhead on the super type end of the line, pointing toward the super type entity. Figure 7-9 shows the same model as Figure 7-8, but in UML notation.

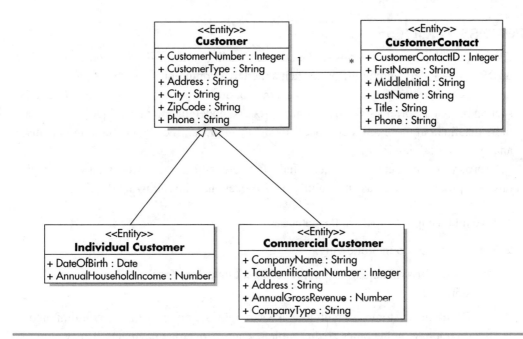

Figure 7-9 Customer subtypes, version 3, converted to UML

Guidelines for Drawing ERDs

Here are some general guidelines to follow when constructing ERDs:

- Do not try to relate every entity to every other entity. Entities should be related only when the *entire* primary key in one entity appears as a foreign key in another.

- Except for subtypes, avoid relationships involving more than two entities. Although drawing fewer lines might seem simpler, it is far too easy to misinterpret relationships drawn from one parent entity to multiple child entities using a single line.

- Be consistent with entity and attribute names. Develop a naming convention and stick with it.

- Use abbreviations in names only when absolutely necessary, and in those cases, use a standard list of abbreviations.

- Name primary keys and foreign keys consistently. Most experts prefer that the foreign key have exactly the same name as the primary key.

- When relationships are named, strive for action words, avoiding nondescriptive terms such as "has," "belongs to," "is associated with," and so on.

Process Models

As mentioned, process design is seldom the responsibility of the database designer or DBA, but understanding the basics helps the DBA communicate with the process designers and ensure that the database design supports the process design. Therefore, this section presents a brief survey of common process model diagram techniques. If you want more detail about these or other process model techniques, find a good book on systems analysis and design.

Throughout this section, the Acme Industries order-fulfillment process, a very simple business process, is used as an example. This process has the following steps:

1. Find all unshipped orders in the database.

2. For each order, do the following:

- Check for available inventory. If sufficient inventory for the order is not available, skip to the next order.

- Check the customer's credit to make sure they are not over their credit limit and do not have some other credit problem, such as overdue payments. This would typically occur at the time the order is entered, but it needs to occur again here because a customer's credit status with Acme Industries can change at any time. If a credit problem is found, skip to the next order.

- Generate the documents required to pack and ship the order (packing slip, shipping labels, and so on) and route them to the shipping department.

- When the shipping department has finished with the order, create the invoice for the order and bill the customer accordingly.

Obviously, this process could be a lot more complicated in a large company, but here it has been reduced to the basics so that it is easier to use for illustration of process models.

The Flowchart

The flowchart (or structure chart) is probably the oldest form of computer systems documentation. Some believe that flowcharts existed when dinosaurs still roamed our planet, and therefore anyone who still uses flowcharts is a dinosaur. Levity aside, flowcharts are often considered outmoded, but they still have much to offer in certain circumstances and are still widely used. Figure 7-10 shows the flowchart for our sample order-fulfillment process.

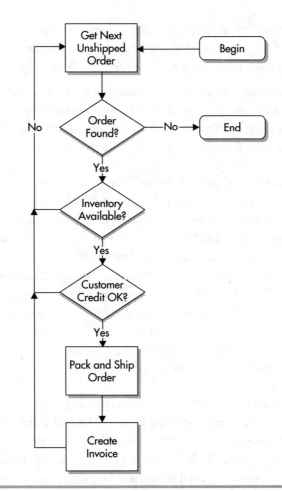

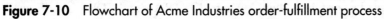

Figure 7-10 Flowchart of Acme Industries order-fulfillment process

Here are the basic components of the flowchart:

- Process steps are shown with rectangles.

- Decision points are shown with diamonds. At each decision point, the logic branches are based on the outcome of the decision. For example, a decision might be "Is today Friday?" with a "Yes" outcome going in one direction and a "No" outcome going in another.

- Lines with arrows show the flow of control through the diagram. When one process completes, it hands over control to the next process or decision point.

- Start and end points are shown with either ellipses or rounded rectangles. Flowcharts can be used to show perpetual processes that have no start and no end, but more often they are used to show finite processes with specific beginning and ending points.

- Connector symbols that look like home plates on a baseball diamond (not shown in Figure 7-10) can be used to connect lines to processes or decision points, on the same or another page. Usually these are given a reference letter with a control flow line assumed between any two connectors that have the same reference letter.

Figure 7-10 shows a very straightforward loop process flow. It begins with a process step that gets the next unshipped order from the database. A decision is added after it to stop the loop (end the flow) if we don't find an unshipped order. If we do find the order, the process continues with decision points that check for available inventory and acceptable customer credit, with a "No" outcome either going back to the top of the loop (the Get Next Unshipped Order process), which essentially skips the order and moves on to find the next one. If we get a "Yes" outcome from all the decision points, the "Pack and ship order" process is invoked next, followed by "Create invoice." After the "Create invoice" process completes, control goes back to "Get next unshipped order," at the top of the loop. The loop continues until no more unshipped orders are found.

Flowcharts have the following strengths:

- Procedural language programmers find them naturally easy to learn and use. A *procedural language* is a programming language by which the programmer must describe the process steps required to do something, as opposed to a *nonprocedural language*, such as SQL, with which the programmer merely describes the desired results. The most commonly used procedural language today is probably C and its variants (C++, C#, and so on), but others, such as FORTRAN and COBOL, still see some use. Also, specialized procedural languages for relational databases, including PL/SQL for Oracle and Transact SQL for Sybase ASE and Microsoft SQL Server, are heavily used.

- Flowcharts are applicable to procedures outside of a programming context. For example, flowcharts are often used to walk repair technicians though troubleshooting procedures for the equipment they service.

- Flowcharts are useful for spotting reusable (common) components. The designer can easily find any process that appears multiple times in the flowcharts for a particular application system.

- Flowcharts may be easily modified and can evolve as requirements change.

On the other hand, flowcharts present these weaknesses:

- They are not applicable to nonprocedural or object-oriented languages.
- They cannot easily model some situations, such as recursive processes (processes that invoke themselves).

The Function Hierarchy Diagram

The *function hierarchy diagram*, as the name suggests, shows all the functions of a particular application system or business process, organized into a hierarchical tree. Figure 7-11 shows this type of process model diagram from our sample order-fulfillment process.

Because the function hierarchy for a single process makes little sense out of context, two other processes have been added to the hierarchy: Order entry and History management. To be effective, a function hierarchy must contain *all* the processes required to carry out the function it describes. Figure 7-11 attempts to show all the processes required for the Order management function at Acme Industries. Order entry is intended to cover all the process steps involved in a customer placing an order and having it recorded in Acme's database. History management is intended to cover all the steps required to archive and purge old (historical) orders and any required reporting on order history. Both of these processes need to be expanded by adding process steps below them (as was done with Order fulfillment) to make this a complete diagram. Under Order fulfillment, the four main process steps involved in fulfilling orders have been added.

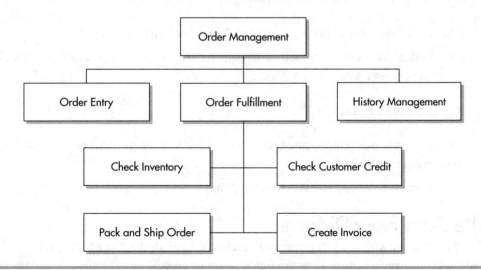

Figure 7-11 Function hierarchy of the Acme order-fulfillment process

The strengths of function hierarchy diagrams are as follows:

- They are quick and easy to learn and use.
- They can quickly document the bulk of the function (they get to 80 percent of the processes quickly).
- They provide a good overview at high and medium levels of detail.

And here are the weaknesses of function hierarchy diagrams:

- Checking quality is difficult and subjective.
- They cannot handle complex interactions between functions.
- They do not clearly show the sequence of process steps or dependencies between steps.
- They are not an effective presentation tool for large hierarchies or at very detailed levels.

The Swim Lane Diagram

The *swim lane diagram* gets its name from the vertical lanes in the diagram, which resemble the lanes in a swimming pool. Each lane represents an organizational unit such as a department, with process steps placed in the lane for the unit that is responsible for the step. Lines with arrows show the sequence or control flow of the process steps. Figure 7-12 shows the swim lane diagram for our sample order-fulfillment process.

Strengths of the swim lane diagram include:

- It has the unmatched ability to show who does what in the organization.
- It's excellent for identifying inefficiencies in existing processes and lends itself well to business process reengineering efforts.

Its weaknesses include:

- It does not represent complicated processes (those with many steps or with complex step dependencies) well.
- It does not show error and exception handling.

The Data Flow Diagram

The *data flow diagram (DFD)* is the most data-centric of all the process diagrams. Instead of showing a control flow through a series of process steps, it focuses on the data that flows through the process steps. By combining diagrams hierarchically, the DFD

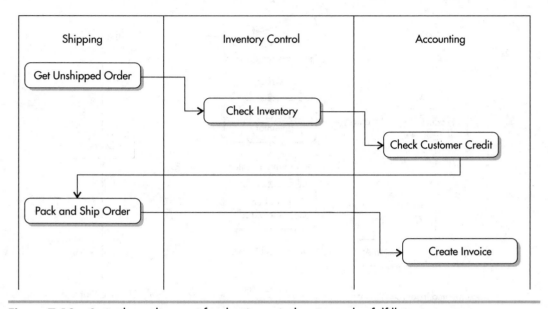

Figure 7-12   Swim lane diagram for the Acme Industries order-fulfillment process

combines the best of the flowchart and the function diagram. DFDs became immensely popular in the late 1970s and early 1980s, largely due to the work of Chris Gane and Trish Sarson. Each process on a DFD can be broken down using another complete page until the desired level of detail is reached. Figure 7-13 shows one page of the DFD for the Acme Industries order-fulfillment process.

The components of a DFD are simple:

- Processes are represented with rounded rectangles. Processes are typically numbered hierarchically. The first page of a DFD might have processes numbered 1, 2, 3, and 4. The next page might break down process number 1 and would have processes numbered 1.1, 1.2, and so forth. If process 1.2 were broken down on yet another page, the processes on that page would be numbered 1.2.1, 1.2.2, and so forth.

- Data stores are represented with an open-ended rectangle. A *data store* is a generic representation of data that is made persistent through being stored somewhere, such as a file, database, or even a written document. The term was chosen so that no particular type of storage is implied. Because we already have an ERD for our example, we should closely align the data stores with the entities we have already identified.

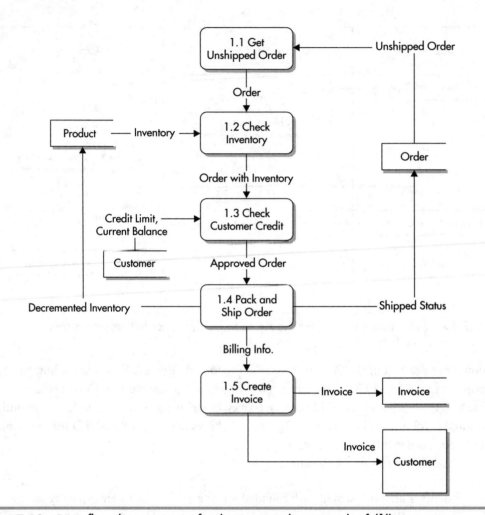
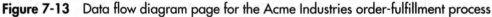

Figure 7-13 Data flow diagram page for the Acme Industries order-fulfillment process

- Sources and destinations of data (external entities in relational terminology) are shown using squares. Figure 7-13 shows the Customer as the destination of the invoice data flow (in addition to a local data store that will hold the invoice data). Try not to confuse data flows with material flows. Yes, the invoice is printed and mailed to the customer, but the data flow is attempting to show that the *data* is sent to the customer with no regard for the medium used to send it.

- Flows of data are shown using lines with arrowheads indicating the direction of flow. Above each flow, words are used to describe the content of the data being sent. Bidirectional flows are permissible but are usually shown as separate flows because the data is seldom exactly the same in both directions.

The strengths of the data flow diagram are as follows:

- It easily shows the overall structure of the system without sacrificing detail (details are shown on subsequent pages that expand on the higher level processes).

- It's good for top-down design work.

- It's good for presentation of systems designs to management and business users.

And here are the weaknesses of the data flow diagram:

- It's time-consuming and labor-intensive to develop for complex systems.

- Top-down design has proved to be ineffective for situations in which requirements are sketchy and continuously evolving during the life of the project.

- It's poor at showing complex logic, but the lowest level diagrams can easily be supplemented with other documents, such as narratives or decision tables.

Ask the Expert

Q: Doesn't UML have process diagrams?

A: Yes, but that's only part of the story. As mentioned, UML 2.x offers 13 different diagrams, 6 of which are *structure diagrams* that emphasize what things must be in the system being modeled, and 7 of which are *behavior diagrams* that emphasize what must happen in the system being modeled. Of these, the class diagram is covered earlier in this chapter. There's not enough space in this book to cover them all,

(continued)

but you'll find lots of information on the Internet and in books on the subject. The following table provides a summary description of each UML diagram:

Type	Name	Description
Structure	Class diagram	Shows a collection of static model elements such as classes and types, their contents, and their relationships
Structure	Component diagram	Depicts the components that make up an application, system, or enterprise
Structure	Composite structure diagram	Depicts that the internal structure of a classifier, (such as a class, component, or use case), including the classifier's interaction points to other parts of the system (added in UML 2.x)
Structure	Deployment diagram	Shows the execution architecture of systems, including nodes, hardware/software environments, and the middleware that connects them
Structure	Object diagram	Depicts objects and their relationships at a point in time
Structure	Package diagram	Shows how model elements are assembled into packages as well as the dependencies between packages
Behavior	Activity diagram	Depicts high-level business processes, including data flow
Behavior	State machine diagram	Describes the states an object or interaction may be in, and the transitions between states
Behavior	Use case diagram	Shows actors, use cases, and their interactions
Behavior	Communication diagram	Shows instances of classes, their interrelationships, and the message flow between them
Behavior	Interaction overview diagram	A variant of an activity diagram that depicts an overview of the control flow within a system or business process (added in UML 2.x)
Behavior	Sequence diagram	Depicts the time ordering of messages between classifiers, essentially showing the sequential logic of the system
Behavior	Timing diagram	Depicts the change in state or condition of a classifier instance or role over time (added in UML 2.x)

Note that some references show a subtype of Interaction Diagram under Behavior Diagram, containing the Sequence, Interaction Overview, Communication, and Timing diagrams.

Relating Entities and Processes

Once the database designer has completed logical database design and an ERD for the proposed database and, in parallel, the process designers have completed their process model, how can we have any confidence that the two will be able to work together in solving the business problem the new project is supposed to address? Part of the answer lies in a charting technique intended to show how the entities and processes interact, known as the CRUD matrix.

Fortunately, CRUD is not slang for a lousy design but rather an acronym formed from the first letters for the words Create, Read, Update, and Delete, which are the letters used in the body of the diagram. The concept of the CRUD matrix is very simple:

- One axis of the matrix represents the major processes of the application system.
- The other axis represents the major entities used by the application system.
- In each cell of the matrix, the appropriate combination of letters is written:
  - *C,* if the process creates new occurrences of the entity
  - *R,* if the process reads information about the entity from a data source
  - *U,* if the process updates one or more attributes for the entity
  - *D,* if the process deletes occurrences of the entity

Here is a sample CRUD matrix for the order management function at Acme Industries, following the major processes shown in the function hierarchy diagram (refer to Figure 7-11). To be effective, only high-level processes and super-type entities should be shown in the matrix. Too much detail clouds the effect of the diagram.

	ENTITY: Product	Order	Customer	Invoice
PROCESS: Order Entry	R	CRU	RU	
Order Fulfillment	RU	RU	R	C
History Management		RD	R	

The CRUD matrix is valuable for verifying the consistency of the process and data (entity) designs. At a glance, one can find the following potential problems:

- Entities that have no Create process
- Entities that have no Delete process

- Entities that are never updated
- Entities that are never read
- Processes that delete or update entities without reading them
- Processes that only read (no Create, Delete, or Update actions)

Our example has multiple problems, which only proves that our process design is incomplete (that is, we are probably missing some key processes for the application system). At the conclusion of the logical design phase of a project, the CRUD matrix is an excellent vehicle for a final review of the work completed. The next step in the database life cycle is to complete the physical database design, which is discussed in Chapter 8.

Try This 7-1   Draw an ERD in Information Engineering (IE) Format

In this Try This exercise, you will draw an ERD that demonstrates most of the concepts presented thus far, including entities (tables), relationships, recursive relationships, and super types and subtypes. You may draw this as either a logical or physical model. However, my solution is in the form of a physical model, and therefore the instructions will use physical model terms (such as table and column).

Step by Step

1. Draw a table for PERSON with columns PERSON_ID (primary key), FIRST_NAME, LAST_NAME, BIRTH_DATE, and GENDER. Leave room for two more columns, which you will be adding in the next step.

2. Draw two one-to-many recursive relationships: one for the person's father and one for the person's mother. Remember that recursive relationships have the same table as both the parent and the child. In this case, the relationships should be optional in both directions because you won't have every person's parents in the database and not all persons have children. The PERSON table will need two foreign keys to support the recursive relationships: one for the father's person ID and another for the mother's person ID.

3. Draw a dependent table called MARRIAGE with columns PERSON_ID_1, PERSON_ID_2, MARRIAGE_DATE, and END_DATE. The primary key must be composed of the first three columns to be unique under all circumstances. PERSON_ID_1 and PERSON_ID_2 will be the foreign keys for the two people who are married.

4. Draw two one-to-many relationships from PERSON to MARRIAGE—one where PERSON_ID_1 is the foreign key and the other where PERSON_ID_2 is the foreign key. These relationships are mandatory-optional (every marriage must have two people, but some people were never married).

5. Draw an EMPLOYEE table with columns PERSON_ID (primary key), EMPLOYEE_ID, HIRE_DATE, and TERMINATION_DATE.

6. Draw a CUSTOMER table with columns CUSTOMER_NUMBER (primary key), NAME, ADDRESS, CITY, STATE, ZIP_CODE, and PHONE.

7. Draw a CUSTOMER_CONTACT table with columns PERSON_ID (primary key) and CUSTOMER_ID.

8. Draw the lines and symbol(s) necessary to make EMPLOYEE and CUSTOMER_CONTACT subtypes of PERSON.

9. Draw a one-to-many mandatory-optional relationship from CUSTOMER to CUSTOMER_CONTACT, making CUSTOMER_ID in CUSTOMER_CONTACT the foreign key.

Try This Summary

In this Try This exercise, you created five tables and five relationships (two of them recursive), and you made two tables subtypes of another table. My solution appears in Appendix B.

Chapter 7 Self Test

Choose the correct responses to each of the multiple-choice and fill-in-the-blank questions. Note that there may be more than one correct response to each question.

1. Why is it important for a database designer to understand process modeling?

    A Process design is a primary responsibility of the DBA.

    B The process model must be completed before the data model.

    C The data model must be completed before the process model.

    D The database designer must work closely with the process designer.

    E The database design must support the intended process model.

2. Peter Chen's ERD format represents "many" with _____.

3. The diamond in Chen's ERD format represents a(n) _____.

4. The relational ERD format represents "many" with _____.

5. The IDEF1X ERD format

    A Was first released in 1983

    B Follows a standard developed by the National Institute of Standards and Technology

    C Has many variants

    D Has been adopted as a standard by many U.S. government agencies

    E Covers both data and process models

6. The IDEF1X ERD format shows

    A Identifying relationships with a solid line

    B Minimal cardinality using a combination of small circles and vertical lines shown on the relationship line

    C Maximum cardinality using a combination of small vertical lines and crow's feet drawn on the relationship line

    D Dependent entities with squared corners on the rectangle

    E Independent entities with rounded corners on the rectangle

7. A subtype

    A Is a subset of the super type

    B Has a one-to-many relationship with the super type

    C Has a conditional one-to-one relationship with the super type

    D Shows various states of the super type

    E Is a superset of the super type

8. Examples of possible subtypes for an Order entity super type include

    A Order line items

    B Shipped order, unshipped order, invoiced order

    C Office supplies order, professional services order

    D Approved order, pending order, canceled order

    E Auto parts order, aircraft parts order, truck parts order

9. In IE notation, subtypes

    A May be shown with a type discriminator attribute name

    B May be connected to the super type via a symbol composed of a circle with a line under it

    C Have the primary key of the subtype shown as a foreign key in the super type

    D Usually have the same primary key as the super type

    E May be shown using a crow's foot

10. When subtypes are being considered in a database design, a tradeoff exists between _____ and _____.

11. In a flowchart, process steps are shown as _____, and decision points are shown as _____.

12. The strengths of flowcharts are

    A They are natural and easy to use for procedural language programmers.

    B They are useful for spotting reusable components.

    C They are specific to application programming only.

    D They are equally useful for nonprocedural and object-oriented languages.

    E They can be easily modified as requirements change.

13. The basic components of a function hierarchy diagram are

    A Ellipses to show attributes

    B Rectangles to show process functions

    C Lines connecting the processes in order of execution

    D A hierarchy to show which functions are subordinate to others

    E Diamonds to show decision points

14. The strengths of the function hierarchy diagram are

   A Checking quality is easy and straightforward.

   B Complex interactions between functions are easily modeled.

   C It is quick and easy to learn and use.

   D It clearly shows the sequence of process steps.

   E It provides a good overview at high and medium levels of detail.

15. The basic components of a swim lane diagram are

   A Lines with arrows to show the sequence of process steps

   B Diamonds to show decision points

   C Vertical lanes to show the organization units that carry out process steps

   D Ellipses to show process steps

   E Open-ended rectangles to show data stores

16. The data flow diagram (DFD)

   A Is the most data centric of all process models

   B Was first developed in the 1980s

   C Combines diagram pages together hierarchically

   D Was first developed by E.F. Codd

   E Combines the best of the flowchart and the function diagram

17. In a DFD, data stores are shown as _____, and processes are shown as _____.

18. The strengths of the DFD are

   A It's good for top-down design work.

   B It's quick and easy to develop, even for complex systems.

   C It shows overall structure without sacrificing detail.

   D It shows complex logic easily.

   E It's great for presentation to management.

19. The components of the CRUD matrix are

    A Ellipses to show attributes

    B Major processes shown on one axis

    C Major entities shown on the other axis

    D Reference numbers to show the hierarchy of processes

    E Letters to show the operations that processes carry out on entities

20. The CRUD matrix helps find the following problems:

    A Entities that are never read

    B Processes that are never deleted

    C Processes that only read

    D Entities that are never updatcd

    E Processes that have no create entity

Chapter 8
Physical Database Design

Key Skills & Concepts

- Designing Tables
- Integrating Business Rules and Data Integrity
- Designing Views
- Adding Indexes for Performance

As introduced in Chapter 5 (Figure 5-1), once the logical design phase of a project is complete, it is time to move on to physical design. Other members of a typical project team will define the hardware and system software required for the application system. We will focus on the database designer's physical design work, which is transforming the logical database design into one or more physical database designs. For situations in which an application system is being developed for internal use, it is normal to have only one physical database design for each logical design. However, if the organization is a software vendor, for example, the application system must run on all the various platform and RDBMS versions that the vendor's customers use, and that requires multiple physical designs. This chapter covers each of the major steps involved in physical database design.

Designing Tables

The first step in physical database design is to map the normalized relations shown in the logical design to tables. The importance of this step should be obvious, because tables are the primary unit of storage in relational databases. However, if adequate work was put into the logical design, then translation to a physical design is much easier. As you work through this chapter, keep in mind that Chapter 2 contains an introduction to each component in the physical database model, and Chapter 4 contains the SQL syntax for the Data Manipulation Language (DML) commands required to create the various physical database components (tables, constraints, indexes, views, and so on). Briefly, the process goes as follows:

1. Each normalized relation becomes a table. A common exception to this occurs when super types and subtypes are involved, as discussed in the next section.

2. Each attribute within the normalized relation becomes a column in the corresponding table. Keep in mind that the column is the smallest division of meaningful data in the

database, so columns should not have subcomponents that make sense by themselves. For each column, the following must be specified:

- *A unique column name within the table.* Generally, the attribute name from the logical design should be adapted as closely as possible. However, adjustments may be necessary to work around database reserved words and to conform to naming conventions for the particular RDBMS being used. You might notice some column name differences between the Customer relation and the CUSTOMER table in the example that follows. The reason for this change is discussed in the "Naming Conventions" section later in this chapter.

- *A data type, and, for some data types, a length and perhaps a precision.* Data types vary from one RDBMS to another, so this is why different physical designs are needed for each RDBMS to be used.

- *Whether column values are required or not.* This takes the form of a NULL or NOT NULL clause for each column. Be careful with defaults—they can fool you. For example, when this clause is not specified, Oracle assumes NULL, but Sybase ASE and Microsoft SQL Server assume NOT NULL (although this default behavior can be changed for an instance or database). It's always better to specify such things and be certain of what you are getting.

- *Check constraints.* These may be added to columns to enforce simple business rules. For example, a business rule specifying that the unit price on an invoice must always be greater than or equal to zero can be implemented with a check constraint, but a business rule requiring the unit price to be lower in certain states cannot use a check constraint. Generally, a check constraint is limited to comparison of a column value with a single value, a range or list of values, or other column values in the same row of table data.

3. The unique identifier of the relation is defined as the primary key of the table. Columns participating in the primary key must be specified as NOT NULL, and in most RDBMSs, the definition of a primary key constraint causes automatic definition of a unique index on the primary key column(s). Foreign key columns should have a NOT NULL clause if the relationship is mandatory; otherwise, they may have a NULL clause.

4. Any other sets of columns that must be unique within the table may have a unique constraint defined. As with primary key constraints, unique constraints in most RDBMSs cause automatic definition of a unique index on the unique column(s). However, unlike primary key constraints, a table may have *multiple* unique constraints, and the columns in a unique constraint may contain null values (that is, they may be specified with the NULL clause).

5. Relationships among the normalized relations become referential constraints in the physical design. For those rare situations for which the logical model contains a one-to-one relationship, you can implement it by placing the primary key of one of the tables as a foreign key in the other (do this for only *one* of the two tables) *and* placing a unique constraint on the foreign key to prevent duplicate values. For example, Figure 2-2 in Chapter 2 shows a one-to-one relationship between Employee and Automobile, and we chose to place EMPLOYEE_ID as a foreign key in the AUTOMOBILE table. We should also place a unique constraint on EMPLOYEE_ID in the AUTOMOBILE table so that an employee may be assigned only to one automobile at any point in time.

6. Large tables (that is, those that exceed several gigabytes in total size) should be partitioned if the RDBMS being used supports it. *Partitioning* is a database feature that permits a table to be broken up into multiple physical components, each stored in separate data files, in a manner that is transparent to the database user. Typical methods of breaking tables into partitions use a range or list of values for a particular table column (called the *partitioning column*) or use a randomizing method known as *hashing* that evenly distributes table rows across available partitions. The benefits of breaking large tables into partitions include easier administration (particularly

Ask the Expert

Q: **For a one-to-one relationship, why should we place a foreign key in only one of the two tables?**

A: The problem with placing a foreign key on both sides of a one-to-one relationship is that it would actually establish two relationships (one for each foreign key) and the redundant relationship could easily lead to data inconsistency. In the Employee–Automobile example, if we place EMPLOYEE_ID in the AUTOMOBILE table and VIN in the EMPLOYEE table, the DBMS cannot guarantee that the foreign key values will always be consistent. For example, the row for employee 125 might contain the VIN for a particular vehicle, but when you look at the row for that vehicle, it might contain a different employee, say 206.

Q: **I see. Does it then matter which of the two tables in the one-to-one relationship has the foreign key defined in it?**

A: Assuming a unique index (or unique constraint) is placed on the foreign key column, there really isn't a performance difference. However, there may be a slight advantage to putting the foreign key in the table that is accessed more frequently.

for backup and recovery operations) and improved performance, achieved when the RDBMS can run an SQL query in parallel against all (or some of the) partitions and then combine the results. Partitioning is solely a physical design issue that is never addressed in logical designs. After all, a partitioned table is still *one* table. There is wide variation in the way database vendors have implemented partitioning in their products, so you need to consult your RDBMS documentation for more details.

7. The logical model may be for a complete database system, whereas the current project may be an implementation of a subset of that entire system. When this occurs, the physical database designer will select and implement only the subset of tables required to fulfill current needs.

Here is the logical design for Acme Industries from Chapter 6:

```
PRODUCT: Product Number (PK), Product Description,
         List Unit Price

CUSTOMER: Customer Number (PK), Customer Name,
          Customer Address, Customer City, Customer State,
          Customer Zip Code, Customer Phone

INVOICE: Invoice Number (PK), Customer Number, Terms,
         Ship Via, Order Date

INVOICE LINE ITEM: Invoice Number (PK), Product Number (PK),
                   Quantity, Sale Unit Price
```

And here is the physical table design we created from the logical design, shown in the form of SQL Data Definition Language (DDL) statements. These statements are written for Oracle and require some modification, mostly of data types, to work on other RDBMSs. If you want to run these on your own Oracle database, I suggest you create a new user account just for this purpose so that the new tables are created in their own schema rather than mixed in with something else in the database. In other RDBMSs such as MySQL and SQL Server, you should create a new database and run these in that database. On databases other than Oracle, you will likely have to adjust data types somewhat. Finally, you may have to run the statements one at a time or in small batches, all depending on the SQL client that you use.

```
CREATE TABLE PRODUCT
  (PRODUCT_NUMBER       VARCHAR(10)    NOT NULL,
   PRODUCT_DESCRIPTION  VARCHAR(100)   NOT NULL,
   LIST_UNIT_PRICE      NUMBER(7,2)    NOT NULL);
```

```
ALTER TABLE PRODUCT
   ADD CONSTRAINT PRODUCT_PK_PRODUCT_NUMBER
      PRIMARY KEY (PRODUCT_NUMBER);

CREATE TABLE CUSTOMER
  (CUSTOMER_NUMBER        NUMBER(5)      NOT NULL,
   NAME                   VARCHAR(25)    NOT NULL,
   ADDRESS                VARCHAR(255)   NOT NULL,
   CITY                   VARCHAR(50)    NOT NULL,
   STATE                  CHAR(2)        NOT NULL,
   ZIP_CODE               VARCHAR(10));

ALTER TABLE CUSTOMER
   ADD CONSTRAINT CUSTOMER_PK_CUST_NUMBER
      PRIMARY KEY (CUSTOMER_NUMBER);

CREATE TABLE INVOICE
  (INVOICE_NUMBER         NUMBER(7)      NOT NULL,
   CUSTOMER_NUMBER        NUMBER(5)      NOT NULL,
   TERMS                  VARCHAR(20)    NULL,
   SHIP_VIA               VARCHAR(30)    NULL,
   ORDER_DATE             DATE           NOT NULL);

ALTER TABLE INVOICE
   ADD CONSTRAINT INVOICE_PK_INVOICE_NUMBER
      PRIMARY KEY (INVOICE_NUMBER);

ALTER TABLE INVOICE
   ADD CONSTRAINT INVOICE_FK_CUSTOMER_NUMBER
      FOREIGN KEY (CUSTOMER_NUMBER)
      REFERENCES CUSTOMER (CUSTOMER_NUMBER);

CREATE TABLE INVOICE_LINE_ITEM
  (INVOICE_NUMBER     NUMBER(7)      NOT NULL,
   PRODUCT_NUMBER     VARCHAR(10)    NOT NULL,
   QUANTITY           NUMBER(5)      NOT NULL,
   SALE_UNIT_PRICE    NUMBER(7,2)    NOT NULL);

ALTER TABLE INVOICE_LINE_ITEM
   ADD CONSTRAINT INVOICE_LI_PK_INV_PROD_NOS
      PRIMARY KEY (INVOICE_NUMBER, PRODUCT_NUMBER);

ALTER TABLE INVOICE_LINE_ITEM
   ADD CONSTRAINT INVOICE_CK_SALE_UNIT_PRICE
      CHECK (SALE_UNIT_PRICE >= 0);

ALTER TABLE INVOICE_LINE_ITEM
   ADD CONSTRAINT INVOICE_LI_FK_INVOICE_NUMBER
```

```
         FOREIGN KEY (INVOICE_NUMBER)
         REFERENCES INVOICE (INVOICE_NUMBER);

ALTER TABLE INVOICE_LINE_ITEM
   ADD CONSTRAINT INVOICE_LI_FK_PRODUCT_NUMBER
         FOREIGN KEY (PRODUCT_NUMBER)
         REFERENCES PRODUCT (PRODUCT_NUMBER);
```

Implementing Super Types and Subtypes

Most data modelers tend to specify every conceivable subtype in the logical data model. This is not really a problem, because the logical design is supposed to encompass not only where things currently stand, but also where things are likely to end up in the future. The designer of the physical database therefore has some decisions to make in choosing to implement or not implement the super types and subtypes depicted in the logical model. The driving motivators here should be reasonableness and common sense. These, along with input from the application designers and business users about their intended uses of the database, will lead to the best decisions.

Looking back at Figure 7-8 in Chapter 7, you will recall that we ended up with two subtypes for our Customer entity: Individual Customer and Commercial Customer. You have basically three choices for physically implementing such a logical design, and we will explore each in the subsections that follow.

Implementing Subtypes As Is

This is called the "three table" solution because it involves creating one table for the super type and one table for each of the subtypes (two in this example). This design is most appropriate when many attributes are particular to individual subtypes. In our example, only two attributes are particular to the Individual Customer subtype (Date of Birth and Annual Household Income), and four are particular to the Commercial Customer subtype. Figure 8-1 shows the physical design for this alternative.

This design alternative is favored when many common attributes (located in the super type table) as well as many attributes particular to one subtype or another (located in the subtype tables) are used. In one sense, this design is simpler than the other alternatives because no one has to remember which attributes apply to which subtype. On the other hand, it is also more complicated to use, because the database user must join the CUSTOMER table either to the INDIVIDUAL_CUSTOMER table or the COMMERCIAL_CUSTOMER table, depending on the value of CUSTOMER_TYPE. The data-modeling purists on your project team are guaranteed to favor this approach, but the application programmers who must write the SQL to access the tables may take a counter position.

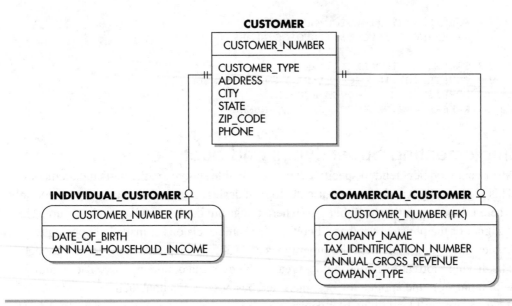

Figure 8-1 Customer subclasses: three-table physical design

Implementing Each Subtype as a Discrete Table

This is called the "two-table" solution because it involves creating one table for each subtype and including all the columns from the super type table in each subtype. At first, this may appear to involve redundant data, but in fact no redundant storage exists, because a given customer can be only one of the two subtypes. However, some columns are redundantly defined. Figure 8-2 shows the physical design for this alternative.

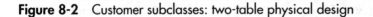

Figure 8-2 Customer subclasses: two-table physical design

This alternative is favored when very few attributes are common between the subtypes (that is, when the super type table contains very few attributes). In our example, the situation is further complicated because of the CUSTOMER_CONTACT table, which is a child of the super type table (CUSTOMER). You cannot (or at least *should* not) make a table the child of two different parents based on the same foreign key. Therefore, if we eliminate the CUSTOMER table, we must create two versions of the CUSTOMER_ CONTACT table—one as a child of INDIVIDUAL_CUSTOMER and the other as a child of COMMERCIAL_CUSTOMER. Although this alternative may be a viable solution in some situations, the complication of the CUSTOMER_CONTACT table makes it a poor choice in this case.

Collapsing Subtypes into the Super Type Table

This is called the "one-table" solution because it involves creating a single table that encompasses the super type and both subtypes. Figure 8-3 shows the physical design for this alternative. Constraints are required to enforce the optional columns. As columns that are mandatory in subtypes are consolidated into the super type table, they usually must be defined to allow null values because they don't apply for all subtypes. For the CUSTOMER_TYPE value that signifies "Individual," DATE_OF_BIRTH and ANNUAL_HOUSEHOLD_INCOME would be allowed to (or required to) contain values, and COMPANY_NAME, TAX_IDENTIFICATION_NUMBER, ANNUAL_GROSS_ INCOME, and COMPANY_TYPE would be required to be null. For the CUSTOMER_ TYPE value that signifies "Commercial," the behavior required would be just the opposite.

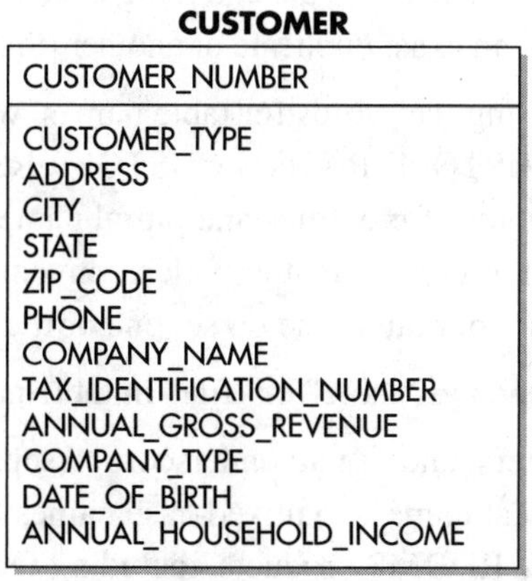

CUSTOMER

CUSTOMER_NUMBER
CUSTOMER_TYPE
ADDRESS
CITY
STATE
ZIP_CODE
PHONE
COMPANY_NAME
TAX_IDENTIFICATION_NUMBER
ANNUAL_GROSS_REVENUE
COMPANY_TYPE
DATE_OF_BIRTH
ANNUAL_HOUSEHOLD_INCOME

Figure 8-3 Customer subclasses: one-table physical design

NOTE

The constraints mentioned here might be implemented in the database using check constraints or triggers, discussed later in this chapter, or in application logic. The decision of which method to use depends a lot on the capabilities of the DBMS.

This alternative is favored when relatively few attributes are particular to any given subtype. In terms of data access, it is clearly the simplest alternative, because no joins are required. However, it is perhaps more complicated in terms of logic, because you must always keep in mind which attributes apply to which subtype (that is, which value of CUSTOMER_TYPE in this example). With only two subtypes, and a total of six subtype-determined attributes between them, this seems a very attractive alternative for this example.

Naming Conventions

Naming conventions are important because they help promote consistency in the names of tables, columns, constraints, indexes, and other database objects. Every organization should develop a standard set of naming conventions (with variations as needed when multiple RDBMSs are in use), publish it, and enforce its use. The conventions offered here are suggestions based on current industry best practices.

Table Naming Conventions

Here are some suggested naming conventions for database tables:

- Table names should be based on the name of the entity they represent. They should be descriptive, yet concise.

- Table names should be unique across the entire organization (that is, across all databases), except where the table is an exact duplicate of another (that is, a replicated copy).

- Some designers prefer singular words for table names, whereas others prefer plural names (for example, CUSTOMER versus CUSTOMERS). Oracle Corporation recommends singular names for entities and plural names for tables (a convention I have never understood). It doesn't matter which convention you adopt as long as you are *consistent* across *all* your tables, so do set one or the other as your standard.

- Do not include words such as "table" or "file" in table names.

- Use only uppercase letters, and use an underscore to separate words. Not all RDBMSs have case-sensitive object names, so mixed-case names limit applicability across multiple vendors. Many RDBMS products, including Oracle and DB2, support mixed-case names in SQL but fold all of them into uppercase when they are processed. The names in the catalog metadata are stored in uppercase, and when you look at them later with one of the popular DBA or developer tools, they become difficult to decipher. For example, a table created with the name EmpJobAsmtHistory would be displayed as EMPJOBASMTHISTORY.

- Use abbreviations when necessary to shorten names that are longer than the RDBMS maximum (typically 30 characters or so). Actually, it is a good idea to stay a few characters short of the RDBMS maximum to allow for suffixes when necessary. All abbreviations should be placed on a standard list and the use of nonstandard abbreviations discouraged.

- Avoid limiting names such as WEST_SALES. Some organizations add a two- or three-character prefix to table names to denote the part of the organization that owns the data in the table. However, this is not considered a best practice because it can lead to a lack of data sharing. Moreover, placing geographic or organizational unit names in table names plays havoc every time the organization changes.

Column Naming Conventions

Here are some suggested naming conventions for table columns:

- Column names should be based on the attribute name as shown in the logical data model. They should be descriptive, yet concise.

- Column names must be unique within the table, but, where possible, it is best if they are unique across the entire organization. Some conventions make exceptions for common attributes such as City, which might describe several entities such as Customer, Employee, and Company Location.

- Use only uppercase letters, and use an underscore to separate words. Not all RDBMSs have case-sensitive object names, so mixed-case names limit applicability across multiple vendors.

- Prefixing column names with entity names is a controversial issue. Some prefer prefixing names. For example, in the CUSTOMER table, they would use column names such as CUSTOMER_NUMBER, CUSTOMER_NAME, CUSTOMER_ ADDRESS, CUSTOMER_CITY, and so forth. Others (including me) prefer to prefix *only* the primary key column name (for example, CUSTOMER_NUMBER), which leads easily to primary key and matching foreign key columns having exactly the same names. Still others prefer no prefixes at all, and end up with a column name such as ID for the primary key of every single table.

- Use abbreviations when necessary to shorten names that are longer than the RDBMS maximum (typically 30 characters or so). All abbreviations should be placed on a standard list and the use of nonstandard abbreviations discouraged.

- Regardless of any other convention, most experts prefer that foreign key columns always have exactly the same name as their matching primary key column. This helps other database users understand which columns to use when coding joins in SQL.

Constraint Naming Conventions

In most RDBMSs, the error message generated when a constraint is violated contains the constraint name. Unless you want to field questions from database users every time one of these messages shows up, you should name the constraints in a standard way that is easily understood by the database users. Most database designers prefer a convention similar to the one presented here.

Constraint names should be in the format *TNAME_TYPE_CNAME*, where:

- *TNAME* is the name of the table on which the constraint is defined, abbreviated if necessary.
- *TYPE* is the type of constraint:
  - PK for primary key constraints.
  - FK for foreign key constraints.
  - UQ for unique constraints.
  - CK for check constraints.
- *CNAME* is the name of the column on which the constraint is defined, abbreviated if necessary. For constraints defined across multiple columns, another descriptive word or phrase may be substituted if the column names are too long (even when abbreviated) to make sense.

Index Naming Conventions

Indexes that are automatically defined by the RDBMS to support primary key or unique constraints are typically given the same name as the constraint name, so you seldom have to worry about them. For other types of indexes, it is wise to use a naming convention so that you know the table and column(s) on which they are defined without having to look up anything. The following is a suggested convention.

Index names should be in the format *TNAME_TYPE_CNAME*, where:

- *TNAME* is the name of the table on which the index is defined, abbreviated if necessary.
- *TYPE* is the type of index:
  - UX for unique indexes.
  - IX for non unique indexes.

- *CNAME* is the name of the column on which the index is defined, abbreviated if necessary. For indexes defined across multiple columns, another descriptive word or phrase may be substituted if the column names are too long (even when abbreviated) to make sense.

Any abbreviations used should be documented in the standard abbreviations list.

View Naming Conventions

View names present an interesting dilemma. The object names used in the FROM clause of SQL statements can be for tables, views, or synonyms. A *synonym* is an alias (nickname) for a table or view. So how does the DBMS know whether an object name in the FROM clause is a table or view or synonym? Well, it doesn't until it looks up the name in a metadata table that catalogs all the objects in the database. This means, of course, that the names of tables, views, and synonyms must come from the same *namespace*, or list of possible names. Therefore, a view name must be unique among all table, view, and synonym names.

Because it is useful for at least some database users to know whether they are referencing a table or a view, and as an easy way to ensure that names are unique, it is common practice to give views distinctive names by employing a standard that appends *VW* to the beginning or end of each name, with a separating underscore. Again, the exact convention chosen matters a lot less than choosing *one* standard convention and sticking to it for all your view names. Here is a suggested convention:

- All view names should end with _*VW* so they are easily distinguishable from table names.

- View names should contain the name of the most significant base table included in the view, abbreviated if necessary.

- View names should describe the purpose of the views or the kind of data included in them. For example, CALIFORNIA_CUSTOMERS_VW and CUSTOMERS_BY_ZIP_CODE_VW are both reasonably descriptive view names, whereas CUSTOMER_LIST_VW and CUSTOMER_JOIN_VW are much less meaningful.

- Any abbreviations used should be documented in the standard abbreviations list.

Integrating Business Rules and Data Integrity

Business rules determine how an organization operates and uses its data. Business rules exist as a reflection of an organization's policies and operational procedures and because they provide control. *Data integrity* is the process of ensuring that data is protected and stays intact through defined constraints placed on the data. We call these *database constraints* because they prevent changes to the data that would violate one or more business rules. The principal benefit of enforcing business rules using data integrity constraints in the database is that database constraints cannot be circumvented. Unlike business rules enforced by application programs, database constraints are enforced no matter *how* someone connects to the database. The only way around database constraints is for the DBA to remove or disable them. On the other hand, developers often prefer to control the rule enforcement themselves rather than relegating them to a DBA, and some rules are best tested before sending the data to the database for processing. In rare cases, usually involving the most important business rules, you might even want to enforce them in both places—in the database, because the rule cannot be circumvented, and in the application, so the user gets fast feedback when he or she violates the rule.

Business rules are implemented in the database as follows:

- NOT NULL constraints
- Primary key constraints
- Referential (foreign key) constraints
- Unique constraints
- Check constraints
- Data types, precision, and scale
- Triggers

The subsections that follow discuss each of these implementation techniques and the effects of the constraints on database processing. Throughout this discussion, the following table definition (in Oracle SQL) is used as an example. A *comment* (a statement beginning with two hyphens) appears above each component to help you identify it. Note that the INVOICE table used here has a column difference—TERMS is replaced with CUSTOMER_PO_NUMBER, which is needed to illustrate some key concepts. A DROP statement is included to drop the INVOICE table in case you created it when following previous examples.

```
--  Drop Invoice Table (in case there already is one)
DROP TABLE INVOICE CASCADE CONSTRAINTS;
--  Create Invoice Table
CREATE TABLE INVOICE
  (INVOICE_NUMBER        NUMBER(7)     NOT NULL,
   CUSTOMER_NUMBER       NUMBER(5)     NOT NULL,
   CUSTOMER_PO_NUMBER    VARCHAR(10)   NULL,
```

```
    SHIP_VIA              VARCHAR(30)    NULL,
    ORDER_DATE            DATE           NOT NULL);

-- Create Primary Key Constraint
ALTER TABLE INVOICE
  ADD CONSTRAINT INVOICE_PK_INVOICE_NUMBER
      PRIMARY KEY (INVOICE_NUMBER);

-- Create Referential Constraint
ALTER TABLE INVOICE
  ADD CONSTRAINT INVOICE_FK_CUSTOMER_NUMBER
      FOREIGN KEY (CUSTOMER_NUMBER)
      REFERENCES CUSTOMER (CUSTOMER_NUMBER);

-- Create Unique Constraint
ALTER TABLE INVOICE
  ADD CONSTRAINT INVOICE_UNQ_CUST_NUMB_PO
      UNIQUE (CUSTOMER_NUMBER, CUSTOMER_PO_NUMBER);

-- Create CHECK Constraint
ALTER TABLE INVOICE
  ADD CONSTRAINT INVOICE_CK_INVOICE_NUMBER
      CHECK (INVOICE_NUMBER > 0);
```

NOT NULL Constraints

As you have already seen, business rules that state which attributes are required translate into NOT NULL clauses on the corresponding columns in the table design. In fact, the NOT NULL clause is how we define a NOT NULL constraint on table columns. Primary keys must always be specified as NOT NULL. (Oracle will automatically do this for you, unlike most other RDBMS products.) And, as already mentioned, any foreign keys that participate in a mandatory relationship should also be specified as NOT NULL.

In our example, if we attempt to insert a row in the INVOICE table and fail to provide a value for any of the columns that have NOT NULL constraints (that is, the INVOICE_NUMBER, CUSTOMER_NUMBER, and ORDER_DATE columns), the insert will fail with an error message indicating the constraint violation. Also, if we attempt to update any existing row and set one of those columns to a NULL value, the update statement will fail.

Primary Key Constraints

Primary key constraints require that the column(s) that make up the primary key contain unique values for every row in the table. In addition, primary key columns must be defined with NOT NULL constraints. A table may have only one primary key constraint. Most RDBMSs will automatically create an index to assist in enforcing the primary key constraint.

In our sample INVOICE table, if we attempt to insert a row without specifying a value for the INVOICE_NUMBER column, the insert will fail because of the NOT NULL constraint on the column. If we instead try to insert a row with a value for the INVOICE_NUMBER column that already exists in the INVOICE table, the insert will fail with an error message that indicates a violation of the primary key constraint. This message usually contains the constraint name—which is why it is such a good idea to give constraints meaningful names. Finally, assuming the RDBMS in use permits updates to primary key values (some do not), if we attempt to update the INVOICE_NUMBER column for an existing row and we provide a value that is already used by another row in the table, the update will fail.

Referential (Foreign Key) Constraints

The referential constraint on the INVOICE table defines CUSTOMER_NUMBER as a foreign key to the CUSTOMER table. It takes some getting used to, but referential constraints are always defined on the child table (that is, the table on the "many" side of the relationship). The purpose of the referential constraint is to make sure that foreign key values in the rows in the child table *always* have matching primary key values in the parent table.

In our INVOICE table example, if we try to insert a row without providing a value for CUSTOMER_NUMBER, the insert will fail due to the NOT NULL constraint on the column. However, if we try to insert a row and provide a value for CUSTOMER_NUMBER that does not match the primary key of a row in the CUSTOMER table, the insert will fail due to the referential constraint. Also, if we attempt to update the value of CUSTOMER_NUMBER for an existing row in the INVOICE table and the new value does not have a matching row in the CUSTOMER table, the update will fail, again due to the referential constraint.

Always keep in mind that referential constraints work in both directions, so they can prevent a child table row from becoming an "orphan," meaning it has a value that does not match a primary key value in the parent table. Therefore, if we attempt to delete a row in the CUSTOMER table that has INVOICE rows referring to it, the statement will fail because it would cause child table rows to violate the constraint. The same is true if we attempt to update the primary key value of such a row. However, many RDBMSs provide a feature with referential constraints written as **ON DELETE CASCADE**, which causes referencing child table rows to be *automatically* deleted when the parent row is deleted. Of course, this option is not appropriate in all situations, but it is nice to have when you need it.

Ask the Expert

Q: **You mentioned that** ON DELETE CASCADE **is not appropriate in all situations. When would it be appropriate?**

A: **ON DELETE CASCADE** is appropriate when the child table rows cannot exist without the parent table rows, a situation known as an *existence dependency*. For example, a line item on an invoice cannot exist without the invoice itself, so it is logical to delete the line items automatically when an SQL statement attempts to delete the invoice. However, this option can be dangerous in other situations. For instance, it would be dangerous to set up the database so that invoices were deleted automatically when someone attempted to delete a customer; because invoices are financial records, it would be safer to force someone first to explicitly delete the invoices. Naturally, these are business rule decisions that depend on requirements.

Unique Constraints

Like primary key constraints, unique constraints ensure that no two rows in the table have duplicate values for the column(s) named in the constraint. However, unique constraints have two important differences:

- Although a table may have only one primary key constraint, it may have as many unique constraints as necessary.

- Columns participating in a unique constraint do not have to have NOT NULL constraints on them.

As with a primary key constraint, an index is automatically created to assist the DBMS in efficiently enforcing the constraint.

In our example, a unique constraint is defined on the CUSTOMER_NUMBER and CUSTOMER_PO_NUMBER columns, to enforce a business rule that states that customers may use a PO (purchase order) number only once. You should realize that the *combination* of the values in the two columns must be unique. Many invoices can exist for any given CUSTOMER_NUMBER, and multiple rows in the INVOICE table can have the same PO_NUMBER (we cannot prevent two customers from using the same PO number, nor do we wish to). However, no two rows for the same customer number may have the same PO number.

As with the primary key constraint, if we attempt to insert a row with values for the CUSTOMER_NUMBER and PO_NUMBER columns that are already in use by another row, the insert will fail. Similarly, we cannot update a row in the INVOICE table if the update would result in the row having a duplicate combination of CUSTOMER_NUMBER and PO_NUMBER.

Check Constraints

Check constraints are used to enforce business rules that restrict a column to a list or range of values or to some condition that can be verified using a simple comparison to a constant, calculation, or a value of another column in the same row. Check constraints may *not* be used to compare column values between different rows, whether in the same table or not. Check constraints are written as conditional statements that must always be true. The terminology comes from the fact that the database must always "check" the condition to make sure it evaluates to true before allowing an insert or update to a row in the table.

In our example, a check constraint requires the INVOICE_NUMBER to be greater than 0. This enforces a business rule that requires positive invoice numbers. Keep in mind that the condition is checked only when we insert or update a row in the INVOICE table, so it will not be applied to existing rows in the table (should there be any) when the constraint is added. With the constraint in force, if we attempt to insert or update a row with an INVOICE_NUMBER set to zero or a negative number, the statement will fail.

Data Types, Precision, and Scale

The data type assigned to the table columns automatically constrains the data to values that match the data type. For example, anything placed in a column with a date format must be a valid date. You cannot put non-numeric characters in numeric columns. However, you can put just about anything in a character column.

For data types that support the specification of the precision (maximum size) and scale (positions to the right of the decimal point), these specifications also constrain the data. You simply cannot put a character string or number larger than the maximum size for the column into the database. Nor can you specify decimal positions beyond those allowed for in the scale of a number.

In our example, CUSTOMER_NUMBER must contain only numeric digits and cannot be larger than 99,999 (five digits) or smaller than –99,999 (again, five digits). Also, because the scale is 0, it cannot have decimal digits (that is, it must be an integer). It may seem silly to allow negative values for CUSTOMER_NUMBER, but no SQL data type restricts a column only to positive integers. However, it is easy to restrict a column only to positive numbers using a check constraint if such a constraint is required.

Triggers

As you may recall, a *trigger* is a unit of program code that executes automatically based on some event that takes place in the database, such as inserting, updating, or deleting data in a particular table. Triggers must be written in a language supported by the RDBMS. For Oracle, this is either a proprietary extension to SQL called PL/SQL (Procedural Language/ SQL) or Java (available in Oracle8*i* or later). For Sybase ASE and Microsoft SQL Server, the supported language is Transact-SQL. Some RDBMSs have no support for triggers, whereas others support a more general programming language such as C. Trigger code must either end normally, which allows the SQL statement that caused the trigger to fire to end normally, or it must raise a database error, which in turn causes the SQL statement that caused the trigger to fire to fail as well.

Triggers can enforce business rules that cannot be enforced via database constraints. Because they are written using a full-fledged programming language, they can do just about anything that can be done with a database and a program (some RDBMSs do place some restrictions on triggers). Deciding whether a business rule should be enforced in normal application code or through the use of a trigger is not always easy. Application developers typically want control of such things, but on the other hand, the main benefit of triggers is that they run automatically and cannot be circumvented (unless the DBA removes or disables them), even if someone connects directly to the database, bypassing the application.

A common use of triggers in RDBMSs that do not support **ON DELETE CASCADE** in referential constraints is to carry out the cascading delete. For example, if we want invoice line items to be automatically removed from the INVOICE_LINE_ITEM table when the corresponding invoice in the INVOICE table is deleted, we could write a trigger that carries that out. The trigger would be set to fire when a delete from the INVOICE table occurs. It would then issue a delete for all the child rows related to the parent invoice (those matching the primary key value of the invoice being deleted) and then end normally, which would permit the original invoice delete to complete (because the referencing child rows will be gone by this time, the delete will not violate the referential constraint).

Designing Views

As covered in Chapter 2, views can be thought of as virtual tables. They are, however, merely stored SQL statements that do not themselves contain any data. Data can be selected from views just as it can from tables, and with some restrictions, data can be inserted into, updated in, and deleted from views. Here are the restrictions:

- For views containing joins, any DML (that is, insert, update, or delete) statement issued against the view must reference only one table.

- Inserts are not possible using views where any required (NOT NULL) column has been omitted.

- Any update against a view may reference only columns that directly map to base table columns. Calculated and derived columns may not be updated.

- Appropriate privileges are required (just as with base tables).

- Various other product-specific restrictions apply to view usage, so the RDBMS documentation should always be consulted.

Views can be designed to provide the following advantages:

- In some RDBMSs, views provide a performance advantage over ordinary SQL statements. Views are precompiled, so the resources required to check the syntax of the statement and prepare it for processing are saved when views are repeatedly referenced. However, there is no such advantage with RDBMSs that provide an automatic SQL statement cache, as Oracle does. Moreover, poorly written SQL can be included in a view, so putting SQL in a view is not a magic solution to performance issues.

- Similarly, in some RDBMSs, stored procedures can outperform views. (A *stored procedure* is a program that is written in a language supported by the RDBMS and stored in the database. They are invoked with an SQL statement and can optionally return a result set much as a view does.) Stored procedures can do a lot more data manipulation than can be accomplished in a view.

- Views may be tailored to individual department needs, providing only the rows and columns needed, and perhaps renaming columns using terms more readily understood by the particular audience.

- Because views hide the real table and column names from their users, they insulate users from changes to those names in the base tables.

- Data usage can be greatly simplified by hiding complicated joins and calculations from the database users. For example, views can easily calculate ages based on birth dates, and they can summarize data in nearly any way imaginable.

- Security needs can be met by filtering rows and columns that users are not supposed to see. Some RDBMS products permit column-level security, where users are granted privileges by column as well as by table, but using views is far easier to implement and maintain. Moreover, a WHERE clause in the view can filter rows easily.

Once created, views must be managed like any other database object. If many members of a database project are creating and updating views, it is very easy to lose control. Moreover, views can become invalid as maintenance is carried out on the database, so their status must be reviewed periodically.

Adding Indexes for Performance

Indexes provide a fast and efficient means of finding data rows in tables, much like the index at the back of a book helps you to quickly find specific references. Although the implementation in the database is more complicated than this, it's easiest to visualize an index as a table with one column containing the key value and another containing a pointer to where the row with that key value physically resides in the table, in the form of a row ID or a relative block address (RBA). For nonunique indexes, the second column contains a list of matching pointers.

Indexes provide faster searches than scanning tables for two reasons: First, index entries are considerably shorter than typical table rows, so many more index entries fit per physical file block than the corresponding table rows. Therefore, when the database must scan the index sequentially looking for matching rows, it can get a lot more index entries with a single read to the file on disk than a corresponding read to the file holding the table. Second, index entries are always maintained in key sequence, which is not at all true of tables. The RDBMS software can take advantage of this by using binary search techniques that remarkably reduce search times and the resources required for searching.

There are no free lunches, however, and indexes come with a price—they take up space and must be maintained. Storage space seems less of an issue with every passing day, because storage devices keep getting cheaper. However, they still cost something, and they require maintenance and must be backed up. Most RDBMS vendors provide tools to help calculate the storage space required for indexes. These will assist you in estimating storage requirements. The more important consideration is maintenance of the index. Whenever a row is inserted into a table, every index defined on that table must have a new entry inserted as well. As rows are deleted, index entries must also be removed. And when columns that have an index defined on them are updated, the index must be updated as well. It's easy to forget this point because the RDBMS does this work automatically, but every index has a detrimental effect on the performance of inserts, updates, and deletes to table data. In essence, this is a typical tradeoff, sacrificing a bit of DML statement performance for considerable gains in SELECT statement performance.

Here are some general guidelines regarding the use of indexes:

- Keep in mind that most RDBMSs automatically create indexes on key columns in primary key constraints and unique constraints.

- Indexes on foreign keys can markedly improve the performance of joins.

- Consider using indexes on columns that are frequently referenced in WHERE clauses.

- The larger the table, the less you want any database query to have to scan the entire table (in other words, the more you want *every* query to use an index).

- The more a table is updated, the fewer the number of indexes you should have on the table, particularly on the columns that are updated most often.

- For relatively small tables (less than 1000 rows or so), sequential table scans are probably more efficient than indexes. Most RDBMSs have optimizers that decide when an index should be used, and typically they will choose a table scan over an index until at least a few hundred rows exist in the table.

- For tables with relatively short rows that are most often accessed using the primary key, consider the use of an *index organized table* (on RDBMSs that support such a table), where all the table data is stored in the index. This can be a highly efficient structure for lookup tables (tables containing little more than code and description columns).

- Consider the performance consequences carefully before you define more than two or three indexes on a single table.

Try This 8-1   Mapping a Logical Model to a Physical Database Design

Implementing subtypes and super types in relational databases is perhaps the most challenging part of physical database design. This Try This exercise gives you an opportunity to practice this essential skill. Illustration 8-1 shows part of the logical model for part of an HR (human resources) application. The steps in this exercise walk you through converting this model to a physical data model.

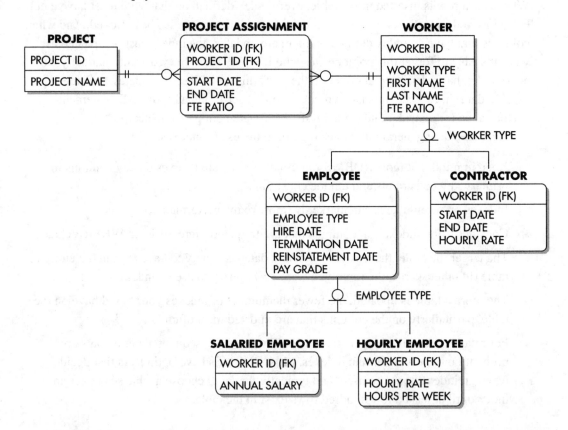

Step by Step

1. Given that the Salaried Employee and Hourly Employee entities have so few attributes, it seems best to collapse them into the Employee relation. Move the Annual Salary and Hourly Rate attributes to Employee.

2. On further analysis, you notice that both the Employee and Contractor entities have an Hourly Rate attribute. Therefore, you need to move Hourly Rate to the Worker entity.

3. After discussion with the business analysts working on your project, you conclude that Hours Per Week can easily be derived from the FTE (Full Time Equivalency) Ratio in the Worker entity. For example, an FTE of 0.5 means the person works 20 hours per week (40 * 0.5 = 20). This was simply missed in earlier analysis passes because Hours Per Week was two layers down the subtype hierarchy from FTE Ratio. You can simply remove Hours Per Week from the model.

4. After discussion regarding the Employee and Contract subtypes, you conclude that they should remain as separate entities (tables) in the physical model. Too many distinct attributes exist between the two subtypes to consider combining them into the Worker entity. At the same time, pushing the Worker super type into the two subtypes is not an attractive option because the many-to-many relationship between Worker and Project applies to both subtypes and therefore would have to be redundantly (and awkwardly) implemented if the Worker entity were eliminated. Create one-to-one relationships between Worker and Employee and between Worker and Contractor.

Try This Summary

In this Try This exercise, you stepped through the considerations that are typical in converting a logical model containing super types and subtypes to a physical model. My solution is shown in Appendix B.

You may have noticed that this particular design does not handle storage of historical data. For example, if a contract employee finished a contract and then returned some time later for another contract, you could not hold both contracts in the database at the same time, because you have only one set of start and end dates per employee. Similarly, if an employee leaves for a time and is rehired at a later time, you cannot hold both employment engagements in the database at the same time. This is typical of modern OLTP (online transaction processing) databases, where you expect to have a different database such as a data warehouse to hold the historical data. Data warehouses and other data structures for OLAP (online analytical processing) are covered in Chapter 12.

✓

Chapter 8 Self Test

Choose the correct responses to each of the multiple-choice and fill-in-the-blank questions. Note that there may be more than one correct response to each question.

1. Business rules are implemented in the database using _____.

2. Two key differences between unique constraints and primary key constraints are _____ and _____.

3. Relationships in the logical model become _____ in the physical model.

4. Constraint names are important because _____.

5. When you're designing tables,

    A Each normalized relation becomes a table.

    B Each attribute in the relation becomes a table column.

    C Relationships become check constraints.

    D Unique identifiers become triggers.

    E Primary key columns must be defined as NOT NULL.

6. Super types and subtypes

    A Must be implemented exactly as specified in the logical design

    B May be collapsed in the physical database design

    C May have the super type columns folded into each subtype in the physical design

    D Usually have the same primary key in the physical tables

    E Apply only to the logical design

7. Table names

    A Should be based on the attribute names in the logical design

    B Should always include the word "table"

    C Should use only uppercase letters

    D Should include organization or location names

    E May contain abbreviations when necessary

8. Column names

    A Must be unique within the database

    B Should be based on the corresponding attribute names in the logical design

    C Must be prefixed with the table name

    D Must be unique within the table

    E Should use abbreviations whenever possible

9. Referential constraints

    A Define relationships identified in the logical model

    B Are always defined on the parent table

    C Require that foreign keys be defined as NOT NULL

    D Should have descriptive names

    E Name the parent and child tables and the foreign key column

10. Check constraints

    A May be used to force a column to match a list of values

    B May be used to force a column to match a range of values

    C May be used to force a column to match another column in the same row

    D May be used to force a column to match a column in another table

    E May be used to enforce a foreign key constraint

11. Data types

    A Prevent incorrect data from being inserted into a table

    B Can be used to prevent alphabetic characters from being stored in numeric columns

    C Can be used to prevent numeric characters from being stored in character format columns

    D Require that precision and scale be specified also

    E Can be used to prevent invalid dates from being stored in date columns

12. View restrictions include which of the following?

    A Views containing joins can never be updated.

    B Updates to calculated columns in views are prohibited.

    C Privileges are required in order to update data using views.

    D If a view omits a mandatory column, inserts to the view are not possible.

    E Any update involving a view may reference columns only from one table.

13. Some advantages of views are

    A Views may provide performance advantages.

    B Views may insulate database users from table and column name changes.

    C Views may be used to hide joins and complex calculations.

    D Views may filter columns or rows that users should not see.

    E Views may be tailored to the needs of individual departments.

14. Indexes

    A May be used to assist with primary key constraints

    B May be used to improve query performance

    C May be used to improve insert, update, and delete performance

    D Are usually smaller than the tables they reference

    E Are slower to sequentially scan than corresponding tables

15. General rules to follow regarding indexes include which of the following?

    A The larger the table, the more important indexes become.

    B Indexing foreign key columns often helps join performance.

    C Columns that are frequently updated should always be indexed.

    D The more a table is updated, the more indexes will help performance.

    E Indexes on very small tables tend not to be very useful.

Part III

Database Implementation

Chapter 9
Connecting Databases to the Outside World

Key Skills & Concepts

- Deployment Models
- Connecting Databases to the Web
- Connecting Databases to Applications

This chapter begins with a look at the evolution of database *deployment models*—the ways that databases have been connected with database users and other computer systems within the enterprise computing *infrastructure* (the internal structure that organizes all the computing resources of an enterprise, including databases, applications, computer hardware, and the network). We then explore the methods used to connect databases to applications that use a web browser as the primary user interface; this is the way many modern application systems are constructed. Finally, we look at current methods for connecting databases to applications, namely using ODBC connections (for most programming languages) and various methods for connecting databases to applications written in Java (a commonly used object-oriented language).

Deployment Models

The history of the information technology (IT) industry is a very interesting study, because it clearly proves the old adage that history repeats itself. Nowhere is this truer than in the ways that we have deployed databases, and computer systems in general, on enterprise networks. The subsections that follow outline the major deployment models that have been used. Most of these models are still in active use.

Centralized Model

The centralized model, shown in Figure 9-1, was the original method used to connect databases to the enterprise computing infrastructure. Database users were originally equipped with "dumb terminals" that offered very little processing power or intelligent programming. The terminals' only functions were to present screens of data that came across the network, move the cursor around the screen, and capture user keystrokes, which were sent back across the network. On the other end of the network was a mainframe or other large centralized server that housed all the other functions, including the business logic (in application programs), the database, and any advanced presentation features,

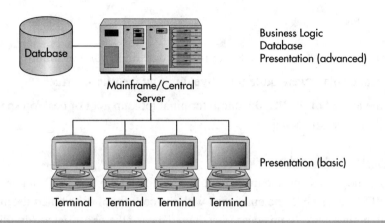

Figure 9-1   The centralized deployment model

such as the ability to compose graphs and charts and select colors to display (if color terminals were connected).

Compared to the technology that is prevalent today, this arrangement might seem primitive, but keep in mind that personal computers had not been invented yet. When PCs came on the scene, some of their first uses were to replace the dumb terminals, giving computer users a desktop device that they could at least use for other purposes, such as word processing (or perhaps playing those early computer games). Programs on the early PCs, called *terminal emulators,* took care of the network connection in such a way that the mainframe still thought it was connected to the original dumb terminal.

The centralized model enjoyed the following benefits:

- **Easy administration**   Upgrades and maintenance were straightforward, because all the application logic and the database were centralized.

- **Lower development labor costs**   Fewer specialists were required, because everything ran on one platform.

- **Potentially higher data input productivity**   Studies have shown that the fancy GUI screens that appeared later actually slowed down experienced users who were performing repetitive tasks. Many an experienced Windows user can perform some tasks much more quickly using the command prompt (DOS window) instead of the available GUI tools. Much of this is due to the time required to move one hand between keys used for typing and the pointing device (mouse, trackball, and so on). If we all had a third hand, or if we could somehow use something else to control the pointing device (for example, eye movements or our feet), perhaps this could be overcome.

Here are the drawbacks:

- The mainframe or centralized server provided a single point of failure.
- Graphical displays were quite primitive, limiting the user interface.
- Until the advent of the PC, the dumb terminal took up a lot of desktop space for the limited purposes it served.

Distributed Model

As computer networks became more readily available in the late 1970s and early 1980s, the IT industry became enamored with the concept of distributed databases and distributed applications. In this case, *distributed* means the partitioning (dividing up) of the application and/or database into parts and the placement of different parts on different computing devices, all connected by a network. When done correctly, this distribution is *transparent* to the users, meaning that the system hides the distribution details from the users, making everything appear to be coming from a single source. Figure 9-2 shows a simple distributed model using two centralized servers.

Unfortunately, the marketing hype attached to the initial appearance of the distributed model never played out due to high costs and performance and reliability issues. Among other things, network technology was not mature enough to handle the load. In many ways, the early versions were solutions in need of problems to solve. Much like the Ford Edsel, these new ideas were simply ahead of their time. This architecture has reappeared since the advent of more advanced networks, including the Internet, and is now successfully used for backup data centers, data warehouses, departmental computer

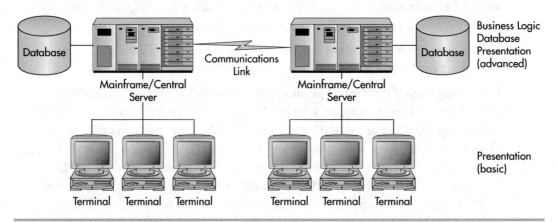

Figure 9-2 The distributed deployment model

systems, and much more. In some object-oriented architectures, an agent known as an *object request broker* manages objects distributed across a network so applications can access objects without regard to their location. Moreover, the current trends in *grid computing (virtual super-computers composed of a clusters of networked, loosely-coupled computers)* can be easily seen as extensions to the original distributed model. History really does repeat itself.

The benefits of the distributed deployment model are as follows:

- Fault tolerance was improved, because any component deployed on more than one device is no longer a single point of failure.

- Potential performance was improved by placing data and application logic closer to the users that need them (that is, departmental computer systems).

Here are the drawbacks:

- It is much more complicated than the centralized model.

- There are potential performance issues related to synchronizing data updates for any redundantly stored data.

- It is far more expensive than the centralized model.

- There is a lack of guidelines and best practices for how to partition data and applications across the available computing devices.

Client/Server Model

The client/server model involves one or more shared computers, called *servers*, that are connected by a network to the individual users' workstations, called *clients*. Client/server computing arrived in the 1980s, riding a wave of marketing hype from hardware and software vendors the likes of which had never before been seen in the IT industry. The original model used is now called the *two-tier client/sever model,* which later evolved into what we call the *three-tier client/server model*, and finally into the *N-tier client/server model*, which is also known as the *Internet computing model*. Each of these is discussed in the following subsections.

Two-Tier Client/Server Model

The two-tier client/server model, shown in Figure 9-3, is almost the opposite of the centralized model in that all the business and presentation logic is placed on the client workstation, which typically is a high-powered personal computer system. The only thing remaining on a centralized server is the database.

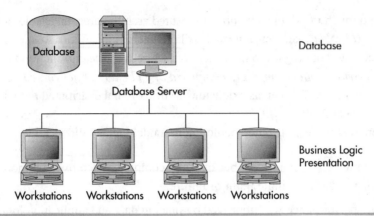

Figure 9-3 The two-tier client/server deployment model

The two-tier model intended to take advantage of the superior presentation and user interface capabilities of the modern workstation. However, the marketing hype of the late 1980s and early 1990s promised *faster* development of *better* application systems at a *lower* cost. It didn't pan out this way, and it's impossible to do so, as discussed in "The Project Triangle" section back in Chapter 5. However, the vendors were offering a "silver bullet" solution, and business managers of the day were far too willing to believe them.

The white lie of the day was in cost comparisons between mainframes and central servers and workstations. The vendors typically showed cost comparisons in dollars per millions of instructions per second (MIPS). The problem was that a given instruction on the personal computers of the day did far less than a given instruction on a mainframe or high-powered server. So it really was comparing apples and oranges. Cynics of the day defined MIPS as "meaningless indicator of processor speed," and they were not far wrong. The other factor that was largely ignored was that personal computers did not read from and write to their disks at anywhere near the rates achieved by mainframes and high-powered servers. So although moving all the application programs (business logic) to the client workstations appeared to be a much less expensive solution, it was, in fact, a false economy.

Nearly every two-tier client/server project finished late and well over budget. Moreover, there were sobering failures. For example, the California Department of Motor Vehicles spent $44 million on a vehicle-registration system that ended up being far slower and less functional than the centralized model system that it was supposed to replace. It was eventually scrapped at a total loss—even the hardware was so specialized that it could not be used for any other purpose, so it too went on the junk pile. There were *some* client/server project successes, however. For example, PeopleSoft built a two-tier client/server human resources system that was successfully deployed by many large enterprises. In the years that followed, incidentally, PeopleSoft (now owned by Oracle) migrated to the N-tier client/server model (described later in this chapter) with no code running on the client workstations aside from a standard web browser, which grew into a full-fledged enterprise resource planning (ERP) suite of applications.

The benefits of the two-tier client/server model include the following:

- It greatly improved the user interface compared with systems using dumb terminals.

- It offered the potential for improved performance because the workstation processor did all the work and did not have to be shared with anyone else.

Here are the drawbacks:

- Very expensive client workstations were required because all the application logic ran on the client. Client workstation costs in the $10,000 to $20,000 range were not unusual. In fairness, hardware prices were considerably higher at that time.

- Administrative nightmares mounted because the application was installed on every client workstation, and all had to be updated with a new software release at the same time.

- Much more complicated (and often more expensive) development resulted because the database server and the client workstation were almost always completely different platforms that required a different set of skills.

Three-Tier Client/Server Model

The many failures of the two-tier client/server model led to some serious rethinking. The result was the three-tier client/server model, which essentially moved the application logic from the client workstation back to a centralized server, now dubbed the *application server*. Figure 9-4 shows this architecture, which proved very workable.

The benefits of the three-tier client/server model include the following:

- It solved the administrative issues of the two-tier model by centralizing application logic on the application server.

- It improved scalability because multiple application servers could be added as needed. (The same could be done with database servers, but that required distributed database technology to synchronize any data updates across all copies of the data.)

- It retained the user interface advantages of the two-tier model.

- The client workstations were far less expensive (standard personal computers could easily do the job).

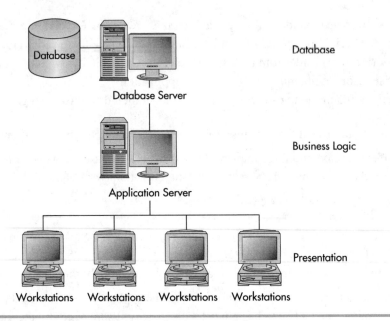

Figure 9-4 The three-tier client/server deployment model

Here are the drawbacks:

- It was still more complicated compared with the centralized model.
- Custom presentation methods and logic added to expense and limited portability across client platforms.

The N-Tier Client/Server (Internet Computing) Model

As web browsers became ubiquitous, business computer systems migrated to using web pages as the primary presentation method. The N-tier client/server model (which some call the *Internet computing model*) is shown in Figure 9-5.

The evolution from three-tier to N-tier involved adding a web server to handle responding to client requests and the rendering (composing) of web pages, as well as swapping proprietary display logic on the workstation to a standard web browser. The interaction between the client and the web server goes something like this:

1. Using the web browser, the client submits a request in the form of a URL (Uniform Resource Locator).

2. The web server processes the request, assembles the requested web page, and sends it to the client.

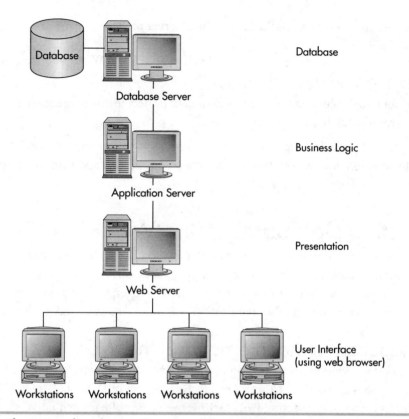

Database

Business Logic

Presentation

User Interface
(using web browser)

Figure 9-5   The N-tier client/server (Internet computing) deployment model

3. The user at the client workstation works with the web page and eventually submits a new request to the web server, and the cycle repeats.

This architecture has been wildly successful in deployment of modern business systems. The benefits of the N-tier client/server model are as follows:

- It offers an industry-standard presentation method using web pages.
- The same architecture can be used for internal (intranet) and external (Internet) applications.
- It retains all the benefits of the three-tier client/server model.
- Client workstations can be scaled all the way down to so-called *network computing devices* that do not have a disk drive—a "smart" version of the original "dumb" terminals, if you will.

Here are the drawbacks of the N-tier client/server model:

- Security challenges exist because the Internet and World Wide Web were not designed with security in mind.

- It potentially necessitates larger development project teams because each layer requires a specialist.

- It potentially requires more hardware. It is possible to combine some of the servers onto common devices, but this is seldom a recommended approach because separation by function improves security.

Connecting Databases to the Web

An extensive "technology stack" is required to deploy an application system and corresponding database on the Internet. The basic components are shown in Figure 9-6. For completeness, we'll review each component. However, our focus is on the database, so you may wish to consult other publications for more details on other components.

Introduction to the Internet and the Web

The *Internet* is a worldwide collection of interconnected computer networks. It began in the late 1960s and early 1970s as the U.S. Department of Defense (DoD) ARPANET, intended as a way of connecting DoD facilities with the colleges and universities that received DoD research grants. Transmission Control Protocol/Internet Protocol (TCP/IP) was adopted as a standard in 1982. Other protocols include File Transfer Protocol (FTP), Simple Mail Transfer Protocol (SMTP), Telnet (remote login protocol), Domain Name System (DNS), and Post Office Protocol (POP).

An *intranet* is a segment of a network, including a website or group of websites, that is accessible only to members of an organization. An *extranet* is an intranet that is accessible to authorized outsiders. Both are typically protected by a *firewall*, which is a dedicated network gateway that applies security precautions such that only network traffic that meets certain criteria is allowed to pass through.

The *World Wide Web* is a hypermedia-based system that provides a simple "point-and-click" means of browsing information on the Internet using *hyperlinks*. Hyperlinks allow users to navigate pages in a nonsequential manner. Clients use a web browser to present pages. The web server hosts (stores and renders) pages and responds to client requests. Web pages may be *static* (always the same) or *dynamic* (changeable and custom built for a particular request). Dynamic pages are of a special interest in the database world

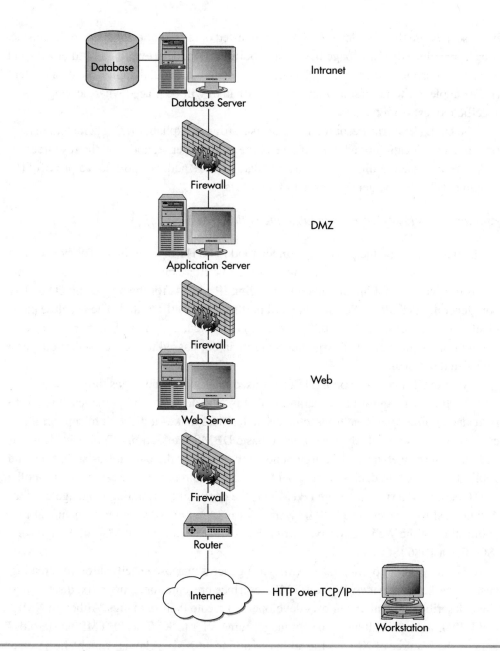

Figure 9-6   Web-connected databases

because they are the vehicles for sending requested data from the database to the business user. Typically, a dynamic page has a static portion (title, help text, data field labels) and a dynamic portion in the form of placeholders where current and applicable data content (for example, customer number and customer name) will be placed when serving a specific request from the client.

The URL (Uniform Resource Locator) is a string of alphanumeric characters that represents the location or address of a resource on the Internet and how the resource should be accessed. It ultimately must translate to an IP address, port, and a protocol (for example, HTTP). The general format of a URL is

<protocol>://<host>[:<port>]/<absolute path> [?arguments]

In most browsers, the protocol is understood to be HTTP if omitted. The host can be an IP address, but it is more commonly a host name (for example, www.Microsoft.com) that is resolved by looking up the corresponding IP address for the host using DNS. The port generally defaults to 80 (the standard port for HTTP) if omitted. The absolute path identifies the specific page (or other resource) requested, and the web server selects a default if the path is omitted. Arguments are variables passed to the web server and are considered optional.

Hypertext Transfer Protocol (HTTP) is used to transfer web pages through the Internet. It uses a request-based paradigm that is "stateless," meaning that each request is treated as an independent transaction. Statelessness makes it difficult to support the concept of a session, which is essential to basic DBMS transactions. Typically, data must be hidden in the web page or in arguments in the URL for the page to assist the web and application servers in distinguishing between pages from one user session versus another.

Hypertext Markup Language (HTML) is the document formatting language used to design most web pages. The HTML system for marking up, or *tagging*, a document for publication on the Web was derived from the Standardized General Markup Language (SGML), a 1986 ISO standard.

Extensible Markup Language (XML) is a general-purpose specification for creating custom markup languages. While HTML describes presentation using a fixed set of tags, XML describes content and allows developers to create their own tags. Although XML and HTML are not at all the same language, some refer to XML as "HTML on steroids." Among the features of XML is the ability to define an XML schema, which allows data to be stored in a hierarchical tree of XML tags within the XML document. Various RDBMS vendors now directly support XML as a data type, and several proprietary XML databases are also on the market. However, businesses have been reluctant to abandon relational databases and undergo a major paradigm shift in the way they organize and store data. So, thus far, XML is most widely used for exchanging data between organizations in industry-standard XML formats. Standards committees are working on standard XML vocabularies (that is, data tags, schema structures, and conventions for using them) for specific data areas, such as HR-XML Consortium, Inc., which works solely on human resources (HR) data. XML is covered in more detail in Chapter 13.

Components of the Web "Technology Stack"

Here's a list of the components shown in Figure 9-6 and what they do:

- The client workstation runs a web browser and communicates on the Internet using HTTP over TCP/IP.

- The website sits behind a *router,* which forwards packets between networks, and a firewall. The router makes decisions on which packets are transferred between the Internet and the subnetwork on which the web server resides. Although some routers perform rudimentary filtering, the additional firewall protection is considered the best way to protect the web server from intruders.

- The web server is responsible for hosting and rendering web pages.

- URLs handled by the web server may cause transactions to be run on the application server (more on this in the next section). The application server typically resides between a pair of firewalls to isolate it from both the web server and the intranet, where the database server typically resides. This area is commonly called the DMZ (demilitarized zone), a term borrowed from buffer zones between countries in dispute.

- The application server submits SQL (or similar language) requests to the database server when data from the database is required.

Invoking Transactions from Web Pages

Information in a web request received by the web server can invoke a transaction on the application server in several ways. These methods are detailed in the following subsections.

Common Gateway Interface

Common Gateway Interface (CGI) is a specification for transferring information between a web server and a CGI program. The CGI program (often called a *CGI script*) runs on either the web server or application server. CGI defines how scripts communicate with web servers. The URL points to the CGI script, and the server launches it. The actual script can be written in a variety of languages, such as Perl, C, or C++. In essence, instead of the URL in the incoming request pointing directly to an HTML document, it points to a script. This script is run, and the output from the script is an HTML document that is then returned to the client in response to the request.

The advantages of CGI include the following:

- Simplicity
- Language and web server independence
- Wide acceptance

Here are the disadvantages:

- Web server is always between the client and the database.
- No transaction support (stateless).
- Not intended for long exchanges.
- Each CGI execution spawns a new process (or thread), which presents resource issues.
- CGI is not inherently secure.

Server Side Includes

Server Side Includes (SSI) has commands embedded in the document that cause the web server to execute a program (as with CGI) and incorporate the output into the document. Essentially, SSI is in an HTML *macro*. The URL in the request points to an HTML document, but the web server parses the document and handles any SSI commands before returning the document to the requesting client. SSI solves some of the CGI performance issues, but it offers few other advantages or disadvantages.

Non-CGI Gateways

Non-CGI gateways work like CGI gateways, except that each is a proprietary extension to a specific vendor's web server. The two most popular choices during the "dot-com" era were the Netscape Server API and Active Server Pages (ASP), part of the Microsoft Internet Information Services (IIS) API. The Netscape Server API was subsequently acquired by Sun Microsystems and incorporated into its product line.

The advantages of non-CGI gateways include the following:

- Improved performance over CGI
- Additional features and functions
- Execution in the server address space instead of as new processes or threads

Here are the disadvantages:

- Proprietary solution that is not portable to another vendor's web server
- Potential instability
- Much more complex compared with CGI

Connecting Databases to Applications

Now that you have seen how the web layer interacts with the application server layer, you need to understand how applications on the application server connect to and interact with the database. Most connections between the application server and remote databases (that is, those running on another server) use a standard *application programming interface, or* API.

An API is a set of calling conventions by which an application program accesses services. Such services can be provided by the operating system or by other software products such as the DBMS. The API provides a *level of abstraction* (a layer of generalization that hides implementation details) that allows the application to be portable across various operating systems and vendors.

Connecting Databases via ODBC

Open Database Connectivity (ODBC) is a standard API for connecting application programs to DBMSs. ODBC is based on a *Call Level Interface (CLI)*, a convention that defines the way calls to services are made, which was first defined by the SQL Access Group and released in September 1992. Although Microsoft was the first company to release a commercial product based on ODBC, it is not a Microsoft standard, and in fact versions are now available for Unix, Macintosh, and other platforms.

ODBC is independent of any particular language, operating system, or database system. An application written to the ODBC API can be ported to another database or operating system merely by changing the ODBC driver. It is the ODBC driver that binds the API to the particular database and platform, and a definition known as the *ODBC data source* contains the information necessary for a particular application to connect with a database service. On Windows systems, the most popular ODBC drivers are shipped with the operating system, as is a utility program to define ODBC data sources (found on the Control Panel or Administrative Tools Panel, depending on the version of Windows).

Most commercial software products and most commercial databases support ODBC, which makes it far easier for software vendors to market and support products across a wide variety of database systems. One notable exception is applications written in Java.

They use a different API known as Java Database Connectivity (JDBC), which is covered in the Connecting Databases to Java Applications section later in this chapter.

A common dilemma is that relational database vendors do not handle advanced functions in the same way. This problem can be circumvented using an escape clause that tells the ODBC driver to pass the proprietary SQL statements through the ODBC API untouched. The downside to this approach, of course, is that applications written this way are not portable to a different vendor's DBMS (and sometimes not even to a different version of the same vendor's DBMS).

Connecting Databases via OLE DB

OLE DB (Object Linking and Embedding, Database—sometimes written as OLE-DB or OLEDB) is an API designed by Microsoft for accessing different types of data stored in a uniform manner. It is intended to be a higher level replacement for ODBC that supports connections to a wide variety of nonrelational databases and files such as object databases and spreadsheets. Although its name includes OLE, the only similarity between OLE and OLE DB is that they both have interfaces that use the Common Object Model (COM).

Connecting Databases to Java Applications

Java started as a proprietary programming language (originally named Oak) that was developed by Sun Microsystems. It rapidly became the de facto standard programming language for web computing, at least in non-Microsoft environments. Java is a type-safe, object-oriented programming language that can be used to build client components (applets) as well as server components (servlets). It has a machine-independent architecture, making it highly portable across hardware and operating system platforms.

You may also run across the terms *JavaScript* and *JScript*. These are scripting languages with a Java-like syntax that are intended to perform simple functions on client systems, such as editing dates. They are not full-fledged implementations of Java and are not designed to handle database interactions, but they can perform the same function as a CGI script if desired.

Java Database Connectivity

JDBC is an API, modeled after ODBC, for connecting Java applications to a wide variety of relational DBMS products. Some JDBC drivers translate the JDBC API to corresponding ODBC calls, and thus connect to the database via an ODBC data source. Other drivers translate directly to the proprietary client API of the particular relational database, such as the Oracle Call Interface (OCI). As with ODBC, an escape clause is available for passing proprietary SQL statements through the interface.

The JDBC API offers the following features:

- **Embedded SQL for Java**   The Java programmer codes SQL statements as string variables, the strings are passed to Java methods, and an embedded SQL processor translates the Java SQL to JDBC calls.

- **Direct mapping of RDBMS tables to Java classes**   The results of SQL calls are automatically mapped to variables in Java classes. The Java programmer may then operate on the returned data as native Java objects.

Java SQL

Java SQL (JSQL) is a method of embedding SQL statements in Java without having to create special coding to put the statements into Java strings. It is an extension of the ISO/ANSI standard for SQL embedded in other host languages, such as C. A special program called a *precompiler* is run on the source program that automatically translates the SQL statements written by the Java programmer into pure Java. This method can save a considerable amount of development effort.

Middleware Solutions

Middleware can be thought of as software that mediates the differences between an application program and the services available on a network, or between two disparate application programs. In the case of Java database connections, middleware products such as Java Relational Binding (JRB) from O2 Technology (acquired by Unidata in 1997) can make the RDBMS look as though it is an object-oriented database running on a remote server. The Java programmer then accesses the database using standard Java methods, and the middleware product takes care of the translation between objects and relational database components.

Try This 9-1   Exploring the World Wide Web

In this Try This exercise, you will explore some aspects of the World Wide Web, observing concepts that were described in this chapter.

Step by Step

1. Access several of your favorite websites, particularly those for which you have an account that lets you review dynamic information such as transactions, travel reward points, auction items, and so forth.

2. Notice which parts of the pages are static and which are dynamic (changing based on your input or the options you select).

(continued)

3. Notice which parts are data listings that likely come from a database. Some of the largest databases in the world support websites for banking, online auctions, and similar functions. However, you probably cannot tell which vendor's DBMS is behind the site by looking at the web pages.

4. Observe the URL displayed by your browser as you navigate pages. Can you spot any arguments (parameters starting with a question mark)? Can you spot any URLs that point to content other than HTML pages (files types such as JSP, PHP, and CGI)? If you see file types that you don't recognize, you can use your favorite search engine to look them up.

Try This Summary

In this Try This exercise, you used the World Wide Web to observe some of the concepts presented in this chapter.

✓ Chapter 9 Self Test

Choose the correct responses to each of the multiple-choice and fill-in-the-blank questions. Note that there may be more than one correct response to each question.

1. In the centralized deployment model,

    A A web server hosts all web pages.

    B A "dumb" terminal is used as the client workstation.

    C Administration is quite easy because everything is centralized.

    D There are no single points of failure.

    E Development costs are often very high.

2. In the distributed deployment model,

    A The database and/or application is partitioned and deployed on multiple computer systems.

    B Initial deployments were highly successful.

    C Distribution can be transparent to the user.

D Costs and complexity are reduced compared with the centralized model.

E Fault tolerance is improved compared with the centralized model.

3. In the two-tier client/server model,

A All application logic runs on an application server.

B A web server hosts the web pages.

C The client workstation handles all presentation logic.

D The database is hosted on a centralized server.

E Client workstations must be high-powered systems.

4. In the three-tier client/server model,

A All application logic runs on an application server.

B A web server hosts the web pages.

C The client workstation handles all presentation logic.

D The database is hosted on a centralized server.

E Client workstations must be high-powered systems.

5. In the N-tier client/server model,

A All application logic runs on an application server.

B A web server hosts the web pages.

C The client workstation handles all presentation logic.

D The database is hosted on a centralized server.

E Client workstations must be high-powered systems.

6. The Internet

A Began as the U.S. Department of Education's ARPANET

B Dates back to the late 1960s and early 1970s

C Always used TCP/IP as a standard

    D Is a worldwide collection of interconnected computer networks

    E Supports multiple protocols, including HTTP, FTP, and Telnet

7. A URL may contain

    A A protocol

    B A host name or IP address

    C A port

    D The absolute path to a resource on the web server

    E Arguments

8. An intranet is available to _____.

9. An extranet is available to _____.

10. The World Wide Web uses _____ to navigate pages.

11. HTTP does not directly support the concept of a session because it is _____.

12. XML is extensible because _____ can be defined.

13. Middleware solutions for Java connections made the RDBMS look like a(n) _____.

14. The web "technology stack" includes

    A A client workstation running a web browser

    B A web server

    C An application server

    D A database server

    E Network hardware (firewalls, routers, and so on)

15. The advantages of CGI are

    A Statelessness

    B Simplicity

    C Inherently secure

    D Widely accepted

    E Language and server independent

16. Server Side Includes (SSI)

    A Are commands embedded in a web document

    B Are non-CGI gateways

    C Are HTML macros

    D Solve some of the CGI performance issues

    E Are inherently secure

17. The advantages of a non-CGI gateway are

    A Known for stability

    B Proprietary solution

    C Improved security over CGI solutions

    D Simpler than CGI

    E Runs in server address space

18. ODBC is

    A A standard API for connecting to DBMSs

    B Independent of any particular language, operating system, or DBMS

    C A Microsoft standard

    D Used by Java programs

    E Flexible in handling proprietary SQL

19. JDBC is

    A A standard API for connecting to DBMSs

    B Independent of any particular language, operating system, or DBMS

    C A Microsoft standard

D Used by Java programs

E Flexible in handling proprietary SQL

20. JSQL is

A A Sun Microsystems standard

B A method of embedding SQL statements in Java

C An extension of an ISO/ANSI standard

D A middleware solution

E Independent of any particular language, operating system, or DBMS

Chapter 10
Database Security

Key Skills & Concepts

- Why Is Security Necessary?

- Database Server Security

- Database Client and Application Security

- Database Access Security

- Security Monitoring and Auditing

Security has become an essential consideration in modern systems. Nothing can be more embarrassing to an organization than a media story regarding sensitive data or trade secrets that were electronically stolen from its computer systems. This chapter discusses the need for security, the security considerations for deploying database servers and clients that access those servers, and methods for implementing database access security. It concludes with a discussion of security monitoring and auditing.

Why Is Security Necessary?

Murphy's Law states that anything that can go wrong will go wrong. Seasoned IT security professionals will tell you that Murphy was an optimist. Servers placed on the Internet with default configurations and passwords have been compromised within *minutes*. Default database passwords and common security vulnerabilities are widely known. In early 2003, the Slammer worm infected tens of thousands of Microsoft SQL Server databases that had been set up with a default SA (system administrator) account that had no password. Oddly, the worst damage was the loss of service when infected computers sent out hundreds of thousands of packets on the network in search of other computers on the network to infect. If you think this cannot happen to you, think again.

Here are some reasons why security must be designed into your computer systems:

- Databases connected to the Internet, or to any other network, are vulnerable to malicious hackers and other criminals who are determined to damage or steal the data. These include the following:

  - Spies from competitors that are after your secrets

  - Hackers interested in a sense of notoriety from penetrating your systems

- Individuals interested in whatever they can obtain that has economic value

- Disgruntled employees—it seems odd that we never hear of gruntled employees (gruntle means "to make happy"), only disgruntled ones

- Zealots interested in making a political statement at the expense of your organization

- The emotionally unbalanced, and just plain evil people

- Employees (or others) may attempt to commit fraud. Any bank auditor will tell you that 80 percent of fraud is committed by employees. Don't assume your system is immune just because the database is not accessible from the Internet.

- Honest mistakes by authorized users can cause security exposures, loss of data, and processing errors.

- Security controls keep people honest in the same way that locks on homes and offices do.

Database Server Security

This section focuses on the security considerations for the database server. When you're considering security, you should start at one end of the network or the other (at either the database user's client workstation or at the database server) and work systematically through all the components in the path. This is the only way you can be sure you don't miss something. In our case, we'll start with the database server and work out from there.

Physical Security

Physically securing the server is an essential ingredient. The server should be located in a locked room, where only authorized personnel have access. Nothing is more embarrassing than having a database server or the disk drives that store the database information stolen or vandalized. Once a thief has made off with the hardware, he has all the time in the world and all the secrecy he needs to crack away at the system until he is able to access the data. Moreover, systems are easier to compromise using the server console than remotely; therefore, "hands-on" access to servers must be tightly controlled. Depending on the sensitivity of the data in the database, the following additional measures might be needed:

- Video surveillance system can be installed.

- "Token" security devices, which administrators must possess to gain access, can be used. These range from cards or keys that must be inserted into the server to gain access, to crypto devices where a PIN must be entered to obtain a password. Some of these devices are synchronized with satellites and change the encryption key used for generating passwords every minute or so.

- Biometric devices can be installed, which require administrators to pass a fingerprint or retinal scan to obtain access.

- Policy provisions can be created that require at least two employees be in the room whenever anyone is locally logged on to the server.

- Policy provisions regarding removal of hardware and software from the workplace can be created. Here's a real-world example: I once worked at a financial institution where employees were searched whenever they left the premises. The removal of any hardware or materials, such as computer listings, microfilmed documents, or media such as tapes and disks, was strictly prohibited. However, there was a laughable loophole. You could put *anything* in an envelope addressed to your home (or anywhere else) and drop it in the outbound mail bins. Not only would the envelope be sent out without inspection, but the firm would even *pay the postage*, no questions asked. Before you get the wrong idea, the only time I saw this technique used was to send computer games offsite, but the security exposure was enormous.

Network Security

It should be obvious that physical security is not enough when the database server is accessible via a network. Intruders who manage to obtain a network connection to the server can work from outside the server room or, for servers connected to the Internet, from anywhere in the world. Moreover, because clients or other servers (such as the application server) are able to connect to the database server, you must take a holistic approach to network security and not only ensure that the network is secure but also that *every* computer system attached to that network is equally secure.

Complete details on how to secure a network are well outside the scope of this book. However, the sections that follow comprise a summary of the network security issues that must be considered. Note that the term *enterprise network* is used here to mean the private network that connects the computing resources for the business enterprise.

Isolate the Enterprise Network from the Internet

If the enterprise network is connected to the Internet, it must be isolated so that malicious hackers on the Internet cannot see the internals of the enterprise network or easily gain access to it. Measures to consider include the following:

Configure the Router   The router that connects the enterprise network to the Internet must be properly configured. Recall that a *router* is a device that forwards data packets between networks using rules contained in a *routing table*. A *packet* is merely a piece of a message that is transmitted over a network. Network devices divide messages into uniformly sized packets for efficient handling. The router must be configured so that only appropriate packets of data are routed from the Internet to the local network. Some routers can perform limited filtering of packets, but typically they do not look at the contents of data packets beyond the destination IP address, contained in the packet header, making decisions on the best way to route the packet based on the destination address and the routing table.

Use a Firewall   Each layer in the enterprise network should be protected by a firewall, with the security rules applied by the firewall getting progressively tighter with each layer. Figure 9-6 in Chapter 9 shows this arrangement. A firewall can be implemented using software on a general-purpose computer or a specialized hardware device that comes with its own operating system and filtering software. The purpose of the firewall is to prevent unauthorized access to the network segment that it protects (that is, computer resources connected to the part of the network that is *inside* the firewall). All data packets passing from the network outside the firewall to the network segment (often called a *subnet*) inside the firewall must pass the security criteria imposed by the firewall or they are simply rejected. The firewall can use the following methods:

- **Packet filtering**   The contents of each packet entering or leaving the network are inspected to make sure user-defined rules are met. Although packet filtering is effective, it is subject to *IP spoofing*, where a hacker masquerades as a legitimate user by planting a legitimate IP address that is acceptable to the firewall in an otherwise illegitimate message. To prevent your network from being used to launch so-called *zombie attacks*, your firewall should always be configured to reject outbound packets that have return IP addresses that are not legitimate for the enterprise network. A zombie attack occurs when an intruder plants a rogue program on one of your servers, which at an appointed time, wakes up and starts sending hundreds or thousands of packets per minute at a target system, typically the website of an enterprise against which the attacker has some grudge, in an attempt to clog the attacked system, rendering it useless. This type of attack is called a *denial of service (DoS)* attack.

- **Application gateway**   Different network applications (HTTP, FTP, Telnet, and so on) use different default ports. For example, HTTP uses port 80 as a default. Ports that are not needed should be shut down. *Always* configure firewalls to open *only* the ports that are *absolutely required* for your normal business.

- **Circuit-level gateway**   For efficiency, this feature applies security mechanisms when a connection is established; then, after the connection is established, it allows packets to flow freely for that established connection. A firewall should normally be configured so that connections can be established *only* from *inside* the firewall—attempts made from outside the firewall to establish connections with resources inside the firewall (other than those specifically authorized) should be rejected.

- **Proxy server** Firewalls can translate all the IP addresses used in the protected network into different addresses as packets pass through, typically assigning each a different port so that any responses to those packets can be sorted out and passed back to the originator. This feature, known as *network address translation (NAT),* hides the internal network from the outside world.

Provide Secure Connections for Employees Working Offsite
These workers present a special risk. If they are connected to a broadband Internet service such as DSL or cable, they essentially reside on a local area network (LAN) with many other users of that particular service. Therefore, if these employees merely plug their personal computers directly into the DSL or cable modem without other precautions, any shared devices they may have (disk drives, printers, and so forth) are automatically shared by all their *neighbors* on the same LAN. All that the intruder has to know is how to click Network Neighborhood and then Entire Network, and all the unprotected systems on the LAN will be there, ripe for picking. Often attackers are only one password away from accessing everything on a target system. Two precautions can circumvent the problem.

A security device, typically a combination router/network switch/firewall, should be placed between the DSL or cable modem and any computers used in the home. A side benefit here is that the user can connect multiple computers to the high-speed service while paying for only one IP address with the Internet service provider (ISP) (note that some ISPs forbid this practice). The device automatically "NATs" any IP address inside the home network to the single IP address assigned by the ISP for the broadband connection, using different ports to differentiate between different connections. I have such a device on my home Internet cable service and have seen firsthand attempts by hackers to scan ports and to ping resources inside my home network. A *port scan* is a technique commonly used by hackers: they launch a special program that tries every conceivable port on an IP address, recording which ones are active so they can try to use the active ports to break into the target system. Intrusion attempts occur with *alarming* frequency, sometimes several times in a single hour. If you install an unprotected home network, your network will likely be penetrated within *hours* of it being activated. Note that Microsoft Windows XP and Vista come with a built-in configurable software firewall. However, most security experts prefer an external firewall on a dedicated hardware device because it offers better protection.

In addition, a secure network technique known as a *virtual private network (VPN)* can be used when connecting from the Internet to the enterprise network. This approach encrypts all data packets and applies other measures to make sure that the packets are useless to any unauthorized party that intercepts them, and that they cannot be altered and retransmitted by hackers. Usually, this technique is implemented using special software from a commercial software vendor in concert with a small device that the remote user employs to generate a unique password each time he connects remotely to the enterprise network. Without the device in his possession (and typically a PIN that goes with the device), the would-be hacker has no chance of penetrating the enterprise network using the VPN.

Secure Any Wireless Network Access

Wireless access points are network devices that receive radio signals from computer devices equipped with wireless network adapters, connecting them to the wired network in the office. Most wireless networks adhere to a version of the network standard protocol known as 802.11. Wireless access points have become inexpensive (less than $100), and therefore prolific, because people like to be able to move around their home or office freely, without having to drag a network cable with them. However, wireless access points require special attention, because an intruder can access a wireless network from outside your premises without going through the routers and firewalls that you have carefully set up to prevent such an intrusion. Horror stories abound in IT trade publications about an unknowing user bringing an unauthorized wireless access point into an office, plugging it into the nearest network jack, and giving everyone within 75 to 150 feet or more open access to the network. By default, many of these devices have *absolutely no* encryption or other access controls enabled, thus providing access to anyone with a wireless-capable computer in a neighboring office, out in the parking lot, or even in a building across the street. Worst of all, once the intruder connects, he can access the intranet, completely *inside* all the firewalls and other controls you so carefully implemented to protect your network from intruders.

If you think this cannot happen to you, following are just a few real-life examples:

● On a recent trip to a medical office, my laptop, which is equipped with an 802.11g wireless network adapter, *automatically* connected to a wireless network in an adjoining doctor's office. I didn't look to see what I might have been able to get to in terms of computers, shared disks, files, and the like, but the office staff was totally unaware that anyone could connect to their wireless network. They didn't understand that walls don't stop wireless networks. Incidentally, a quick look at the wireless adapter's site survey showed two other vulnerable networks accessible from the same waiting room. One of those even had the default network name that comes with the wireless access point, so the password to the router was probably also the factory default. An intruder could reconfigure their entire network before they knew what happened.

- On a recent drive down Market Street in San Francisco, the wireless adapter in the same laptop detected an average of three wireless networks in every block, a surprising number of them wide open to anyone who would want to connect.

- An IT manager reported that after she discovered her company's network had been inappropriately accessed from an unauthorized wireless access point, she went hunting for it, failing to find it in several attempts. Finally, she brought in a consultant who had a device to track down the rogue signal. (Believe it or not, a potato chip tube covered with aluminum foil makes an excellent directional antenna for "sniffing out" wireless access points.) The consultant found it hidden in the suspended ceiling of a conference room. The person who installed it knew it was against the rules, but he just didn't want to bother to cable-connect his laptop to a nearby jack. Needless to say, that person lost his job, but who knows what the intruders got before the unauthorized access point was shut down.

Establish a Wireless Security Policy   Your organization's security policy should address wireless connections, forbidding anyone other than trained network administrators from installing them, and setting standards for their proper installation.

Mandate Encryption   Standards should mandate that encryption be enabled on every wireless access point. All the access points on the market have encryption capability built into them, and it takes only a few minutes to enable the feature and to input a pass phrase that any device trying to connect must supply in order to gain access to the network.

Limit Access Using a MAC Address List   Every network device currently manufactured has a unique Media Access Control (MAC) address assigned to it by the manufacturer. Most wireless access points permit the entry of a MAC address list that restricts network access *only* to the devices that appear in the list. Alternatively, the MAC address list can list devices that are *not* allowed to connect.

System-Level Security

Once the network is as secure as you can make it, the next area of focus is the system that will run the DBMS. A poorly secured database server can provide many unchecked paths for intruders to use. Here are some measures worth considering:

Install Minimal Operating System Software   Install only the minimal software components required to get the job done, especially on a production server. Avoid default or "typical" installation options and use the "custom" installation option to choose only the components needed. For example, on production Unix servers, you should be in the habit of removing the "make" utility and C language compilers after you complete an installation. Hackers have a difficult time installing things when the tools needed to perform software installations do not exist on the server.

Use Minimal Operating System Services   Shut down or remove operating system services that are not required. In particular, communications services such as FTP should not be running unless they are expressly required. On Windows systems, it's a good idea to set Startup Type to Disabled for services that are not required. This makes it impossible to start these services unless you have Administrator privileges.

Install Minimal DBMS Software   The fewer the features of the DBMS that you have installed, the less exposure you'll have to problems such as buffer overflow vulnerabilities. The DBA should work with the application developers to create a consolidated list of the DBMS functions needed. Once you have the list, use the custom installation option for the DBMS and perform only minimal installations.

Apply Security Patches in a Timely Manner   Establish a program wherein security alerts are reviewed as they are announced and countermeasures, including patches and workarounds, are applied in a timely manner. Patches should be shaken down in a development environment for a finite period of time before application to a production environment.

Change All Default Passwords   Default passwords should be changed to new passwords that are difficult to guess or discover via *brute force*, a method that repeatedly tries possibilities until access is finally achieved.

Database Client and Application Security

A *database client* is any computer system that signs on directly to the database server. Therefore, the application server is nearly always a database client, along with the client workstation of any person in the organization who has sign-on privileges for the database. Typically, the DBMS requires installation of client software on these systems to facilitate communication between the database client and the DBMS using any specialized communications mechanisms required by the DBMS.

Login Credentials

Every database user who connects to the database must supply appropriate credentials to establish the connection. Typically this is in the form of a user ID (or login ID) and a password. Use care to establish credentials that are not easily compromised. Here are some considerations:

- Credentials must not be shared by multiple database users.

- Passwords should be selected that are not easy to guess. A security policy should establish minimum standards for password security, including minimum length, the mixture of uppercase/lowercase letters, numbers and special characters, and avoiding words that can be found in a dictionary.

- Passwords should be changed on a regular basis, such as every 30 or 45 days. There is some disagreement among security experts as to the effectiveness of periodic password changes, but most IT auditors insist on this practice.

- Any exposed password should be immediately changed.

- Passwords should never be written down and must be encrypted whenever they are electronically stored.

Data Encryption

Encryption is the translation of data into a secret code that cannot be read without the use of a password or secret key. Unencrypted data is called *plain text,* whereas encrypted data is called *cipher text.*

Some encryption schemes use a *symmetric key,* which means that a single key is used both to encrypt plain text and to decrypt cipher text. This form is considered less secure compared with the use of *asymmetric keys,* where a pair of keys is used—a *public* key and a *private* key. What the public key encrypts, the private key can decrypt, and vice versa. The names come from the expected use of the keys: the public key is given to anyone with which an enterprise does business, and the private key remains confidential and internal to the enterprise.

Here are some guidelines to follow regarding encryption:

- Encryption keys should be a minimum of 128 bits in length. The longer the key, the more secure it is considered to be (within reason). However, longer keys lengthen the decryption process, so there is a tradeoff.

- The loss of an encryption key should be treated with the same seriousness as the loss of the data that it was used to encrypt.

- Sensitive data should be encrypted whenever it is permanently stored. Which data is considered sensitive is a judgment call that should be made by the business people who own the data, not by the DBA. In general, however, any personal data (such as Social Security numbers and birthdates) that can be used for identity theft should be considered sensitive.

- All data not considered public knowledge should be encrypted whenever transported electronically across network connections that are not otherwise encrypted. For example, if a company sends a purchase order file to a trading partner via FTP, the file should be encrypted. There is no guarantee that the bad guys are not monitoring public networks.

- E-mail is not considered secure, so any sensitive information to be sent via e-mail should be in an encrypted attachment instead of the main body of the e-mail message. Alternatively, some e-mail systems support encrypted and signed messages.

Other Client Considerations

Database clients require special scrutiny in terms of security precautions, because if compromised, they provide an easy pathway for the intruder to gain access to data in the database. Here are some additional client considerations:

Web Browser Security Level   Modern web browsers allow the setting of a security level for the browser. For Microsoft Internet Explorer, the security settings are controlled using the Security tab on the Internet Options panel, which is accessible using the Tools option on the main toolbar. This security level should be set to the highest possible level that still permits normal use of the database applications. Two considerations are related to the web browser:

Cookies provide the ability for the web browser to store textual information on the client, which can be automatically retrieved later by the web browser and sent to the web server that requested them. Cookies are not very secure and can be used to spy on users of the client system. Furthermore, there is no guarantee that unauthorized persons and software will have no access to information in cookies. The organization's security policy should address this issue and set a clear standard for cookie use, which is one of the facilities controlled by the web browser's security level. Also, it is not wise to design application systems that require cookies, because they are not supported by all web browsers and not permitted by all users. In Microsoft Internet Explorer, options for cookies are controlled using the Privacy tab on the Internet Options panel.

Scripting languages such as VBScript, JavaScript, and JScript provide nice features for assisting with a user's interaction with a web page. However, they can and have been used for injecting malicious code into systems, so you should be careful when allowing such languages to be used on the client. VBScript is especially notorious for its misuse and has been used to transport viruses in e-mail attachments.

Minimal Use of Other Software   Software that is not required for the normal functioning of the client should not be installed. Security policies should forbid employees from installing unauthorized software.

Virus Scanner   All computer systems running operating systems that are susceptible to computer viruses should have appropriate virus-scanning software installed. Virus scanners that automatically update their virus profiles on a regular basis offer the most effective protection.

Test Application Exposures   Web-based applications should be thoroughly tested using a client configured just the way your real business users' client workstations will be configured. Hacker tricks such as the following should be attempted to verify that the exposures do not exist:

- **SQL injection**   SQL commands are entered into normal data fields in web pages in such a way that the application server or web server hands them off to the database for processing. Application programs should include precautions against such attacks, such as using stored procedures for all updates or testing for and rejecting any input fields that contain control characters such as semicolons, ampersands, and backslashes that can be used to format escape sequences necessary for SQL injection.

- **URL spoofing**   The URL in the web browser is manually overtyped in such a way that unauthorized data is revealed. Designs in which session IDs are assigned sequentially by the application server and then passed back to the web browser as an argument in the URL are especially susceptible to this approach. If you can guess another user's session ID, you can hijack the user's session just by overtyping the session ID in the URL.

- **Buffer overflows**   Published exposures such as buffer overflows should be thoroughly tested once the vendor's patch has been installed to ensure that the problem really was corrected. A *buffer overflow* is a condition in which a process attempts to store data beyond the boundaries of a fixed-length buffer. The result is that the extra data overwrites adjacent memory locations. The overwritten data can include malicious code that can then be used to compromise security controls.

Database Access Security

With the confidence that our clients, servers, and network are now secure, we can focus on database access. The goal here is to determine precisely the data that each database user needs to conduct business, and what the user is permitted to do with the data (that is, select, insert, update, or delete). Each database user should be given *exactly* the privileges required—nothing more and nothing less. Recall that an application program with database access is a database user, as is an employee who directly queries the database.

In terms of database security, all database users should be treated in the same way (that is, the same standards should be applied to all), whether the database user is software or "liveware." In this section, we will explore the options and challenges related to securing access to the database and its data.

Database Security Architectures

For DBAs who support databases from multiple vendors, one of the challenges is that, with the exception of Microsoft SQL Server and Sybase Adaptive Server Enterprise (ASE), no two databases have the same architecture for database security. And of course, this is a side effect of the overall database architectures being different. The only reason that Microsoft SQL Server and Sybase ASE have such similar architectures is that the former was derived from the later.

Because Microsoft SQL Server/Sybase ASE and Oracle are among the most popular databases today, let's have a quick look at how each implements database security.

Database Security in Microsoft SQL Server and Sybase ASE

With Microsoft SQL Server and Sybase ASE, once the DBMS software is installed on the server, a database server is created. "Server" is a confusing term, of course, because we call the hardware a "server." In this case, the term *SQL server* is a copy of the DBMS software running in memory as a set of processes (usually installed as *services* in Windows environments) with related control information that is stored in a special database on the *database server*. We will use the term *SQL server* to mean the DBMS software and the term *database server* to mean the hardware platform on which the database is running. In this architecture, each SQL server manages many databases, with each database representing a logical grouping of data as determined by the database designer. Figure 10-1 shows a simplified view of the security architecture for Microsoft SQL Server and Sybase ASE.

Login   A user account on the SQL server, a login is also called a *user login*. This is not the same as any operating system account the user may have on the database server. However, on database servers running Microsoft Windows, the login can use Windows authentication, meaning the Windows operating system stores the credentials (login name and password) and authenticates users when they attempt to connect to the SQL server. An obvious advantage to Windows authentication is that user access to the various SQL servers in the enterprise can be centrally managed through the Windows account, rather than locally managed on each SQL server. Note that once a login is defined in the SQL server, the database user may connect to the SQL server, but a login alone does *not* give the user access to any database information. There is, however, a master login

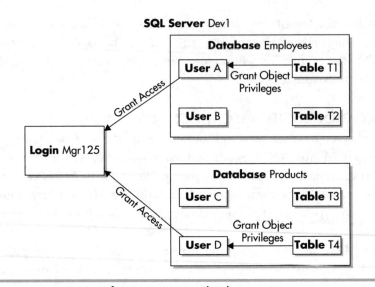

Figure 10-1   Security in Microsoft SQL Server and Sybase ASE

called *sa* (system administrator) that, similar to root in Unix and Administrator in Microsoft Windows, has full privileges to everything in the SQL Server environment. Figure 10-1 shows only one user login, called Mgr125.

Database   A database is a logical collection of database objects (tables, views, indexes, and so on) as defined by the database designer. Figure 10-1 shows two databases: Employees and Products. You must understand that a login is allowed to connect to a database only after it has been granted that privilege by an administrator. (See the "User" topic that follows.) In addition to databases holding system data, some special databases are created when the SQL server is created (not shown in Figure 10-1) and are used by the DBMS to manage the SQL server. Among these are the following databases:

- **master**   The master database contains system-level information, initialization settings, configuration settings, login accounts, the list of databases configured in the SQL server, and the location of primary database data files.

- **tempdb**   The tempdb database contains temporary tables and temporary stored procedures.

- **model**   The model database contains a template for all other databases created on the system.

- **msdb**   In Microsoft SQL Server databases only, the msdb database contains information used for scheduling jobs and alerts.

User   Each database has a set of users assigned to it. Each database user maps to a login, so each user is a "pseudo-account" that is an alias to an SQL Server login account. User accounts do not necessarily have to have the same user name as their corresponding login accounts. When an administrator grants access to a database for a particular login account, the user account corresponding to the login account is created by the DBMS. In Figure 10-1, the Mgr125 login corresponds to User A in the Employees database and to User D in the Products database. These privileges permit the login to connect to the database(s), but they do not give the user any privileges against objects in those databases. How this happens is covered in the next topic.

Privileges   Each user account in a database may be granted any number of privileges (also called *permissions*). *System privileges* are general privileges applied at the database level. Microsoft SQL Server divides these into *server privileges,* which include such permissions as starting up, shutting down, and backing up the SQL server, and *statement privileges*, which include such permissions as creating a database and creating a table. *Object privileges* allow specific actions on a specific object, such as allowing select and update on table T1. Figure 10-1 contains arrows that show the granting of object privileges on Table T1 to User A in the Employees database, and on Table T4 to User D in the Products database. These privileges work in much the same way across all relational databases, thanks to ANSI standards, and are therefore covered in the "System Privileges" and "Object Privileges" sections a little later in this chapter.

Database Security in Oracle

Oracle's security architecture, shown in Figure 10-2, is markedly different compared to that of Microsoft SQL Server and Sybase ASE. The differences between the two are highlighted as each component is introduced:

Instance   This is a copy of the Oracle DBMS software running in memory. Each instance manages only *one* database.

Database   This is the collection of files managed by a single Oracle instance. Taken together, the Oracle instance and database make up what Microsoft SQL Server and Sybase ASE call the *SQL server*. Figure 10-2 depicts the Dev1 database.

User   Each database account is called a *user*. As with Microsoft SQL Server and Sybase ASE, the user account may be authenticated externally (that is, by the operating system) or internally (by the DBMS). Each user is automatically allocated a *schema* (defined next), and this user is the *owner* of that schema, meaning the user automatically has full privileges over any object in the schema. The following predefined users are created automatically when the database is created (not shown in Figure 10-2):

- The SYS user is the owner of the Oracle instance and contains objects that Oracle uses to manage the instance. This user is equivalent to the sa user in Microsoft SQL Server and Sybase ASE.

- The SYSTEM user is the owner of the Oracle database and contains objects that Oracle uses to manage the database. This user's schema is similar to the master database in Microsoft SQL Server and Sybase ASE.

- Many Oracle database options create their own user accounts when those options are installed.

Schema   The schema is the collection of database objects that belong to a specific Oracle user. The Oracle schema is equivalent to what Microsoft SQL Server and Sybase ASE call a *database*. Figure 10-2 shows the Employees, Products, and Mgr125 schemas, which are owned by the Employees, Products, and Mgr125 users, respectively. Schema and user names are *always* identical in Oracle. Mgr125 is a workaround to a special challenge we face with Oracle's security architecture, as discussed in the "Schema Owner Accounts" section that follows.

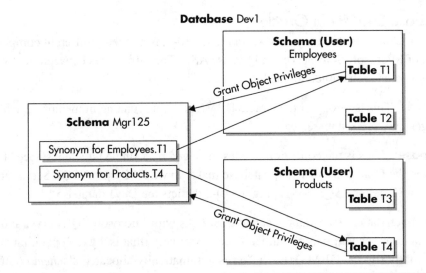

Figure 10-2   Database security in Oracle

Privileges   As with Microsoft SQL Server and Sybase ASE, privileges are divided into system and object privileges. These are covered in the "System Privileges" section a bit later.

Schema Owner Accounts

With all databases, you should avoid giving database users more privileges than they need to do their job. This not only prevents errors made by humans (including those contained in the application programs and database queries they write) from becoming data disasters, but it also keeps people honest.

In Microsoft SQL Server and Sybase ASE, database users should not be allowed to connect as the sa user. You should create database logins that have the minimal privileges required. Sadly, this is often not done, and applications connect as sa or to a database with a user account that has the DBO (database owner) or DBA (database administrator) role. *Roles* are collections of privileges and are discussed in an upcoming section. Whether it occurs due to a lack of understanding or because of laziness, this practice represents a *huge* security exposure that should be forbidden as a matter of policy.

In Figure 10-2, note that the Mgr125 user owns no tables but does have some privileges granted to it by the Employees and Products users. This is to work around a fundamental challenge with Oracle's security architecture. If we allowed a database user to connect to the database using a user such as Employees or Products, the user would automatically have full privileges to every object in the schema, including insert, delete, and update against any table, and the user would also be able to create and alter tables without restriction. This is fundamentally the same issue as allowing use of the sa user or the DBO and DBA roles in Microsoft SQL Server and Sybase ASE. The Mgr125 user mimics the behavior of the login with the same name, as shown in Figure 10-1. With the right system privileges, we can prevent the Mgr125 user in Oracle from being able to create any tables of its own.

You may have noticed the synonyms for user Mgr125 in Figure 10-2. A *synonym* is merely an alias or nickname for a database object. Synonyms are for the convenience of the user so that names do not have to be qualified with their schema name. To select from the T1 tables in the Employees schema directly, user Mgr125 would have to refer to the table name as Employees.T1 in the SQL statement. This is not only inconvenient, but it can also cause seemingly endless problems if we ever decide to change the name of the Employees user. By creating a synonym called T1 in the Mgr125 schema that points to Employees.T1, the user may now refer to the table as just T1. Incidentally, you may recall that all user and object names in Oracle are case-insensitive, so the use of mixed case here is only for illustration. The syntax for creating this synonym is as follows:

```
CREATE SYNONYM T1 FOR EMPLOYEES.T1;
```

System Privileges

System privileges are general permissions to perform functions in managing the server
and the database(s). Hundreds of permissions are supported by each database vendor,
with most of those being system privileges. As with object privileges, system privileges
are granted using the SQL GRANT statement and rescinded using the SQL REVOKE
statement. Some of the most commonly used privileges are listed in the sections that
follow. Complete details can be found in vendor-supplied documentation.

Microsoft SQL Server System (Server and Statement) Privilege Examples

Here are some commonly used Microsoft SQL Server system privileges:

- **SHUTDOWN**   Provides the ability to issue the server shutdown command.
- **CREATE DATABASE**   Provides the ability to create new databases on the SQL server.
- **BACKUP DATABASE**   Provides the ability to run backups of the databases on
  the SQL server.

Oracle System Privilege Examples

Here are some commonly used Oracle system privileges:

- **CREATE SESSION**   Provides the ability to connect to the database.
- **CREATE TABLE**   Provides the ability to create tables in your own schema. Similar
  privileges exist for other object types, such as indexes, synonyms, procedures, and so on.
- **CREATE ANY TABLE**   Provides the ability to create tables in *any* user's schema.
  Similar privileges are available for other object types, such as indexes, synonyms,
  procedures, and so on.
- **CREATE USER**   Provides the ability to create new users in the database.

Object Privileges

Object privileges are granted to users with the SQL GRANT statement and revoked with
the REVOKE statement. The database user (login) who receives the privileges is called
the *grantee*. These statements are also covered in Chapter 4. The GRANT statement may
include a WITH GRANT OPTION clause that allows the recipient to grant the privilege
to others. If the privilege is subsequently revoked, a cascading revoke takes place if this
user has, in turn, granted the permission to any other user. I do *not* recommend use of the
WITH GRANT OPTION clause because it is far too easy to lose control over who has
which privileges.

The general syntax of the **GRANT** and **REVOKE** statements are shown here, along with some examples:

```
GRANT <privilege list> ON <object> TO <grantee list>
   [WITH GRANT OPTION];
GRANT SELECT, UPDATE, INSERT ON T1 TO Mgr125;
GRANT SELECT ON T2 TO User1, User2, User3;

REVOKE <privilege list> ON <object> FROM <grantee list>;
REVOKE SELECT, UPDATE, INSERT ON T1 FROM Mgr125;
REVOKE SELECT ON T2 FROM User1, User2, User3;
```

Roles

A *role* is a named collection of privileges that can, in turn, be granted to one or more users. Most RDBMS systems have predefined roles that come with the system, and database users with the CREATE ROLE privilege may create their own. Roles have the following advantages:

- *Roles may exist before user accounts do.* For example, you can create a role that contains all the privileges required to work on a particular development project. When a new hire joins the project team, one GRANT statement gives his or her new user account all the required permissions.

- *Roles relieve the administrator of a lot of tedium.* Many privileges can be granted (or revoked) with a single command when a role is used.

- *Roles survive when user accounts are dropped.* If the DBA must drop and re-create a user account, it can be a lot of work to reinstate all the privileges, which is simplified if all the privileges are assembled into one role.

For administrators, a common role is DBA, which conveys a lot of powerful privileges (more than 125 separate privileges in Oracle). Obviously, such a high-powered privilege must be granted judiciously.

Views

One of the common security issues to be addressed is how to allow database users access to some rows and columns in a table while preventing access to other rows and columns.

Ask the Expert

Q: I haven't noticed any SQL statements to create user accounts. Isn't some SQL available to do so?

A: Yes and no. Some SQL implementations such as Oracle provide a CREATE USER statement. However, others, such as SQL Server and Sybase ASE, do not and rely instead on vendor-supplied stored procedures and GUI tools for the creation of user accounts. The ANSI/ISO SQL Standard provides no standard syntax for creating user accounts, so each vendor is free to implement the function as it sees fit.

Views are an excellent way to accomplish this. Here are some of the benefits of using views to accomplish security objectives:

- *Columns that a database user does not require may be omitted from the view.* Assuming the user has been granted access to the view rather than the underlying table, this method totally prevents the user from seeing the information in the columns that were omitted from the view.

- *A WHERE clause may be included in the view to limit returned rows.* Joins may be included to match to other tables as a way of limiting rows. For example, the view could limit Product table rows only to those products for a Division ID that matches the division in which the employee works.

- *Joins to lookup tables can be used to replace code values in a table with their corresponding descriptions.* A lookup table typically contains a list of code values (for example, department codes, transaction codes, status codes) and their descriptions, and it's used to "look up" the descriptions for the codes. Although this is a minor point, employees trying to hack database records during fraud attempts have a much more difficult time if they cannot see the codes used to categorize the transactions. Furthermore, employees trying to do their best usually have a better time reading and understanding code descriptions than the corresponding code values.

Security Monitoring and Auditing

Security policies and controls are typically not enough to ensure compliance. A monitoring system must also be in place to detect security breaches so that corrective measures can be taken. Multiple intrusion-detection tools are on the market and are capable of monitoring a server and detecting unauthorized changes to files stored in the file system. Also, all the major RDBMS products have provisions for setting up auditing so that selected actions in the database are silently logged, typically into audit tables that can subsequently be used for reporting. Consult your RDBMS documentation for a full description of these auditing features.

It is also a good idea to have an independent auditor review your organization's security policies and procedures when they are initially written and at periodic intervals thereafter. Furthermore, it is wise to have your auditors, or a consultant who specializes in information systems security, perform an onsite audit, including testing the site for vulnerabilities that have not yet been addressed. System intrusions, including fraud, can cost you many times more than a system audit, which may save you any embarrassment before your employees and customers.

Try This 10-1 Database Object Privileges

In this Try This exercise, you will try out the SQL statements that grant and revoke database privileges, including performing some tests to demonstrate that privileges are properly granted.

Step by Step

1. Two user accounts are needed for this exercise: one that will own the database object and another that will be given privileges on that database object. Create an account named Data1 and another named User1. Use database authentication instead of operating system authentication. If you are working in SQL Server or Sybase ASE, you will also need to create a database, make the Data1 account the owner of the database, grant User1 account access to the database, and make the new database the default database for both accounts when they connect. Each RDBMS product supports user account creation in a unique way, so if you are unfamiliar with this function in your RDBMS, consult your documentation.

2. Grant accounts Data1 and User1 any system privileges required for connecting to the database and creating database objects. In Oracle, the CONNECT and RESOURCE roles should be granted to them. In SQL Server and Sybase ASE, the steps you performed in Step 1 should suffice.

3. Connect to the database using account User1.

(continued)

4. Objects must exist before privileges may be granted for them. We will use a simple Department table that holds department codes and names. Create the DEPARTMENT table by running the following SQL statement. In SQL Server and Sybase ASE, make sure you create the table in the database you created in Step 1 of this exercise.

```
CREATE TABLE DEPARTMENT
   (DEPARTMENT_CODE    CHAR(3),
    DEPARTMENT_NAME    VARCHAR(50));
```

5. Use the following SQL statement to grant the SELECT and INSERT privileges on the DEPARTMENT table to User1:

```
GRANT SELECT, INSERT ON DEPARTMENT TO USER1;
```

6. Connect to the database as User1.

7. Use the following statement to insert a row for Department 001 into the table:

```
INSERT INTO DATA1.DEPARTMENT
VALUES ('001','Executive');
```

NOTE
In this step and in steps 8–10, for SQL Server and Sybase ASE, the table name should not be qualified with DATA1.

8. Retrieve the row you just inserted using the following statement:

```
SELECT * FROM DATA1.DEPARTMENT
 WHERE DEPARTMENT_CODE = '001';
```

9. Attempt to delete the row you just inserted using the following statement. The delete should fail because account User1 does not have delete privileges on the object.

```
DELETE FROM DATA1.DEPARTMENT
 WHERE DEPARTMENT_CODE = '001';
```

10. Attempt to drop the table using the following statement. The drop should fail because account User1 does not have drop privileges on the object.

```
DROP TABLE DATA1.DEPARTMENT;
```

11. Connect as account Data1 (the account that owns the DEPARTMENT table).

12. Drop the table using the following statement (note that this time it does not have to be qualified with DATA1 because you are connected as that account):

```
DROP TABLE DEPARTMENT;
```

13. To finish the cleanup task, drop user accounts Data1 and User1, and any database you created for this Try This exercise.

Try This Summary

In this Try This exercise, you created two user accounts. Then you created a table in one of the accounts and granted some privileges on the table to the other count. Next, you tried various SQL statements on the table to demonstrate that lack of proper privileges prevented some of the statements from working. Finally, you dropped the table and user accounts you created to put the data back to where it was when you started.

Chapter 10 Self Test

Choose the correct responses to each of the multiple-choice and fill-in-the-blank questions. Note that there may be more than one correct response to each question.

1. A collection of privileges that can be granted to multiple users is called a _____.

2. Privileges are rescinded using the SQL _____ command.

3. For database servers connected to a network, physical security alone is _____.

4. Employees connecting to the enterprise network from home or another remote work location should have a _____ between the computer and their cable or DSL modem.

5. When login credentials are stored in the computer system, they must always be _____.

6. Network security

    A Can be handled by routers alone

    B Can be handled by firewalls alone

    C Must include provisions for remotely located employees

    D Should be mandatory for all computer systems connected to any network

7. Firewall protection may include

    A Packet filtering

    B Packet selection using a routing table

    C Network address translation

    D Limiting ports that may be used for access

    E IP spoofing

8. Wireless networks need to be secured because

　　A Inexpensive wireless access points are readily available.

　　B Anyone with a wireless network adapter can connect to an unprotected network.

　　C Employees may use the wireless network to communicate secretly with hackers.

　　D Radio waves penetrate walls to adjoining offices.

　　E Radio waves may carry to public roads outside the building.

9. Components of wireless access point security include

　　A Network address translation

　　B The organization's security policy

　　C Encryption

　　D Virtual private networks

　　E MAC address lists

10. System-level security precautions include

　　A Installing the minimal software components necessary

　　B Granting only table privileges that users require

　　C Applying security patches in a timely manner

　　D Changing all default passwords

　　E Using simple passwords that are easy to remember

11. Encryption

　　A Should be used for all sensitive data

　　B Should use keys of at least 28 bits in length

　　C Should be used for sensitive data sent over a network

　　D Can use symmetric or asymmetric keys

　　E Should never be used for login credentials

12. Client security considerations include which of the following?

　　A MAC address lists

　　B Web browser security level

   C Granting only database table privileges that are absolutely necessary

   D Use of a virus scanner

   E Testing of application exposures

13. In Microsoft SQL Server, a login (user login)

   A Can connect to any number of databases

   B Automatically has database access privileges

   C Can use Windows authentication

   D Can be authenticated by Microsoft SQL Server

   E Owns a database schema

14. In Microsoft SQL Server, a database

   A Is owned by a login

   B May have one or more users assigned to it

   C May contain system data (for example, master) or user (application) data

   D May be granted privileges

   E Is a logical collection of database objects

15. In Oracle, a user account

   A Can connect (log in) to any number of databases

   B Automatically has database privileges

   C Can use operating system authentication

   D Can be authenticated by the Oracle DBMS

   E Owns a database schema

16. In Oracle, a database

   A Is owned by a user

   B May have one or more user accounts defined in it

   C May contain system data (for example, system schema) and user (application) data

   D Is the same as a schema

   E Is managed by an Oracle instance

17. System privileges

    A Are granted in a similar way in Oracle, Sybase ASE, and Microsoft SQL Server

    B Are specific to a database object

    C Allow the grantee to perform certain administrative functions on the server, such as shutting it down

    D Are rescinded using the SQL REMOVE statement

    E Vary across databases from different vendors

18. Object privileges

    A Are granted in a similar way in Oracle, Sybase ASE, and Microsoft SQL Server

    B Are specific to a database object

    C Allow the grantee to perform certain administrative functions on the server, such as shutting it down

    D Are rescinded using the SQL REMOVE statement

    E Are granted using the SQL GRANT statement

19. Using **WITH GRANT OPTION** when granting object privileges

    A Allows the grantee to grant the privilege to others

    B Gives the grantee DBA privileges on the entire database

    C Can lead to security issues

    D Will cascade if the privilege is subsequently revoked

    E Is a highly recommended practice because it is so convenient to use

20. Views may assist with security policy implementation by

    A Restricting the table columns to which a user has access

    B Restricting the databases to which a user has access

    C Restricting table rows to which a user has access

    D Storing database audit results

    E Monitoring for database intruders

Chapter 11
Deploying Databases

Key Skills & Concepts

- Cursor Processing
- Transaction Management
- Performance Tuning
- Change Control

This chapter covers considerations regarding the development of applications that use the database system. These include cursor processing, transaction management, performance tuning, and change control.

Cursor Processing

Before we embark on *transaction management*, which includes a discussion of the locking mechanisms required to support concurrent updates of the database, we must explore the way application programs handle database queries. The collection of rows returned by the execution of a database query is called the *result set*. When you're selecting data from the database, application programming languages such as C and Java present a dilemma when the result set contains multiple rows of data. These programming languages are designed to handle one record at a time (one object instance at a time in the case of Java). So a mismatch occurs, which must be addressed.

To overcome the mismatch, most relational databases support the concept of a *cursor*, which is merely a pointer to a single row in the result set. In Oracle, cursor support is included in a SQL extension called PL/SQL (Procedural Language/SQL), and similarly in Transact-SQL for Sybase ASE and Microsoft SQL Server. The examples in this chapter use Oracle, so some of them may require minor modification before they will work on other RDBMS products. The use of a cursor parallels the use of a traditional flat file in that the cursor must be defined and opened before it may be used, it may be read from by fetching rows in a programming loop, and it should be closed when the program no longer needs it.

Following is an example of a cursor declaration. For clarity, all the keywords are shown in uppercase and database object names in lowercase. In Oracle, this makes no difference because all database object names are case-insensitive. You may, however, have a different experience with other RDBMS products.

```
DECLARE CURSOR ny_customers AS
   SELECT customer_number, name, address, city, zip_code
     FROM customer
    WHERE state = 'NY';
```

NOTE

The cursor handling statements shown in this section are intended to be embedded in application programs. They generally cannot be run using an interactive SQL client.

You may recognize the customer table from Chapter 8. If you ignore the first line, the statement looks like any ordinary SQL query—it selects some columns from a table and, in this case, has a WHERE clause that limits the rows returned to those from New York state. This is very nice, because it means we can test the query using any interactive SQL client tool before we paste it into a program and turn it into a cursor declaration. The DECLARE CURSOR clause defines the cursor for us, which has been named ny_ customers. Cursor declarations are not executable statements, meaning that when they are processed by the RDBMS, they do nothing but set up a definition that can be subsequently referenced. The declaration is checked for syntax and some other internal details, but the database does not need to access any table rows until the cursor is opened.

The cursor must be opened before it can be used. In this example, the RDBMS may not have to retrieve any rows when we open the cursor, but for efficiency, it might decide to retrieve some number of rows and place them in a buffer for us. A *buffer* is merely an area of computer memory used to hold data temporarily. It is far more efficient to use a buffer to hold some number of prefetched rows rather than going to the database files for every single row, because computers can access memory so much faster than files in the file system. In some cases, however, the RDBMS *must* fetch all the rows matching a query and sort them before the first row can be returned to the application program. You may have guessed that these are queries containing an ORDER BY to sequence the returned rows. If there is no index on the column(s) we use for sequencing, then the RDBMS must find and sort all of them before it knows which one is the correct one to return as the *first* row (the one that sorts first in the requested sequence).

Although a lot goes on when we open a cursor, the statement itself is quite simple. Here is the OPEN CURSOR statement for our example:

```
OPEN CURSOR ny_customers;
```

Each time our program requires a new row from the result set, we simply issue a **FETCH** command against the cursor. This is very much like reading the next record from a file in an older flat file system. Remember that the cursor is merely a pointer into the result set. Every time a **FETCH** is issued, the row currently pointed to is returned to the calling program (that is, the program that issued the **FETCH**), and the cursor is advanced one row to point to the next row to be returned. If no more rows exist in the result set, a code is returned to the calling program to so indicate. Another detail handled by the **FETCH** is mapping the columns returned to programming language variables (called *host language variables*, or just *host variables*). This is done with the INTO clause, and naturally the syntax of the variable names will vary from one programming language to another. Our example uses very simple names to stay away from programming language issues, but in real life you would want the names to be as descriptive as possible. It's also good programming practice to use names that are *not* exactly the same as the database column names, so as to avoid confusion when someone else reads the program. The variable names in this example are prefixed with **v_** (for *variable*) for this reason. Here is the fetch of the ny_customers cursor:

```
FETCH ny_customers
 INTO v_customer_number, v_name, v_address, v_city,
    v_zip_code;
```

Notice that the FETCH statement refers only to the cursor name and the host variables. The cursor declaration ties the cursor to the table(s) and column(s) being referenced. As stated, you should always close the cursor when the program no longer needs it because this frees up any resources the cursor has used, including memory for buffers. The CLOSE statement is as simple as the OPEN statement:

```
CLOSE ny_customers;
```

The topic of cursor processing has been introduced before the discussion of transaction management because cursors play a key role in some transaction events.

Transaction Management

To support the database users successfully, the DBMS must include provisions to manage the transactions carried out by the application systems using the database.

What Is a Transaction?

A *transaction* is a discrete series of actions that must be either completely processed or not processed at all. Some call a transaction a *unit of work* as a way of further emphasizing its all-or-nothing nature. Transactions have properties that can be easily remembered using the acronym *ACID* (Atomicity, Consistency, Isolation, Durability):

- **Atomicity**   A transaction must remain whole. That is, it must completely succeed or completely fail. When it succeeds, all changes that were made by the transaction must be preserved by the system. Should a transaction fail, all changes that were made by it must be completely undone. In database systems, we use the term *rollback* for the process that backs out any changes made by a failed transaction and the term *commit* for the process that makes transaction changes permanent.

- **Consistency**   A transaction should transform the database from one consistent state to another. For example, a transaction that creates an invoice for an order transforms the order from a *shipped* order to an *invoiced* order, including all the appropriate database changes.

- **Isolation**   Each transaction should carry out its work independent of any other transaction that might occur at the same time.

- **Durability**   Changes made by completed transactions should remain permanent, even after a subsequent shutdown or failure of the database or other critical system component. In object terminology, the term *persistence* is used for permanently stored data. The concept of permanence here can be confusing, because nothing ever seems to stand still for long in an online transaction processing (OLTP) database. Just keep in mind that *permanent* means the change will not disappear when the database is shut down or fails—it does *not* mean that the data is in a permanent state that can never be changed again.

DBMS Support for Transactions

Aside from personal computer database systems, most DBMSs provide transaction support. This includes provisions in SQL for identifying the beginning and end of each transaction, along with a facility for logging all changes made by transactions so that a rollback can be performed when necessary. As you might guess, standards lagged behind the need for transaction support, so support for transactions varies a bit across RDBMS vendors. As examples, let's look at transaction support in Microsoft SQL Server and Oracle, followed by discussion of transaction logs.

Transaction Support in Microsoft SQL Server

Microsoft SQL Server supports transactions in three modes: autocommit, explicit, and implicit. All three modes are available when you're connected directly to the database using a client tool designed for this purpose. However, if you plan to use an ODBC or JDBC driver, you should consult the driver's documentation for information on the transaction support it provides. Here are descriptions of the three modes:

- **Autocommit mode**   In autocommit mode, each SQL statement is automatically committed as it completes. Essentially, this makes every SQL statement a discrete transaction. Every connection to Microsoft SQL Server uses autocommit until either an explicit transaction is started or the implicit transaction mode is set. In other words, autocommit is the default transaction mode for each SQL Server connection.

- **Explicit mode**   In explicit mode, each transaction is started with a BEGIN TRANSACTION statement and ended with either a COMMIT TRANSACTION statement (for successful completion) or a ROLLBACK TRANSACTION statement (for unsuccessful completion). This mode is used most often in application programs, stored procedures, triggers, and scripts. The general syntax of the three SQL statements follows:

```
BEGIN TRAN[SACTION] [tran_name | @tran_name_variable]

COMMIT [TRAN[SACTION] [tran_name | @tran_name_variable]]

ROLLBACK [TRAN[SACTION] [tran_name | @tran_name_variable |
         savepoint_name | @savepoint_name_variable]]
```

- **Implicit mode**   Implicit transaction mode is toggled on or off with the command **SET IMPLICIT_TRANSACTIONS {ON | OFF}**. When implicit mode is on, a new transaction is started whenever any of a list of specific SQL statements is executed, including DELETE, INSERT, and UPDATE, among others. Once a transaction is implicitly started, it continues until the transaction is either committed or rolled back. If the database user disconnects before submitting a transaction-ending statement, the transaction is automatically rolled back.

Microsoft SQL Server records all transactions and the modifications made by them in the *transaction log*. The before and after image of each database modification made by a transaction is recorded in the transaction log. This facilitates any necessary rollback, because the before images can be used to reverse the database changes made by the transaction. A transaction commit is not complete until the commit record has been written to the transaction log. Because database changes are not always written to disk immediately, the transaction log is sometimes the only means of recovery when there is a system failure.

Transaction Support in Oracle

Oracle supports only two transaction modes: autocommit and implicit. As with Microsoft SQL Server, support varies when ODBC and JDBC drivers are used, so the driver vendor's documentation should be consulted in those cases. Here are descriptions of these two modes in Oracle:

● **Autocommit mode**   As with Microsoft SQL Server, each SQL statement is automatically committed as it completes. Autocommit mode is toggled on and off using the **SET AUTOCOMMIT** command, as shown here, and is off by default:

```
SET AUTOCOMMIT ON
SET AUTOCOMMIT OFF
```

● **Implicit mode**   A transaction is implicitly started when the database user connects to the database (that is, when a new database session begins). This is the default transaction mode in Oracle. When a transaction ends with a commit or rollback, a new transaction is automatically started. Unlike Microsoft SQL Server, nested transactions (transactions within transactions) are not permitted. A transaction ends with a commit when any of the following occurs: the database user issues the SQL COMMIT statement, the database session ends normally (that is, the user issues an **EXIT** or **DISCONNECT** command), or the database user issues an SQL Data Definition Language (DDL) statement (that is, a CREATE, DROP, or ALTER statement). A transaction ends with a rollback when either of the following occurs: the database user issues the SQL ROLLBACK statement, or the database session ends abnormally (that is, the client connection is canceled or the database crashes or is shut down using one of the shutdown options that aborts client connections instead of waiting for them to complete).

Try This 11-1   SQL Transaction Support

In this Try This exercise, you will explore transaction support statements in your RDBMS.

Step by Step

1. Use the same Department table that was used in Try This 10-1. If you have already created one, drop it and re-create it so your query results in this exercise will be predictable. Run the following statements (the DROP statement is unnecessary if the table does not exist):

```
DROP TABLE DEPARTMENT;

CREATE TABLE DEPARTMENT
   (DEPARTMENT_CODE    CHAR(3),
    DEPARTMENT_NAME    VARCHAR(50));
```

(continued)

2. Set the database in implicit transaction mode. For Oracle, this is the default, provided you have not set autocommit mode on. Consult your RDBMS documentation for how this is done. If you are using SQL Server, use the following statement:

```
SET IMPLICIT_TRANSACTIONS ON
```

3. Insert one row into the table using the following statement, but do not commit the change:

```
INSERT INTO DEPARTMENT
VALUES ('001','Executive');
```

4. Run a SELECT statement to confirm that the row exists:

```
SELECT * FROM DEPARTMENT;
```

5. If you know how to connect to the database a second time in a different client session, do so and run the select query from Step 4 in it. You should not be able to find the row because it is uncommitted data, and it is therefore available only in the session that created it. Depending on how your DBMS handles locking, it may appear as if this query is stalled while the SQL client waits for the DBMS to return the row (particularly in SQL Server). Locking is covered in the next section of this chapter.

6. Run a ROLLBACK statement as follows:

```
ROLLBACK;
```

7. Run the SELECT from Step 4 again. Notice that the row is now gone.

8. Run the INSERT from Step 3 again, followed by a commit:

```
INSERT INTO DEPARTMENT
VALUES ('001','Executive');

COMMIT;
```

9. Run the SELECT from Step 4 again to confirm that the row is there.

10. Run a ROLLBACK as you did in Step 6. In SQL Server, you may get an error that tells you that no transaction is in progress (the previous commit ended your implicit transaction).

```
ROLLBACK;
```

11. Try the SELECT one more time. Notice that the row is still there. A ROLLBACK has no effect on data that has already been committed to the database.

12. Drop the Department table to return your database (schema in Oracle) to where you started. In Oracle, DDL statements are never part of transactions, but they are in SQL Server, so you will need to run a COMMIT after the DROP statement in SQL Server:

```
DROP TABLE DEPARTMENT;
COMMIT;
```

Try This Summary

In this Try This exercise, you used the implicit transaction mode along with INSERT, SELECT, COMMIT, and ROLLBACK statements to demonstrate transaction support in SQL.

Locking and Transaction Deadlock

Although the simultaneous sharing of data among many database users has significant benefits, a serious drawback can cause updates to be lost. Fortunately, database vendors have worked out solutions to the problem. This section presents the concurrent update problem and various solutions.

The Concurrent Update Problem

Figure 11-1 illustrates the concurrent update problem that occurs when multiple database sessions are allowed to concurrently update the same data. Recall that a session is created every time a database user connects to the database, which includes the same user connecting to the database multiple times. The concurrent update problem happens most often between two different database users who are unaware that they are making conflicting updates to the same data. However, database users with multiple connections can trip themselves up if they apply updates using more than one of their database sessions.

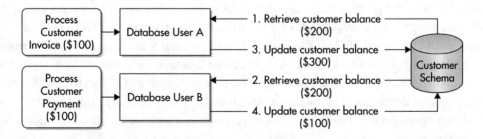

Figure 11-1 The concurrent update problem

The scenario presented features a fictitious company that sells products and creates an invoice for each order shipped, similar to Acme Industries in the normalization examples from earlier chapters. Figure 11-1 illustrates user A, a clerk in the shipping department who is preparing an invoice for a customer, which requires updating the customer's data by adding to the customer's balance due. At the same time, user B, a clerk in the accounts receivable department, is processing a payment from the very same customer, which requires updating the customer's balance due by subtracting the amount the customer paid. Here is the exact sequence of events, as illustrated in Figure 11-1:

1. User A queries the database and retrieves the customer's balance due, which is $200.

2. A few seconds later, user B queries the database and retrieves the same customer's balance, which is still $200.

3. In a few more seconds, user A applies her update, adding the $100 invoice to the balance due, which makes the new balance $300 in the database.

4. Finally, user B applies his update, subtracting the $100 payment from the balance due he retrieved from the database ($200), resulting in a new balance due of $100. He is unaware of the update made by user A and thus sets the balance due (incorrectly) to $100.

The balance due for this customer should be $200, but the update made by user A has been overwritten by the update made by user B. The company is out $100 that either will be lost revenue or will take significant staff time to uncover and correct. As you can see, allowing concurrent updates to the database without some sort of control can cause updates to be lost. Most database vendors implement a locking strategy to prevent concurrent updates to the exact same data.

Locking Mechanisms

A *lock* is a control placed in the database to reserve data so that only one database session may update it at any one time. When data is locked, no other database session can update the data until the lock is released, which is usually done with a COMMIT or ROLLBACK SQL statement. Some DBMSs also block attempts to read locked data. Any other session that attempts to update locked data will be placed in a *lock wait* state, and the session will stall until the lock is released. Some database products, such as IBM's DB2, will time out a session that waits too long and return an error instead of completing the requested update. Others, such as Oracle, will leave a session in a lock wait state for an indefinite period of time.

By now it should be no surprise that there is significant variation in how locks are handled by different vendors' database products. A general overview is presented here with the recommendation that you consult your database vendor's documentation for details on how locks are supported. Locks may be placed at various levels (often called *lock granularity*), and some database products, including Sybase ASE, Microsoft SQL Server, and IBM's DB2, support multiple levels with automatic *lock escalation,* which raises locks to higher levels as a database session places more and more locks on the same database objects. Locking and unlocking small amounts of data requires significant overhead, so escalating locks to higher levels can substantially improve performance. Typical lock levels are as follows:

- **Database**   The entire database is locked so that only one database session may apply updates. This is obviously an extreme situation that should not occur very often, but it can be useful when significant maintenance is being performed, such as upgrading to a new version of the database software. Oracle supports this level indirectly when the database is opened in exclusive mode, which restricts the database to one user session only.

- **File**   An entire database file is locked. Recall that a file can contain part of a table, an entire table, or parts of many tables. This level is less favored in modern databases because the data locked can be so diverse.

- **Table**   An entire table is locked. This level is useful when you're performing a table-wide change, such as reloading all the data in the table, updating every row, or altering the table to add or remove columns. Oracle calls this level a *DDL lock,* and it is used when DDL statements (CREATE, DROP, and ALTER) are submitted against a table or other database object.

- **Block or page**   A block or page within a database file is locked. A *block* is the smallest unit of data that the operating system can read from or write to a file. On most personal computers, the block size is called the *sector size*. Some operating systems use pages instead of blocks. A *page* is a virtual block of fixed size, typically 2K or 4K, which is used to simplify processing when multiple storage devices support different block sizes. The operating system can read and write pages and let hardware drivers translate the pages to appropriate blocks. As with file locking, block (page) locking is less favored in modern database systems because of the diversity of the data that may happen to be written to the same block in the file.

- **Row**   A row in a table is locked. This is the most common locking level, with virtually all modern database systems supporting it.

- **Column**   One or more columns within a row in the table are locked. This method sounds terrific in theory, but it's not very practical because of the resources required to place and release locks at this level of granularity. Very sparse support for it exists in modern commercial database systems.

Locks are always placed when data is updated or deleted. Most RDBMSs also support the use of a FOR UPDATE OF clause on a SELECT statement to allow locks to be placed when the database user declares an *intent* to update something. Some locks may be considered *read-exclusive,* which prevents other sessions from even reading the locked data. Many RDBMSs have session parameters that can be set to help control locking behavior. One of the locking behaviors to consider is whether all rows fetched using a cursor are locked until the next COMMIT or ROLLBACK, or whether previously read rows are released when the next row is fetched. Consult your database vendor's documentation for more details.

The main problem with locking mechanisms is that locks cause *contention,* meaning that the placement of locks to prevent loss of data from concurrent updates has the side effect of causing concurrent sessions to compete for the right to apply updates. At the least, lock contention slows user processes as sessions wait for locks. At the worst, competing lock requests can stall sessions indefinitely, as you will see in the next section.

Deadlocks

A *deadlock* is a situation in which two or more database sessions have locked some data and then each has requested a lock on data that another session has locked. Figure 11-2 illustrates this situation.

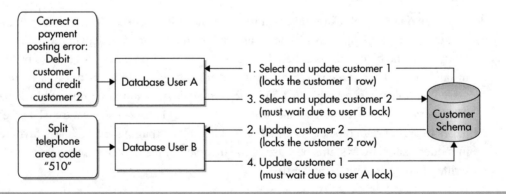

Figure 11-2   The deadlock

This example again uses two users from our fictitious company, cleverly named A and B. User A is a representative in the customer service department and is attempting to correct a payment that was credited to the wrong customer account. He needs to subtract (debit) the payment from Customer 1 and add (credit) it to Customer 2. User B is a database specialist in the IT department, and she has written an SQL statement to update some of the customer phone numbers with one area code to a new area code in response to a recent area code split by the phone company. The statement has a WHERE clause that limits the update to those customers having a phone number with certain prefixes in area code 510 and updates those phone numbers to the new area code. User B submits her SQL UPDATE statement while user A is working on his payment credit problem. Customers 1 and 2 both have phone numbers that need to be updated. The sequence of events (all happening within seconds of each other), as illustrated in Figure 11-2, takes place as follows:

1. User A selects the data from Customer 1 and applies an update to debit the balance due. No commit is issued yet because this is only part of the transaction that must take place. The row for Customer 1 now has a lock on it due to the update.

2. The statement submitted by user B updates the phone number for Customer 2. The entire SQL statement must run as a single transaction, so there is no commit at this point, and thus user B holds a lock on the row for Customer 2.

3. User A selects the balance for Customer 2 and then submits an update to credit the balance due (same amount as debited from Customer 1). The request must wait because user B holds a lock on the row to be updated.

4. The statement submitted by user B now attempts to update the phone number for Customer 1. The update must wait because user A holds a lock on the row to be updated.

These two database sessions are now in deadlock. User A cannot continue due to a lock held by user B, and vice versa. In theory, these two database sessions will be stalled forever. Fortunately, modern DBMSs contain provisions to handle this situation. One method prevents deadlocks. Few DBMSs have this capability due to the considerable overhead this approach requires and the virtual impossibility of predicting what an interactive database user will do next. However, the theory is to inspect each lock request for the potential to cause contention and not permit the lock to take place if a deadlock is possible. The more common approach is deadlock detection, which aborts one of the requests that caused the deadlock. This can be done either by timing lock waits and giving up after a preset time interval or by periodically inspecting all locks to find two sessions that have each other locked out. In either case, one of the requests must be terminated and the transaction's changes rolled back to allow the other request to proceed.

Performance Tuning

Any seasoned DBA will tell you that database performance tuning is a never-ending task. Something always needs to be tweaked to make the database run more quickly and/or efficiently. The key to success is managing your time and the expectations of the database users, and setting the performance requirements for an application before it is even written. Simple statements such as "every database update must complete within 4 seconds" are usually the best. With that done, performance tuning becomes a simple matter of looking for things that do not conform to the performance requirement and tuning them until they do. The law of diminishing returns applies to database tuning, and you can put lots of effort into tuning a database process for little or no gain. The beauty of having a standard performance requirement is that you can stop when the process meets the requirement and then move on to the next problem.

Although components other than SQL statements can be tuned, these components are so specific to a particular DBMS that it is best not to attempt to cover them here. Suffice it to say that memory usage, CPU utilization, and file system I/O all must be tuned along with the SQL statements that access the database. The tuning of SQL statements is addressed in the sections that follow.

Tuning Database Queries

About 80 percent of database query performance problems can be solved by adjusting the SQL statement. However, you must understand how the particular DBMS being used processes SQL statements before you can know what to tweak. For example, placing SQL statements inside stored procedures can yield remarkable performance improvements in Microsoft SQL Server and Sybase ASE, but the same is usually not true in Oracle.

A query *execution plan* is a description of how a DBMS will process a particular query, including index usage, join logic, and estimated resource cost. It is important to learn how to use the "explain plan" utility in your DBMS, if one is available, because it will show you exactly how the DBMS will process the SQL statement you are attempting to tune. In Oracle, the SQL EXPLAIN PLAN statement analyzes an SQL statement and posts analysis results to a special plan table. The plan table must be created exactly as specified by Oracle, so it is best to use the script Oracle provides for this purpose. After running the EXPLAIN PLAN statement, you must retrieve the results from the plan table using a SELECT statement. Fortunately, Oracle tools such as SQL Developer have a GUI version available that makes query tuning a lot easier. The Query tool contained in Microsoft SQL Server Management Studio (SQL Server 2005 and 2008) has buttons labeled Display Estimated Execution Plan and Include Actual Execution Plan that graphically display how the SQL statement will be executed. These options are also accessible from the Query menu. In older versions of Microsoft SQL Server, these options (with different names) can be found in the Query Analyzer tool.

Following are some general tuning tips for SQL that apply to most implementations. You should consult a tuning guide for the particular DBMS you are using, because techniques, tips, and other considerations vary by DBMS product.

Avoid table scans of large tables. For tables larger than 1000 rows or so, scanning all the rows in the table instead of using an index can be expensive in terms of resources required. And, of course, the larger the table, the more expensive table scans become. Full table scans occur in the following situations:

- The query does not contain a WHERE clause to limit rows.

- None of the columns referenced in the WHERE clause match the leading column of an index on the table.

- Index and table statistics have not been updated. Most RDBMS query optimizers use statistics to evaluate available indexes, and without statistics, a table scan may be seen as more efficient than using an index.

- At least one column in the WHERE clause does match the first column of an available index, but the comparison used obviates the use of an index. These cases include the following:

  - Use of the NOT operator (for example, **WHERE NOT CITY = 'New York'**). In general, indexes can be used to find what *is* in a table, but they cannot be used to find what is *not* in a table.

  - Use of the NOT EQUAL operator (for example, **WHERE CITY <> 'New York'**).

  - Use of a wildcard in the first position of a comparison string (for example, **WHERE CITY LIKE '%York%'**).

  - Use of an SQL function in the comparison (for example, **WHERE UPPER(CITY) = 'NEW YORK'**).

Create indexes that are selective. Index selectivity is a ratio of the number of distinct values a column has, divided by the number of rows in a table. For example, if a table has 1000 rows and a column has 800 distinct values, the selectivity of the index is 0.8, which is considered good. However, a column such as gender that has only two distinct values (M and F) has very poor selectivity (.002 in this case). Unique indexes always have a selectivity of 1.0, which is the best possible. With some RDBMSs such as DB2, unique indexes are so superior that DBAs often add otherwise unnecessary columns to an index just to make the index unique. However, always keep in mind that indexes take storage space and must be maintained, so they are never a "free lunch."

Evaluate join techniques carefully. Most RDBMSs offer multiple methods for joining tables, with the query optimizer in the RDBMS selecting the one that appears best based on table statistics. In general, creating indexes on foreign key columns gives the optimizer more options from which to choose, which is always a good thing. Run an explain plan and consult your RDBMS documentation when tuning joins.

Pay attention to views. Because views are stored SQL queries, they can present performance problems just like any other query.

Tune subqueries in accordance with your RDBMS vendor's recommendations.

Limit use of remote tables. Tables connected to remotely via database links never perform as well as local tables.

Very large tables require special attention. When tables grow to millions of rows in size, any query can be a performance nightmare. Evaluate every query carefully, and consider partitioning the table to improve query performance. Table partitioning is addressed in Chapter 8. Your RDBMS may offer other special features for very large tables that will improve query performance.

Ask the Expert

Q: I often don't know what case was used in the database for proper names such as city names. You mentioned that using a function such as UPPER in the predicate (for example, WHERE UPPER(CITY) = 'NEW YORK') obviates the use of an index on that column. Are there any workarounds for this?

A: I can think of several. First, if you use a DBMS that supports case-insensitive comparisons, such as SQL Server, Sybase ASE, or Microsoft Access, the function isn't needed because it doesn't matter what case you use in the **WHERE** predicate. Second, if the DBMS supports what is known as a *function-based index*, you can create an index on an expression such as **UPPER(CITY)** and then predicates that use the same function on the same column can use the index. Oracle supports this feature. Third, you can store the data in two columns: one as entered by the user, and the other folded either to uppercase or lowercase for searching. While this is not a great idea in a transaction-processing database, it is a common technique in data warehouses and data marts, where the redundant data typically doesn't lead to any data consistency issues. (These types of databases are discussed in detail in Chapter 12).

Tuning DML Statements

Data Manipulation Language (DML) statements generally produce fewer performance problems than query statements. However, there can be issues.

INSERT statements have two main considerations:

- **Ensuring adequate free space in the tablespaces to hold new rows**   Tablespaces that are short on space present problems as the DBMS searches for free space to hold rows being inserted. Moreover, inserts do not usually put rows into the table in primary key sequence because free space isn't usually available in exactly the right places. Therefore, reorganizing the table, which is essentially a process of unloading the rows to a flat file, re-creating the table, and then reloading the table, can improve both insert and query performance.

- **Index maintenance**   Every time a row is inserted into a table, a corresponding entry must be inserted into every index built on the table (null values are never indexed, however). The more indexes, the more overhead every insert will require. Index free space can usually be tuned just as table free space can.

UPDATE statements have the following considerations:

- **Index maintenance**   If columns that are indexed are updated, the corresponding index entries must also be updated. In general, updating primary key values has particularly bad performance implications, so much so that some RDBMSs prohibit it.

- **Row expansion**   When columns are updated in such a way that the row grows significantly in size, the row may no longer fit in its original location, and sufficient free space around the row may not be available for it to expand in place (other rows might be right up against the one just updated). When this occurs, the row must either be moved to another location in the data file where it will fit or be split with the expanded part of the row placed in a new location, connected to the original location by a pointer. Both of these situations are not only expensive when they occur but are also detrimental to the performance of subsequent queries that touch those rows. Table reorganizations can resolve the issue, but it is better to prevent the problem by designing the application so that rows tend not to grow in size after they are inserted.

DELETE statements are the least likely to present performance issues. However, a table that participates as a parent in a relationship that is defined with the ON DELETE CASCADE option can perform poorly if there are many child rows to delete.

Change Control

Change control (also known as *change management*) is the process used to manage the changes that occur after a system is implemented. A change control process has the following benefits:

- It helps you understand when it is acceptable to make changes and when it is not.

- It provides a log of all changes that have been made to assist with troubleshooting when problems occur.

- It can manage versions of software components so that a defective version can be smoothly backed out.

Change is inevitable. Not only do business requirements change, but new versions of database and operating system software and new hardware devices eventually must be incorporated. Technologists should devise a change control method suitable to the organization, and management should approve it as a standard. Anything less leads to chaos when changes are made without the proper coordination and communication. Although terminology varies among standard methods, they all have common features:

- **Version numbering**   Components of an application system are assigned version numbers, usually starting with 1 and advancing sequentially every time the component is changed. Usually a revision date and the identifier of the person making the change are carried with the version number.

- **Release (build) numbering**   A *release* is a point in time at which all components of an application system (including database components) are promoted to the next environment (for example, from development to system test) as a bundle that can be tested and deployed together. Some organizations use the term *build* instead. Database environments are discussed in Chapter 5. As releases are formed, it is important to label each component included with the release (or build) number. This allows you to tell which version of each component was included in a particular release.

- **Prioritization**   Changes may be assigned priorities to allow them to be scheduled accordingly.

- **Change request tracking**   Change requests can be placed into the change control system, routed through channels for approval, and marked with the applicable release number when the change is completed.

● **Check-out and check-in**   When a developer or DBA is ready to apply changes to a component, he should be able to check it out (reserve it), which prevents others from making potentially conflicting changes to the same component at the same time. When work is complete, the developer or DBA checks the component back in, which essentially releases the reservation.

A number of commercial and freeware software products can be deployed to assist with change control. However, it is important that you establish the process *before* choosing tools. In this way, the organization can establish the best process for their needs and find the tool that best fits that process rather than trying to retrofit a tool to the process.

From the database perspective, the DBA should develop DDL statements to implement all the database components of an application system and a script that can be used to invoke all the changes, including any required conversions. This deployment script and all the DDL should be checked into the change control system and managed just like all the other software components of the system.

Chapter 11 Self Test

Choose the correct responses to each of the multiple-choice and fill-in-the-blank questions. Note that there may be more than one correct response to each question.

1. A cursor is _____.

2. A result set is _____.

3. The *I* in the ACID acronym stands for _____.

4. Before rows may be fetched from a cursor, the cursor must first be

   A Declared

   B Committed

   C Opened

   D Closed

   E Purged

5. A transaction

   A May be partially processed and committed

   B May not be partially processed and committed

   C Changes the database from one consistent state to another

   D Is sometimes called a *unit of work*

   E Has properties described by the ACID acronym

6. Microsoft SQL Server supports the following transaction modes:

   A Autocommit

   B Automatic

   C Durable

   D Explicit

   E Implicit

7. Oracle supports the following transaction modes:

   A Autocommit

   B Automatic

   C Durable

   D Explicit

   E Implicit

8. The SQL statements (commands) that end a transaction are

   A **SET AUTOCOMMIT**

   B **BEGIN TRANSACTION** (in SQL Server)

   C **COMMIT**

   D **ROLLBACK**

   E **SAVEPOINT**

9. The concurrent update problem

   A Is a consequence of simultaneous data sharing

   B Cannot occur when **AUTOCOMMIT** is set to **ON**

   C Is the reason that transaction locking must be supported

   D Occurs when two database users submit conflicting SELECT statements

   E Occurs when two database users make conflicting updates to the same data

10. A lock

   A Is a control placed on data to reserve it so that the user may update it

   B Is usually released when a COMMIT or ROLLBACK takes place

   C Has a timeout set in DB2 and some other RDBMS products

   D May cause contention when other users attempt to update locked data

   E May have levels and an escalation protocol in some RDBMS products

11. A deadlock

   A Is a lock that has timed out and is therefore no longer needed

   B Occurs when two database users each request a lock on data that is locked by the other

   C Can theoretically put two or more users in an endless lock wait state

   D May be resolved by deadlock detection on some RDBMSs

   E May be resolved by lock timeouts on some RDBMSs

12. Performance tuning

   A Is a never-ending process

   B Should be used on each query until no more improvement can be realized

   C Should be used only on queries that fail to conform to performance requirements

   D Involves not only SQL tuning but also CPU, file system I/O, and memory usage tuning

   E Should be requirements based

13. SQL query tuning

   A Can be done in the same way for all relational database systems

   B Usually involves using an explain plan facility

   C Always involves placing SQL statements in a stored procedure

   D Applies only to SQL SELECT statements

   E Requires detailed knowledge of the RDBMS on which the query is to be run

14. General SQL tuning tips include which of the following?

   A Avoid table scans on large tables.

   B Use an index whenever possible.

   C Use an ORDER BY clause whenever possible.

   D Use a WHERE clause to filter rows whenever possible.

   E Use views whenever possible.

15. SQL practices that obviate the use of an index are

   A Use of a WHERE clause

   B Use of a NOT operator

   C Use of table joins

   D Use of the NOT EQUAL operator

   E Use of wildcards in the first column of LIKE comparison strings

16. Indexes work well at filtering rows when

   A They are very selective.

   B The selectivity ratio is very high.

   C The selectivity ratio is very low.

   D They are unique.

   E They are not unique.

17. The main performance considerations for INSERT statements are

   A Row expansion

   B Index maintenance

   C Free space usage

   D Subquery tuning

   E Any very large tables that are involved

18. The main performance considerations for UPDATE statements are

A Row expansion

B Index maintenance

C Free space usage

D Subquery tuning

E Any very large tables that are involved

19. A change control process

A Can prevent programming errors from being placed into production

B May also be called *change management*

C Helps with understanding when changes may be installed

D Provides a log of all changes made

E Can allow defective software versions to be backed out

20. Common features of change control processes include which of the following?

A Transaction support

B Version numbering

C Deadlock prevention

D Release numbering

E Prioritization

Chapter 12

Databases for Online Analytical Processing

Key Skills & Concepts

- Data Warehouses
- Data Marts
- Data Mining

Starting in the 1980s, businesses recognized the need for keeping historical data and using it for analysis to assist in decision making. It was soon apparent that data organized for use by day-to-day business transactions was not as useful for analysis. In fact, storing significant amounts of history in an *operational* database (a database designed to support the day-to-day transactions of an organization) could have serious detrimental effects on performance. William H. (Bill) Inmon pioneered work in a concept known as *data warehousing,* in which historical data is periodically trimmed from the operational database and moved to a database specifically designed for analysis. It was Inmon's dedicated promotion of the concept that earned him the title "father of data warehousing."

The popularity of the data warehouse approach grew with each success story. In addition to Inmon, others made significant contributions, notably Ralph Kimball, who developed specialized database architectures for data warehouses (covered in the "Data Warehouse Architecture" section, later in this chapter). E.F. (Ted) Codd added his endorsement to the data warehouse approach and coined two important terms in 1993:

- **Online transaction processing (OLTP)**   Systems designed to handle high volumes of transactions that carry out the day-to-day activities of an organization
- **Online analytical processing (OLAP)**   Analysis of data (often historical) to identify trends that assist in making strategic decisions regarding the business

Up to this point, the chapters of this book have dealt almost exclusively with OLTP databases. This chapter, on the other hand, is devoted exclusively to OLAP database concepts.

Data Warehouses

Using Inmon's definition, a *data warehouse* is a subject-oriented, integrated, time-variant, and nonvolatile collection of data intended to support management decision making. Here are some important properties of data warehouses:

- They are organized around major subject areas of an organization, such as sales, customers, suppliers, and products. OLTP systems, on the other hand, are typically organized around major processes, such as payroll, order entry, billing, and so forth.
- They are integrated from multiple operational (OLTP) data sources.
- They are not updated in real time, but periodically, based on an established schedule. Data is pulled from operational sources as often as needed, such as daily, weekly, monthly, and quarterly.

The potential benefits of a well-constructed data warehouse are significant, including the following:

- Competitive advantage
- Increased productivity of corporate decision makers
- Potential high return on investment as the organization finds the best ways to improve efficiency and/or profitability

However, there are significant challenges to creating an enterprise-wide data warehouse, including the following:

- Underestimation of the resources required to load the data
- Hidden data integrity problems in the source data
- Omitting data, only to find out later that it is required
- Ever-increasing end user demands (each new feature spawning ideas for even more features)
- Consolidating data from disparate data sources
- High resource demands (huge amounts of storage; queries that process millions of rows)
- Ownership of the data
- Difficulty in determining what the business really wants or needs to analyze
- "Big bang" projects that seem never-ending

OLTP Systems Compared with Data Warehouse Systems

Data warehouse systems and OLTP systems are fundamentally different. Here is a comparison:

OLTP Systems	Data Warehouse Systems
Hold current data	Hold historic data
Store current data	Store detailed data along with lightly and highly summarized data
Data is dynamic	Data is static, except for periodic additions
Database queries are short-running and access relatively few rows of data	Database queries are long-running and access many rows of data
High transaction volume	Medium to low transaction volume
Repetitive processing; predictable usage pattern	Ad hoc and unstructured processing; unpredictable usage pattern
Transaction driven; support day-to-day operations	Analysis driven; support strategic decision making
Process oriented	Subject oriented
Serve a large number of concurrent users	Serve a relatively low number of managerial users (decision makers)

Data Warehouse Architecture

Two schools of thought reign as to the best way to organize OLTP data into a data warehouse: the *summary table approach* and the *star schema approach*. The following subsections take a look at each approach, along with the benefits and drawbacks of each.

Summary Table Architecture

Inmon originally developed the summary table data warehouse architecture. This data warehouse approach involves storing data not only in detail form, but also in summary tables so that analysis processes do not have to summarize the same data continually. This is an obvious violation of the principles of normalization, but because the data is historical—and therefore is not expected to change after it is stored—the data anomalies (insert, update, and delete) that drive the need for normalization simply don't exist. Figure 12-1 shows the summary table data warehouse architecture.

Data from one or more operational data sources (databases or flat file systems) is periodically moved into the data warehouse database. A major key to success is determining the appropriate level of detail that must be carried in the database and anticipating the necessary levels of summarization. Using Acme Industries as an example,

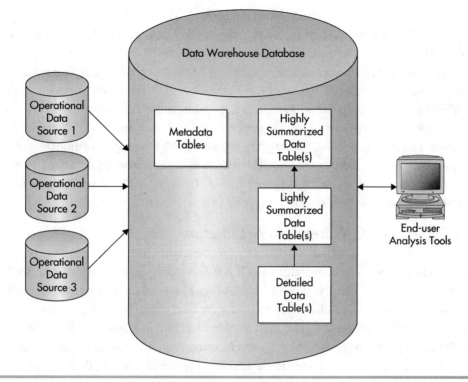

Figure 12-1   Summary table data warehouse architecture

if the subject of the data warehouse is sales, it may be necessary to keep every single invoice, or it may be necessary to keep only those invoices that exceed a certain amount—or perhaps only those that contain certain products. If requirements are not understood, it is unlikely that the data warehouse project will be successful. Failure rates of data warehouse projects are higher than most other types of IT projects, and the most common cause of failure is poorly defined requirements.

In terms of summarization, we might summarize the transactions by month in one summary table and by product in another. At the next level of summarization, we might summarize the months by quarter in one table and the products by department in another. An *end user* (the person using the analysis tools to obtain results from the OLAP database) might look at sales by quarter and notice that one particular quarter doesn't look quite right. The user can expand the quarter of concern and examine the data for months within it. This process is known as "drilling down" to more detailed levels. The user may then choose a particular month of interest and drill down to the detailed transactions for that month.

The metadata (data about data) shown in Figure 12-1 is very important and, unfortunately, often a missing link. Ideally, the metadata defines every data item in the data warehouse, along with sufficient information so its source can be tracked all the way back to the original source data in the operational database. The biggest challenge with metadata is that, lacking standards, each vendor of data warehouse tools has stored metadata in its own way. When multiple analysis tools are in use, metadata must usually be loaded into each one of them using proprietary formats. For end-user analysis tools (also called OLAP tools or business intelligence tools), not only are tools embedded in major relational database products such as SQL Server and Oracle, but literally dozens of specialized commercial products are available, including Business Objects (now owned by SAP), Cognos (an IBM company), Actuate, Hyperion (now owned by Oracle), and many more.

Star Schema Data Warehouse Architecture

Kimball developed a specialized database structure known as the *star schema* for storing data warehouse data. His contribution to OLAP data storage is significant. Red Brick, the first DBMS devoted exclusively to OLAP data storage, used the star schema. In addition, Red Brick offered SQL extensions specifically for data analysis, including moving averages, this year versus last year, market share, and ranking. Informix acquired Red Brick's technology, and later IBM acquired Informix, so IBM now markets the Red Brick technology as part of its data warehouse solution. Figure 12-2 shows the basic architecture of a data warehouse using the star schema.

The star schema uses a single detailed data table, called a *fact table*, surrounded by supporting reference data tables called *dimension tables*, forming a starlike pattern. Compared with the summary table data warehouse architecture, the fact table replaces the detailed data tables, and the dimension tables logically replace the summary tables. Aside from the primary key, each attribute in the fact table must be either a *fact* (a metric that can be summarized) or a foreign key to a dimension table. Keep in mind that facts must be additive, such as quantities, scores, time intervals, and currency amounts. A new star schema is constructed for each additional fact table. Dimension tables have a one-to-many relationship with the fact table, with the primary key of the dimension table appearing as a foreign key in the fact table. However, dimension tables are not necessarily normalized because they may have an entire hierarchy, such as layers of an organization or different subcomponents of time, compressed into a single table. The dimension tables may or may not contain summary information, such as totals, but they generally should not contain facts.

Using our prior Acme Industries sales example, the fact table would contain the invoices from the table, and typical dimension tables would be time (days, months,

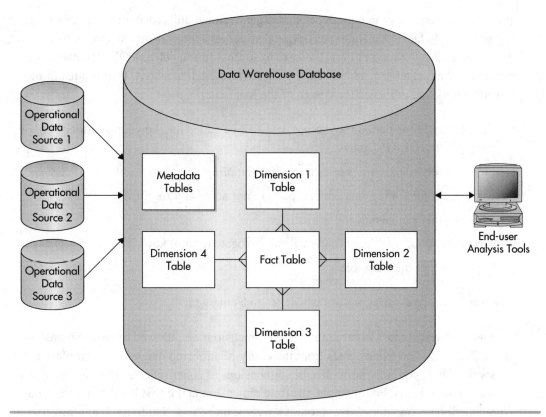

Figure 12-2   Star schema data warehouse architecture

Ask the Expert

Q: I've heard that star schemas can be very difficult to use when analysis requires combining data from multiple fact tables. Is there a way around these issues?

A: Yes, indeed, but the solution is to design the dimensions correctly rather than employing workarounds after the data warehouse is implemented. If, for example, the time dimension in one schema uses calendar months, and another uses fiscal months, it may be impossible to combine them unless individual days are somehow available. The trick is to use what Kimball calls *conformed dimensions*, which are dimensions that have identical structure, attributes, domain values, definitions, and concepts. Following that tenet, every time dimension in the database would be identically defined, perhaps by calendar day, which can easily be rolled up to calendar or fiscal weeks, months, and quarters.

quarters, and perhaps years), products, and organizational units (departments, divisions, and so forth). In fact, time and organizational structure appear as dimensions in most star schemas. As you might guess, the keys to success in star schema OLAP databases are getting the fact table right and using only conformed dimensions. Here's a list of the considerations that influence the design of the fact table:

- The required time period (how often data will be added and how long history must remain in the OLAP database)
- Storing every transaction versus statistical sampling
- Columns in the source data table(s) that are not necessary for OLAP
- Columns that can be reduced in size
- The best uses of intelligent (natural) and surrogate (dumb) keys
- Partitioning of the fact table

Over time, some variations of the star schema emerged:

- **Snowflake schema**   A variant in which dimensions are allowed to have dimensions of their own. The name comes from the entity-relationship diagram's resemblance to a snowflake. If you fully normalize the dimensions of a star schema, you end up with a snowflake schema. For example, the time dimension at the first level could track days, with a dimension table above it to track weeks, one above that to track months, one above that one to track quarters, and so forth. Similar arrangements could be used to track the hierarchy of an organization (departments, divisions, and so on).
- **Starflake schema**   A hybrid arrangement containing a mixture of (denormalized) star and (normalized) snowflake dimensions.

Multidimensional Databases

Multidimensional databases evolved from star schemas. They are sometimes called multidimensional OLAP (MOLAP) databases. A number of specialized multidimensional database systems are on the market, including Oracle Express, Microsoft SQL Server Analysis Services, and Oracle Essbase. MOLAP databases are best visualized as cubes, where each dimension forms a side of the cube. To accommodate additional dimensions, the cube (or set of cubes) is simply repeated for each.

Figure 12-3 shows a four-column fact table for Acme Industries. Product Line, Sales Department, and Quarter are dimensions, and they would be foreign keys to a dimension

Product Line	Sales Department	Quarter	Quantity
Helmets	Corporate Sales	1	2250
Helmets	Corporate Sales	2	2107
Helmets	Corporate Sales	3	5203
Helmets	Corporate Sales	4	5806
Helmets	Internet Sales	1	1607
Helmets	Internet Sales	2	1812
Helmets	Internet Sales	3	4834
Helmets	Internet Sales	4	5150
Springs	Corporate Sales	1	16283
Springs	Corporate Sales	2	17422
Springs	Corporate Sales	3	21288
Springs	Corporate Sales	4	32768
Springs	Internet Sales	1	12
Springs	Internet Sales	2	24
Springs	Internet Sales	3	48
Springs	Internet Sales	4	48
Rockets	Corporate Sales	1	65
Rockets	Corporate Sales	2	38
Rockets	Corporate Sales	3	47
Rockets	Corporate Sales	4	52
Rockets	Internet Sales	1	2
Rockets	Internet Sales	2	1
Rockets	Internet Sales	3	6
Rockets	Internet Sales	4	9

Figure 12-3   Four-column fact table for Acme Industries

table in a star schema. Quantity contains the number of units sold for each combination of Product Line, Sales Department, and Quarter.

Figure 12-4 shows the multidimensional equivalent of the table shown in Figure 12-3. Note that Sales Department, Product Line, and Quarter all become edges of the cube, with the single fact Quantity stored in each grid square. The dimensions displayed may be changed by simply rotating the cube.

When the dimensions contain data that mutates over time, such as a product being moved from one product family to another, we call this a *slowly changing dimension*. These present

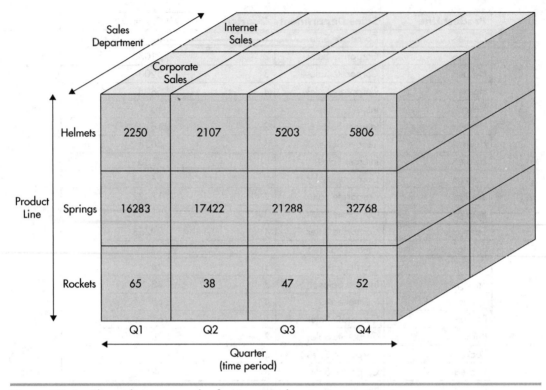

Figure 12-4 Three-dimension cube for Acme Industries

a special challenge when designing multidimensional schemas. Several solution methods, known as *types* of slowly changing dimensions, are listed in the following table:

Method Type	Description
1	Old data is overwritten with new data, so no tracking of history occurs.
2	A new row is created every time any data in the dimension changes, which provides unlimited history. A version number or effective dates are included in each row to record the sequence of the changes.
3	Multiple columns are provided for each attribute for which changes must be tracked, with each new value written into the next available column for the attribute. Naturally, the amount of history is limited to the number of columns provided.
4	Current data is kept in one table, and a history table is used to record some or all of the previous data values.

You can find more information on slowly changing dimensions in the many articles published on the Internet.

Data Marts

A *data mart* is a subset of a data warehouse that supports the requirements of a particular department or business function. In part, data marts evolved in response to some highly visible multimillion-dollar data warehouse project failures. When an organization has little experience building OLTP systems and databases, or when requirements are very sketchy, a scaled-down project such as a data mart is a far less risky approach. Here are a few characteristics of data marts:

- Focus on one department or business process
- Do not normally contain any operational data
- Contain much less information than a data warehouse

Here are some reasons for creating a data mart:

- Data may be tailored to a particular department or business function.
- Overall costs are lower than that of a full data warehouse.
- Project is lower risk than a full data warehouse project.
- A limited number of end-user analysis tools (usually just one) allow data to be tailored to the particular tool to be used.
- For departmental data marts, the database may be placed physically near the department, reducing network delays.

Three basic strategies can be used to build data marts:

- *Build the enterprise-wide data warehouse first, and use it to populate data marts.* The problem with this approach is that you will never get to build the data marts if the data warehouse project ends up being canceled or put on indefinite hold.
- *Build several data marts and build the data warehouse later, integrating the data marts into the enterprise-wide data warehouse at that time.* This is a lower risk strategy, at least in terms of delivery, because it does not depend on completion of a major data warehouse project. However, it may cost more because of the rework required to integrate the data marts after the fact. Moreover, if several data marts are built containing similar data without a common data warehouse to integrate all the data, the same query may yield different results depending on the data mart used. Imagine, for example, the finance department quoting one revenue number and the sales department another, only to find they are both correctly quoting their data sources.

Ask the Expert

Q: Are data marts built using summary tables or star schemas?

A: Data marts are built almost exclusively using star schemas. This is most likely because almost all the popular end-user analysis tools expect star schemas, including pivot tables supported by spreadsheet tools such as Microsoft Excel.

● *Build the data warehouse and data marts simultaneously.* This sounds great on paper, but when you consider that the already complex and large data warehouse project now has the data marts added to its scope, you begin to appreciate the enormity of the project. In fact, this strategy practically *guarantees* that the data warehouse project will be the never-ending project from hell.

Data Mining

Data mining is the process of extracting valid, previously unknown, comprehensible, and actionable information from large databases and using it to make crucial business decisions. The biggest benefit is that it can uncover correlations in the data that were never suspected. The caveat is that it normally requires very large data volumes in order to produce accurate results. Most commercial OLAP/business intelligence (BI) tools include some data-mining features.

One of the commonly cited stories of an early success with data mining involves an NCR Corporation employee who produced a study for American Stores' Osco Drugs in 1992. The study noted a correlation between beer sales and diaper sales between 5 P.M. and 7 P.M., meaning that the two items were found together in a single purchase more often than pure randomness would suggest. This correlation was subsequently mentioned in a speech, and the "beer and diapers" story quickly became a bit of an urban legend in data warehouse circles. Countless conference speakers have related the story of young fathers sent out for diapers who grab a six-pack at the same time, often embellished well beyond the facts. However, the story remains an excellent example of how unexpected the results of data mining can be.

Once you discover a correlation, the organization must decide the best action to take to capitalize on the new information. In the "beer and diapers" example, the company could either strategically place the diaper display near the beer chillers for that quick impulse sale or perhaps place coupon dispensers for beer near the diaper display, strategically locating the beer and diapers products at opposite corners of the store in hopes of more impulse buys as the shopper picks up one item and heads across the store for the other. For the newly found information to be of benefit, the organization must be agile enough to take some action, so data mining itself isn't a silver bullet by any measure.

Try This 12-1 Design Star Schema Fact and Dimension Tables

In this Try This exercise, you will design a star schema fact for the BOOK table for the Computer Books Company schema from Try This 6-2, along with its associated dimension tables. For easy reference, here are the normalized OLTP tables that need consideration:

```
BOOK: ISBN (PK), BOOK TITLE, SUBJECT CODE, PUBLISHER ID,
      EDITION CODE, EDITION COST, SELLING PRICE,
      QUANTITY ON HAND, QUANTITY ON ORDER,
      RECOMMENDED QUANTITY, PREVIOUS EDITION ISBN

SUBJECT: SUBJECT CODE (PK), DESCRIPTION

AUTHOR: AUTHOR ID (PK), AUTHOR NAME

BOOK-AUTHOR: AUTHOR ID (PK), ISBN (PK)

PUBLISHER: PUBLISHER ID (PK), PUBLISHER NAME, STREET ADDRESS,
      CITY, STATE, ZIP CODE, AMOUNT PAYABLE
```

Step by Step

1. Design the fact table:

    a. Identify the facts that will go in your fact table. For the BOOK table, the only attributes that can be facts are EDITION COST, SELLING PRICE, QUANTITY ON HAND, QUANTITY ON ORDER, and RECOMMENDED QUANTITY.

    b. Among the remaining attributes in the BOOK table, identify those that are foreign keys to dimension tables. These are SUBJECT CODE and PUBLISHER ID.

    c. The remaining attributes are BOOK TITLE and PREVIOUS EDITION ISBN. What can be done with these? One choice is simply to eliminate them for your star schema. But another is to make a dimension out of them, called something like BOOK TITLE. The fact table can then be joined with the dimension using ISBN when you want to include the title or previous edition ISBN in our query results.

    d. List the contents of the fact table.

(continued)

2. Design the dimension tables:

   a. From Step 1.c, design a dimension table to hold BOOK TITLE and PREVIOUS EDITION ISBN.

   b. SUBJECT becomes a dimension just as it is.

   c. AUTHOR and BOOK_AUTHOR pose a small challenge because they form a hierarchy. However, if you collapse them into a single table, they form a dimension that lists every author for every book. The dimension table will include a second normal form violation (AUTHOR NAME will depend only on the AUTHOR ID), but you need not be concerned about such things in star schemas. In fact, were it not for the possibility of two different authors having the same name, you could remove AUTHOR ID from the dimension altogether.

   d. PUBLISHER looks straightforward enough, but there is a minor issue with AMOUNT PAYABLE. It's a fact, and facts don't belong in dimension tables. So you should eliminate it from this star schema. It may be useful when the fact table is about publisher purchases or something like that, but it has no bearing on our book inventory.

   e. List the contents of each dimension table.

Try This Summary

In this Try This exercise, you designed a fact table and several dimension tables. My solution is in Appendix B.

✓ Chapter 12 Self Test

Choose the correct responses to each of the multiple-choice and fill-in-the-blank questions. Note that there may be more than one correct response to each question.

1. OLTP databases are designed to handle _____ transaction volumes.

2. OLAP queries typically access _____ amounts of data.

3. Compared with OLTP systems, data warehouse systems tend to have _____ running queries.

4. Data warehousing was pioneered by _____.

5. The process of moving from more summarized data to more detailed data is known as
_____.

6. The snowflake schema allows dimensions to have _____.

7. The starflake schema is a hybrid containing both _____ and _____
dimensions.

8. A data warehouse is

   A Subject oriented

   B Integrated from multiple data sources

   C Time variant

   D Updated in real time

   E Organized around one department or business function

9. Challenges with the data warehouse approach include

   A Updating operational data from the data warehouse

   B Underestimation of required resources

   C Diminishing user demands

   D Large, complex projects

   E High resource demands

10. The summary table architecture

   A Was originally developed by Bill Inmon

   B Includes a fact table

   C Includes dimension tables

   D Includes lightly and highly summarized tables

   E Should include metadata

11. The star schema

   A Was developed by Ralph Kimball

   B Includes a dimension table and one or more fact tables

C Always has fully normalized dimension tables

D Was a key feature of the Red Brick DBMS

E Involves multiple levels of dimension tables

12. Factors to consider in designing the fact table include

A Adding columns to the fact table

B Reducing column sizes between the source and fact tables

C Partitioning the fact table

D How often it must be updated

E How long history must remain in it

13. Multidimensional databases

A Use a fully normalized fact table

B Are best visualized as cubes

C Have fully normalized dimension tables

D Are sometimes called MOLAP databases

E Accommodate dimensions beyond the third by repeating cubes for each additional dimension

14. A data mart

A Is a subset of a data warehouse

B Is a shop that sells data to individuals and businesses

C Supports the requirements of a particular department or business function

D Can be a good starting point for organizations with no data warehouse experience

E Can be a good starting point when requirements are sketchy

15. Reasons to create a data mart include

A It is more comprehensive than a data warehouse.

B It is a potentially lower risk project.

C Data may be tailored to a particular department or business function.

    D It contains more data than a data warehouse.

    E The project has a lower overall cost than a data warehouse project.

16. Building a data warehouse first, followed by data marts

    A Will delay data mart deployment if the data warehouse project drags on

    B Has lower risk than trying to build them all together

    C Has the lowest risk of the three possible strategies

    D Has the highest risk of the three possible strategies

    E May require a great deal of rework

17. Building one or more data marts first, followed by the data warehouse

    A May delay data warehouse delivery if the data mart projects drag on

    B Has the potential to deliver some OLAP functions more quickly

    C Has the lowest risk of the three possible strategies

    D Has the highest risk of the three possible strategies

    E May require a great deal of rework

18. Building the data warehouse and data marts simultaneously

    A Creates the largest single project of all the possible strategies

    B Has the potential to take the longest to deliver any OLAP functions

    C Has the lowest risk of the three possible strategies

    D Has the highest risk of the three possible strategies

    E May require a great deal of rework

19. Data mining

    A Creates a scaled-down data warehouse

    B Extracts previously unknown data correlations from the data warehouse

    C Can be successful with small amounts of data

    D Is most useful when the organization is agile enough to take action based on the information

    E Usually requires large data volumes in order to produce accurate results

20. Properties of data warehouse systems include

   A Holding historic rather than current information

   B Long-running queries that process many rows of data

   C Support for day-to-day operations

   D Process orientation

   E Medium to low transaction volume

Chapter 13

Integrating XML Documents and Objects into Databases

Key Skills & Concepts

- Learn the Basics of XML
- Learn About SQL/XML
- Object-Oriented Applications
- Object-Relational Databases

A long with the explosive growth in the use of databases, particularly relational databases, the need to store more complex data types has increased sharply. This is especially true for databases that support websites that render images and formatted documents as well as sound and video clips. Furthermore, as the use of object programming languages such as C++ and Java has grown, so has the need to store the objects that these languages manipulate. (Objects were briefly introduced in Chapter 1.) In this chapter, we'll look at a number of ways to integrate such content into databases.

Learn the Basics of XML

The Extensible Markup Language (XML) is a general-purpose markup language used to describe data in a format that is convenient for display on web pages and for exchanging data between different parties. In 2003, the specifications for storing XML data in SQL (relational) databases were added to the ANSI/ISO SQL Standard as Part 14, named SQL/XML. Part 14 was expanded further in 2006.

NOTE
SQL/XML is not at all the same as Microsoft's SQLXML, which is a proprietary technology used in SQL Server. As you can imagine, the unfortunately similar names have caused much confusion. Microsoft participated in the standards proceedings for SQL/XML but then chose not to implement it.

To understand SQL/XML, you must first understand the basics of XML. While a complete explanation of XML is well beyond the scope of this book, I'll provide a brief overview. You can find a lot more information by searching on the Internet.

You may already be familiar with HTML, the markup language used to define web pages. If so, the syntax of XML will look familiar. This is because both are based on the Standard Generalized Markup Language (SGML), which itself is based on Generalized

Markup Language (GML), developed by IBM in the 1960s. A *markup language* is a set of annotations, often called *tags*, that are used to describe how text is to be structured, formatted, or laid out. The tagged text is intended to be human-readable. One of the fundamental differences between HTML and XML is that HTML provides a predefined set of tags, while XML allows the author to create his or her own tags.

Let's look at a sample XML document that contains the results of an SQL query. Figure 13-1 shows a DEPARTMENT table containing two departments and a COURSE table containing five educational courses offered by those departments. As you learned in Chapter 4, the two tables can be easily joined using an SQL SELECT statement like this one:

```
SELECT a.DEPT_NAME, b.COURSE_TITLE, b.COURSE_ID
  FROM DEPARTMENT a JOIN COURSE b
      ON a.DEPT_ID = b.DEPT_ID
 ORDER BY a.DEPT_NAME, b.COURSE_TITLE;
```

Note that I used the ORDER BY clause to specify the order of the rows in the result set. The query results should look something like this:

```
DEPT_NAME                COURSE_TITLE                      COURSE_ID
--------------------     ------------------------------    ---------
Business                 Accounting 101                    101
Business                 Concepts of Marketing             102
Information Technology   C Programming I                   401
Information Technology   C Programming II                  402
Information Technology   Introduction to Computer Systems  400
```

The query results are well suited for display or printing, but they are not in a form that would be easy to display on a web page or to pass to another computer application for

DEPARTMENT

DEPT_ID	DEPT_NAME
BUS	Business
IT	Information Technology

COURSE

COURSE_ID	COURSE_TITLE	DEPT_ID
101	Accounting 101	BUS
102	Concepts of Marketing	BUS
400	Introduction to Computer Systems	IT
401	C Programming I	IT
402	C Programming II	IT

Figure 13-1 The DEPARTMENT and COURSE tables

further processing. One way to make this easier is to convert the query results into XML, as shown here:

```
<departments>
   <department name="Business">
      <courses>
         <course title="Accounting 101"><id>101</id></course>
         <course title ="Concepts of Marketing">
            <id>102</id></course>
      </courses>
   </department>
   <department name="Information Technology">
      <courses>
         <course title="C Programming I"><id>401</id></course>
         <course title="C Programming II"><id>402</id></course>
         <course title="Introduction to Computer Systems">
            <id>400</id></course>
      </courses>
   </department>
   <!-- Additional departments available soon -->
</departments>
```

As you can see in the code listing, tags are enclosed in angle brackets, and each start tag has a matching end tag that is identical, except for the slash (/) used in the end tag. (HTML uses an identical convention; however, HTML is a lot more forgiving if you do something like omit an end tag.) For example, the tag **<departments>** starts the list of academic departments, while the end tag **</departments>** ends it. Within the list of departments, the information for each individual department begins with the **<department>** tag, which includes a data value for the name attribute, and ends with the **</department>** tag. It is customary (and considered a best practice) to name a list using the plural of the tag name used for each item in the list. Comments can be added using a special tag that begins with **<!--** and ends with **-->**, as shown in the next to last line of the example.

Data items and values, such as those that would be stored in a relational table column, can be coded as name and value pairs in one of two ways. The first way is using an XML *attribute,* by naming the attribute inside another tag, followed by the equal sign and the data value enclosed in double quotation marks, such as I did with the name and title attributes. The second way is using an XML *element,* by creating a separate tag for the data item with the data value sandwiched between the start and end tags, such as I did with the **id** attribute within the **course** tag. The question of which form to use has been the subject of much debate among XML developers. However, the general consensus is to use elements whenever the data item might later be broken down into additional elements, such as splitting a person's name into first name and last name, or dividing a single data element containing a comma-separated list of prerequisite course names into a list of elements. An additional consideration is whether you want to allow the XML processor to ignore insignificant whitespace, as it would do for attributes, but not for elements.

You likely noticed that, unlike the SQL result set, XML can show the hierarchy of the data. In this case, the list of courses offered by each department is nested within the information about the department. I have indented the XML statements to make the nesting more obvious. And while indentation of nested tags is a best practice, it is not significant, because whitespace between tags is ignored when the XML is processed.

XML coding can be quite tedious. Fortunately, tools are available to help you convert between XML and plain text, and SQL/XML functions (covered later in this chapter) to convert relational database data into XML. For a time, specialized databases for storing and retrieving XML were gaining popularity, but the major relational database vendors added features to permit native XML to be stored directly in their databases. At the same time, the SQL standard was expanded to include provisions for XML data, as I discuss in the next section of this chapter.

Ask the Expert

Q: Is there a standard for the XML language itself?

A: While ISO does not currently publish a standard for XML, ISO 8879 provides a standard for SGML, and XML is based on SGML. More importantly, the World Wide Web Consortium (W3C) publishes XML specifications that make up the standard that is generally accepted throughout the IT industry.

Q: You mentioned that XML is a convenient way for different parties to exchange information. Does that mean that two companies can freely exchange data without having to create elaborate interface software so long as they both use XML?

A: Well, not exactly. XML provides only a standard way to format the data. For one company to correctly interpret the XML data that another company has sent them, the receiving company must know the names and definitions of the tags the sending company formatted for them, particularly the elements and attributes that contain the data. Fortunately, a number of industry standards can help. For example, HR/XML provides a standard for exchanging human resources (HR) data, so that a company can, for example, send employee data to a vendor that provides medical insurance for those employees. In some industries, XML is beginning to replace an older standard known as EDI (Electronic Data Interchange).

Learn About SQL/XML

As mentioned, XML is commonly used to represent data on web pages, and that data often comes from relational databases. However, as you have seen, the two models in use are quite different, in that relational data is stored in tables where neither hierarchy nor sequence have any significance, while XML is based on hierarchical trees in which order is considered significant. The term *forest* is often used to refer to a collection of XML tree structures. XML is used for web pages because its structure so closely matches the structure that would be used to display the same data in HTML. In fact, many web pages are a mixture of HTML for the static portions and XML for the dynamic data. It is perhaps this widespread implementation that has led many of the major vendors, including Oracle, Microsoft, and IBM, to support XML extensions. However, only Oracle and IBM's DB2 UDB support the SQL/XML commands covered in this topic—the Microsoft SQL Server XML extension is markedly different, and I have not included it in this book because it is proprietary.

SQL/XML can be divided into three main parts: the XML data type, SQL/XML functions, and SQL/XML mapping rules. I cover each of these as the major topics in the remainder of this chapter.

The XML Data Type

The XML data type is handled in the same general way as all the other data types discussed in Chapter 2. Storing data in XML format directly in the database is not the only way to use SQL and XML together. However, it is a very simple way to get started, because it is a logical extension of the earliest implementations where SQL developers simply stored the XML text in a column defined with a general character data type such as CHARACTER VARYING (VARCHAR). It is far better to tell the DBMS that the column contains XML, and the particular way the XML is coded, so that the DBMS can provide additional features tailored to the XML format.

The specification for the XML data type has this general format:

XML (<type modifier> {(<secondary type modifier>)})

The type modifier is required and must be enclosed in a pair of parentheses as shown, while the secondary type modifier is optional, and in fact is not supported for all type modifiers. The standard is not specific about how a particular SQL implementation should treat the various types, but some conventions and syntax rules are specified. The valid type modifiers are as follows:

- **DOCUMENT** The DOCUMENT type is intended for storage of text documents formatted using XML. In general, the data values are expected to be composed of human-readable characters such as letters, numbers, and symbols as they would appear in an unstructured text document.

- **CONTENT** The CONTENT type is intended for more complex data that can include binary data such as images and sound clips.

- **SEQUENCE** The SEQUENCE type is intended for XQuery documents, which are often called XQuery sequences. XQuery is an advanced topic that is beyond the scope of this book.

The secondary type modifier, used only with the DOCUMENT and CONTENT primary type modifiers, can have one of these values:

- **UNTYPED** The XML data is not of a particular type.

- **ANY** The XML data is of any of the types supported by the SQL implementation.

- **XMLSCHEMA** The XMLSCHEMA type refers to a registered XML schema that has been made known to the database server. The three most common are shown in the following table:

Common Prefix	Target Namespace URI (Uniform Resource Identifier)
Xs	www.w3.org/2001/XMLSchema
Xsi	www.w3.org/2001/XMLSchema-instance
Sqlxml	standards.iso.org/iso/9075/2003/sqlxml

For SQL implementations that do not support the secondary type modifier, ANY is assumed as a default.

NOTE

Because SQL/XML is a relatively new standard, vendor implementation support varies. Oracle supports a XMLType data type instead of the XML type, but it applies at the table level so that the entire table is stored as XML. IBM's DB2 UDB supports an XML type, but without the type modifiers. As mentioned, Microsoft SQL Server supports XML and an XML data type, but in a manner a bit different from the SQL/XML standard. As of version 5.0, MySQL provides no support for XML, but it is expected to be included in a future release.

Suppose we want to add the course syllabus to our course table that can be displayed on a web page. If the syllabus could come from several different sources, and thus be formatted differently depending on the source, XML might be a good way to store the data in our course table. In the following example, I have added the column to the definition of the COURSE table that appears in Figure 13-1:

```
CREATE TABLE COURSE
( COURSE_ID          INT,
  COURSE_TITLE       VARCHAR(60),
  DEPT_ID            CHAR(3),
  COURSE_SYLLABUS    XML(DOCUMENT(UNTYPED)) );
```

NOTE
Although the ISO/ANSI SQL Standard specifies an XML data type in the form shown here, no major SQL implementations seem to support this syntax. However, the standard is quite new, so hopefully this syntax will be supported in the near future.

SQL/XML Functions

An SQL/XML function (also called an XML value function) is simply a function that returns a value as an XML type. For example, a query can be written that selects non-XML data (that is, data stored in data types other than XML) and formats the query results into XML suitable for inclusion in an XML document that can be displayed on a web page or transmitted to some other party. In other words, SQL/XML does not always format complete documents—sometimes additional elements must be added to wrap the XML returned by the DBMS into a complete document. Table 13-1 shows the basic SQL/XML functions.

More functions exist than are listed here, and all these SQL/XML functions can be used in combinations to form extremely powerful (if not complicated) queries. Also, the functions available vary across SQL implementations. Let's look at a simple example to clarify how these functions can be used. This example lists the courses for the Business department using the DEPARTMENT and COURSE tables shown in Figure 13-1. Here is the SQL statement, using the XMLELEMENT and XMLFOREST functions:

```
SELECT XMLELEMENT("DepartmentCourse",
       XMLFOREST(a.DEPT_NAME as Department, a.DEPT_ID, b.COURSE_ID,
                 b.COURSE_TITLE))
  FROM DEPARTMENT a JOIN COURSE b
       ON a.DEPT_ID = b.DEPT_ID
 WHERE a.DEPT_ID = 'BUS'
 ORDER BY b.COURSE_ID;
```

Function	Value Returned
XMLAGG	A single XML value containing an XML forest formed by combining (aggregating) a collection of rows that each contain a single XML value
XMLATTRIBUTES	An attribute in the form *name=value* within an XMLELEMENT
XMLCOMMENT	An XML comment
XMLCONCAT	A concatenated list of XML values, creating a single value containing an XML forest
XMLDOCUMENT	An XML value containing a single document node
XMLELEMENT	An XML element, which can be a child of a document node, with the name specified in the name parameter
XMLFOREST	An XML element containing a sequence of XML elements formed from table columns, using the name of each column as the corresponding element name
XMLPARSE	An XML value formed by parsing the supplied string without validating it
XMLPI	An XML value containing an XML processing instruction
XMLQUERY	The result of an XQuery expression (XQuery is a sublanguage used to search XML stored in the database; it is beyond the scope of this book)
XMLTEXT	An XML value containing a single XML text node, which can be a child of a document node
XMLVALIDATE	An XML sequence that is the result of validating an XML value

Table 13-1   SQL/XML Functions

The results returned should look something like this:

```
<DepartmentCourse>
  <Department>Business</Department>
  <DEPT_ID>BUS</DEPT_ID>
  <COURSE_ID>101</COURSE_ID>
  <COURSE_TITLE>Accounting 101</COURSE_TITLE>
</DepartmentCourse>
<DepartmentCourse>
  <Department>Business</Department>
  <DEPT_ID>BUS</DEPT_ID>
  <COURSE_ID>102</COURSE_ID>
  <COURSE_TITLE>Concepts of Marketing</COURSE_TITLE>
</DepartmentCourse>
```

Notice that the XML element names are taken from the column names, in uppercase with underscores as is customary in SQL. However, using the column alias, as I did for the DEPT_NAME column, you can change the column names to just about anything you want. Keep in mind that the result set is not necessarily a complete document (an XML developer would say the XML may not be "well formed"). To turn the XML in the last example into a complete document, at the very least a root element is needed, along with its corresponding end tag. If we were to add the element **<DepartmentCourses>** at the beginning of the results and **</DepartmentCourses>** at the end of the results, we would have a well-formed document.

SQL/XML Mapping Rule

Thus far I have not discussed how SQL values are translated and represented as XML values and vice versa. The SQL standard describes in detail how SQL values can be mapped to and from XML values. This topic contains an overview of the SQL/XML mapping rules.

Mappings from SQL to XML

The mappings in this topic apply to translating data in SQL data types to XML.

Mapping SQL Character Sets to Unicode *Unicode* is an industry standard that allows computer systems to consistently represent (encode) text characters expressed in most of the world's written languages. XML is often encoded as Unicode characters to allow for text in multiple languages. SQL character data is stored in whatever character set is specified when the table or database is created, and while most SQL implementations support Unicode, many other character sets can also be used. The SQL standard requires that each character in an SQL character set have a mapping to an equivalent Unicode character.

Mapping SQL Identifiers to XML Names It is necessary to define a mapping of SQL identifiers, such as table and column names, to XML names, because not all SQL identifiers are acceptable XML names. Characters that are not valid in XML names are converted to a sequence of hexadecimal digits derived from the Unicode encoding of the character, bracketed by an introductory underscore and lowercase x and a trailing underscore. For example, a colon (:) in an SQL identifier might be translated to _x003A_ in an XML name.

Mapping SQL Data Types to XML Schema Data Types This is perhaps the most complicated of the mapping forms. For each SQL type or domain, the SQL implementation is required to provide a mapping to the appropriate XML schema type. Detailed mapping of standard SQL types to XML schema data types is provided in the standard in exhaustive detail. I summarize them in Table 13-2.

SQL Type	XML Schema Type	Notes
CHARACTER, CHARACTER VARYING, CHARACTER LARGE OBJECT	xs:string	The XML facet xs:length is used to specify length for fixed length strings. (A *facet* is an element used to define a property of another element.)
NUMERIC DECIMAL	xs:decimal	Precision and scale are specified using XML facets xs:precision and xs:scale.
INTEGER SMALLINT BIGINT	xs:integer	This mapping is listed as implementation-defined, meaning it is optional.
FLOAT REAL DOUBLE PRECISION	xs:float, xs:double	For precisions up to 24 binary digits (bits) and an exponent between −149 and 104 inclusive, xs:float is used; otherwise xs:double is used.
BOOLEAN	xs:Boolean	
DATE	xs:date	The xs:pattern facet is used to exclude the use of a time zone displacement.
TIME WITH TIME ZONE TIME WITHOUT TIME ZONE	xs:time	The xs:pattern facet is used to exclude or specify the time zone displacement, as appropriate.
TIMESTAMP WITH TIME ZONE; TIMESTAMP WITHOUT TIME ZONE	xs:dateTime	The xs:pattern facet is used to exclude or specify the time zone displacement, as appropriate.
Interval types	xdt:yearMonthDuration, xdt:dayTimeDuration	
Row type	XML schema complex type	The XML document contains one element for each field of the SQL row type.
Domain	XML schema data type	The domain's data type is mapped to XML with an annotation that identifies the name of the domain.
SQL distinct type	XML schema simple type	
SQL collection type	XML schema complex type	The complex type has a single element named *element*.
XML type	XML schema complex type	

Table 13-2　Mapping of SQL Data Types to XML Schema Types

Mapping Values of SQL Data Types to Values of XML Schema Data Types   For each SQL type or domain, with the exception of structured types and reference types, is a mapping of values for the type to the value space of the corresponding XML schema type. Null values are representing either using absence (skipping the element) or using the facet **xsi:nil="true"** to explicitly set the null value.

Mapping an SQL Table to an XML Document and an XML Schema Document   The SQL standard defines a mapping of an SQL table to one or both of two documents: an XML schema document that describes the structure of the mapped XML, and either an XML document or a sequence of XML elements. This mapping applies only to base tables and viewed tables, and only columns visible to the database user can be mapped. The implementation may provide options for the following:

- Whether to map the table to a sequence of XML elements or as an XML document with a single root name derived from the table name

- The target namespace of the XML schema to be mapped

- Whether to map null values as absent elements or elements marked with facet **xsi:nil="true"**

- Whether to map the table into XML data, an XML schema document, or both

Mapping an SQL Schema to an XML Document and an XML Schema Document   The SQL standard defines the mapping between the tables of an SQL schema and either an XML document that represents the data in the tables, an XML schema document, or both. Only tables and columns visible to the database user can be mapped. The implementation may provide options for the following:

- Whether to map each table as a sequence of XML elements or as an XML document with a single root name derived from the table name

- The target namespace of the XML schema to be mapped

- Whether to map null values as absent elements or elements marked with facet **xsi:nil="true"**

- Whether to map the schema into XML data, an XML schema document, or both

Mapping an SQL Catalog to an XML Document and an XML Schema Document   The SQL standard defines the mapping between the tables of an SQL catalog and either an XML document that represents the data in the catalog's tables or an XML schema document, or both. However, this part of the standard specifies no syntax for invoking such mapping because it is intended to be used by applications or referenced by other standards. Only schemas visible to the SQL user can be mapped. The implementation may provide options for the following:

- Whether to map each table as a sequence of XML elements or as an XML document with a single root name derived from the table name

- The target namespace of the XML schema and data to be mapped

- Whether to map null values as absent elements or elements marked with facet **xsi:nil="true"**

- Whether to map the catalog into XML data, an XML schema document, or both

Mappings from XML to SQL   This topic contains two mappings from XML back to SQL.

Mapping Unicode to SQL Character Sets   As with the mapping of SQL character sets to Unicode, the SQL standard requires that there be an implementation-defined mapping of Unicode characters to the characters in each SQL character set supported by the SQL implementation.

Mapping XML Names to SQL Identifiers   This is the reverse of the mapping of SQL identifiers to XML names, where characters that were converted because they were not valid in XML names are converted back to their original form. So, if a colon in an SQL identifier was converted to _x003A_ when translating the SQL identifier into XML, it would be converted back into a colon when the process was reversed. The SQL standard further recommends that the SQL implementation use a single algorithm for translation in both directions.

Try This 13-1   Using SQL/XML Functions

In this Try This exercise, you will use XML functions to select XML formatted data from the Oracle HR sample schema used in Chapter 4. Obviously, if you chose to use a different RDBMS, your SQL implementation has to provide XML support in order for you to complete the exercise, and, as usual, you may have to modify the code included in this exercise to run it on your DBMS. As of this writing, Oracle and DB2 UDB are the only other DBMSs that support SQL/XML. For SQL Server, some recoding is required to use the Microsoft proprietary FOR XML clause instead of the SQL/XML functions. You can download the Try_This_13.txt file from the website (details in Appendix B), which contains not only the SQL statement used in this Try This exercise (with an alternative

(continued)

statement for use with SQL Server), but also the statements required to create the EMPLOYEES table and populate it with the data required for this exercise (in case you are not using the Oracle HR sample schema).

Step by Step

1. Open the client application for your RDBMS.

2. If you are not using an Oracle database that already has the HR sample schema installed, do the following to create a schema with the EMPLOYEES table and data needed to complete this exercise:

   a. If you are using Oracle, create a user named HR (this will create a schema with the same name). Consult Oracle documentation if you don't know how to do this. Note that many of the GUI client tools such as SQL Developer have functions built in for creating new users.

   b. If you are using SQL Server or DB2, create a database called HR. (In these products, a database is the logical equivalent of a schema in Oracle.) Consult vendor documentation if you need help with this step.

   c. Connect to the schema (or database) that you just created. Many of the GUI tools provide a simple drop-down menu of available schemas for this purpose.

   d. Copy and paste the CREATE TABLE statement and the three INSERT statements from the Try_This_13.txt file into your SQL client and run them as a script.

3. If you have not already done so, connect to the HR schema (Oracle) or database (SQL Server, DB2, and others).

4. You are going to create an SQL query that uses three SQL/XML functions to format XML that contains an element for each employee of Department 90 in the EMPLOYEES table. Each element will include the ID of the employee, followed by separate elements containing the first name, last name, and phone number of the employee. Enter and execute the following statement (or copy and paste if from the Try_This_13.txt file). For SQL Server, the Try_This_13.txt file contains an alternative version that includes the Microsoft proprietary FOR XML clause.

```
SELECT XMLELEMENT("Employee",
       XMLATTRIBUTES(EMPLOYEE_ID AS ID),
       XMLFOREST(FIRST_NAME AS "FirstName",
                 LAST_NAME AS "LastName",
                 PHONE_NUMBER AS "Phone"))
```

```
FROM EMPLOYEES
WHERE DEPARTMENT_ID = 90
ORDER BY EMPLOYEE_ID;
```

5. The output produced should look something like the following. Note that the XML for each employee is output as a single line in the result set—I added the line breaks and indentation to make the results more understandable.

```
<Employee ID="100">
    <FirstName>Steven</FirstName>
    <LastName>King</LastName>
    <Phone>515.123.4567</Phone>
</Employee>
<Employee ID="101">
    <FirstName>Neena</FirstName>
    <LastName>Kochhar</LastName>
    <Phone>515.123.4568</Phone>
</Employee>
    <Employee ID="102">
    <FirstName>Lex</FirstName>
    <LastName>De Haan</LastName>
    <Phone>515.123.4569</Phone>
</Employee>
```

6. Close the client application.

Try This Summary

In this Try This exercise, the SQL SELECT statement used three SQL/XML functions to format data from the EMPLOYEES table into XML. The XMLELEMENT function was used to create an element for each Employee. The XMLATTRIBUTES function was used to include the EMPLOYEE_ID value with the name ID as a value within the Employee element. Finally, the XMLFOREST function was used to create elements for the FIRST_NAME, LAST_NAME, and PHONE_NUMBER columns.

Object-Oriented Applications

This section assumes that you have read and understood the section "The Object-Oriented Model" in Chapter 1. You may want to review it before continuing.

Object-oriented (OO) applications are written in an object-oriented programming language. These OO languages usually come with a predefined object class structure and predefined methods—but, of course, the developers can create their own classes and methods. Some come with a complete development environment that includes not only the language elements, but also an integrated OO database. It is important for you to understand that OO applications can be created without an OO database, and an OO database can exist (at least in theory) without an OO application to access it.

Object-Oriented Programming

Object-oriented programming uses *messages* as the vehicle for object interaction. A *message* in the OO context is composed of the identifier of the object that is to receive the message, the name of the method to be invoked by the receiving object, and, optionally, one or more parameters. You will recall from Chapter 1 that a *method* is a piece of application program logic that operates on a particular object and provides a finite function. The notion that all access to an object's variables is done via its methods is essential to the OO paradigm. Therefore, OO programming involves writing methods that encompass the *behavior* of the object (that is, what the object does) and crafting messages within those methods whenever an object must interact with other objects. OO application development includes object and class design in addition to the aforementioned programming tasks.

The OO paradigm also supports *complex* objects, which are objects composed of one or more other objects. Usually, this is implemented using an object *reference*, where one object contains the identifier for one or more other objects. For example, a Customer object might contain a list of Order objects that the customer has placed, and each Order object might contain the identifier of the customer who placed the order. The unique identifier for an object is called the *object identifier* (*OID*), the value of which is automatically assigned to each object as it is created and is then invariant (that is, the value never changes).

Object-Oriented Languages

Let's have a look at three of the most popular OO programming languages: Smalltalk, C++, and Java.

Smalltalk

The pioneering OO system was Smalltalk, developed in 1972 by the Software Concepts Group at the Xerox Palo Alto Research Center (PARC), led by Alan Kay. It was Kay who coined the term "object-oriented." Smalltalk includes a language, a programming environment, an "image file system" to store objects and methods (more or less a database), and an extensive object library. Smalltalk's innovations include a bitmap display, a windowing system, and the use of a mouse. In an interesting twist of history, Xerox funded and owned the first commercial OO programming environment, the original windowing system, the mouse, and many other technical computing innovations. Yet, Xerox never figured out how to market any of them, so the company's innovations fell into other hands over time and were eventually "introduced" into the market by other companies. Although not nearly as popular as it once was, Smalltalk is still around today, and you can find much more about it at www.smalltalk.org.

C++

As the name suggests, C++ is based on the C programming language. In fact, ++ is the operator in C that increments a variable by 1, so C++ literally means "C plus 1." This superset of C was developed primarily by Bjarne Stroustrup at AT&T Bell Laboratories in 1986. Classes are implemented as user-defined types—a *struct* (structure) in C syntax. Methods are implemented as member functions of a struct. Object purists frown upon C++, claiming it's not an OO language because programmers can ignore the object paradigm when they choose to and do such things as manipulating data directly using C language commands. C++ aficionados, on the other hand, see this as a huge benefit because it gives them a great deal of flexibility.

Java

Java is a simple, portable, general-purpose OO language that was developed by Sun Microsystems around 1995. It took the market by storm immediately after its introduction, largely because of its support for Internet programming in the form of platform-independent "applets." Another advantage of Java is that it can run on very small computers due to the small size of its interpreter. Unlike Smalltalk and C++, Java is an *interpretive* language, which means that each statement is evaluated at runtime instead of being compiled ahead of time. A *compiler* is a program that converts a computer program from the source language the programmer used to write it to the machine language of the computer on which it is to be run. Initially, the interpreter hampered performance compared with compiled languages, but recent innovations, such as *just-in-time* compilers, which compile statements just prior to their execution, have helped enormously.

Object Persistence

Persistence is the OO property that preserves the state of an object between executions of an application and across the shutdown and startup of the computer system itself. In most cases, a database is used to store objects permanently, so it is the database that implements persistence. Objects must be loaded into memory for an application to access them, and any changes must be saved back to persistent storage when they are no longer required.

Object loading into memory is an *indirect* process, which means the application does not specifically request that an object be loaded—the application environment works with the database environment to load objects into memory automatically whenever they are accessed by an application. This access is usually in the form of a message that is sent to the object, but, as discussed in the next subsection, it may also occur when an object contains a reference to another object.

Let's look at two methods for implementing object persistence using a database—the OO database and the relational database. In the next section, we explore a hybrid approach that combines features of both object-oriented and relational databases.

Persistence Using an OO Database

Figure 13-2 shows the retrieval of an object from persistent storage in an OO database. For the purposes of illustration, the specific components that execute each of the illustrated steps have been omitted, thereby showing what happens without worrying about how it happens. This is actually a very good way to think about OO databases,

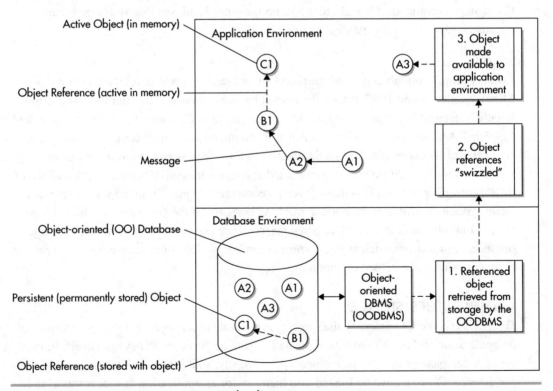

Figure 13-2 Persistence using an OO database

because a common property of OO systems is to hide implementation details. As shown in Figure 13-2, the database contains persistent copies of objects A1, A2, A3, B1, and C1. Assume that the first letter denotes the object class to which the objects belong. Note that object B1 references object C1 as illustrated, using a broken line to connect them. This is a typical arrangement in which one object, such as an order, contains the object ID (OID) of a related object, such as the customer who placed the order. In an equivalent relational database, this relationship would be implemented using a foreign key in the order.

As shown in Figure 13-2, the sequence of events that takes place when an object is first referenced by the application is as follows:

1. A request to retrieve the object is sent to the OO database, typically because a message in the application environment referenced the object. The OODBMS retrieves the object from persistent storage and passes it to the application environment. If the object contains references to other objects, the OODBMS may also automatically retrieve those objects, depending on the architecture of the OODBMS.

2. If an object contains references to other objects, those references must be changed into memory addresses when the objects are loaded into memory. This process is known as *swizzling* the references. (The origin of the term *swizzle* is unknown, but it may have been derived from swizzle sticks that are used to stir drinks.) In persistent storage, the OID can be used as the reference because other storage structures similar to indexes can be used by the OODBMS to locate the related objects. For example, object B1 contains the OID of object C1, and the OODBMS has no difficulty using the OID to locate the related object in the database's persistent storage. However, the OID is of little use in locating the related object once the objects are loaded into memory because objects are loaded into any available memory location, which means there is no simple way to know the locations they occupy. Therefore, the OID is translated (swizzled) into the actual address that the related object occupies in memory to allow direct access of the related object in memory. The original OID is retained within the object because it will be needed when the object is stored back into the database.

3. The object is made available to the application environment. That is, it is placed in a memory location, and any messages addressed to the object are routed to it. Usually, this also involves registering the object with the application environment so it can easily be found in memory the next time it is referenced.

The reverse process of storing an object back into the OO database when the application no longer needs to access it is exactly that—a *reverse* of the original process. The conditions that trigger moving the object back to persistent storage vary from one OODBMS to another but typically involve a *least recently used* (*LRU*) algorithm. The LRU algorithm is a process that is invoked when space must be freed up for the loading of more objects into memory locations. The algorithm finds the objects that were accessed the longest time ago (that is, least recently), and it removes those objects from memory. And, of course, a request to shut down the database requires that every object in memory be made persistent before the database is shut down. The sequence of events to move an object from memory to persistent storage is as follows:

1. The object is removed from its memory location, and any registration of the object in the application environment is deleted.

2. Any memory addresses added to the object when references were swizzled are removed.

3. If the object was modified while it was in memory, it is sent back to the OODBMS, which stores the new version.

Persistence Using a Relational Database

When the object data is stored in a relational database, some important differences are the result. First, everything in a relational database must be stored in a table. Therefore, objects must be translated to and from relational tables. Typically, each class is stored in a different relational table, with the rows in the tables representing object instances for the corresponding classes. Second, relational tables cannot store objects in their native format, because objects are composed of methods and a class hierarchy along with the data itself. The methods and class hierarchy are usually not stored in the relational database at all, but rather are maintained in a file system location (directory) that is managed by the application environment. Figure 13-3 illustrates this arrangement.

Take note of the differences between Figures 13-2 and 13-3. First, in the latter figure, the object data is stored in the database in tables. Second, an additional step is required when retrieving objects and making them available in memory—the data from the relational database must be mapped to object classes and variables. This can be accomplished in many different ways. A common approach with applications written in Java is to issue the relational SQL directly from a Java method using a Java Database Connectivity (JDBC) driver (introduced in Chapter 9), and within the same method, to relate the results returned by the JDBC driver to one or more objects. This is a manual and very labor-intensive approach for Java programmers. Fortunately, more automated solutions are available, wherein an application server or middleware product handles all the details of persistently storing objects in the relational database, including the translation between relational tables and objects. Figure 13-3 has been simplified to

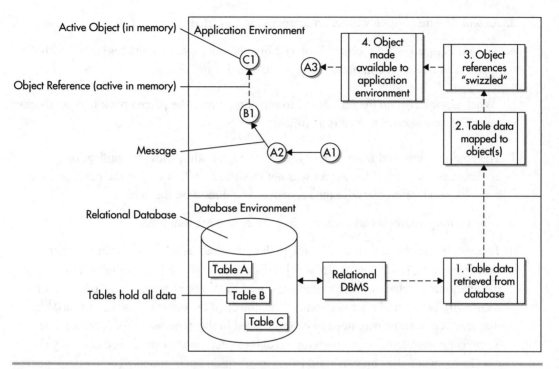

Figure 13-3 Persistence using a relational database

show the steps required to assemble an object stored in a relational database and make it available in the application environment without any details as to which components handle the various steps.

As illustrated in Figure 13-3, here is the sequence of events required to assemble an object from data stored in a relational database:

1. An SQL query is sent to the RDBMS to retrieve the table data (typically one row) from the database. The query is executed by the RDBMS and the resultant data sent to the application environment.

2. The table data is mapped to the object. Typically, this involves assigning the table data to a class and the individual columns to variables within that class, along with retrieving the methods defined for the class from wherever they are stored in the file system. This mapping step is the proverbial Achilles heel of this architecture—it is expensive in terms of resources, and it requires design compromises because object data cannot always be perfectly represented in relational database tables.

3. As with Figure 13-2, any object references are swizzled.

4. As with Figure 13-2, the object is placed in a memory location and registered with the application environment, making it available to the application.

When an object is no longer needed in memory, it must be placed back into persistent storage. The sequence of events is as follows:

1. The object is removed from memory, and any registration with the application environment deleted. If the object was not modified while it was in memory, no other action is necessary; otherwise the sequence continues with the next step.

2. Any memory addresses added for object references are removed.

3. The data in the object is mapped back to the relational table row(s) from which it came. One or more SQL statements (INSERT, UPDATE, or DELETE) are formed to change the relational database data to match the object data. For efficiency, this often involves comparing before and after versions of the object (if available) so that only variables that changed in some way need to be referenced in the generated SQL statement(s). There is no need to do anything with the class structure or methods because they do not change when the object is used in the application environment. These components change only when a new version of the application is installed.

4. The SQL statement(s) is (are) passed to the relational DBMS to be processed. If the object was not changed while it was in memory, this step is not required.

Object-Relational Databases

This section assumes you have read and understood the section "The Object-Relational Model" in Chapter 1. You may wish to review it before continuing. The object-relational DBMS (ORDBMS) evolved in response to the difficulties of mapping objects to relational databases and to market pressure from OODBMS vendors. Relational database vendors, such as Informix (subsequently acquired by IBM) and Oracle, added object extensions in hopes of preventing any loss of market share to the OODBMS vendors. To a large degree, this tactic appears to have worked, with pure OO databases gaining ground only in niche markets. Moreover, the lack of ad-hoc query capability in pure OO databases has certainly not helped it in the marketplace. The ORDBMS provides a blend of desirable features from the object world, such as the storage of complex data types, with the relative simplicity and ease of use of the relational model. Most industry experts believe that object-relational technology will continue to gain market share.

The advantages of an object-relational database are as follows:

- Complex data types (that is, data types formed by combining other data types) are directly supported while preserving ad-hoc query capability.

- The DBMS may be extended to perform common functions (methods) centrally, which improves program logic reuse compared with a pure relational DBMS.

- Storing object functions (methods) in the database makes them available to all applications, which improves object sharing compared with a pure relational DBMS.

- Ad-hoc query capability is fully supported, which is a feature that is not supported in pure OO databases.

Here are the disadvantages of the object-relational approach:

- The combination is more complex than either pure relational or pure OO databases, leading to increased development costs.

- Objects are *table-centric,* meaning that all persistent objects must be stored within a table.

- Relational purists argue that the essential simplicity of the relational model is clouded by the object extensions.

- Object purists are not attracted to the extension of objects into relational databases, arguing that the ORDBMS is little more than a relational database with user-defined data types added.

- Current ORDBMSs lack the class structure and inheritance that are at the foundation of OODBMSs.

- Object applications are not as data-centric as relational applications, and therefore pure OO databases may better serve the needs of object applications.

In terms of deciding which database model is the best fit for a given application, consider the following points:

- Simple data with no requirement for ad-hoc query capability, such as static web pages, can be adequately stored in ordinary file system files.

- Simple data that requires ad-hoc query capability, such as customer data, fits well into a relational database.

- Complex data that does not require ad-hoc query capability, such as images, maps, and drawings, fits well into an object-oriented database.

- Complex data that requires ad-hoc query capability, such as purchase orders stored as composite data types, fits well into an object-relational database.

✓ ## Chapter 13 Self Test

Choose the correct responses to each of the multiple-choice and fill-in-the-blank questions. Note that there may be more than one correct response to each question.

1. XML is _____.

2. How do SQL databases and XML documents vary in terms of data structure?

3. If two organizations are both using XML, does that mean that they have a standard way of exchanging data without having to create interface software?

4. The valid secondary type modifiers for the SEQUENCE type modifier are _____.

5. The _____ XML schema type is mapped from the SQL NUMERIC data type.

6. The _____ XML schema type is mapped from the SQL DATE data type.

7. The two ways that null values from the database can be represented in SQL/XML are _____ and _____.

8. Which of the following are common uses of XML?

   A Display database data on a web page

   B Create static web pages

   C Transmit database data to another party

   D Enforce business rules on documents

9. Which of the following are valid type modifiers for the XML data type?

   A DOCUMENT

   B SEQUENCE

   C SQLXML

   D CONTENT

10. Which of the following SQL/XML functions creates an element based on a table column?

   A XMLQUERY

   B XMLELEMENT

   C XMLFOREST

D XMLDOCUMENT

E XMLPARSE

11. Object-oriented programming

A Uses messages as a vehicle for object interaction

B Allows an object to directly access the variables in a related object

C Uses methods to define the behavior of an object

D Requires objects to have a primary key

E Supports the use of complex objects

12. Object-oriented (OO) applications

A Require the use of an OO database

B Are written in an OO language

C Use development environments that usually come with predefined classes

D Use development environments that usually come with predefined methods

E May be written in the C programming language

13. Smalltalk

A Was developed by Linus Torvalds

B Was developed in 1972

C Was developed at the Xerox PARC facility

D Is based on the C programming language

E Was the first OO programming language to include a windowing system and use of a mouse

14. C++

A Was developed by Alan Kay

B Was developed in 1976

C Was developed at AT&T Bell Laboratories

D Is based on the Java programming language

E Allows programmers to ignore the object paradigm if they wish

15. Java

    A Was developed by Sun Microsystems

    B May be run only on large systems with lots of memory

    C Was developed around 1995

    D Is an interpretive language

    E Is a general-purpose OO language

16. Object persistence

    A Preserves the state of an object between executions of an application

    B Preserves the state of an object across the shutdown and startup of the computer system

    C Loads objects into memory to preserve them permanently

    D Occurs when the application requests that an object be saved

    E Can be accomplished only with an OO database

17. The events necessary to retrieve an object from an OO database include

    A A message is sent to the object, so the object must be loaded into memory.

    B A request to retrieve the object is sent to the OO database.

    C Object references are swizzled into memory addresses.

    D Relational data is assigned to an object class.

    E The object is made available to the application environment.

18. The advantages of object-relational databases include

    A Objects are stored within tables.

    B Complex data types are supported.

    C Ad-hoc query capability is fully supported.

    D Class structures and inheritance are fully supported.

    E Centrally stored functions (methods) improve reuse.

19. The disadvantages of object-relational databases include

   A The combination is more complex than either pure object-oriented or pure relational databases.

   B Ad-hoc query capability is limited.

   C Objects are table-centric.

   D Neither relational purists nor object purists are enamored with this combination.

   E Object applications are not as data-centric as relational ones.

20. When considering the selection of a database model, which of the following facts should be taken into account?

   A Ordinary file system files can handle simple data, provided there are no ad-hoc query requirements.

   B Relational databases can handle simple data that has ad-hoc query requirements.

   C Object-oriented databases are best at handling complex data.

   D Object-relational databases can handle complex data that has ad-hoc query requirements.

   E Object-oriented databases can handle complex data, provided there are no ad-hoc query requirements.

Part IV

Appendices

Appendix A

Answers to Self Tests

Chapter 1: Database Fundamentals

1. **The logical layer of the ANSI/SPARC model provides which of the following?**

   A. Physical data independence

   B. Parent-child relationships

   C. Logical data independence

   D. Encapsulation

   A is the correct answer.

2. **The external layer of the ANSI/SPARC model provides which of the following?**

   A. Physical data independence

   B. Parent-child relationships

   C. Logical data independence

   D. Encapsulation

   C is the correct answer.

3. **Which of the following is *not* true regarding user views?**

   A. Application programs reference them.

   B. People querying the database reference them.

   C. They can be tailored to the needs of the database user.

   D. Data updates are shown in a delayed fashion.

   D is the correct answer.

4. **The database schema is contained in the _____ layer of the ANSI/SPARC model.**

   logical

5. **User views are contained in the _____ layer of the ANSI/SPARC model.**

   external

6. **When application programs use flat file systems, where do the file definitions reside?**

   In the application programs

7. **Which of the following is true regarding the hierarchical database model?**

   A. It was first developed by Peter Chen.

   B. Data and methods are stored together in the database.

C. Each node may have many parents.

D. Records are connected using physical address pointers.

> **D** is the correct answer.

8. Which of the following is true regarding the network database model?

A. It was first developed by E.F. Codd.

B. Data and methods are stored together in the database.

C. Each node may have many parents.

D. Records are connected using common physical address pointers.

> **C** and **D** are correct answers.

9. Which of the following is true of the relational database model?

A. It was first developed by Charles Bachman.

B. Data and methods are stored together in the database.

C. Records are connected using physical address pointers.

D. Records are connected using common data items in each record.

> **D** is the correct answer.

10. Which of the following is true regarding the object-oriented model?

A. It was first developed by Charles Bachman.

B. Data and methods are stored together in the database.

C. Data is presented as two-dimensional tables.

D. Records are connected using common data items in each record.

> **B** is the correct answer.

11. Which of the following is true regarding the object-relational model?

A. It serves only a niche market and most experts believe it will stay that way.

B. Records are connected using physical address pointers.

C. It was developed by adding object-like properties to the relational model.

D. It was developed by adding relational-like properties to the object-oriented model.

> **C** is the correct answer.

12. According to advocates of the relational model, which of the following describe the problems with the CODASYL model?

A. It is too mathematical.

B. It is too complicated.

    C. Set-oriented queries are too difficult.

    D. It has no formal underpinnings in mathematical theory.

        B, **C**, and **D** are correct answers.

13. **According to advocates of the CODASYL model, which of the following describe the problems with the relational model?**

    A. It is too mathematical.

    B. Set-oriented queries are too difficult.

    C. Application systems need record-at-a-time processing.

    D. It is less efficient than CODASYL model databases.

        A, **C**, and **D** are correct answers.

14. **The ability to add a new object to a database without disrupting existing processes is an example of _____.**

    logical data independence

15. **The property that most distinguishes a relational database table from a spreadsheet is the ability to present multiple users with their own _____.**

    views of the data

Chapter 2: Exploring Relational Database Components

1. **Examples of an entity are**

    A. A customer

    B. A customer order

    C. An employee's paycheck

    D. A customer's name

        A, **B**, and **C** are correct answers.

2. **Examples of an attribute are**

    A. An employee

    B. An employee's name

    C. An employee's paycheck

    D. An alphabetical listing of employees

        B is the correct answer.

3. **Which of the following denotes the cardinality of "zero, one, or more" on a relationship line?**

A. A perpendicular tick mark near the end of the line and a crow's foot at the line end

B. A circle near the end of the line and a crow's foot at the end of the line

C. Two perpendicular tick marks near the end of the line

D. A circle and a perpendicular tick mark near the end of the line

   B is the correct answer.

4. **Valid types of relationships in a relational database are**

A. One-to-many

B. None-to-many

C. Many-to-many

D. One-to-one

   A, **C**, and **D** are correct answers.

5. **If a product can be manufactured in many plants, and a plant can manufacture many products, this is an example of which type of relationship?**

A. One-to-one

B. One-to-many

C. Many-to-many

D. Recursive

   C is the correct answer.

6. **Which of the following are examples of recursive relationships?**

A. An organizational unit made up of departments

B. An employee who manages other employees

C. An employee who manages a department

D. An employee who has many dependents

   B is the correct answer.

7. **Examples of a business rule are**

A. A referential constraint must refer to the primary key of the parent table.

B. An employee must be at least 18 years old.

C. A database query eliminates columns an employee should not see.

D. Employees below pay grade 6 are not permitted to modify orders.

   B and **D** are correct answers.

8. **A relational table**

A. Is composed of rows and columns

B. Must be assigned a data type

C. Must be assigned a unique name

D. Is the primary unit of storage in the relational model

A, **C**, and **D** are correct answers.

9. **A column in a relational table**

A. Must be assigned a data type

B. Must be assigned a unique name within the table

C. Is derived from an entity in the conceptual design

D. Is the smallest named unit of storage in a relational database

A, **B**, and **D** are correct answers.

10. **A data type**

A. Assists the DBMS in storing data efficiently

B. Provides a set of behaviors for a column that assists the database user

C. May be selected based on business rules for an attribute

D. Restricts characters allowed in a database column

A, **B**, **C**, and **D** are correct answers.

11. **A primary key constraint**

A. Must reference one or more columns in a single table

B. Must be defined for every database table

C. Is usually implemented using an index

D. Guarantees that no two rows in a table have duplicate primary key values

A, **C**, and **D** are correct answers.

12. **A referential constraint**

A. Must have primary key and foreign key columns that have identical names

B. Ensures that a primary key does not have duplicate values in a table

C. Defines a many-to-many relationship between two tables

D. Ensures that a foreign key value always refers to an existing primary key value in the parent table

D is the correct answer.

13. **A referential constraint is defined**

    A. Using the Relationships panel in Microsoft Access

    B. Using SQL in most relational databases

    C. Using the referential data type for the foreign key column(s)

    D. Using a database trigger

    A and **B** are correct answers.

14. **Major types of integrity constraints are**

    A. CHECK constraints

    B. One-to-one relationships

    C. NOT NULL constraints

    D. Constraints enforced with triggers

    A, **C**, and **D** are correct answers.

15. _____ **tables are used to resolve many-to-many relationships.**

    Intersection

16. **An entity in the conceptual design becomes a(n)** _____ **in the logical design.**

    table

17. **An attribute in the conceptual design becomes a(n)** _____ **in the logical design.**

    column

18. **Items in the external level of the ANSI/SPARC model become** _____ **in the logical model.**

    views

19. **A relationship in the conceptual design becomes a(n)** _____ **in the logical design.**

    referential constraint

20. **A primary key constraint is implemented using a(n)** _____ **in the logical design.**

    index

Chapter 3: Forms-based Database Queries

1. **A forms-based query language**

    A. Was first developed by IBM in the 1980s

    B. Describes how a query should be processed rather than what the results should be

    C. Resembles SQL

D. Uses a GUI (graphical user interface)

E. Was shown to be clearly superior in controlled studies

D is the correct answer.

2. **The object types in Microsoft Access that relate strictly to database management (as opposed to application development) are**

A. Tables

B. Queries

C. Forms

D. Macros

E. Modules

A and **B** are correct answers.

3. **When a table is deleted from the Microsoft Access Relationships panel, what happens next?**

A. It is immediately deleted from the database.

B. It remains unchanged in the database and is merely removed from the Relationships panel.

C. It remains in the database, but all data rows are deleted.

D. Relationships belonging to the table are also deleted.

B is the correct answer.

4. **Relationships on the Microsoft Access Relationships panel represent _____ in the database.**

referential constraints

5. **A column in the results of a Microsoft Access query can be formed from**

A. A table column

B. A query column

C. A constant

D. A calculation

E. All of the above

E is the correct answer.

6. **When a query with no criteria included is executed, the result is**

A. An error message

B. No rows being displayed

C. All the rows in the table being displayed

D. None of the above

    C is the correct answer.

7. **When sequencing (sorting) of rows is not included in a database query, the rows returned by the query are in _____ order.**

no particular

8. **In a query, the search criteria REGION NOT = "CA" OR REGION NOT ="NV" will display**

A. An error message

B. All the rows in the table

C. Only the rows in which Region is equal to "CA" or "NV"

D. All the rows in the table except those in which Region is NULL

E. All the rows in the table except those in which the Region is "CA" or "NV"

    D is the correct answer.

9. **Criteria on different lines in a Microsoft Access query are connected with the _____ logical operator.**

OR

10. **The join connector between tables in a Microsoft Access query may**

A. Be manually created by dragging a column from one table or view to a column of another table or view

B. Be inherited from the metadata defined on the Relationships panel

C. Be altered to define left, right, and full outer joins

D. Cause a Cartesian product if not defined between two tables or views in the query

E. All of the above

    E is the correct answer.

11. **When an outer join is used, column data from tables (or views) in which no matching rows were found will contain _____.**

null values

12. **An aggregate function**

A. Combines data from multiple columns together

B. Combines data from multiple rows together

C. May be applied to table columns but not to calculated columns

D. Requires that every column in a query be either an aggregate function or named in the GROUP BY list for the query

E. All of the above

> **B** and **D** are correct answers.

13. Self-joins in a query are a method of resolving a _____.

recursive relationship

14. The column name of a calculated column in the query results is _____ when not provided in the query definition.

automatically assigned by Microsoft Access

15. Tables may be joined

A. Using only the primary key in one table and a foreign key in another

B. Using any column in either table (theoretically)

C. Only to themselves

D. Only to other tables

E. Only using the Cartesian product formula

> **B** is the correct answer.

Chapter 4: Introduction to SQL

1. SQL may be divided into the following subsets:

A. Data Selection Language (DSL)

B. Data Control Language (DCL)

C. Data Query Language (DQL)

D. Data Definition Language (DDL)

> **B** and **D** are correct answers.

2. SQL was first developed by _____.

IBM

3. A program used to connect to the database and interact with it is called a(n) _____.

SQL client

4. A SELECT without a WHERE clause

A. Selects all rows in the source table or view

B. Returns no rows in the result set

C. Results in an error message

D. Lists only the definition of the table or view

    A is the correct answer.

5. **In SQL, row order in query results**

    A. Is specified using the **SORTED BY** clause

    B. Is unpredictable unless specified in the query

    C. Defaults to descending when sequence is not specified

    D. May be specified only for columns in the query results

    B is the correct answer.

6. **The BETWEEN operator**

    A. Includes the end-point values

    B. Selects rows added to a table during a time interval

    C. Can be rewritten using the <= and **NOT =** operators

    D. Can be rewritten using the <= and >= operators

    A and **D** are correct answers.

7. **The LIKE operator uses _____ as positional wildcards and _____ as nonpositional wildcards.**

underscores (_), percent signs (%)

8. **A subselect**

    A. May be corrugated or noncorrugated

    B. Allows for the flexible selection of rows

    C. Must not be enclosed in parentheses

    D. May be used to select values to be applied to **WHERE** clause conditions

    B and **D** are correct answers.

9. **A join without a WHERE clause or JOIN clause**

    A. Results in an error message

    B. Results in an outer join

    C. Results in a Cartesian product

    D. Returns no rows in the result set

    C is the correct answer.

10. **A join that returns all rows from both tables whether or not matches are found is known as a(n) _____.**

full outer join

11. **A self-join**

    A. Involves two different tables

    B. Can be either an inner or outer join

    C. Resolves recursive relationships

    D. May use a subselect to further limit returned rows

    B, **C**, and **D** are all correct responses.

12. **An SQL statement containing an aggregate function**

    A. Must contain a **GROUP BY** clause

    B. May also include ordinary columns

    C. May not include both **GROUP BY** and **ORDER BY** clauses

    D. May also include calculated columns

    B and **D** are correct answers.

13. **A(n) _____ causes changes made by a transaction to become permanent.**

    COMMIT

14. **An INSERT statement**

    A. Must contain a column list

    B. Must contain a VALUES list

    C. May create multiple table rows

    D. May contain a subquery

    C and **D** are correct answers.

15. **An UPDATE statement without a WHERE clause**

    A. Results in an error message

    B. Updates no rows in a table

    C. Updates every row in a table

    D. Results in a Cartesian product

    C is the correct answer.

16. **A DELETE statement with a column list**

    A. Results in an error message

    B. Deletes data only in the listed columns

    C. Deletes every column in the table

D. Can be used to delete from a view

    A is the correct answer.

17. A CREATE statement

A. Is a form of DML

B. Creates new user privileges

C. Creates a database object

D. May be reversed later using a DROP statement

    C and **D** are correct answers.

18. An ALTER statement

A. May be used to add a constraint

B. May be used to drop a constraint

C. May be used to add a view

D. May be used to drop a table column

    A, **B**, and **D** are correct answers.

19. The _____ mode causes each SQL statement to commit as soon as it completes.

autocommit

20. Database privileges

A. May be changed with an ALTER PRIVILEGE statement

B. May be either system or object privileges

C. Are best managed when assembled into groups using **GROUP BY**

D. Are managed using **GRANT** and **REVOKE**

    B and **D** are correct answers.

Chapter 5: The Database Life Cycle

1. The phases of a systems development life cycle (SDLC) methodology include which of the following?

A. Physical design

B. Logical design

C. Prototyping

D. Requirements gathering

E. Ongoing support

    A, **B**, **D**, and **E** are correct responses.

2. During the requirements phase of an SDLC project,

A. User views are discovered.

B. The quality assurance (QA) environment is used.

C. Surveys may be conducted.

D. Interviews are often conducted.

E. Observation may be used.

A, **C**, **D**, and **E** are correct responses.

3. The advantages of conducting interviews are

A. Interviews take less time than other methods.

B. Answers may be obtained for unasked questions.

C. A lot can be learned from nonverbal responses.

D. Questions are presented more objectively compared to survey techniques.

E. Entities are more easily discovered.

B and **C** are correct responses.

4. The advantages of conducting surveys include

A. A lot of ground can be covered quickly.

B. Nonverbal responses are not included.

C. Most survey recipients respond.

D. Surveys are simple to develop.

E. Prototyping of requirements is unnecessary.

A is the correct response.

5. The advantages of observation are

A. You always see people acting normally.

B. You are likely to see lots of situations in which exceptions are handled.

C. You may see the way things really are instead of the way management and/or documentation presents them.

D. The Hawthorne effect enhances your results.

E. You may observe events that would not be described to you by anyone.

C and **E** are correct responses.

6. **The advantages of document reviews are**

   A. Pictures and diagrams are valuable tools for understanding systems.

   B. Document reviews can be done relatively quickly.

   C. Documents will always be up to date.

   D. Documents will always reflect current practices.

   E. Documents often present overviews better than other techniques can.

   A, **B**, and **E** are correct responses.

7. **Application program modules are specified during the SDLC _____ phase.**

   conceptual design

8. **A feasibility study is often conducted during the _____ phase of an SDLC project.**

   planning

9. **Normalization takes place during the _____ phase of an SDLC project.**

   logical design

10. **DDL is written to define database objects during the _____ phase of an SDLC project.**

    physical design

11. **Program specifications are written during the _____ phase of an SDLC project.**

    logical design

12. **During implementation and rollout,**

    A. Users are placed on the live system.

    B. Enhancements are designed.

    C. The old and new applications may be run in parallel.

    D. Quality assurance testing takes place.

    E. User training takes place.

    A, **C**, and **E** are correct responses.

13. **During ongoing support,**

    A. Enhancements are immediately implemented.

    B. Storage for the database may require expansion.

    C. The staging environment is no longer required.

    D. Bug fixes may take place.

    E. Patches may be applied if needed.

    B, **D**, and **E** are correct responses.

14. **When requirements are sketchy, _____ can work well.**

prototyping

15. **Rapid Application Development develops systems rapidly by skipping _____.**

20 percent of the requirements

16. **The three objectives depicted in the application triangle are _____, _____, and _____.**

Quality, cost, delivery time (or good, fast, and cheap)

17. **The database is initially constructed in the _____ environment.**

development

18. **Database conversion is tested during the _____ phase of an SDLC project.**

implementation and rollout

19. **User views are analyzed during the _____ phase of an SDLC project.**

requirements gathering

20. **The relational database was invented by _____.**

E.F. (Ted) Codd

Chapter 6: Database Design Using Normalization

1. **Normalization**

A. Was developed by E.F. Codd

B. Was first introduced with five normal forms

C. First appeared in 1972

D. Provides a set of rules for each normal form

E. Provides a procedure for converting relations to each normal form

A, **C**, **D**, and **E** are correct answers.

2. **The purpose of normalization is**

A. To eliminate redundant data

B. To remove certain anomalies from the relations

C. To provide a reason to denormalize the database

D. To optimize data-retrieval performance

E. To optimize data for inserts, updates, and deletes

B and **E** are correct answers.

3. **When implemented, a third normal form relation becomes a(n) _____.**

table

4. **The insert anomaly refers to a situation in which**

A. Data must be inserted before it can be deleted.

B. Too many inserts cause the table to fill up.

C. Data must be deleted before it can be inserted.

D. A required insert cannot be done due to an artificial dependency.

E. A required insert cannot be done due to duplicate data.

D is the correct answer.

5. **The delete anomaly refers to a situation in which**

A. Data must be deleted before it can be inserted.

B. Data must be inserted before it can be deleted.

C. Data deletion causes unintentional loss of another entity's data.

D. A required delete cannot be done due to referential constraints.

E. A required delete cannot be done due to lack of privileges.

C is the correct answer.

6. **The update anomaly refers to a situation in which**

A. A simple update requires updates to multiple rows of data.

B. Data cannot be updated because it does not exist in the database.

C. Data cannot be updated due to lack of privileges.

D. Data cannot be updated due to an existing unique constraint.

E. Data cannot be updated due to an existing referential constraint.

A is the correct answer.

7. **The roles of unique identifiers in normalization are**

A. They are unnecessary.

B. They are required once you reach third normal form.

C. All normalized forms require designation of a primary key.

D. You cannot normalize relations without first choosing a primary key.

E. You cannot choose a primary key until relations are normalized.

C and **D** are correct answers.

8. **Writing sample user views with representative data in them is**

   A. The only way to normalize the user views successfully

   B. A tedious and time-consuming process

   C. An effective way to understand the data being normalized

   D. Only as good as the examples shown in the sample data

   E. A widely used normalization technique

       B, **C**, and **D** are correct responses.

9. **Criteria useful in selecting a primary key from among several candidate keys are**

   A. Choose the simplest candidate.

   B. Choose the shortest candidate.

   C. Choose the candidate most likely to have its value change.

   D. Choose concatenated keys over single attribute keys.

   E. Invent a surrogate key if that is the best possible key.

       A, **B**, and **E** are correct responses.

10. **First normal form resolves anomalies caused by _____.**

    multivalued attributes

11. **Second normal form resolves anomalies caused by _____.**

    partial dependencies

12. **Third normal form resolves anomalies caused by _____.**

    transitive dependencies

13. **In general, violations of a normalization rule are resolved by**

    A. Combining relations

    B. Moving attributes or groups of attributes to a new relation

    C. Combining attributes

    D. Creating summary tables

    E. Denormalization

        B is the correct answer.

14. **A foreign key in a normalized relation may be**

    A. The entire primary key of the relation

    B. Part of the primary key of the relation

C. A repeating group

D. A non-key attribute in the relation

E. A multivalued attribute

    A, B, and **D** are correct answers.

15. Boyce-Codd Normal Form deals with anomalies caused by _____.

determinants that are not primary or candidate keys

16. Fourth normal form deals with anomalies caused by _____.

multivalued attributes

17. Fifth normal form deals with anomalies caused by _____.

join dependencies

18. Domain key normal form deals with anomalies caused by _____.

constraints that are not the result of the definitions of domains and keys

19. Most business systems require that you normalize only as far as _____:

third normal form

20. Proper handling of multivalued attributes when converting relations to first normal form usually prevents subsequent problems with _____.

fourth normal form

Chapter 7: Data and Process Modeling

1. Why is it important for a database designer to understand process modeling?

A. Process design is a primary responsibility of the DBA.

B. The process model must be completed before the data model.

C. The data model must be completed before the process model.

D. The database designer must work closely with the process designer.

E. The database design must support the intended process model.

    D and **E** are correct answers.

2. Peter Chen's ERD format represents "many" with _____.

the symbol *M* placed near the end of the relationship line

3. The diamond in Chen's ERD format represents a(n) _____.

relationship

4. **The relational ERD format represents "many" with _____.**

   a crow's foot

5. **The IDEF1X ERD format**

   A. Was first released in 1983

   B. Follows a standard developed by the National Institute of Standards and Technology

   C. Has many variants

   D. Has been adopted as a standard by many U.S. government agencies

   E. Covers both data and process models

   B and **D** are correct answers.

6. **The IDEF1X ERD format shows**

   A. Identifying relationships with a solid line

   B. Minimal cardinality using a combination of small circles and vertical lines shown on the relationship line

   C. Maximum cardinality using a combination of small vertical lines and crow's feet drawn on the relationship line

   D. Dependent entities with squared corners on the rectangle

   E. Independent entities with rounded corners on the rectangle

   A is the correct answer.

7. **A subtype**

   A. Is a subset of the super type

   B. Has a one-to-many relationship with the super type

   C. Has a conditional one-to-one relationship with the super type

   D. Shows various states of the super type

   E. Is a superset of the super type

   A and **C** are correct answers.

8. **Examples of possible subtypes for an Order entity super type include**

   A. Order line items

   B. Shipped order, unshipped order, invoiced order

   C. Office supplies order, professional services order

   D. Approved order, pending order, canceled order

E. Auto parts order, aircraft parts order, truck parts order

C and **E** are correct answers.

9. **In IE notation, subtypes**

A. May be shown with a type discriminator attribute name

B. May be connected to the super type via a symbol composed of a circle with a line under it

C. Have the primary key of the subtype shown as a foreign key in the super type

D. Usually have the same primary key as the super type

E. May be shown using a crow's foot

A, **B**, and **D** are correct answers.

10. **When subtypes are being considered in a database design, a tradeoff exists between _____ and _____.**

generalization, specialization

11. **In a flowchart, process steps are shown as _____ and decision points are shown as _____.**

rectangles, diamonds

12. **The strengths of flowcharts are**

A. They are natural and easy to use for procedural language programmers.

B. They are useful for spotting reusable components.

C. They are specific to application programming only.

D. They are equally useful for nonprocedural and object-oriented languages.

E. They can be easily modified as requirements change.

A, **B**, and **E** are correct answers.

13. **The basic components of a function hierarchy diagram are**

A. Ellipses to show attributes

B. Rectangles to show process functions

C. Lines connecting the processes in order of execution

D. A hierarchy to show which functions are subordinate to others

E. Diamonds to show decision points

B and **D** are correct answers.

14. **The strengths of the function hierarchy diagram are**

A. Checking quality is easy and straightforward.

B. Complex interactions between functions are easily modeled.

C. It is quick and easy to learn and use.

D. It clearly shows the sequence of process steps.

E. It provides a good overview at high and medium levels of detail.

C and **E** are correct answers.

15. **The basic components of a swim lane diagram are**

A. Lines with arrows to show the sequence of process steps

B. Diamonds to show decision points

C. Vertical lanes to show the organization units that carry out process steps

D. Ellipses to show process steps

E. Open-ended rectangles to show data stores

A, C, and **D** are correct answers.

16. **The data flow diagram (DFD)**

A. Is the most data-centric of all process models

B. Was first developed in the 1980s

C. Combines diagram pages together hierarchically

D. Was first developed by E.F. Codd

E. Combines the best of the flowchart and the function diagram

A, C, and **E** are correct answers.

17. **In a DFD, data stores are shown as _____ and processes are shown as _____.**

open-ended rectangles, rounded rectangles

18. **The strengths of the DFD are**

A. It's good for top-down design work.

B. It's quick and easy to develop, even for complex systems.

C. It shows overall structure without sacrificing detail.

D. It shows complex logic easily.

E. It's great for presentation to management.

A, C, and **E** are correct answers.

19. **The components of the CRUD matrix are**

A. Ellipses to show attributes

B. Major processes shown on one axis

C. Major entities shown on the other axis

D. Reference numbers to show the hierarchy of processes

E. Letters to show the operations that processes carry out on entities

B, **C**, and **E** are correct answers.

20. **The CRUD matrix helps find the following problems:**

A. Entities that are never read

B. Processes that are never deleted

C. Processes that only read

D. Entities that are never updated

E. Processes that have no create entity

A, **C**, and **D** are correct answers.

Chapter 8: Physical Database Design

1. **Business rules are implemented in the database using _____.**

constraints

2. **Two key differences between unique constraints and primary key constraints are _____ and _____.**

a table may have only one primary key constraint; columns referenced in primary key constraints must be defined as NOT NULL

3. **Relationships in the logical model become _____ in the physical model.**

referential constraints

4. **Constraint names are important because _____.**

they appear in error messages

5. **When you're designing tables,**

A. Each normalized relation becomes a table.

B. Each attribute in the relation becomes a table column.

C. Relationships become check constraints.

D. Unique identifiers become triggers.

E. Primary key columns must be defined as NOT NULL.

A, **B**, and **E** are correct answers.

6. Super types and subtypes

A. Must be implemented exactly as specified in the logical design

B. May be collapsed in the physical database design

C. May have the super type columns folded into each subtype in the physical design

D. Usually have the same primary key in the physical tables

E. Apply only to the logical design

  B, **C**, and **D** are correct answers.

7. Table names

A. Should be based on the attribute names in the logical design

B. Should always include the word "table"

C. Should use only uppercase letters

D. Should include organization or location names

E. May contain abbreviations when necessary

  C and **E** are correct answers.

8. Column names

A. Must be unique within the database

B. Should be based on the corresponding attribute names in the logical design

C. Must be prefixed with the table name

D. Must be unique within the table

E. Should use abbreviations whenever possible

  B and **D** are correct answers.

9. Referential constraints

A. Define relationships identified in the logical model

B. Are always defined on the parent table

C. Require that foreign keys be defined as NOT NULL

D. Should have descriptive names

E. Name the parent and child tables and the foreign key column

  A and **D** are correct answers.

10. Check constraints

A. May be used to force a column to match a list of values

B. May be used to force a column to match a range of values

C. May be used to force a column to match another column in the same row

D. May be used to force a column to match a column in another table

E. May be used to enforce a foreign key constraint

A, **B**, and **C** are correct answers.

11. Data types

A. Prevent incorrect data from being inserted into a table

B. Can be used to prevent alphabetic characters from being stored in numeric columns

C. Can be used to prevent numeric characters from being stored in character format columns

D. Require that precision and scale be specified also

E. Can be used to prevent invalid dates from being stored in date columns

B and **E** are correct answers.

12. View restrictions include which of the following?

A. Views containing joins can never be updated.

B. Updates to calculated columns in views are prohibited.

C. Privileges are required in order to update data using views.

D. If a view omits a mandatory column, inserts to the view are not possible.

E. Any update involving a view may reference columns only from one table.

B, **C**, **D**, and **E** are correct answers.

13. Some advantages of views are

A. Views may provide performance advantages.

B. Views may insulate database users from table and column name changes.

C. Views may be used to hide joins and complex calculations.

D. Views may filter columns or rows that users should not see.

E. Views may be tailored to the needs of individual departments.

A, **B**, **C**, **D**, and **E** are correct answers.

14. Indexes

A. May be used to assist with primary key constraints

B. May be used to improve query performance

C. May be used to improve insert, update, and delete performance

D. Are usually smaller than the tables they reference

E. Are slower to sequentially scan than corresponding tables

A, **B**, and **D** are correct answers.

15. **General rules to follow regarding indexes include which of the following?**

    A. The larger the table, the more important indexes become.

    B. Indexing foreign key columns often helps join performance.

    C. Columns that are frequently updated should always be indexed.

    D. The more a table is updated, the more indexes will help performance.

    E. Indexes on very small tables tend not to be very useful.

    A, **B**, and **E** are correct answers.

Chapter 9: Connecting Databases to the Outside World

1. **In the centralized deployment model,**

    A. A web server hosts all web pages.

    B. A "dumb" terminal is used as the client workstation.

    C. Administration is quite easy because everything is centralized.

    D. There are no single points of failure.

    E. Development costs are often very high.

    B and **C** are correct answers.

2. **In the distributed deployment model,**

    A. The database and/or application is partitioned and deployed on multiple computer systems.

    B. Initial deployments were highly successful.

    C. Distribution can be transparent to the user.

    D. Costs and complexity are reduced compared with the centralized model.

    E. Fault tolerance is improved compared with the centralized model.

    A, **C**, and **E** are correct answers.

3. **In the two-tier client/server model,**

    A. All application logic runs on an application server.

    B. A web server hosts the web pages.

    C. The client workstation handles all presentation logic.

    D. The database is hosted on a centralized server.

E. Client workstations must be high-powered systems.

C, **D**, and **E** are correct answers.

4. In the three-tier client/server model,

A. All application logic runs on an application server.

B. A web server hosts the web pages.

C. The client workstation handles all presentation logic.

D. The database is hosted on a centralized server.

E. Client workstations must be high-powered systems.

A, **C**, and **D** are correct answers.

5. In the N-tier client/server model,

A. All application logic runs on an application server.

B. A web server hosts the web pages.

C. The client workstation handles all presentation logic.

D. The database is hosted on a centralized server.

E. Client workstations must be high-powered systems.

A, **B**, **C**, and **D** are correct answers.

6. The Internet

A. Began as the U.S. Department of Education's ARPANET

B. Dates back to the late 1960s and early 1970s

C. Always used TCP/IP as a standard

D. Is a worldwide collection of interconnected computer networks

E. Supports multiple protocols, including HTTP, FTP, and Telnet

B, **D**, and **E** are correct answers.

7. A URL may contain

A. A protocol

B. A host name or IP address

C. A port

D. The absolute path to a resource on the web server

E. Arguments

A, **B**, **C**, **D**, and **E** are correct answers.

8. **An intranet is available to _____.**

   authorized internal members of an organization

9. **An extranet is available to _____.**

   authorized outsiders

10. **The World Wide Web uses _____ to navigate pages.**

    hyperlinks

11. **HTTP does not directly support the concept of a session because it is _____.**

    stateless

12. **XML is extensible because _____ can be defined.**

    custom tags

13. **Middleware solutions for Java connections made the RDBMS look like a(n) _____.**

    object-oriented database

14. **The web "technology stack" includes**

    A. A client workstation running a web browser

    B. A web server

    C. An application server

    D. A database server

    E. Network hardware (firewalls, routers, and so on)

    A, B, C, D, and **E** are correct answers.

15. **The advantages of CGI are**

    A. Statelessness

    B. Simplicity

    C. Inherently secure

    D. Widely accepted

    E. Language and server independent

    B, D, and **E** are correct answers.

16. **Server Side Includes (SSI)**

    A. Are commands embedded in a web document

    B. Are non-CGI gateways

    C. Are HTML macros

D. Solve some of the CGI performance issues

E. Are inherently secure

   A, **C**, and **D** are correct answers.

17. **The advantages of a non-CGI gateway are**

A. Known for stability

B. Proprietary solution

C. Improved security over CGI solutions

D. Simpler than CGI

E. Runs in server address space

   C and **E** are correct answers.

18. **ODBC is**

A. A standard API for connecting to DBMSs

B. Independent of any particular language, operating system, or DBMS

C. A Microsoft standard

D. Used by Java programs

E. Flexible in handling proprietary SQL

   A, **B**, and **E** are correct answers.

19. **JDBC is**

A. A standard API for connecting to DBMSs

B. Independent of any particular language, operating system, or DBMS

C. A Microsoft standard

D. Used by Java programs

E. Flexible in handling proprietary SQL

   A, **D**, and **E** are correct answers.

20. **JSQL is**

A. A Sun Microsystems standard

B. A method of embedding SQL statements in Java

C. An extension of an ISO/ANSI standard

D. A middleware solution

E. Independent of any particular language, operating system, or DBMS

   B and **C** are correct answers.

Chapter 10: Database Security

1. A collection of privileges that can be granted to multiple users is called a _____.

   role

2. Privileges are rescinded using the SQL _____ command.

   REVOKE

3. For database servers connected to a network, physical security alone is _____.

   inadequate

4. Employees connecting to the enterprise network from home or another remote work location should have a _____ between the computer and the cable or DSL modem.

   firewall

5. When login credentials are stored in the computer system, they must always be _____.

   encrypted

6. Network security

   A. Can be handled by routers alone

   B. Can be handled by firewalls alone

   C. Must include provisions for remotely located employees

   D. Should be mandatory for all computer systems connected to any network

   C and **D** are correct responses.

7. Firewall protection may include

   A. Packet filtering

   B. Packet selection using a routing table

   C. Network address translation

   D. Limiting ports that may be used for access

   E. IP spoofing

   A, **C**, and **D** are correct responses.

8. Wireless networks need to be secured because

   A. Inexpensive wireless access points are readily available.

   B. Anyone with a wireless network adapter can connect to an unprotected network.

   C. Employees may use the wireless network to communicate secretly with hackers.

   D. Radio waves penetrate walls to adjoining offices.

E. Radio waves may carry to public roads outside the building.

A, **B**, **D**, and **E** are correct responses.

9. **Components of wireless access point security include**

A. Network address translation

B. The organization's security policy

C. Encryption

D. Virtual private networks

E. MAC address lists

B, **C**, and **E** are correct responses.

10. **System-level security precautions include**

A. Installing the minimal software components necessary

B. Granting only table privileges that users require

C. Applying security patches in a timely manner

D. Changing all default passwords

E. Using simple passwords that are easy to remember

A, **C**, and **D** are correct responses.

11. **Encryption**

A. Should be used for all sensitive data

B. Should use keys of at least 28 bits in length

C. Should be used for sensitive data sent over a network

D. Can use symmetric or asymmetric keys

E. Should never be used for login credentials

A, **C**, and **D** are correct responses.

12. **Client security considerations include which of the following?**

A. MAC address lists

B. Web browser security level

C. Granting only database table privileges that are absolutely necessary

D. Use of a virus scanner

E. Testing of application exposures

B, **D**, and **E** are correct responses.

13. In Microsoft SQL Server, a login (user login)

    A. Can connect to any number of databases

    B. Automatically has database access privileges

    C. Can use Windows authentication

    D. Can be authenticated by Microsoft SQL Server

    E. Owns a database schema

        A, **C**, and **D** are correct responses.

14. In Microsoft SQL Server, a database

    A. Is owned by a login

    B. May have one or more users assigned to it

    C. May contain system data (for example, master) or user (application) data

    D. May be granted privileges

    E. Is a logical collection of database objects

        B, **C**, and **E** are correct responses.

15. In Oracle, a user account

    A. Can connect (log in) to any number of databases

    B. Automatically has database privileges

    C. Can use operating system authentication

    D. Can be authenticated by the Oracle DBMS

    E. Owns a database schema

        B, **C**, **D**, and **E** are correct responses.

16. In Oracle, a database

    A. Is owned by a user

    B. May have one or more user accounts defined in it

    C. May contain system data (for example, system schema) and user (application) data

    D. Is the same as a schema

    E. Is managed by an Oracle instance

        B, **C**, and **E** are correct responses.

17. System privileges

    A. Are granted in a similar way in Oracle, Sybase ASE, and Microsoft SQL Server

    B. Are specific to a database object

C. Allow the grantee to perform certain administrative functions on the server, such as shutting it down

D. Are rescinded using the SQL REMOVE statement

E. Vary across databases from different vendors

    A, **C**, and **E** are correct responses.

18. Object privileges

A. Are granted in a similar way in Oracle, Sybase ASE, and Microsoft SQL Server

B. Are specific to a database object

C. Allow the grantee to perform certain administrative functions on the server, such as shutting it down

D. Are rescinded using the SQL REMOVE statement

E. Are granted using the SQL GRANT statement

    A, **B**, and **E** are correct responses.

19. Using WITH GRANT OPTION when granting object privileges

A. Allows the grantee to grant the privilege to others

B. Gives the grantee DBA privileges on the entire database

C. Can lead to security issues

D. Will cascade if the privilege is subsequently revoked

E. Is a highly recommended practice because it is so convenient to use

    A, **C**, and **D** are correct responses.

20. Views may assist with security policy implementation by

A. Restricting the table columns to which a user has access

B. Restricting the databases to which a user has access

C. Restricting table rows to which a user has access

D. Storing database audit results

E. Monitoring for database intruders

    A and **C** are correct responses.

Chapter 11: Deploying Databases

1. A cursor is _____.

a pointer into a result set

2. A result set is _____.

the collection of rows returned by a database query

3. The *I* in the ACID acronym stands for _____.

isolation

4. Before rows may be fetched from a cursor, the cursor must first be

A. Declared

B. Committed

C. Opened

D. Closed

E. Purged

A and **C** are correct responses.

5. A transaction

A. May be partially processed and committed

B. May not be partially processed and committed

C. Changes the database from one consistent state to another

D. Is sometimes called a unit of work

E. Has properties described by the ACID acronym

B, **C**, **D**, and **E** are correct responses.

6. Microsoft SQL Server supports the following transaction modes:

A. Autocommit

B. Automatic

C. Durable

D. Explicit

E. Implicit

A, **D**, and **E** are correct responses.

7. Oracle supports the following transaction modes:

A. Autocommit

B. Automatic

C. Durable

D. Explicit

E. Implicit

A and **E** are correct responses.

8. The SQL statements (commands) that end a transaction are

A. SET AUTOCOMMIT

B. BEGIN TRANSACTION (in SQL Server)

C. COMMIT

D. ROLLBACK

E. SAVEPOINT

    C and **D** are correct responses.

9. The concurrent update problem

A. Is a consequence of simultaneous data sharing

B. Cannot occur when AUTOCOMMIT is set to ON

C. Is the reason that transaction locking must be supported

D. Occurs when two database users submit conflicting SELECT statements

E. Occurs when two database users make conflicting updates to the same data

    A, C, and **E** are correct responses.

10. A lock

A. Is a control placed on data to reserve it so that the user may update it

B. Is usually released when a COMMIT or ROLLBACK takes place

C. Has a timeout set in DB2 and some other RDBMS products

D. May cause contention when other users attempt to update locked data

E. May have levels and an escalation protocol in some RDBMS products

    A, B, C, D, and **E** are correct responses.

11. A deadlock

A. Is a lock that has timed out and is therefore no longer needed

B. Occurs when two database users each request a lock on data that is locked by the other

C. Can theoretically put two or more users in an endless lock wait state

D. May be resolved by deadlock detection on some RDBMSs

E. May be resolved by lock timeouts on some RDBMSs

    B, C, D, and **E** are correct responses.

12. Performance tuning

A. Is a never-ending process

B. Should be used on each query until no more improvement can be realized

C. Should be used only on queries that fail to conform to performance requirements

D. Involves not only SQL tuning but also CPU, file system I/O, and memory usage tuning

E. Should be requirements based

A, **C**, **D**, and **E** are correct responses.

13. **SQL query tuning**

A. Can be done in the same way for all relational database systems

B. Usually involves using an explain plan facility

C. Always involves placing SQL statements in a stored procedure

D. Applies only to SQL SELECT statements

E. Requires detailed knowledge of the RDBMS on which the query is to be run

B and **E** are correct responses.

14. **General SQL tuning tips include which of the following?**

A. Avoid table scans on large tables.

B. Use an index whenever possible.

C. Use an ORDER BY clause whenever possible.

D. Use a WHERE clause to filter rows whenever possible.

E. Use views whenever possible.

A, **B**, and **D** are correct responses.

15. **SQL practices that obviate the use of an index are**

A. Use of a WHERE clause

B. Use of a NOT operator

C. Use of table joins

D. Use of the NOT EQUAL operator

E. Use of wildcards in the first column of LIKE comparison strings

B, **D**, and **E** are correct responses.

16. **Indexes work well at filtering rows when**

A. They are very selective.

B. The selectivity ratio is very high.

C. The selectivity ratio is very low.

D. They are unique.

E. They are not unique.

> **A**, **B**, and **D** are correct responses.

17. **The main performance considerations for INSERT statements are**

    A. Row expansion

    B. Index maintenance

    C. Free space usage

    D. Subquery tuning

    E. Any very large tables that are involved

    > **B** and **C** are correct responses.

18. **The main performance considerations for UPDATE statements are**

    A. Row expansion

    B. Index maintenance

    C. Free space usage

    D. Subquery tuning

    E. Any very large tables that are involved

    > **A** and **B** are correct responses.

19. **A change control process**

    A. Can prevent programming errors from being placed into production

    B. May also be called change management

    C. Helps with understanding when changes may be installed

    D. Provides a log of all changes made

    E. Can allow defective software versions to be backed out

    > **B**, **C**, **D**, and **E** are correct responses.

20. **Common features of change control processes include which of the following?**

    A. Transaction support

    B. Version numbering

    C. Deadlock prevention

    D. Release numbering

    E. Prioritization

    > **B**, **D**, and **E** are correct responses.

Chapter 12: Databases for Online Analytical Processing

1. **OLTP databases are designed to handle _____ transaction volumes.**

   high

2. **OLAP queries typically access _____ amounts of data.**

   large

3. **Compared with OLTP systems, data warehouse systems tend to have _____ running queries.**

   longer

4. **Data warehousing was pioneered by _____.**

   Bill Inmon

5. **The process of moving from more summarized data to more detailed data is known as _____.**

   drilling down

6. **The snowflake schema allows dimensions to have _____.**

   dimensions of their own

7. **The starflake schema is a hybrid containing both _____ and _____ dimensions.**

   normalized, denormalized

8. **A data warehouse is**

   A. Subject oriented

   B. Integrated from multiple data sources

   C. Time variant

   D. Updated in real time

   E. Organized around one department or business function

   A, **B**, and **C** are correct answers.

9. **Challenges with the data warehouse approach include**

   A. Updating operational data from the data warehouse

   B. Underestimation of required resources

   C. Diminishing user demands

   D. Large, complex projects

   E. High resource demands

   B, **D**, and **E** are correct answers.

10. **The summary table architecture**

A. Was originally developed by Bill Inmon

B. Includes a fact table

C. Includes dimension tables

D. Includes lightly and highly summarized tables

E. Should include metadata

A, **D**, and **E** are correct answers.

11. **The star schema**

A. Was developed by Ralph Kimball

B. Includes a dimension table and one or more fact tables

C. Always has fully normalized dimension tables

D. Was a key feature of the Red Brick DBMS

E. Involves multiple levels of dimension tables

A and **D** are correct answers.

12. **Factors to consider in designing the fact table include**

A. Adding columns to the fact table

B. Reducing column sizes between the source and fact tables

C. Partitioning the fact table

D. How often it must be updated

E. How long history must remain in it

B, **C**, **D**, and **E** are correct answers.

13. **Multidimensional databases**

A. Use a fully normalized fact table

B. Are best visualized as cubes

C. Have fully normalized dimension tables

D. Are sometimes called MOLAP databases

E. Accommodate dimensions beyond the third by repeating cubes for each additional dimension

B, **D**, and **E** are correct answers.

14. **A data mart**

A. Is a subset of a data warehouse

B. Is a shop that sells data to individuals and businesses

C. Supports the requirements of a particular department or business function

D. Can be a good starting point for organizations with no data warehouse experience

E. Can be a good starting point when requirements are sketchy

A, C, D, and **E** are correct answers.

15. **Reasons to create a data mart include**

A. It is more comprehensive than a data warehouse.

B. It is a potentially lower risk project.

C. Data may be tailored to a particular department or business function.

D. It contains more data than a data warehouse.

E. The project has a lower overall cost than a data warehouse project.

B, C, and **E** are correct answers.

16. **Building a data warehouse first, followed by data marts**

A. Will delay data mart deployment if the data warehouse project drags on

B. Has lower risk than trying to build them all together

C. Has the lowest risk of the three possible strategies

D. Has the highest risk of the three possible strategies

E. May require a great deal of rework

A and **B** are correct answers.

17. **Building one or more data marts first, followed by the data warehouse**

A. May delay data warehouse delivery if the data mart projects drag on

B. Has the potential to deliver some OLAP functions more quickly

C. Has the lowest risk of the three possible strategies

D. Has the highest risk of the three possible strategies

E. May require a great deal of rework

B, C, and **E** are correct answers.

18. **Building the data warehouse and data marts simultaneously**

A. Creates the largest single project of all the possible strategies

B. Has the potential to take the longest to deliver any OLAP functions

C. Has the lowest risk of the three possible strategies

D. Has the highest risk of the three possible strategies

E. May require a great deal of rework

    A, **B**, and **D** are correct answers

19. Data mining

A. Creates a scaled-down data warehouse

B. Extracts previously unknown data correlations from the data warehouse

C. Can be successful with small amounts of data

D. Is most useful when the organization is agile enough to take action based on the information

E. Usually requires large data volumes in order to produce accurate results

    B, **D**, and **E** are correct answers.

20. Properties of data warehouse systems include

A. Holding historic rather than current information

B. Long-running queries that process many rows of data

C. Support for day-to-day operations

D. Process orientation

E. Medium to low transaction volume

    A, **B**, and **E** are correct answers.

Chapter 13: Integrating XML Documents and Objects into Databases

1. XML is _____.

a general-purpose markup language used to describe data

2. How do SQL databases and XML documents vary in terms of data structure?

XML defines sequence and a hierarchical tree structure, while SQL does not.

3. If two organizations are both using XML, does that mean that they have a standard way of exchanging data without having to create interface software?

Not necessarily. The two organizations must use a common definition for the elements within the XML documents to be exchanged before they can process them without the need to perform any interpretation or conversion.

4. The valid secondary type modifiers for the SEQUENCE type modifier are _____.

The SEQUENCE type modifier cannot have a secondary type modifier.

5. The _____ XML schema type is mapped from the SQL NUMERIC data type.

   xs:decimal

6. The _____ XML schema type is mapped from the SQL DATE data type.

   xs:date

7. The two ways that null values from the database can be represented by SQL/XML are _____ and _____.

   Absent element, **xsi:nil="true"**

8. Which of the following are common uses of XML?

   A. Display database data on a web page

   B. Create static web pages

   C. Transmit database data to another party

   D. Enforce business rules on documents

   A and **C** are correct answers.

9. Which of the following are valid type modifiers for the XML data type?

   A. DOCUMENT

   B. SEQUENCE

   C. SQLXML

   D. CONTENT

   A, **B**, and **D** are correct answers.

10. Which of the following SQL/XML functions creates an element based on a table column?

    A. XMLQUERY

    B. XMLELEMENT

    C. XMLFOREST

    D. XMLDOCUMENT

    E. XMLPARSE

    C is the correct answer.

11. **Object-oriented programming**

    A. Uses messages as a vehicle for object interaction

    B. Allows an object to directly access the variables in a related object

    C. Uses methods to define the behavior of an object

D. Requires objects to have a primary key

E. Supports the use of complex objects

A, C, and E are correct answers.

12. **Object-oriented (OO) applications**

A. Require the use of an OO database

B. Are written in an OO language

C. Use development environments that usually come with predefined classes

D. Use development environments that usually come with predefined methods

E. May be written it the C programming language

B, C, and D are correct answers.

13. **Smalltalk**

A. Was developed by Linus Torvalds

B. Was developed in 1972

C. Was developed at the Xerox PARC facility

D. Is based on the C programming language

E. Was the first OO programming language to include a windowing system and use of a mouse

B, C, and E are correct answers.

14. **C++**

A. Was developed by Alan Kay

B. Was developed in 1976

C. Was developed at AT&T Bell Laboratories

D. Is based on the Java programming language

E. Allows programmers to ignore the object paradigm if they wish

C and E are correct answers.

15. **Java**

A. Was developed by Sun Microsystems

B. May be run only on large systems with lots of memory

C. Was developed around 1995

D. Is an interpretive language

E. Is a general-purpose OO language

A, C, D, and E are correct answers.

16. **Object persistence**

    A. Preserves the state of an object between executions of an application

    B. Preserves the state of an object across the shutdown and startup of the computer system

    C. Loads objects into memory to preserve them permanently

    D. Occurs when the application requests that an object be saved

    E. Can be accomplished only with an OO database

    A, **B**, and **D** are correct answers.

17. **The events necessary to retrieve an object from an OO database include**

    A. A message is sent to the object, so the object must be loaded into memory.

    B. A request to retrieve the object is sent to the OO database.

    C. Object references are swizzled into memory addresses.

    D. Relational data is assigned to an object class.

    E. The object is made available to the application environment.

    A, **B**, **C**, and **E** are correct answers.

18. **The advantages of object-relational databases include**

    A. Objects are stored within tables.

    B. Complex data types are supported.

    C. Ad-hoc query capability is fully supported.

    D. Class structures and inheritance are fully supported.

    E. Centrally stored functions (methods) improve reuse.

    B, **C**, and **E** are correct answers.

19. **The disadvantages of object-relational databases include**

    A. The combination is more complex than either pure object-oriented or pure relational databases.

    B. Ad-hoc query capability is limited.

    C. Objects are table-centric.

    D. Neither relational purists nor object purists are enamored with this combination.

    E. Object applications are not as data-centric as relational ones.

    A, **C**, **D**, and **E** are correct answers.

20. **When considering the selection of a database model, which of the following facts should be taken into account?**

A. Ordinary file system files can handle simple data, provided there are no ad-hoc query requirements.

B. Relational databases can handle simple data that has ad-hoc query requirements.

C. Object-oriented databases are best at handling complex data.

D. Object-relational databases can handle complex data that has ad-hoc query requirements.

E. Object-oriented databases can handle complex data, provided there are no ad-hoc query requirements.

A, B, C, D, and E are correct answers.

Appendix B

Solutions to the Try This Exercises

This appendix contains my solutions to the Try This exercises contained in various chapters. In any design endeavor, many solutions are possible. Database design is no different in this regard; it is not an exact science, and therefore there is some latitude for alternative solutions. If your solution is different from mine, that does not necessarily mean that your solution is incorrect, provided your solution meets the requirements stated in the exercise.

The source files for these solutions may also be downloaded from the McGraw-Hill Professional website. Follow these steps to download the files:

1. Open your web browser and go to www.mhprofessional.com.

2. In the Search box, near the top of the page, type Databases A Beginner's Guide and click SEARCH.

3. Click on the displayed image of the book to display the book's information page.

4. Find the download links under the image of the book along the left margin. Select the files you want and either click to open them or right-click to save them to your personal computer.

Try This 5-1 Solution: Project Database Management Tasks

Project Phase	Task
Planning	w. Evaluate available DBMS options
Requirements Gathering	f. Determine the views required by the business users
	r. Identify the attributes required by the business users
	t. Identify and document business data requirements
Conceptual Design	l. Specify a logical name for each entity and attribute
	q. Document business rules that cannot be represented in the data model
	s. Identify the relationships between the entities
Logical Design	a. Normalization
	b. Add foreign keys to the database
	d. Specify the unique identifier for each relation
	g. Remove data that is easily derived
	h. Resolve many-to-many relationships
	l. Specify a logical name for each entity and attribute
	p. Translate the conceptual data model into a logical model

	q. Document business rules that cannot be represented in the data model
	s. Identify the relationships between the entities
Physical Design	c. Specify the physical placement of database objects on storage media
	e. Specify the primary key for each table
	j. Modify the database to meet business requirements
	m. Specify a physical name for each table and column
	o. Specify database indexes
Construction	i. Define views in the database
	u. Ensure that user data requirements are met
Implementation and Support	k. Denormalize the database for performance
	n. Add derivable data to improve performance
	v. Tune the database to improve performance
Ongoing Support	j. Modify the database to meet business requirements
	k. Denormalize the database for performance
	n. Add derivable data to improve performance
	u Ensure that user data requirements are met
	v. Tune the database to improve performance

Try This 6-1 Solution: UTLA Academic Tracking

Here are the normalized relations for Try This 6-1, with (**PK**) denoting primary key attributes:

```
COURSE: COURSE ID (PK), TITLE, DESCRIPTION, NUMBER OF CREDITS

INSTRUCTOR: INSTRUCTOR ID (PK), INSTRUCTOR NAME, HOME ADDRESS STREET,
            HOME ADDRESS CITY, HOME ADDRESS STATE,
            HOME ADDRESS ZIP CODE, HOME PHONE, OFFICE PHONE

COURSE SECTION: SECTION ID (PK), CALENDAR_YEAR, SEMESTER, COURSE ID,
                BUILDING, ROOM, MEETING DAY, MEETING TIME,
                INSTRUCTOR ID

STUDENT: STUDENT ID (PK), STUDENT NAME, HOME ADDRESS,
         HOME ADDRESS CITY, HOME ADDRESS STATE,
         HOME ADDRESS ZIP CODE, HOME PHONE

STUDENT SECTION: STUDENT ID (PK), SECTION ID (PK), GRADE

COURSE PREREQUISITE: COURSE ID (PK), PREREQUISITE COURSE ID (PK)

COURSE INSTRUCTOR QUALIFIED: INSTRUCTOR ID (PK), COURSE ID (PK)
```

A few notes on this particular solution are in order:

- No simple natural key exists for the Course Section relation, so a surrogate key was added.

- The Course Prerequisite relation can be quite confusing. This is the intersection relation for a many-to-many recursive relationship. A course can have many prerequisites, which may be found by joining COURSE ID in the COURSE relation with COURSE ID in the COURSE PREREQUISITE relation. At the same time, any course may be a prerequisite for many other courses. These may be found by joining COURSE ID in the COURSE relation with PREREQUISITE COURSE ID in the COURSE PREREQUISITE relation. This means that *two* relationships exist between the COURSE and COURSE PREREQUISITE: one in which COURSE ID is the foreign key and another in which PREREQUISITE COURSE ID is the foreign key. Comparing the upcoming illustrations for the COURSE and COURSE_ PREREQUISITE tables should help make this point clear.

To assist you in visualizing how all this works, the following illustrations show each of the tables as implemented in a Microsoft Access database, each loaded with the data from the original user view (report) examples. The last illustration shows the ERD for the solution, using the Microsoft Relationships panel as the presentation media.

COURSE table:

INSTRUCTOR table:

COURSE_SECTION table:

SECTION_ID	CALENDAR_YEAR	SEMESTER	COURSE ID	BUILDING	ROOM	MEETING_DAY	MEETING_TIME	INSTRUCTOR_ID
1	2008	Spr	X408	Evans	70	Tu	7-10	756
2	2008	Spr	X408	SFO	7	We	7-10	756
3	2008	Spr	X100	Evans	70	M,Fr	7-9	801

STUDENT table:

STUDENT_ID	STUDENT_NAME	HOME_ADDRESS	HOME_ADDRESS_CITY	HOME_ADDRESS_STATE	HOME_ADDRESS_ZIP_CODE	HOME_PHONE
4567	Helen Wheels	127 Essex Drive	Hayward	CA	94545	510-555-2859
4973	Barry Bookworm	P.O. Box 45	Oakland	CA	94601	510-555-9403
6758	Carla Coed	South Hall #23	Berkeley	CA	94623	510-555-8742

STUDENT_SECTION table:

STUDENT_ID	SECTION_ID	GRADE
4567	1	A
4973	2	B+
6758	1	B+
6758	2	A-

COURSE_PREREQUISITE table:

COURSE_ID	PREREQUISITE_COURSE_ID
X301	X100
X302	X301
X408	X301
X408	X422
X422	X301

COURSE_INSTRUCTOR_QUALIFIED table:

ERD for TLA University:

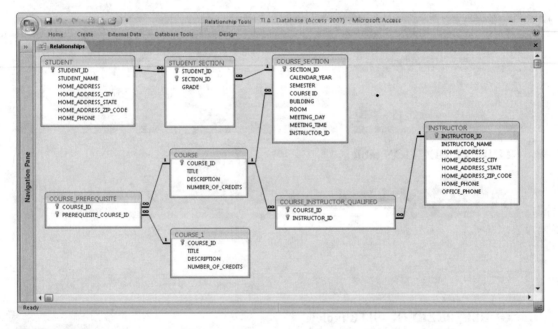

Try This 6-2 Solution: Computer Books Company

Here are the normalized relations for Try This 6-2, with primary keys noted with (**PK**):

```
BOOK: ISBN (PK), BOOK TITLE, SUBJECT CODE, PUBLISHER ID,
      EDITION CODE, EDITION COST, SELLING PRICE,
      QUANTITY ON HAND, QUANTITY ON ORDER,
      RECOMMENDED QUANTITY, PREVIOUS EDITION ISBN

CUSTOMER ORDER: CUSTOMER ORDER NUMBER (PK), CUSTOMER ID,
      ORDER DATE

CUSTOMER ORDER BOOK: CUSTOMER ORDER NUMBER (PK), ISBN (PK),
      QUANTITY, BOOK PRICE
```

SUBJECT: SUBJECT CODE (PK), DESCRIPTION

AUTHOR: AUTHOR ID (PK), AUTHOR NAME

BOOK-AUTHOR: AUTHOR ID (PK), ISBN (PK)

CUSTOMER: CUSTOMER ID (PK), CUSTOMER_NAME, STREET ADDRESS, CITY,
      STATE, ZIP CODE, PHONE NUMBER, BALANCE DUE

PUBLISHER: PUBLISHER ID (PK), PUBLISHER NAME, STREET ADDRESS,
      CITY, STATE, ZIP CODE, AMOUNT PAYABLE

SHIPPED ORDER (RECEIVABLE): SALES INVOICE NUMBER (PK),
      CUSTOMER ORDER NUMBER, SALES TAX, SHIPPING CHARGES

SHIPPED ORDER BOOK: SALES INVOICE NUMBER (PK), ISBN (PK),
      PRICE_AT_SALE, QUANTITY

PURCHASE (PAYABLE): PURCHASE INVOICE NUMBER (PK), PUBLISHER_ID,
      INVOICE DATE, INVOICE AMOUNT

PURCHASE BOOK: PURCHASE INVOICE NUMBER (PK), ISBN (PK), QUANTITY,
      COST EACH

Here is an ERD that shows the complete design, implemented in Microsoft Access:

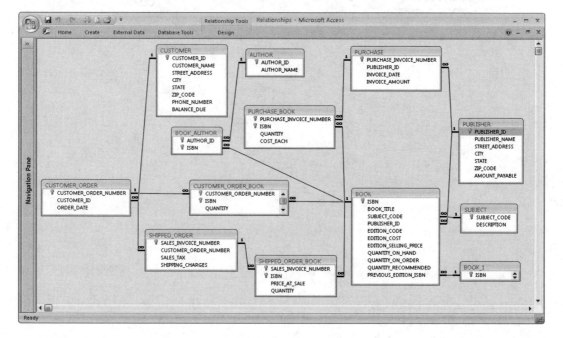

Try This 7-1 Solution: Draw an ERD in Information Engineering (IE) Format

The following illustration shows my solution to Try This 7-1:

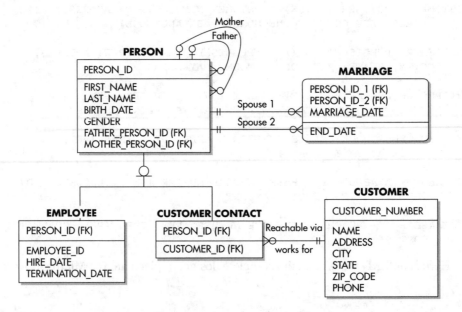

Try This 8-1 Solution: Mapping a Logical Model to a Physical Database Design

The following illustration shows my solution to Try This 8-1:

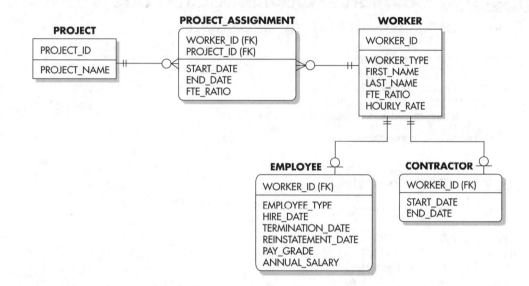

Try This 10-1 Solution: Database Object Privileges

Here are the SQL statements used in Try This exercise 10-1:

```
CREATE TABLE DEPARTMENT
   (DEPARTMENT_CODE     CHAR(3),
    DEPARTMENT_NAME     VARCHAR(50));


GRANT SELECT, INSERT ON DEPARTMENT TO USER1;

INSERT INTO DATA1.DEPARTMENT
VALUES ('001','Executive');

SELECT * FROM DATA1.DEPARTMENT
 WHERE DEPARTMENT_CODE = '001';

DELETE FROM DATA1.DEPARTMENT
 WHERE DEPARTMENT_CODE = '001';
```

```
DROP TABLE DATA1.DEPARTMENT;

DROP TABLE DEPARTMENT;
```

Try This 11-1 Solution: SQL Transaction Support

Here are the SQL statements used in Try This exercise 11-1:

```
DROP TABLE DEPARTMENT;

CREATE TABLE DEPARTMENT
   (DEPARTMENT_CODE     CHAR(3),
    DEPARTMENT_NAME     VARCHAR(50));

SET IMPLICIT_TRANSACTIONS ON

INSERT INTO DEPARTMENT
VALUES ('001','Executive');

SELECT * FROM DEPARTMENT;

ROLLBACK;

INSERT INTO DEPARTMENT
VALUES ('001','Executive');

COMMIT;

ROLLBACK;

SELECT * FROM DEPARTMENT;

DROP TABLE DEPARTMENT;
COMMIT;
```

Try This 12-1 Solution: Design Star Schema Fact and Dimension Tables

Here are the fact and dimension tables designed in Try This exercise 12-1:

```
BOOK (FACT):  ISBN (PK), SUBJECT CODE(FK), PUBLISHER ID(FK),
     EDITION COST, SELLING PRICE, QUANTITY ON HAND, QUANTITY ON ORDER,
     RECOMMENDED QUANTITY

BOOK TITLE (DIMENSION):  BOOK TITLE, EDITION CODE, PREVIOUS ISBN
SUBJECT (DIMENSION):  SUBJECT CODE (PK), DESCRIPTION
```

AUTHOR (DIMENSION): ISBN (PK), AUTHOR ID (PK), AUTHOR NAME

PUBLISHER (DIMENSION): PUBLISHER ID (PK), PUBLISHER NAME, STREET ADDRESS,
        CITY, STATE, ZIP CODE

Try This 13-1   Solution: Using SQL/XML Functions

If you are not using an Oracle database with Oracle's HR sample schema, here is the SQL
code to create an Employees table with the necessary columns and populate it with the
three rows needed for this exercise:

```
CREATE TABLE EMPLOYEES
  (EMPLOYEE_ID    NUMBER(6)  NOT NULL,
   FIRST_NAME     VARCHAR(20),
   LAST_NAME      VARCHAR(20),
   PHONE_NUMBER   VARCHAR(20),
   DEPARTMENT_ID  NUMBER(4));

INSERT INTO EMPLOYEES
  VALUES(100,'Steven','King','515.123.4567',90);
INSERT INTO EMPLOYEES
  VALUES(101,'Neena','Kochhar','515.123.4568',90);
INSERT INTO EMPLOYEES
  VALUES(102,'Lex','DeHaan','515.123.4569',90);
COMMIT;
```

Here is the SQL statement used in Try This 13-1:

```
SELECT XMLELEMENT("Employee",
       XMLATTRIBUTES(EMPLOYEE_ID AS ID),
       XMLFOREST(FIRST_NAME AS "First Name",
                 LAST_NAME AS "Last Name",
                 PHONE_NUMBER AS "Phone"))
  FROM EMPLOYEES
 WHERE DEPARTMENT_ID = 90
 ORDER BY EMPLOYEE_ID;
```

Index

N